Oedipal God

Oedipal God

The Chinese Nezha and His Indian Origins

Meir Shahar

University of Hawai'i Press
Honolulu

Printed in the United States of America

20 19 18 17 16 15 6 5 4 3 2 1

Library of Congress Cataloging-in-Publication Data

Shahar, Meir, author.
Oedipal God : the Chinese Nezha and his Indian origins / Meir Shahar.
pages cm
Includes bibliographical references and index.
ISBN 978-0-8248-4760-9 (cloth : alk. paper)
1. Nezha (Chinese deity) 2. Nezha (Chinese deity)—In literature. 3. Oedipus complex—Cross-cultural studies. 4. Tantric Buddhism—China. I. Title.
BL1812.G63S42 2015
299'.5112113—dc23 2014048857

University of Hawaiʻi Press books are printed on acid-free paper and meet the guidelines for permanence and durability of the Council on Library Resources.

Designed by Integrated Composition Systems, Spokane, Washington

Printed by Sheridan Books, Inc.

Contents

Acknowledgments

I am indebted to Ye Derong (A'de), who accompanied me on research trips to Henan and Hebei, and I am grateful to Wang Ch'iu-kui for his hospitality and guidance during my visit to Jinmen Island. I wish to express my thanks to John Kieschnick, John Lagerwey, and the anonymous readers for the press for their suggestions. For references, assistance, and rare materials I am much indebted to Yael Bentor, Cai Rongying, Chen Tianqi, Avi Darshani, Mark Gamsa, Noga Ganany, Erez Joskovich, Paul Katz, Einor Keinan-Segev, Ernest Kozin, Lin Fushi, Lü Jianfu, Steven Sangren, Noga Zhang Hui Shahar, Shulamith Shahar, Shang Wei, David Shulman, Wu Jen-shu, and Zhuang Zhengong. Patricia Crosby, my editor at the University of Hawai'i Press, has been helpful and encouraging, like her entire crew of Drew Bryan, Emma Ching, and Stephanie Chun.

My research benefited from Israel Science Foundation Grants (no. 586/07 and no. 188/11) and from the support of the Chiang Ching-kuo Foundation for International Scholarly Exchange (project number RG006-P-06).

Introduction

Traditional Chinese culture has accorded filial piety paramount significance. The virtue has been the cornerstone of Chinese ethics and political theory, informing every aspect of a person's life, from familial roles and social conduct to religious practice. It is striking therefore that one of the most beloved Chinese folk heroes has attempted to kill his father. The legend of this book's protagonist, Nezha, has him locked in familial conflict from the moment of his birth. Culminating in suicide and attempted patricide, the child-god's visceral myth has enjoyed tremendous popularity throughout late imperial and modern times. Despite his brazen disregard for the hegemonic Confucian ethics, the patricidal Nezha has been celebrated in written and in oral fiction, and the story of his familial revolt has been adapted to diverse media from regional operas and puppet plays to television serials, movies, and cartoons. The unruly infant has risen to become one of the most popular gods in the Chinese pantheon. Straddling the boundaries between Buddhism, Daoism, and the popular religion, the oedipal deity's cult flourishes to this day.

This book examines the legend of the patricidal prodigy set against the background of the Confucian ethics that he so flagrantly violates. It analyzes the child's oedipal myth in Freudian psychological terms, taking into account its culture-specific significance. Nezha attempted to kill his father not before killing himself: In an exemplary act of martyrdom he sacrificed his own life (ostensibly for his father's sake). Shortly thereafter he was miraculously reborn, confronting his progenitor. Even though the two recognized each other, the infant no longer acknowledged his father as such. Instead, Nezha attempted to avenge his self-immolation by patricide.

The legend's climactic moments of self-immolation and familial murder are examined in their Chinese context. The social perception of self-murder as protest (by an inferior against his superior) and the late imperial legal implications of parricide are charted as a prelude to the comparative analysis of the oedipal theme. The Freudian hypothesis is tested against the Chinese cultural background. The psychological investigation of the legend is followed by an ethnographic survey of its protagonist's flourishing cult. Fieldwork and textual research chart the diverse forms of Nezha worship, exploring the possible meanings of the child-god to his burgeoning clientele. Finally, the book attempts a comprehensive history of the legend and the cult, reaching back more than two thousand years, for originally Nezha had been an Indian mythological being named Nalakūbara, whose sexual misadventures had been celebrated in the Sanskrit epics as early as the first centuries BCE.

The book is written backwards in time. Its starting point is the contemporary myth in its varied written, dramatic, and cinematic adaptations. The contours of the Nezha legend are then traced back through stories and plays dating from the Ming period (1368–1644) to hints strewn in the "recorded sayings" of Chan masters who taught during the Song period (960–1279). Heading further back, the image of the protean prodigy is examined in the writings of eighth-century Tantric ritual masters, who harnessed his powers to fight the demonic hordes. Translated from the Sanskrit, the Tantric manuals betray the Indian ancestry of the Chinese Nezha. The exploits of his predecessor, Nalakūbara, are explored, first in the purāṇic compendiums of the first centuries CE, then in the great epics that predated them by half a millennium. Because this reverse chronological order might be confusing, let us preface it by a temporal one. Here, before we begin, is a brief chronological summary of the Asian god's history:

Nezha began his career as a semidivine semidemonic *yakṣa* spirit called Nalakūbara. The Sanskrit epics of the first millennium BCE identified him as the son of the great *yakṣa* king Vaiśravaṇa (also known as Kubera), guardian of the gods' treasures. The earliest legend of the *yakṣa* prince had his lover, the beautiful courtesan Rambhā, raped by his uncle, the reckless demon Rāvaṇa. Bearing oedipal shades, other stories likewise involved Nalakūbara in sexual competition with his elders. The most famous one associated the youthful *yakṣa* with the baby-god Kṛṣṇa. Elaborated upon in the purāṇic literature of the first centuries CE, the legend likely had a significant impact upon the emergence of the Chinese Nezha. It appears that Nalakūbara arrived in China colored in the captivating hues of Bāla-Kṛṣṇa ("The Child Kṛṣṇa"), creating a link between the two Asian toddler divinities: Kṛṣṇa and Nezha.

Nalakūbara was introduced to China by Tantric ritual masters such as Vajrabodhi (671–741) and Amoghavajra (704–774), who gave him his Chinese name Nezha (a shortened and slightly corrupt transcription of the original Sanskrit). Embraced by the Tang Dynasty (618–907), Tantric Buddhism (also known as esoteric Buddhism) featured a vast array of Indian divinities, including the *yakṣa* king Vaiśravaṇa, who was worshiped as a god of riches and of war alike. The *yakṣa* king communicated with his devotees by means of his offspring angel. Nalakūbara (Nezha) figured in Tantric literature as his father's messenger. He was called upon to bestow Vaiśravaṇa's wealth upon the faithful, or else lead the Heavenly King's troops in their defense. As such, the child-god contributed to the affluence of the Tang Dynasty as much as to the success of its military campaigns.

Nezha's Tantric legacy had a decisive impact upon his cult during the ensuing Song period (960–1279). By the twelfth century at the latest, Daoist priests had adopted the Tantric warrior into their divine ranks. The Buddhist stalwart was called upon to battle the enemies of the Daoist faith. Appointed as the "General of the Middle Altar," he was to figure in Daoist rites of exorcism all through modern times. Simultaneously with his growing Daoist significance, the young god was emulated by Buddhist monastics. The "recorded sayings" of Song-period Chan masters reveal that they considered the story of his self-immolation emblematic of the conflict between Confucian family values and Buddhist celibacy. The child-god was venerated by Buddhist clerics as one who was willing to pay the highest price (suicide) for his spiritual freedom.

The lore of the Yuan period (1279–1368) attests to Nezha's attraction to a lay clientele. According to a fourteenth-century legend, Beijing (then Dadu) had been fashioned in the Tantric deity's image, its eleven gates corresponding to his three heads, six arms, and two legs. The Yuan Dynasty capital, therefore, was referred to in prose and poetry as "Nezha City." The child-god had been elevated to the post of the metropolitan tutelary-deity because of his invincible martial skills, which were celebrated in contemporaneous drama. A substantial body of fourteenth- and fifteenth-century plays had Nezha vanquishing a wide assortment of monstrous creatures. Blurring the distinctions between hagiographic literature and entertainment, the divine warrior battled on stage many of the same demons that he exorcised in Daoist scriptures.

The oedipal Nezha legend evolved through Ming-period (1368–1644) fiction, drama, and hagiographic literature, receiving its present-day shape in the early seventeenth-century *The Canonization of the Gods* (*Fengshen yanyi*). The novel has made a tremendous contribution to the spread of the unruly infant's legend and the proliferation of his religious cult. Among the most popular Chinese mythological epics, it went through at least twenty extant editions during the Qing period (1644–1911) and dozens more in the twentieth century. Furthermore, *Canonization* has served as a source for a vast body of oral, dramatic, and cinematic adaptations that variously interpreted the Nezha trope in psychological, social, and political terms. The People's Republic of China has transformed Nezha into a revolutionary martyr; Taiwanese cinema has depicted him as an alienated youth à la James Dean; and Japanese cartoons have redesigned the venerable Tantric warrior as a futuristic mega-robot, a snazzy hybrid of the human race and its computerized machines.

By the turn of the twenty-first century, Nezha had become a household name. A cursory survey of the cartoon shelves in any Chinese bookstore reveals that his popularity is rivaled only by another prototypical rebel, the monkey king Sun Wukong. At the same time, the cult of the unruly infant has spread throughout the Chinese-speaking world. Nezha is among the most widely encountered deities in spirit-medium cults. He appears as an ancillary divinity in countless temples throughout Southeast Asia, even as the number of temples dedicated to him as the principal god is far from negligible. The patricidal prodigy is among the most prominent figures in Chinese religion and popular culture alike.

Questions and Chapter Outline

Two themes underlie my study of the unruly Nezha: First is the question of whether or not the Freudian hypothesis is applicable to Chinese culture. I examine the similarities and differences between the Chinese expression of the oedipal drive and the classical Greek one. Second is the impact that esoteric Buddhism (also known as Tantric Buddhism) has had upon the Chinese imagination of divinity. Admittedly, the two topics might well have been studied independently of each other. They happen to coincide, however, in the fetching figure of this book's protagonist. Nezha is a perfect example not only of the oedipal drive but also of the unique cultural vocabulary by which it is masked. The child-god's patricidal tendencies are camouflaged by the hegemonic discourse of filial piety. At the same time, he demonstrates the role of esoteric Buddhism as a vehicle for the Indian culture's passage to China. Nezha is but one of the many Indian mythological beings who, imported by the Tantric movement, have left an indelible mark upon the Chinese supernatural.

Even though they are occasionally intermingled, the two topics each occupy roughly half the book. The question of the Oedipus complex in Chinese culture is discussed in the opening four chapters, whereas the remaining five are increasingly concerned with religion, and hence with the Chinese domestication of esoteric Buddhism. The first chapter places the Nezha legend in the context of the seventeenth-century *The Canonization of the Gods,* arguing for an intimate link between the child's attempted patricide and the novel's overriding plot of regicide. The story of Nezha's familial revolt corresponds to the Zhou Dynasty's rebellion against the Shang regime, both of which are celebrated in *Canonization.* The novel features other victims of familial aggression, which are similarly analyzed. Particular attention is given to the cannibalistic tale of the august King Wen, who did not flinch from eating his own son. The pathetic Bo Yikao set on a filial journey to rescue the imprisoned king only to end up as a meatball on his plate. Reminiscent of the Greek Cronus (who devoured his offspring lest they depose him), the gruesome tale of King Wen is traced back to the first centuries BCE. It occasions a discussion of cannibalism in China (practiced as well as imagined) from the historical writings of Sima Qian (ca. 145–86 BCE) to the bitter fiction of Lu Xun (1881–1936).

The second chapter analyzes the cultural vocabulary of the late imperial Nezha myth. I argue that the survival of the disturbing legend in its Confucian environment hinged upon the ambivalence of the child's suicide, which preceded his attempt parricide. Nezha's self-immolation was presented as heroic self-sacrifice for his parents' sake, even though it was recognizable as protest against them. Phrased differently, the oedipal myth masqueraded as a filial piety tale. Other cultural tropes that are ironically reversed by the audacious infant are likewise examined, including the late imperial practice of filial cannibalism, by which children fed their own flesh to their ailing parents. The chapter surveys the hagiographic genre of filial piety tales (which has served as a foil to the seditious myth) as well as the legal codes that the oedipal Nezha has so flagrantly disregarded. Qing law stipulated the harshest punishment of death by slicing for father killers.

The third chapter broadens the discussion of the Chinese Oedipus by various other examples drawn from literary and religious texts. Incestuous drives and familial animosities are found lurking under the surface of canonical works of literature, from the *Dream of the Red Chamber* (whose iconic protagonist is prey to his father's virulent jealousy) to the Buddhist legend of the devoted Mulian, who sets upon a chivalric journey in search of his beloved mother. Even as it supports the universality of the Oedipus complex, the chapter highlights the weight of the Confucian ethics that distorted its Chinese manifestations. The primacy of filial piety dictated that most tales of familial conflict culminate in infanticide rather than patricide. Furthermore, aggression and sexual libido have often been masked by Confucian rhetoric, their hapless victims paraded—like Nezha—as paragons of filial piety. The chapter also includes brief forays into the reception of Freudian theory in twentieth-century China, and into the social conditions that might have contributed to the Oedipus complex as a lived psychological reality during the late imperial period. Drawing upon the works of Chinese historians and psychologists, it points out the familial conditions that might have estranged sons and fathers, fostering the bond of mothers and their male offspring.

The claim for the applicability of the Freudian hypothesis to the Chinese legend does not imply its identity with the Greek one. A significant difference between the tales of Oedipus and Nezha concerns the sexual intimacy with the mother, which in the latter case is merely implied. Whereas the animosity between the Chinese infant and his father is laid bare, the erotic attraction to the mother is not explicitly acknowledged. More generally, Chinese oedipal tales differ from Freud's Greek prototype by the high degree of repression that is applied to them. Claude Lévi-Strauss has commented on psychoanalysis—to which he has been deeply indebted—that "the nature of true reality is already apparent in the care which it takes to evade our detection."[1] The observation is certainly applicable to the Chinese case, in which the hegemony of the Confucian ethics required that the oedipal drive masquerade as filial piety.

The fourth chapter explores the significant diversity that characterizes the late imperial and modern adaptations of the Nezha legend. Some nineteenth-century oral narratives accentuate the cruelty of Nezha's father, their undivided sympathy reserved for the heroic infant. Reflecting the familial concerns of the middle or lower urban classes, a Qing-period Beijing drum ballad is remarkable for its overt hostility to patriarchal authority. By contrast, recent cinematic versions have sometimes muffled the myth's oedipal tension, transmuting the familial conflict into the social and political spheres. The mainland animation classic *Nezha Wreaks Havoc in the Ocean* (1979) has replaced the legend's psychological discourse with the vocabulary of revolutionary struggle. Nezha is portrayed as a socialist hero who sacrifices his life for the toiling masses. Drawing upon American cinema rather than socialist ideology, the Taiwanese *Teenaged Nezha* (1992) has shed a different light upon the malleability of the Nezha trope. Its protagonist is a disoriented youth, partially fashioned after the Los Angeles delinquents in Nicholas Ray's *Rebel Without a Cause* (1955).

The fifth chapter charts Nezha's military career from the Southern Song period (1127–1279) down to the present. His role of divine warrior has been central to the child's image in fiction and drama no less than to his religious cult. Nezha's martial feats have been a major attraction to the aficionados of his novels and plays, just as his unsurpassed military skills have been relied upon by Daoist exorcists. The chapter surveys the evolution of the toddler's martial mythology from thirteenth-century hagiographic literature and theatrical pieces all the way to contemporary Japanese manga cartoons (which pronounce the young warrior's name "Nataku"). Written and visual evidence is used to date the child's heroic feats, which have been celebrated since the Song period: His subjugation of the dragon king and his bending of a mythic bow that none but the gods had been able to draw. Particular attention is given to the emergence of the child-god's martial iconography. Some of his magic weapons have accrued to Nezha from the arsenal of Daoist exorcism, illustrating the impact of the native faith upon the originally Buddhist deity.

The sixth chapter is dedicated to the child-god's flourishing cult. Nezha's ubiquitous presence in contemporary Chinese religion is demonstrated by anthropological research. Drawing upon my own fieldwork and the extensive records of other scholars, the chapter describes the multifarious ways of worshiping the infant divinity. The cult's geographic scope is charted, and selected Nezha temples are surveyed (from Henan and Macau to Fujian and Taiwan); the young warrior's role of General of the Middle Altar is examined (he has been appointed the commander of the invisible spirit armies that protect Chinese villages); and his widespread cults of possession are analyzed (the toddler-divinity has been a favorite of Chinese spirit mediums, who are themselves conceived of as children). Attention is paid to the quintessential features of a child deity's cult (such as the toys and candies that are offered him), as well as to the persistent apologetics that accompany the veneration of a god who defies paternal authority. The custodians of the Nezha cult—temple managers, ritual masters, and even mediums in trance—struggle to present an immaculate image of the god. Nezha's rebellious features, the very source of his attraction, are glossed over in deference of the hegemonic ethics of filial piety.

The seventh chapter surveys the references to Nezha in Song period literature. Launching the search for the origins of the protean prodigy, it examines his image in the "recorded sayings" of Chan masters. By the tenth century at the latest, Buddhist monks venerated Nezha for his choice of a spiritual father (the Buddha) over the biological one. His myth served to illustrate the conflict between the monastic ideal and Confucian family values. The chapter explores the similarities between the legend of the defiant prince Nezha and the roughly contemporaneous myth of the rebellious princess Miaoshan, who similarly defied paternal authority for the sake of spiritual liberation. The Buddhist motif of lotus birth is examined, as is the Chinese (and universal) trope of the religiously inclined third offspring.

The eighth chapter examines the role of esoteric Buddhism in shaping the Asian cult of Vaiśravaṇa and his son Nezha. It argues for the functional equivalents—in Tantric Buddhism—of the Western angels. Much as the monotheistic god communicates with his devotees by means of messengers, some Tantric divinities are so remote as to require the intermediacy of angels. Nezha (and his siblings) made their debut on the Chinese stage as their father's envoys. Tantric ritual masters summoned them to lead Vaiśravaṇa's awesome *yakṣa* troops to battle, or else distribute the Heavenly King's fabulous wealth to the faithful. His Tantric role of military commander has been the source of Nezha's martial image in Chinese religion and literature. The chapter surveys the growth of Vaiśravaṇa's Asian cult—and the crystallization of his offspring's image—through written scriptures and visual art. Particular attention is given to the fearful image of the three-headed and six-armed Nezha. The typically Indian iconography has held a spell upon the Chinese imagination, so much so that the capital Beijing has been fashioned after the multiheaded and multilimbed Tantric divinity.

The ninth chapter describes the figure of Nezha's Indian predecessor Nalakūbara in Sanskrit literature. Nalakūbara's dubious identity of a *yakṣa* might have contributed to the semidivine, semidemonic traits of his Chinese descendant. Particular attention is given to the *pūraṇic* tradition that associates Nalakūbara with the baby-god Kṛṣṇa. Among the most widely worshiped Indian deities, Kṛṣṇa and his mythology shares striking similarities with that of the Chinese infant Nezha. The legends of the two child-gods pivot upon the concealment of divine might under a misleadingly fragile appearance. Kṛṣṇa and Nezha are motivated by similar oedipal drives, and they perform identical heroic feats, subduing a dragon (or *nāga*) and bending a divine mythic bow. The chapter explores the Song-period

Tantric literature that evinces the possible fusion of Kṛṣṇa and Nalakūbara. The Chinese Nezha might have been partially fashioned after Kṛṣṇa, creating a link between the Asian story cycles of the two divine infants.

The epilogue places Nezha's history in the context of contemporary research on Chinese esoteric Buddhism. It argues for the enduring impact that the Tantric movement has had upon Chinese religion and for its role introducing to China creatures of the Indian imagination. That Chinese literature and drama are to this day imbued with Indian supernatural beings is partially due to the contribution of medieval esoteric Buddhism.

1

Sons and Fathers

The legend of Nezha may be summarized as follows:

Nezha was the son of General Li Jing. His mother had been ominously pregnant for three years before giving birth to a ball of flesh. Considering it monstrous, the alarmed father hacked the ball with his sword, whereupon a tiny child, armed with a magic ring and wrapped in a red sash, emerged from within. Shortly thereafter, the Daoist Immortal Taiyi arrived on the scene, naming the newborn Nezha.

When he was seven years old (and six feet tall) the child went bathing in a river. Laundering his girdle, he caused the water to boil all the way to the underwater palace of the dragon king, who dispatched his son to check the cause of the disturbance. In the ensuing fray, the infant killed the awesome heir of the dragon king, making a belt from its sinews.

Playing in the garden, Nezha came upon a bow that no one but the mythic Yellow Emperor of old had been able to bend. The child effortlessly drew the bowstring, shooting an arrow that killed the acolyte of the ogress Lady Rock (Shiji Niangniang). The harpy pursued the boy, who was narrowly rescued by the Immortal Taiyi.

The enraged dragon king threatened to annihilate Li Jing's family if he were not compensated for his lost offspring. The general blamed his wife for bearing him a monster and his son for bringing a disaster upon him. A murderous conflict between Nezha and his father ensued, at the height of which the child committed suicide, returning to his parents the body he had owed them. Satisfied that his son's murderer had paid for his crime, the dragon king (and his brothers who had gathered to his cause) returned to their oceanic abode.

Nezha's disembodied soul sought help from his master Taiyi, who recommended that a temple be built for him. The incense offerings, he explained, would bring the child back to life. Nezha appeared in his mother's dream, demanding that she build him one. Consenting to her son's request, Lady Yin established a Nezha Temple, which attracted pilgrims far and wide. Fearful of her husband, she did not inform him of it.

Discovering the teeming Nezha Temple, Li Jing was infuriated. He ordered the crowds dispersed, whipped the hateful image of his son, and burned the temple to ashes. Seeking revenge, the enraged Nezha was incarnated on earth. Equipped with a lotus body fashioned for him by the Immortal Taiyi, he confronted his dad, whom he no longer addressed as such: "Li Jing" he vowed, "I will not be satisfied until I kill you."

The invincible child pursued his helpless father, who begged the gods for mercy. An immortal appeared on the scene, bestowing upon Li Jing a magic stupa that enabled him to control his son. An uneasy compromise—but no sincere truce—was established between Nezha and his father.[1]

The legend is remarkable for its naked display of father-son animosity. The hatred of offspring and progenitor originated with Nezha's birth and lasted all through his suicide and attempted patricide. Li Jing appears to have loathed his extraordinary child from the moment he emerged from the womb as a ball of flesh (which he promptly hacked in two), whereas the son's lust for revenge lived on through his self-immolation and reincarnation in a lotus body. Significantly, the boy felt no remorse for his attempted patricide, even after the gods had forced him to apologize for it. "Even as his mouth uttered an excuse, his heart did not comply. He merely gnashed his teeth."[2]

Which psychological and social tensions does the Nezha legend betray? How has it survived in a society that sanctions filial piety? We begin our investigation with the novel that recorded it.

The Canonization of the Gods

The legend of Nezha received its present-day form in the seventeenth-century *The Canonization of the Gods* (*Fengshen yanyi*). The mythological novel belongs to the late Ming genre of "fiction on the supernatural" (*ling'guai xiaoshuo*). The sixteenth and seventeenth centuries witnessed the publication of vernacular novels that blurred the distinction between hagiography and entertainment. Some celebrated the epiphanies of one deity only. Others featured an entire pantheon of gods and demons involved in intricate plots of mythological warfare. The two largest and most influential novels were *The Journey to the West* (1592) and *The Canonization of the Gods* (ca. 1625). The former advocated a Buddhist framework of enlightenment, whereas the latter constructed a largely Daoist pantheon of divinities.

Novels such as *The Canonization of the Gods* offer us a window into the religion of late imperial China. Revealing the gods that had captured the imagination of the people, the novels further spread their cults. Deriving for the most part from oral literature, the written fiction on the supernatural has served itself as a source for oral narratives, drama, and, in recent times, television serials and movies.

Reaching every segment of society—literate and illiterate alike—sixteenth- and seventeenth-century novels have played a significant role in shaping Chinese conceptions of the supernatural down to the present. The protagonists of *The Canonization of the Gods* are worshiped to this day in Daoist temples and the shrines of the popular religion alike.[3]

The novel's divine cast of characters is involved in a historical conflict. Just as the Greek poet had the gods take part in the Trojan Wars, so did the creators of the *Canonization* place their mythic protagonists in the historical context of China in the second millennium BCE. Like the Homeric gods descending into the battlefield, the Chinese divinities participate in the historical confrontation between the Shang Dynasty (ca. 1600–ca. 1066 BCE) and the Zhou Dynasty that succeeded it (ca. 1066–221 BCE). Modern scholarship interprets the Shang-Zhou war as a conflict between two states—two centers of geopolitical power. Traditional Chinese historiography conceived of it as a rebellion on the part of a vassal (Zhou) against its lord (Shang). It is this rebellion that serves as historical background for *The Canonization of the Gods.*

The significance of loyalty in Chinese political thought made it exceedingly difficult to accept the Zhou victory over the Shang. Nonetheless, the war had been justified by the cruelty of the Shang kings and the virtue of their Zhou opponents (who had been described as forced into rebellion as a last resort). In *The Canonization of the Gods,* the righteous divinities—including Nezha *and* his father—fight for the just cause of the Zhou, whereas a host of demons and evil spirits are incarnated into the wicked Shang camp. As the Zhou emerges victorious, its deified warriors are rewarded with heavenly posts. Their divine commander Jiang Ziya canonizes each in the Roster of the Gods (Fengshen bang), hence the novel's title: *The Canonization of the Gods.*

The wicked defenders of the evil Shang regime are promoted to heavenly positions as well. The novel's villains are canonized like the heroes that subjugate them. In this respect the novel mirrors the Daoist process of sublimation (*liandu*), by which demons are transmuted into deities. As Mark Meulenbeld has pointed out, the noxious spirits are redeemed by the very gods that annihilate them. They are incarnated into the evil Shang camp in order to be vanquished. Subjugated, they are subsequently elevated into the pantheon of divinities. *The Canonization of the Gods* betrays therefore the ghostly origins of many Chinese divinities, revealing the abhorrent aspect that lurks behind their dignified mien. In Daoist ritual, the supplication of a benevolent god is often hard to distinguish from the pacification of an evil spirit.[4]

The novel's dating has been the subject of a scholarly dispute. The earliest edition of *Canonization* does not bear a date, and it has been suggested that it might have been authored as early as the sixteenth century.[5] The bulk of the evidence, however, indicates a seventeenth-century time frame: *The Canonization of the*

Gods postdates the 1592 edition of *The Journey to the West* (from which it freely borrows); its publisher, the Shu Family of Suzhou, is known to have issued popular fiction in the 1620s; and the novel is missing from bibliographic lists all through the 1630s, when it made its earliest appearance in records of vernacular fiction. Judging by these and other considerations, Zhang Peiheng has convincingly argued for a mid-1620s date of composition.[6]

Hardly anything is known about the novel's authors. The earliest edition carries a preface by one Li Yunxiang, who describes the publisher's commission that he fill the gaps and annotate the novel. The second volume (*juan*), however, gives the author as Xu Zhonglin. We may surmise that Xu likely compiled the core of the opening chapters, whereas Li was responsible for editing and expanding the narrative. Unfortunately, nothing beyond their native places is known about either: Xu is described as the Old Recluse from Mount Zhong (in Nanjing), and Li identifies himself as a Yangzhou native.[7]

Whereas precious little is known about the novel's compilers, the source they drew upon can be ascertained. Li Yunxiang's preface leaves no doubt that the subject matter of *Canonization* had evolved in oral literature. "The popular saying has Jiang Ziya beheading the [evil] generals and appointing the gods," he tells us. "However, this story has never been written down in book form. It has been transmitted by storytellers only."[8] The adaptation of the oral narrative into a written text probably took place in several stages. Xu Zhonglin might have recorded the opening sections of the story cycle, which Li Yunxiang might have supplemented and edited, giving the novel its current form. That their novel is replete with historical anachronisms and geographical errors might be taken as further evidence of its origins in oral lore. The storytellers who created the *Canonization* cycle were likely not highly educated.

The Zhou rebellion against the Shang had been celebrated in oral literature centuries before the novel was written. It is the subject of the *Popular Tale of King Wu Punishing King Zhou* (*Wu wang fa Zhou pinghua*) (ca. 1320), which derives from fourteenth-century storytelling.[9] A comparison of the Yuan narrative with its late Ming sequel suggests the story cycle's evolution. Not only is the *Popular Tale of King Wu* one-tenth as long, it lacks *The Canonization of the Gods*' mythological aspect. Instead of gods battling demons with deadly charms, its protagonists are for the most part human. Evidently, the dimension of fantasy had been added to the narrative in the course of the Ming period. The historical fiction that had been narrated by fourteenth-century storytellers gradually gave way to the fantastic legends that are recorded in the seventeenth-century novel.

The Canonization of the Gods' derivation from oral literature sheds significant light on the history of the Nezha legend. It suggests that the story of the oedipal boy had been popular with storytellers as early as the Ming period. What had been its appeal to the creators of *Canonization*? Why did they choose to incorporate the story of the naughty child into the narrative of the Zhou rebellion? The likely answer is the common theme of insubordination that underlies them both.

Patricide and Regicide

Nezha figures in *The Canonization of the Gods* as one of the Zhou's greatest heroes. The brave boy plays a prominent role in countless battles against the Shang tyrant. Riding on wheels of fire, he emerges from the clouds to strike his helpless foes with his divine spear and cosmic ring (*qiankun quan*), "like lightning traveling in empty space, like the wind howling through a jade forest."[10] Having shed his earthly body and human soul, Nezha is invulnerable to his adversaries' magic warfare. Neither poisonous pills, nor soul stealing, nor high-pitched sound waves can harm the child prodigy, who overcomes plague gods and awesome sorcerers alike.

His contribution to the Zhou campaign notwithstanding, the story of Nezha's conflict with his father is not directly related to the plot of *Canonization*. The hostility of father and son is irrelevant to the dynasty's cause, and its elaborate telling over three chapters is not linked to surrounding episodes. The very identity of Nezha's father belies his affiliation with the Zhou Dynasty. Li Jing (571–649) was a historical Tang general, and his association with a war fought fifteen hundred years earlier is anachronistic. Not surprisingly, neither he nor his rebellious son figure in earlier narratives of the Shang-Zhou period. Nezha and his father are not mentioned either in the Yuan-period *Popular Tale of King Wu Punishing King Zhou* or in the late-Ming *Romance of the Feudal States* (*Lieguo zhi zhuan*).[11]

We will see in the following chapters that the Nezha legend had evolved independently of the Shang-Zhou cycle for more than a millennium. The myth of the defiant infant was likely incorporated into the narratives of the Zhou wars no earlier than the late Ming. Its appeal to the authors of *Canonization* was likely the theme of rebellion that runs through it. The naughty child disregards his father's orders, just as the Earl of the West (King Wen)—leader of the Zhou armies—disobeys his lord. Subversion of authority is the key to the Nezha myth and to the Zhou epic alike, whether a son defying paternal rule or a vassal upsetting royal sovereignty.

Chinese political thought had created an inextricable link between the private realm of filial piety (*xiao*) and the political sphere of loyalty (*zhong*). The assumption was that a filial son would be a conscientious minister. He who scrupulously attended to his parents could be trusted to faithfully serve his lord. The argument had been put forth in the *Analects:* "It is rare for a man whose character is such that he is good as a son and obedient as a young man to have the inclination to transgress against his superiors."[12] Conflicting demands by state and parents notwithstanding, the virtues of filial piety and political loyalty had been firmly wedded in imperial ideology. *The Classic of Filial Piety* (ca. second century BCE) had elevated the moral into a cosmic principle that governs the familial, the political, and the natural spheres alike: "Filial Piety is the constant method of Heaven, the righteousness of Earth."[13] It is by nurturing the primary virtue at home that one is able to assume his political duties abroad: "The filial piety with which the superior man serves his parents may be transferred as loyalty to the ruler.... Therefore, when his conduct is thus successful in his inner (private) circle, his name will be established (and transmitted) to future generations."[14]

Even though they considered filial piety a precondition for political loyalty, Chinese thinkers were fully aware that the two virtues might conflict. Under given historical circumstances, the service to one's lord might compromise one's attention to his parents and vice versa. The historical novel *Three Kingdoms* tells of Mother Xu, whose son Shan Fu had been an adviser to Liu Bei. Determined to obtain the services of the brilliant strategist, Liu Bei's rival Cao Cao took Mother Xu captive and pressured her to convince her son to switch allegiances. When the righteous mother refused, Cao Cao forged a letter in her name, urging Shan Fu to come to her rescue. The flustered son arrived at Cao Cao's capital only to be berated by his mother for his ignorance. Mother Xu accused Shan Fu of failing to verify the letter's authenticity and more broadly of misjudging his duties. "As a scholar" she cried, "you should have known that loyalty and filial piety may conflict."[15]

Filial piety and political loyalty could be similarly challenged by a wrongheaded or abusive authority. Sons and ministers alike were permitted to remonstrate but were forbidden to rebel. A son could caution misguided parents, but was expected to obey them: "To obey with no admonition is unfilial; to admonish and disobey is equally unfilial" was the maxim.[16] An official was allowed—and even required—to admonish his ruler, but he could not forsake him for another. "A loyal minister would not serve two monarchs, even if he had to give up his life," stated Sima Guang (1019–1086).[17] Confucius singled out for praise three officials who had been willing to pay the highest price for their loyalty—chastising the king, but refusing to depose him: Bi Gan chose to give up his life; Ji Zi was sold as a slave; and Wei Zi hid among the common people.[18] A minister whose advice remained unheeded could escape, feign madness, or commit suicide. He could not, however, rebel against his lord.

If filial piety and political loyalty were interlinked, their violations had been associated. The same vocabulary was applied to those who transgressed against paternal authority and political authority. *Ni* (disobedient) equally described an unfilial son (*nizi*), a traitorous official (*nichen*), and a rebel outlaw (*nitu*). The most heinous crimes, patricide and regicide, were identically termed *shi* (sometimes modified as *shifu* ("patricide") and *shijun* ("regicide")). Those who committed the one crime were imagined capable of the other. The *Classic of Changes* discussed the two sins as expressions of the same pathology: "The situation in which a minister kills his lord, or a son his father, does not arise in one day."[19] When, in the greatest of all Chinese novels, Baoyu's father savagely beats him, he justifies the near infanticide as not only self-defense, but as the prevention of a political crime. Jia Zheng exclaims to those remonstrating with him in the *Dream of the Red Chamber* (ca. 1760): "Would you like me to wait until Baoyu commits *patricide* or *regicide* (*shifu shijun*). Would you still intercede for him then?"[20]

We may conclude that the naughty child Nezha and the august Zhou leader share the same crime of *shi* (attempted patricide by the former; regicide by the latter). But whereas the endearing toddler goes about the business of his revenge with narcissistic self-fulfillment—no qualms nor hesitations whatsoever—the pious Earl of the West performs his against constant groaning and moaning, indulging in self-righteous protestations on the vassal's duty to obey his lord. All too often, the Earl of the West (and his heir King Wu) allows his advisers to shoulder the moral responsibility for the accelerating war against the Shang. Nezha and King Wen, therefore, represent two modes of response to tyrannical authority: outright rejection with no regard to the social norms of filial piety on the one hand, versus an (ultimately failed) struggle to accommodate virtue and loyalty on the other hand.[21]

The Chinese Cronus

The Canonization of the Gods is replete with stories of familial conflict, which evince an interest in the relationship of fathers and sons. Exploring the boundaries of loyalty and filial piety, the novel places parents and children in extreme situations of mutual expectations, mutual sacrifice, and mutual hatred. Abused by the Shang tyrant, General Huang Feihu defects to the Zhou camp, only to be accused by his father, a loyal Shang vassal, of betraying state and parent. The father demands that Huang Feihu kill him; he would rather die at his son's hands than see the family's reputation of loyalty tarnished. (A tragic outcome is prevented by a successful ploy that forces the father to join the Zhou camp.) The sad fate of the Shang ruler's two sons is the subject of another story. Driven from the palace by the machinations of their father's wicked concubine, the expelled princes wonder whether to fight for or against him. Filial piety gaining the upper hand, they die at the hands of the Zhou rebels.[22]

The most dramatic story that pits a father against his son is that of the paragon of virtue King Wen, who knowingly consumes his child's flesh. The cannibalistic tale is narrated in some detail over three chapters of *Canonization*. It will serve as a prelude for our discussion of the Nezha legend, for it similarly betrays the novel's concern with the hidden animosity of fathers and sons. Even though the two legends are very different—King Wen eats his son, whereas Nezha rebels against his father—they equally labor to disguise the familial discord under the veneer of the Confucian ethics. Furthermore, we will see in following chapters that the cannibalistic trope is not irrelevant to the Nezha legend. Even though he is *not* eaten by his father, Nezha's suicide draws upon the discourse of filial slicing, by which children fed their own flesh to ailing parents.

The protagonists of the gruesome tale—in which a son is eaten by his father—are the Zhou leader King Wen (traditional dates 1152–1056 BCE), who was known in his lifetime as the Earl of the West (the title of king had been posthumously bestowed upon him by his son, King Wu); the evil last ruler of the Shang Dynasty, King Zhou (written with a character different from the Zhou Dynasty that would depose him); the inevitable femme fatale, Daji (who is identified as a fox-spirit); and the Earl of the West's filial, and pathetic, eldest son, Bo Yikao. The story's setting is the Youli jail, where, prior to his rebellion, the Earl of the West had been imprisoned and where, according to a tradition dating back to the first centuries BCE, he had invented the hexagram divination system (recorded in the *Classic of Changes*).[23]

Having learned of his father's imprisonment, Bo Yikao rushes to the Shang capital to ransom him. A renowned *qin* player, he is invited to perform at the palace, where the king's consort Daji falls in love with him. In a plot reminiscent of the Joseph and Potiphar biblical tale, the mistress's attraction to her slave turns into venom. When she tries to seduce him, the handsome Bo Yikao strikes the queen with his musical instrument, a gesture likely fashioned after the blind musician's injury to the Qin emperor in the *Historical Records*. Rejected and enraged, Daji accuses him of trying to rape her. She demands that the king mince the righteous youth to pieces, offering his flesh to the imprisoned father. The punishment would serve the added purpose of testing the Earl of the West's purported sagacity: If he identifies his son's flesh, refusing to eat it, he should be eliminated forthwith for his (potentially seditious) wisdom; if he fails to recognize it, he poses no danger, in which case he would be released. Blinded by lust, the lecherous king follows her advice, and Bo Yikao ends up as meat paste.

Meanwhile in his prison cell, the Earl of the West casts the hexagrams, divining his first-born's tragic fate. Preparing to receive the king's culinary gift, he composes a lament for his son: "Alone, harboring loyalty and virtue, he journeyed ten thousand miles to relieve his kin's misfortune. . . . Hurling his *qin* at the evil woman, in a fit of anger rejecting her. Alas, the young traveler's sad fate, his soul turning into ashes."[24] When the envoy arrives, the earl receives him with the ceremony due a royal emissary. Kneeling down to receive the monarch's gift, he eats three balls of the child's flesh. Suppressing his grief, he goes on to express his gratitude: "Could I trouble Your Excellency to convey my thanks for a heavenly favor, as this sinful official is unable to express it himself."[25] Elated that his enemy has been proven a fool, King Zhou orders his release. The way to the rebellion that would topple his regime has been paved.

The story of the Earl of the West (King Wen) eating his son has ancient origins. In all likelihood it was already well known during the Warring States Period (475–221 BCE), when it served as the topic of a popular riddle. The *Heavenly Questions* (ca. fourth century BCE) features a conundrum that associates the butchering of Bo Yikao with the fall of the Shang Dynasty: "When [King] Zhou bestowed his son's flesh on him, the Earl of the West declared it to heaven. Why did Zhou invite God's chastisement so that the dominion of Yi [Shang] could not be saved?"[26] Apparently, it was their rendering of the earl's son into a sauce that brought upon the Shang people the wrath of the supreme god Shangdi.

The gruesome story that is hinted at in the *Heavenly Questions* is narrated in full in medieval anthologies such as the sixth-century *Collection of Classified Literature* and the tenth-century *Encyclopedia of the Taiping Era*. The earliest complete record is the third-century *Chronologies of Emperors and Kings* by Huangfu Mi (215–282), who elaborates on King Zhou's gleeful mockery of his nemesis: "A sage would not consume his offspring's flesh. . . . Who could say now that the Earl of the West is a sage? He ate his son's stew, without even realizing it!"[27] By the fourteenth century, the cannibalistic tale penetrated vernacular fiction, becoming a favorite topic of Ming historical novels. In addition to *The Canonization of the Gods*, it had been featured in the successive versions of the *Romance of the Feudal States* (which had served as a textual source for the former's lament on Bo Yikao).[28] A remarkably detailed version is preserved in the Yuan-period *Popular Tale of King Wu Punishing King Zhou*, which minces no words in its description of the earl's cunning artifice. Even though he knows full well that the chopped flesh is his son's, the future King Wen politely inquires after its source: "What is this stew made of? The meat is delicious!"[29]

The legend of the earl eating his son had been meant to demonstrate the viciousness of his tormentor, King Zhou. As early as twenty-five centuries ago, historians noted that the last Shang ruler "had not been as wicked as all that."[30] Rather, King Zhou's cruelty had been exaggerated to justify the uprising against him. The question is: Why did tradition demonstrate his evil by means of anthropophagy? Why, of all possible crimes, was he accused of cooking human flesh? The likely answer is the role of cannibalism—imagined and practiced—in ancient Chinese culture.

"I hate you so much that I could eat you," was more than a figure of speech during the Zhou period, when cannibalism was a sanctioned form of political violence. Victorious Zhou armies sometimes exhibited their ferociousness by dismembering and devouring their humiliated adversaries. Rather than mutilating the corpse of a hateful enemy—as Achilles does to Hector in the *Iliad*—ancient Chinese warriors would sometimes eat him. As Mark Lewis has suggested, "the designation of warriors as tigers marked not only their power and speed but also their tendency to slide back into the animal realm, as demonstrated by the supreme bestiality of man eating."[31] Political rivals were occasionally cannibalized as well. Rebels and assassins would be boiled in a soup or rendered into a meat paste (*hai*), their flesh ceremoniously divided between members of the ruling elite. The communal consumption suggests that the slaughter was at once capital punishment and ritual. In this respect Zhou-period cannibalism was a continuation of the widespread human sacrifices of the preceding Shang period. As in other forms of sacrifice, the flesh of the victims was shared between the gods to whom it was offered and the humans who conducted the ritual. Immortals and mortals feasted together on the human fare.[32]

That the cooking of political rivals was well known into the first centuries BCE is suggested by the famous story of the Han Dynasty founder Liu Bang (256–195 BCE), who was reported willing to eat his own father. Like the Earl of the West's, the story pivots on the familial price of a political ambition. Xiang Yu had captured Liu Bang's father, threatening to cannibalize him if his rival did not surrender. The unflustered Liu Bang responded, "As we had once sworn brotherhood, my father is also yours. If you are determined to boil him, be sure to send me a ball of the soup."[33] The story could be read as an expression of the future emperor's political acumen. An experienced player, he called Xiang Yu's bluff, estimating that he would not dare to carry out his threat. From another angle, Sima Qian's account might have served to illustrate Liu Bang's extraordinary personality that qualified him to rule "all under heaven." The cruelty of the Han founder demonstrated that he was made of imperial stuff. Those willing to eat their family members, the anecdote implies, could aspire to gain the empire.

Chinese authors of the first centuries BCE were fascinated by leaders so power-hungry they would devour their own kin. The eating of one's family was a recurring measure of political determination, so much so that cannibalism became a trope of ambition. Whereas in Liu Bang's case the father was the victim, Yue Yang (fl. 410 BCE) demonstrated resolution by eating his own son. According to a story narrated in several Warring States sources, General Yue Yang was commissioned by the king of Wei to attack the neighboring state of Zhongshan. At the time, Yue Yang's son was staying in Zhongshan. He was taken captive and shown to Yue Yang in the battlefield to weaken his morale. When the latter remained unmoved, the king of Zhongshan cooked the son in a stew. The dish was sent to the father who, eating it forthwith, proceeded to destroy the Zhongshan army and conquer its kingdom. Interestingly, Yue Yang's brutality did not earn him the trust he was seeking from his own ruler. A minister to the Wei king wryly noted, "Eating his own son, whom would he not eat?"[34]

The cannibalistic trope figured in Chinese literature all through the late imperial period. Short stories and novels celebrated heroes who proved their virility feeding on their adversaries' flesh. In some works of fiction, cannibalism is the yardstick of bravery. Those who do not flinch from eating a human liver or a human heart qualify for the fraternity of the "rivers and lakes" (*jianghu*), the heroic brotherhood of the wandering martial artists. In the Tang period, "Curly-Bearded Hero" Li Jing gains the confidence of a mysterious warrior, sharing with him tidbits made of the latter's nemesis.[35] In the Ming-period *Water Margin*, Wu Song becomes best friends with those aiming to devour him. Zhang Qing and his daring witch of a wife run an establishment in which they drug their customers and mince their flesh into meat paste. The fare is served to other patrons as dumpling filling. The couple fails in their attempt on the mighty Wu Song, only to have their appreciative victim turn into a sworn brother. Wu Song treats the bid for his flesh as a practical joke. He takes the couple's cannibalistic livelihood as proof that they are worthy of his friendship.[36]

The violence of man eating expressed intensity of emotions, whether hatred and vengeance or piety and love. All through the late imperial period, exceptional sons, daughters, and daughters-in-law sliced pieces of their own flesh and offered it as medicine to ailing parents. The filial practice was known as "cutting the thigh" (*gegu*), which was the favored body part, but it sometimes extended to the liver, the heart, and other organs. Whereas at times the gesture might have been symbolic, at others it involved real injuries to its devoted performers. A medical procedure premised upon the assumption that vitality could be transmitted through the consumption of a person's flesh, "cutting the thigh" was a ritual that could strengthen familial ties. If the communal consumption of defeated enemies created a sense of solidarity between the victors, a bride cooking her thigh for her mother-in-law established a ritual bond with her marital family. Cannibalism was thus part of a cultural repertoire that could be diversely applied.[37]

We will return below to filial cannibalism, for it had a direct bearing upon the Nezha myth. The rebellious child offered his flesh to his parents as the paragons of filial virtue had done, except that his motivation was more complex. Even if he had harbored gratitude to his father and mother, Nezha's self-immolation was driven by spite. Here suffice it to note that the cannibalistic paradigm has held a tenacious grip upon the Chinese imagination all through the modern period. It is probably not accidental that two of Lu Xun's (1881–1936) most expressive stories revolve around the consumption of human flesh. The sad irony of "Medicine" has a miserably superstitious couple purchase the flesh of a hanged revolutionary in the vain hope that it would cure their consumptive child, whereas the biting symbolism of "A Madman's Diary" has a protagonist paralyzed by phobias of familial cannibalism: "I have only just realized," the madman asserts, "that I have been living all these years in a place where for four thousand years they have been eating human flesh."[38]

> Lu Xun's fiction should not be taken as evidence that Chinese people commonly eat each other. In China, as elsewhere, cannibalism is rare. But the stories do corroborate the testimony of classical literature, historical records, and folklore, suggesting that the consumption of human flesh figured in the Chinese imagination as a cultural option that, under extreme conditions, could be materialized. As Donald Sutton has convincingly argued, "a culture of cannibalism was rooted in Chinese written records and folk ways. . . . This is not to say that the leap from cultural familiarity to practice, from imagery and metaphor to reality, was an easy one. There had to be an extraordinary political atmosphere and particular local reasons."[39] Such an exceptional political climate was provided by the Cultural Revolution when, during the harrowing spring of 1968, dozens of labeled "counterrevolutionaries" were cannibalized in poor and remote Southern Guangxi. The unique but well-documented events at Guangxi reveal a terrible merging of Maoist-style political struggle with an ancient sacrificial rite that can be traced back to the Zhou period, as party cadres solidified their victory over the humiliated enemies of the people by feasting on their human flesh.[40]

Returning to Bo Yikao's sad fate, we might suggest that it reflected the cannibalism—metaphorical and real—of the Zhou period. The Earl of the West had been forced to eat his son as a form of political vengeance. At the same time, the tale of the father consuming his son bore religious connotations. Bo Yikao was the Earl of the West's eldest son, and his slaughter might have mirrored the immolation of the firstborns. The sacrifice of the eldest offspring had been practiced in many cultures, including the ancient Near East, where it might have served as the background for Abraham's trial: God demanded that his prophet sacrifice his only son to him.[41] It has been suggested that similar human offerings figured in Shang, or early Zhou, culture. If it had been practiced in ancient China, the sacrifice of the firstborns might have contributed to the story of the earl immolating his eldest son.

Sacrificial infanticide was not unknown in China's peripheries. Mozi (ca. 460–390 BCE) described the custom to the south of China: "The cannibals' state of Qiao is situated south of Chu. When the first-son is born, they dismember his body and eat him. They call this: 'Proper behavior towards the younger brother.' If the flesh is tasty, they reserve a portion for the ruler. If he enjoys it, he rewards the father."[42] The question is whether similar practices had existed in the Chinese cultural sphere. Drawing on hints in the historical records—such as Yiya cooking his son for the pleasure of the gourmet Lord Huan (reigned 685–643 BCE)—Qiu Xigui has suggested that they did: "The sacrifice of the first-born sons was quite common in China's border regions. Moreover, after being slaughtered, the child would be dismembered and eaten, a portion being offered to the ruler. We may estimate that at an earlier period, the practice likely existed in the Central Plains as well."[43]

Assuming that it figured in Chinese antiquity, how should sacrificial infanticide be understood? Qiu Xigui has linked the (possible) custom to the well-documented rites of the early crops. The Chinese classics of ritual—like the Hebrew Bible—required that the yields be offered to the gods before they were consumed. "Unless tasted [by the deities] the new crops can-not be eaten" declares the *Book of Rites* (which was edited during the Han period).[44] The cruel logic of the "tasting" rites (*chang*) likely underscored the slaughtering of the firstborns. Just as the gods were permitted to choose from the freshest agricultural products, they were favored with the flavor of the eldest sons. Before they could enjoy the fruits of their labor, farmers and parents alike had to proffer them to the gods. That the offering would subsequently be divided accorded with Chinese ritual custom. Sacrificial meat was known as *zuo,* a term that carried the added meaning of "good fortune," for the food that had been graced by the gods was thought to bring prosperity to their devotees. The offerings of which the deities had partaken were communally consumed in ritual feasts. Sometimes, sacrificial meat was sent long-distance as a token of friendship or political alliance, which would explain why—according to Mozi—the Qiao people were careful to reserve a portion of each immolated child for their ruler.[45]

The evidence for sacrificial infanticide in Chinese antiquity could be disputed, but if the slaughter of the firstborns did figure in Shang or early Zhou culture, it would shed new light on the legend of the Earl of the West. The story of a parent being coerced into eating his son might conceal a ritual that was its structural opposite. Instead of a brutal king forcing a child's flesh on a helpless father, the myth might have borne ancient memories of parents who sacrificed their eldest son, offering a portion of the meat to the ruler.

Whereas the Chinese evidence of sacrificial infanticide is equivocal, we possess solid testimony of other forms of human sacrifice that have lasted in China all through modern times. Paul Katz has shown that during the late imperial period and into the early twentieth century, Chinese rebels have not infrequently made offerings of human flesh to their military banners. The flag that symbolized the insurgent fraternity would be proffered the blood of a sacrificial victim, usually a captive government soldier or a member of the local elite. In much the same way, the imperial troops would slaughter imprisoned rebels, smearing the blood on their own martial banners. The brutal practice, Katz suggests, might have served to dehumanize the victim no less than to foster the bond of his tormentors. From the regime's perspective, human sacrifice might have effected the re-establishment of imperial authority, whereas when performed by rebels it might have furthered group solidarity. Much as in Chinese fiction cannibalism qualified the perpetrator to the fraternity of rivers and lakes, in the blood-stained reality of warfare, human sacrifices might have functioned as a rite of passage.[46]

Stories of parents who had been tricked into eating their progeny's flesh are found in cultures other than China. Sharing significant similarities with the gruesome tale of the Earl of the West, they can illuminate it from a comparative perspective. Greek mythology features at least three fathers who had been fed their offspring: Harpagus, Thyestes, and Tereus. The earliest detailed account is the first. According to the fifth-century BCE historian Herodotus, Harpagus was a general in the court of King Astyages (r. 585–550 BCE). A prophetic dream had warned the king that his daughter's son would depose him. Hence, he ordered Harpagus to murder the newborn. Afraid of committing the crime himself, Harpagus instructed a herdsman to expose the baby on a mountaintop. Taking pity on the child, the herdsman raised him as his own instead. Learning of his grandson's survival, the king was enraged. Inviting Harpagus to a grisly feast, he inflicted upon him a gruesome punishment:

> Astyages . . . took the son of Harpagus, and slew him, after which he cut him in pieces, and roasted some portions before the fire, and boiled others; and when all were duly prepared, he kept them ready for use. The hour for the banquet came, and Harpagus appeared, and with him the other guests, and all sat down to the feast. Astyages and the rest of the guests had joints of meat served up to them; but on the table of Harpagus, nothing was placed except the flesh of his own son. This was all put before him, except the hands and feet and head, which were laid by themselves in a covered basket. When Harpagus seemed to have eaten his fill, Astyages called out to him to know how he had enjoyed the repast. On his reply that he had enjoyed it excessively, they whose business it was brought him the basket, in which were the hands and feet and head of his son, and bade him open it, and take out what he pleased. Harpagus accordingly uncovered the basket, and saw within it the remains of his son. The sight, however, did not scare him, or rob him of his self-possession. Being asked by Astyages if he knew what beast's flesh it was that he had been eating, he answered that he knew very well, and that whatever the king did was agreeable. After this reply, he took with him such morsels of the flesh as were uneaten, and went home, intending, as I conceive, to collect the remains and bury them.[47]

The story of Harpagus's dreadful punishment demonstrated that a tyrant's cruelty would lead to his downfall. Shortly after he had been treated to the grisly repast, Harpagus—like the Earl of the West—participated in a revolt that led to his tormentor's demise. He convinced Astyages's grandson, who in the meantime had settled in Persia, to rise against him. Known as Cyrus the Great (reigned ca. 550–530 BCE), the grandchild deposed the cruel Astyages, just as the Zhou Dynasty overthrew the vicious Shang regime. The Greek and the Chinese myths alike exemplified the heavenly punishment awaiting those who feed children to their parents.

Beneath the ethical surface of crime and punishment, the Earl of the West and the Harpagus tales might have been equally related to sacrificial practices. It has been suggested that the Greek myth reflected the Mediterranean child sacrifices that were practiced by such Semitic peoples as the Canaanites and the Phoenicians. The intriguing reference to the slaughtered child's head, hands, and feet—appearing also in the parallel myths of Thyestes and Tereus—might allude to the collocation of bodily organs that followed the victims' immolation.[48] The Greek and the Chinese myths had been premised upon a similar association of slaughtered meat and sacrifice. The cannibalistic feasts they depicted might have been equally related to religious offerings.

The context of the Harpagus myth is unmistakably oedipal. The father is coerced into eating his son because he has failed to slaughter the king's grandson. In both cases familial violence is directed from progenitor to a (potentially threatening) offspring. It has been pointed out that the Herodotus tale of Harpagus is textually related to Sophocles's contemporaneous play *Oedipus Rex*. The two share not only a harrowing tale of intergenerational conflict, but also a quintessential episode. Samuel Bassett has argued convincingly that the playwright had borrowed the scene of the herdsman taking pity on the foundling Oedipus from Herodotus's history of Harpagus.[49] The textual overlap between the play and the chronicle underscore their concern with identical unconscious desires. The Oedipus and the Harpagus myths alike pivot upon the rivalry of sons and fathers.

The oedipal aspect of the Harpagus story alerts us to its significance in the Chinese myth. The story of the Earl of the West devouring his filial offspring likely mirrored unconscious familial tensions. It has been noted that in most Chinese oedipal tales—the Nezha myth excluded—the violence is directed from father to son. Rather than killing his progenitor, the offspring is eliminated by him. The morality of filial piety entailed that the progeny would be the victim of the generational conflict. We will return to the oedipal interpretation of the earl's cannibalistic feast in chapter 3. Here suffice it to note that from a psychoanalytic perspective it reflects the father's fear of his son replacing him as much as the latter's terror of castration by his competitor for the mother's love.

Whichever its origins, the legend of the earl eating his son was hard to swallow, so much so that future generations labored to take off its cannibalistic edge. Popular lore sought to make the myth more digestible, suggesting that the ingested Bo Yikao somehow re-emerged from his father's stomach. The seventeenth-century *The Canonization of the Gods* reminds the Earl of the West—after his release from jail and following his family reunion—of his son's tragic fate, whereupon, fainting to the ground, he vomits the meat. Three rabbits emerge from the spewed flesh, scampering happily away. Apparently, something of the earl's son lived on in the bunnies.[50]

The suggestion that Bo Yikao re-emerged as a rabbit from his father's gorge was made already by the fourteenth-century *Popular Tale of King Wu Punishing King Zhou*.[51] The crude association of rabbit (*tu*) and vomit (*tu*) was based upon their identical pronunciation. The pun had an ancient history, for as early as the Han period, the animal was supposed to reproduce by spewing. In his *Record of Extensive Things*, Zhang Hua (232–300) noted the tradition that the rabbit conceives after gazing at the full moon (in the mountainous texture of which the Chinese, like the Indians, had perceived a rabbit). The animal goes on to vomit its litter. The third-century author was careful to acknowledge, however, that he had not verified the hearsay by personal observation.[52]

The legend of the vomited son has been preserved through an association with a sacred place. The myth became part of the local lore of Youli (in today's Henan Province) where, according to tradition, the Earl of the West had been imprisoned. The disgorged remains of the earl's child were enshrined at the Vomited-Son Tomb (Tu'er Zhong), which survives to this day. Recently renovated, the traditionally circular grave commemorates the courageous son, who had been eaten—only to be vomited—by his father. It had been shown to pilgrims as early as the fourteenth century, when the historian of Mongolian descent Naxin (fl. 1345) referred to it in the classical idiom as the Disgorged-Offspring Tomb (Ouzi Zhong).[53]

Youli is situated some fifteen miles south of the historical Shang capital of Anyang (Henan Province). Its "Tomb of the Vomited Son" is located within the imposing grounds of a temple dedicated to the Earl of the West (King Wen). The positioning of the grave within the sumptuous temple demonstrates the pathetic fate of the filial son. It is hidden behind the stately halls dedicated to his father's epoch-making achievements: the establishment of the Zhou Dynasty and the creation of the *Classic of Changes*. The legend of the vomited child was not part of official history, and it had not been engraved on the temple's grand steles. Even though popular sentiment required that the cannibalized offspring be commemorated with a grave, it was not the sanctioned center of the father's temple.[54]

Hagiographic literature is often driven by contradictory urges. It wishes to record a saint's burial place, even as it argues for his immortality (which would necessarily dissociate him from any given grave). On the one hand the devotees believe in the martyr's eternal presence, and on the other hand they require a sacred location in which they would pay him homage. Perhaps for this reason, saintly tombs are often conceived of as empty. Jesus miraculously emerged from his Jerusalem grave and, bidding farewell to the apostles, rose to heaven. Attracting pilgrims from around the world, his burial place at the Church of the Holy Sepulchre contains no coffin. Buddhist saints have similarly walked away from their tombs. Resurrected from his Chinese grave, Bodhidharma returned to his native India. Opened by his alarmed devotees, the tomb of the Chan founder has been found empty.[55]

The legend of the pathetic Bo Yikao—like the myths of his august counterparts—equivocates on the fate of his bodily remains. The Youli lore of the vomited son betrays an inconsistency regarding his burial. Bo Yikao is at once described as entombed in the "Vomited-Son Grave," and as emerging from it as a rabbit. It

Figure 1: Bo Yikao resurrected as a scampering rabbit. Wall painting dated 2009. Youli, Henan. Photo by Ye Derong (A'de).

appears that popular sentiment wanted the courageous son to have a proper tomb, even as it fancied his bunny epiphany. The Youli sanctuary features a beautiful fresco (dated 2009) that shows the rabbits emerging from the earl's vomit (figure 1). When I visited the temple on a chilly December morning in 2010, I was told that the local rabbit population is teeming, for it is forbidden to hunt the epiphanies of the courageous son who had been eaten by his father.

In the context of the seventeenth-century *The Canonization of the Gods,* the story of the Earl of the West complements that of Nezha. If the former is reminiscent of the Greek Cronus (who devoured his sons lest they depose him), the latter resembles Oedipus (who murdered his father). The violence of the two myths shuttles along the same axis of father and son, even though it is exerted in opposite directions. The legends of Nezha and of the Earl of the West betray a similar familial conflict, to which we will now turn.

2

Patricide and Suicide

There are various measures for the primacy of filial piety in traditional Chinese culture. The virtue had been accorded paramount significance in the Confucian classics, which served as the cornerstone of the education system. It had been adopted as official ideology by the state, which institutionalized the veneration of one's elders by such means as obligatory mourning periods. Filial piety underlay the legal system (which rewarded those who observed it), and it provided the moral underpinning to the extended family that guaranteed the elderly the care of sons and daughters-in-law. The veneration of the living parents extended to the worship of the deceased ancestors, linking the ethical and the religious spheres. Informing every aspect of life, filial piety has been considered by some scholars the foundation of Chinese culture.[1]

The efforts of the state and of educators had internalized the veneration of parents. "Among the various forms of virtuous conduct, filial piety comes first" (*baixing xiao weixian*) went the popular proverb, indicating that people had accepted the primacy of the Confucian virtue. Throughout the imperial period "Chinese largely defined good behavior in terms of whether or not one was a good son or daughter."[2] Anthropological research shows that down to the present filial piety has earned its practitioners moral capital. Fieldwork in diverse East Asian communities has revealed that those who exert themselves as dedicated offspring are considered by neighbors and relations as honorable and trustworthy persons. Filial behavior has been a source of personal as well as familial pride. The memorial arches constructed in the late imperial period for exemplary daughters-in-law testify that observance of the sanctioned virtue could shed glory on an entire community. By the same token, those who failed in the role of son or daughter suffered psychological as well as social injuries. Falling short of the internalized ideal led to a sense of worthlessness and a loss of communal reputation. Just as the paragons of filial virtue honored their families, those who violated the Confucian ethic were a source of familial shame.[3]

Filial piety had been inculcated in part by hagiographic literature. *Accounts of*

Filial Offspring, as they were called, enjoyed tremendous popularity beginning in the first centuries CE. The genre extolled individuals who went to extremes of self-denial in providing for their parents' well-being. A typical story would combine an act of self-sacrifice with a miracle, affirming heaven's satisfaction with the filial protagonist. Those who for their parents sought fish in the depths of winter would be rewarded with carps jumping into their hands, and those who out of season looked for the bamboo shoots their mothers craved would be blessed with the plant sprouting under their feet. Particularly well known were the filial fables collected in Guo Jujing's (1295–1321) *Twenty-Four Filial Exemplars* (*Ershisi xiao*). The subject of oral and dramatic adaptations, the tract reached all layers of society. Everybody was familiar with the twenty-four paragons, whose stories were a favorite topic of folk art and temple decoration.[4]

The *Twenty-Four Filial Exemplars* dedicate themselves to the service of their parents. No task is too severe in their selfless practice of the familial virtue. The male protagonist of one story goes as far as tasting his father's stool to check on his health, whereas the heroine of another breastfeeds her toothless mother-in-law. To be sure, such excessive devotion was beyond the pale of the average person. Nevertheless, the hagiographic literature offers us a window into the mental landscape of imperial China. Its saintly protagonists carry to the extreme values that had been common throughout the culture. Even though ordinary people were incapable of the filial paragon's asceticism, they did venerate his ideals. The didactic tales were meant to influence society at large. Their extraordinary examples reveal to us—as if by a magnifying glass—norms that had been widespread throughout the culture.[5]

Nutrition is a principal concern of the filial piety tales. Just as he had been nourished by them in his infancy, a filial offspring should nurture his elderly parents. In times of natural calamity or social upheaval, a child would go hungry making sure his parents were well-fed. One story has the protagonist eating brambles and feeding his parents with rice. Many tales revolve around a child's intrepid quest of the delicacy (or medicine) his father and mother require. The hero of one story dresses as a deer to milk the wild animal for his parents, whereas the protagonist of another lies naked on a frozen river, melting the ice to obtain the fish his stepmother desires. Repaying his parents' kindness, a filial offspring would chew the food for them. It was not uncommon for Chinese mothers to masticate solid food for their babies; hence they could expect to be requited by the same gesture. The medieval tale of Xing Qu had its moral exemplar regurgitate food, putting it into his father's toothless mouth. The inevitable miracle that followed had the old man growing a new set of choppers.[6]

Humility marks the saint. The literature of filial piety associates self-fulfillment with self-abasement. Like their Christian counterparts, the Confucian exemplars sought glory by humbling themselves. Many stories have the filial offspring engage in socially demeaning occupations to provide for his parents. He may, for example, hire himself out as a servant or a slave. Other tales have him overcome his disgust and take care of an aging parent's bodily excretions. Even in a household full of servants, a filial offspring would insist on attending himself to his parents' washing. One story has a high-ranking official rinse daily his mother's chamber pot. Another has a prince suck the pus from his father's sores. The filial child would willingly undergo physical pain to assure his parent's bodily comfort. One exemplar would sleep naked, attracting mosquitoes to feed on his flesh. The filial offspring would not wave the bloodthirsty insects away, lest they attack his parents who were sleeping nearby. In this, as in other stories, the love for parents is realized through physical torture. The hagiography of filial piety links pain and attainment, asceticism and spiritual fulfillment.

The ultimate sacrifice is that of children. In some tales, the filial child gives up his own offspring for the sake of his parent. He sacrifices the life of his child, providing for his father and mother. Beginning in the first centuries CE, the hagiographic literature subjected its protagonists to a moral dilemma. The hero would be able to save one person only: either his parent or his child. The family might be escaping from enemy forces, or might not have enough food for one additional mouth (the option of suicide not being available since the protagonist must stay alive to provide for them). In such circumstances, the filial offspring would inevitably give up his children. As horrible as these moral parables might seem to us, they did make sense to medieval society. Keith Knapp has convincingly argued that the children in these stories were regarded as extensions of oneself. Giving up his offspring, the hero was relinquishing his self-interest for the communal interest of the agnatic family (symbolized by the parent). He was yielding his private good for the greater benefit of the clan (i.e., the parents whom he shared with his brothers).[7]

The tale of Guo Ju typifies the moral offspring's dilemma. Living with his elderly mother and only child, the filial protagonist lacks enough food for them both. He resolves to bury his son alive, whereupon he is rewarded by a miracle that exempts him from the sacrifice he was willing to make. The story had originated in the first centuries CE and because it had been incorporated into Guo Jujing's *Twenty-Four Filial Exemplars* was well known into the twentieth century. As early as the Ming period some scholars found Guo Ju's immolation of his innocent child unacceptable, and by modern times the filial exemplar became the subject of bitter criticism. The leading reformer Lu Xun (1881–1936) noted caustically that the story had bred loathing—rather than love—of one's elders. It was not until his grandmother passed away, the biting essayist recalled, that he overcame the fear of his father emulating Guo Ju.[8] Here is the filial tale that terrified the young Lu Xun:

> The family of Guo Ju in the Han dynasty was poor. He had a three-year-old son. His mother reduced what she ate to give more food to him. Ju said to his wife, "Because we are very poor, we cannot provide for Mother. Moreover, our son is sharing mother's food. We ought to bury this son." When he had dug the hole three feet deep he found a great pot of gold. On it were the words "Officials may not take it, commoners may not seize it."[9]

The Confucian hagiography bears striking similarities to the biblical tale of Abraham's immolation of his son Isaac (Gen. 22:1–19). In both stories, the protagonist sacrifices that which is dearest to him for a higher cause. In both, he is rewarded by a miracle that exempts him from the terrible price he was willing to pay. In Abraham's case this is the ram caught in the thicket (which will be substituted for Isaac); In Guo Ju's, it is the pot of gold that brings the family's misfortune to an end. The difference lies in the object of the sacrifice: Abraham's devotion is to a transcendental god, whereas Guo Ju worships his immanent mother.[10] The religiosity of the filial offspring is directed toward his parents, reminding us that Confucianism has had no other gods for its devotees to adore. Unlike Buddhism and Daoism with their vast pantheons of divinities, Confucian doctrine recognized no objects of veneration beyond one's ancestors (the worship of heaven being the prerogative of the emperor alone).

Stories of a filial offspring giving up a child for a parent involve three generations: grandparent, parent, and child. The genre considers the middle one (the parent) as the "child," ignoring the sacrificed grandchild altogether. As such, the filial tales reveal that the definition of *zi* (translated here as "child" or "offspring") was, more often than not, social. No matter his age, a man was a "child" as long as his parents were alive. Anyone in a junior or a subservient position was labeled a "child," attesting the term's cultural—instead of biological—meaning.[11] The protagonist of one filial piety tale is a seventy-year-old man who dresses up in baby clothes to entertain his ninety-year-old parents. Allowing his parents to relive their fondest memories, the old man acts the role of a toddler.

Inasmuch as their protagonists were often grown-ups, the filial piety tales were intended for adult emulation. Although it was sown in childhood, the virtue was supposed to ripen in adulthood. These were for the most part grown-up offspring who were expected to take care of their elderly parents. Hence, filial piety had to be inculcated in adults. The very persistence of the didactic genre indicates that its intended audience had not been invariably responsive to the moral message. Chinese, like other people, were not always eager to shoulder the difficult task of caring for their elderly. We might imagine that siblings deferred the unpleasant responsibility to each other. As Charlotte Ikels has noted, "[T]he relentless insistence on the value of filial piety in pre-modern official discourse suggests the existence of a counter-discourse, one that said the elderly are a burden and it would be better to be rid of them."[12]

The filial piety tales permit us to appreciate the boldness of the Nezha myth. Here was a hero who, far from subjugating himself to his parents, expressed his grievances by attempted patricide. The legend's appeal probably lay in its defiance of the hegemonic Confucian discourse. Nezha has been relished as an antidote to the meek filial exemplars and venerated precisely because he disregarded paternal authority. The Nezha myth reflected the tensions created by familial hierarchy. Venting the frustrations caused by the sanctioned moral order, it provided symbolic resources for resisting it.

No less than a foil for the Nezha legend, the Confucian hagiographies have been means for its survival. The myth of the rebellious child masqueraded as a filial piety tale. Recall that Nezha's attempted patricide had been preceded by suicide. Shouldering responsibility for the murder of the dragon king's son, the brave child killed himself, thereby sparing his parents. The myth of the patricidal son, therefore, could be read as a filial hagiography. The ambivalence of filial piety and defiance, suicide and patricide, has been key for the legend's survival in a society that sanctions the veneration of one's elders.

Patricide

The Canonization of the Gods was among the most widely read Chinese novels. During the Qing period (1644–1911), it went through some twenty extant editions, which were followed by dozens more in the twentieth century.[13] Nevertheless, successive publishers felt continuous unease about—arguably—its most successful episode. Prefaces and running commentaries acknowledged that the Nezha myth was socially unacceptable, even as they struggled to justify its inclusion in the novel. As early as the first edition, Li Yunxiang expressed his discomfort with the patricidal myth he had borrowed from oral literature and suggested that the father-son conflict could have been avoided had Nezha's master dispensed with the requirement that his disciple be dedicated a shrine (for Nezha tried to kill his father following the demolition of his temple):

> Gods and immortals possess the miraculous method of bringing people back to life. At the very beginning, the immortal Taiyi should have relied upon it to rescue Nezha. Why did he have him go to Cuiping Mountain to receive some incense or other, causing friction between father and son? If, as he had claimed, the immortal had done this intentionally—to vent Nezha's murderous instincts—it is clearly gibberish.[14]

In his preface to the 1695 edition, Chu Renhuo expressed similar unease with the novel's eccentric protagonist. The influential editor of vernacular fiction acknowledged that such deviant divinities as Nezha would never be accepted by Confucian educators. Unconventional and weird, they would not be canonized by the state. In addition to the rebellious child, Chu mentioned two other antinomian deities: the winged Thunder God (Leizhen) (who likely derived from the Tantric Garuḍa bird)[15] and the simian Sun Tuxing (who was fashioned after the mischievous monkey protagonist of *The Journey to the West*):

> *The Canonization of the Gods* tells of strange spirits and unruly gods (*guai li luan shen*), none of whom had been mentioned by Confucius. The characters portrayed in the book—such as Nezha and Leizhen—are exceedingly strange. The miraculous powers recorded—such as Sun Tuxing's seventy-two transformations—are even stranger. Weird and improper (*guai'dan bujing*), they should probably be rejected by Zhongni's [Confucius] disciples.[16]

Even as they questioned his propriety, editors defended aspects of the child-god's personality. Li Yunxiang commended his bravery: "Nezha was a straightforward hero, not the kind of person who hides his head, displaying his tail. When challenged by the dragon king, he immediately confessed [killing his son]. Had this happened today, most people would have denied responsibility."[17] Elsewhere in his running commentary, Li compared Nezha to other rebellious figures in Chinese vernacular fiction. "In his naughtiness, Nezha was not inferior to the Handsome Monkey King [Sun Wukong]. . . . In his fierce intensity he resembled the Tattooed Monk [Lu Zhishen] and Li Tieniu [Li Kui]. *The Canonization of the Gods* belongs in the same class as *The Journey to the West* and *The Water Margin*."[18] Li's analogy is apt. The novels he mentions did challenge the social order as the Nezha legend did. Their protagonists shared Nezha's explosive mixture of courage and violence. Nezha, Sun Wukong, Lu Zhishen, and Li Tieniu (Li Kui) disregarded social hierarchies and accepted norms of behavior. All four inhabited a tumultuous realm that fits Bakhtin's notion of a "carnival" world: "A second life, a second world of folk culture, is thus constructed; it is to a certain extent a parody of the extra-carnival life, a 'world inside out.'"[19]

It is easy to understand the editors' unease with their child protagonist. Nezha attempted the most heinous crime in the Chinese book. As we have seen in chapter 1, patricide was a political sin as much as a familial crime. Shaking the foundations of the social order, the homicide of a parent was the equivalent of regicide. During the late imperial period, patricide was classified as one of the "Ten Abominations" (*shi'e*), which included such political crimes as treason and rebellion. Yet the infant Nezha went about the business of killing his father with narcissistic self-fulfillment. Following the insult he had suffered—Li Jing's destruction of his temple—Nezha was determined to annihilate him. His was patricide with a vengeance:

> Arriving at Chentang Pass, Nezha headed straight to his father's mansion. "Li Jing!" he roared, "Come out and face me!" The attending officers hurried inside to report: "Your third son is outside. He is riding wheels of fire and is wielding a fire-tipped spear. We do not know why he is shouting your tabooed first name. Your lordship, what should we do?" "Nonsense!" retorted Li Jing. "Who ever heard of the dead coming back to life!" He had not finished shouting, when another group of men scurried in: "If your lordship does not hurry," they reported, "your son is sure to break in forcibly.'
>
> "This cannot be," thought the infuriated Li Jing. Grasping his painted halberd, and mounting his dappled steed, he hastened out to see his son facing him. Riding fire-wheels and wielding a fire-tipped spear, Nezha seemed much bigger than before. Li Jing was flabbergasted. "You beast!" he screamed. "A monster in your previous life, how dare you come back to pester me as a ghost!" "I have returned you my flesh and bones," answered Nezha, "and I have caused you no harm. Why did you go to Cuiping Mountain, whip my golden statue, and burn my temple? Today you will taste my hatred for that whipping!"
>
> Lifting his shining spear, Nezha aimed it straight at his father's breast. Li Jing met it with his painted halberd. Horse and fire-wheels circled each other; halberd and spear clashed together. Nezha possessed limitless strength. After three to five rounds, his adversary was so worn out that the horse stirred and its rider fell off. His strength exhausted, and his muscles spent, Li Jing felt the sweat trickling down his spine. He had no alternative but to turn on his heels, escaping southeastwards. Nezha's shouts followed him: "Li Jing! Do not imagine I will spare you. If I do not kill you, I will not go back empty-handed. . . . Even if you escape to the immortal isles, I will get your head before I am through with my anger."[20]

Despite his determination, Nezha failed to kill his father. Even as he vowed revenge, he had been foiled by divine intervention. Arriving on the scene, the Immortal Randeng sheltered Li Jing, preventing the heinous crime of patricide. A thinly disguised adaptation of the Buddha Dīpaṃkara (Randengfo), the immortal bestowed on Li Jing a magic stupa (pagoda) that protected him from his son's wrath. It sufficed for the father to intone a spell for the implement to capture and burn his rebellious offspring. A similar method of control had been applied to another defiant protagonist of late imperial fiction. *The Journey to the West*'s mischievous monkey had been constrained by a metal band attached to his skull. Whenever he got out of hand, his Buddhist master recited a charm that caused the impish Sun Wukong insufferable headaches.[21]

The magic pagoda had been invoked to prevent Nezha's patricide as early as the eleventh century. It is mentioned in a poem on the rebellious child by Su Zhe (1039–1112): "The Buddha, knowing Nezha was crazy and hard to be told, ordered the father a magic stupa in his left hand to hold"[22] We will see in following chapters that the disciplinary method provided an etiological explanation for the father's iconographic attribute. The Buddhist god Vaiśravaṇa had been equipped with a stupa centuries before he was identified with the Tang general Li Jing. Medieval works of art invariably depicted the martial god holding a stupa in his left hand. The Nezha legend integrated the emblem into the tale of the patricidal son, assigning it a restrictive function (see figure 2).

Constraining Nezha by means of the magic stupa, the Daoist immortal insisted that he apologize to Li Jing. He demanded, furthermore, that the rebellious child address his father as such. Nezha, who following his suicide had pointedly called Li Jing by his first name, was forced to comply. "Father," he said, "your son is guilty of a crime." The perfunctory—and brief—excuse entailed no repentance. Nezha felt no remorse for his attempted patricide: "Even as his mouth uttered an excuse, his heart did not comply. He merely gnashed his teeth."[23] The apology extracted from him notwithstanding, Nezha would have attempted to kill his father again had he been given the opportunity.

The Immortal Randeng exacted from Nezha an apology, but he did not punish him. His leniency stands in sharp contrast to late imperial Chinese law, which stipulated the harshest punishments to those who attempted—not to mention succeeded—to kill a father. The Ming and Qing codes deemed capital punishment insufficient and specified "death by slicing" (*lingchi*) for patricide. The cutting would begin while the condemned was still alive, lasting long after his death until his entire body had been dismembered. The lesser penalty of decapitation had been reserved for those—like Nezha—who took action to kill a parent but failed.[24] As one of the "Ten Abominations" (or gravest crimes), patricide was beyond amnesty. Its redress, moreover, affected a wide circle of people. Living in Fujian in the 1850s, the Protestant missionary Justus Doolittle enumerated the consequences of the crime:

> If a son should murder his parent, either father or mother, and be convicted of the crime, he would not only be beheaded, but his body would be mutilated by being cut into small pieces; his house would be razed to the ground, and the earth under it would be dug up for several feet deep; his neighbors living on the right and the left would be severely punished; his principal teacher would suffer capital punishment; the district magistrate of the place would be deprived of his office and disgraced; the prefect, the governor of the province, and the viceroy would all be degraded three degrees in rank. All this is done and suffered to mark the enormity of the crime of parricide.[25]

As the gravest of all crimes, patricide recognized no mitigating circumstances. The harshest punishment was applied even when the culprit was known to have suffered from mental illness. During the Qing period, insane people who committed parricide were invariably sentenced to "death by slicing." Luca Gabbiani has shown that the sanctity of filial piety was such that it overruled the tendency

Figure 2:
Vaiśravaṇa in a Tang-period (ninth-century) painting on silk. The stupa (pagoda) he holds in his right hand has been assigned a disciplinary function by the Nezha legend. © The Trustees of the British Museum. Stein painting 138.

of the Qing courts to consider madness a mitigating factor. Even though special procedures for insane homicide did exist, they were not applied to patricide. The question of the crime's intentionality was disregarded, contrary to the Chinese legal tradition that weighed the culprit's awareness of his deed. Gabbiani shows that the state's concern for its own legitimacy was one reason for the severity meted out for patricide. The legal tools that would have allowed for leniency were not applicable to the felony that threatened the ideological foundations of the imperial regime.[26]

Why was Nezha spared punishment for his heinous crime, faring so differently from the miserable father killers of the Ming and Qing periods? How could Chinese society adopt a patricidal son as a folk hero and a god? As Ho Kin-chung has suggested, the answer lies in the child's self-sacrifice, which preceded his attempted murder.[27] We turn to the ambivalent meanings of Nezha's suicide.

Suicide

Let us recall the circumstances leading to Nezha's suicide: Bathing in a river and laundering his magic girdle in it, the child caused the water to boil all the way to the underwater palace of the dragon king Ao Guang, who dispatched first a *yakṣa* spirit named Li Gen, then his own son Ao Bing, to check the cause of the disturbance. In the ensuing fray the infant killed both monsters. Adding insult to injury, he pulled out the precious tendons from the dragon Ao Bing's body, mutilating his corpse. The enraged dragon king demanded reparations from Nezha's father, threatening to annihilate his family. Seeking the guidance of the Immortal Taiyi, Nezha headed for the Golden-Light Cavern atop the Mountain of Heavenly Origins. After consulting with his master, he rushed back to his parents' residence:

> Approaching the commander's residence, Nezha heard the din of confused shouts. The officers quickly reported to Li Jing that his son had arrived. "The young lord has returned," they said. The four ocean dragon kings were surveying the scene, when they heard Nezha's stern command: "One person's crime is one person's punishment. I have killed Ao Bing and Li Gen; I will pay for it with my life. How would I dare implicate my parents in my misdeeds?" Addressing Ao Guang, he said: "I am not just anybody. I am the Numinous Pearl (Ling Zhuzi). Bearing divine tallies, I have been ordered into this world. Today, I will slash open my belly, gouge out my intestines, and scrape the meat off my bones, returning it to my parents. This way they would not be implicated. Do you accept the proposal? If you do not, we will head together for the Hall of Divine Mists, where I will have a lot to say to the Emperor of Heaven." "All right," replied Ao Guang, "Since you are ready to save your parents, you will be renowned for your filial behavior."
>
> The four dragon kings proceeded to release Li Jing and his wife, whereupon Nezha,

> grasping the sword in his right arm, cut off his left arm. He slashed open his belly, gouged out his intestines, and scraped the bones. His heavenly and earthly souls dispersing, he returned to the netherworld. The four dragon kings departed as he had instructed. Taking her son's corpse, Lady Yin placed it in a wooden coffin and buried it; but of that no more.[28]

Why did Nezha commit suicide? Why did the narrative require the boy to give up his life? On the most immediate level, the suicide served to separate the filial offspring that came before it, from the patricidal ghost that followed. Nezha's self-immolation implied that the attack on paternal authority had taken place outside of the mortal realm, for which reason it had no consequences for ordinary human relations. Significantly, the human boy (as distinct from the subsequent divinity) was not devoid of filial sentiments. Even Nezha's most outrageous deed, tearing off the dragon Ao Bing's tendons, was motivated by the love of his father. Bursting into Li Jing's studio, the excited child told the horrified parent—in the presence of the stupefied dragon king—that he had made him a belt of the precious ophidian's sinews. Nezha had mutilated the dragon prince in order to make of him a filial present.

To be sure, there is an element of pretense in the separation of the human Nezha from the ghost—or incarnated divinity—that followed. His suicide caused Nezha no disjunction of identity; he remained the same person, endowed with the identical fiery temperament. The child carried with him the memories of his previous incarnation, acting upon the grievances of his former life. Nezha's physical appearance, like his psychological makeup, hardly altered, his newly fashioned lotus body was easily recognizable. To the novel's protagonists—and readers—the divine Nezha was the same old boy. Still, the relegation of the (thwarted) patricide to the netherworld permitted society to accept it. What is forbidden to humans is permissible to their gods. With no more than slight self-deception, the myth of the patricidal divinity could be accepted as irrelevant to the sanctioned social order.

Tzvetan Todorov has argued that the fantastic permits authors to explore realms that have been tabooed by their community. The resort to the supernatural enables novelists to escape both their superegos and the censorship of society. What is prohibited by society, and forbidden by one's conscience, may be tried in the divine realm: "The function of the supernatural is to exempt the text from the action of the law, and thereby to transgress the law."[29] The Nezha legend is a perfect example. The rebellious child was permitted to attack his father in the realm of the spirits only. In order for him to fulfill society's unconscious dreams, he had to be made into a ghost.

We may pause here to consider the different mechanisms that are employed to mitigate the heinous crimes of Oedipus and Nezha respectively. In the Greek play, it is the flesh-and-blood Oedipus who kills his father (and lies with his mother). Sophocles, however, alleviates his protagonist's responsibility by having him commit his crime unconsciously: Oedipus neither knows that the man he murders is his father, nor that the woman he makes love to is his mother. By contrast, Nezha goes about the business of his patricide consciously; he recognizes full well that Li Jing is his father. The extenuating circumstances for *his* crime are provided by the pretense that it is not he who commits it. Instead of the human Nezha, he is a ghost who—after the child's suicide—attempts to avenge his death by murder.

More than a separation between the divine realm (which would tolerate patricide) and the human world (which abhorred it), Nezha's suicide was an act of filial piety. Shouldering the responsibility for killing the dragon prince, Nezha ransomed his parents. By killing himself, he saved their lives. The brave child could be canonized as a filial exemplar, as the dragon king himself consented: "since you are ready to save your parents, you will be renowned for your filial behavior." Versions of the Nezha legend that end with the child's self-immolation, omitting the ensuing patricide, would fit the hagiographic genre of filial piety. We will examine in chapter 4 a Taiwanese opera rendition of the Nezha legend that presents him as an exemplary offspring. Culminating with the child's suicide (rather than the ensuing revenge), the protagonist of Jiang Qingliu's (1935–2004) *Nezha Story* is lauded as a paragon of filial devotion.

Even as Nezha's suicide ransomed his parents, it violated a cardinal aspect of filial piety: the preservation of the body. Confucianism considered the body a gift from one's parents, which it was forbidden to mutilate. The sanctity of the paternal endowment had been stated in the opening paragraph of the *Classic of Filial Piety*: "Our bodies—to every hair and bit of skin—are received by us from our parents, and we must not presume to injure or wound them: This is the beginning of filial piety."[30] That Nezha chose to dispose of the sacred gift suggests that his self-immolation might have involved more than filial sentiments. It might have been driven by spite. Returning his flesh and bones to his parents, the boy was released from his obligation to them. His suicide settled Nezha's filial debt, paving the way for an outright break with his parents. From this angle, the self-immolation had been motivated by anger. Even as it saved his parents, Nezha's suicide had been meant as a protest.

The sanctity of the body had figured prominently in the late imperial debate over filial cannibalism. Beginning in the seventh century, exceptional sons, daughters, and daughters-in-law would cut off pieces of their own flesh and offer it as medicine to ailing parents. The practice was known as "cutting the thigh" (*gegu*), but it extended to various other body parts including arms, fingers, liver, heart, and bone marrow. The wound would be treated with incense ashes, Artemisia leaves, paper, or cloth to stop the bleeding, while the sliced flesh was boiled in a soup for the needy elder. The treatment originated among the uneducated, and it might have reflected medical despair. Unable to afford expensive physicians and costly medications, the poor might have resorted to cutting their own flesh. Nevertheless, the therapeutic procedure was gradually incorporated into various compendiums of *materia medica,* and by the late imperial period it had penetrated at least some segments of the literati elite. As Jimmy Yu has noted, "during the late-Ming [filial slicing] was part of mainstream society."[31] When the Nezha legend took shape, it was not unheard of for people of all walks of life to slice their bodies for their parents' sake. Their flesh was returned as a drug to the father and the mother who had bestowed it upon them in the first place.

Children volunteering the flesh to their parents are mentioned in Dante Alighieri's (1265–1321) *Inferno.* Imprisoned at the dreadful Pisa Tower, Count Ugolino and his four sons are being starved to death. Seeing the gaunt aspect of their dying father, the children offer him their bodies to eat. Much like the *gegu* practitioners, they reason that the flesh should be returned to its progenitor: "O Father, It will hurt much less if you of us eat: Take what once you gave to clothe us this flesh of our wretchedness."[32] Dante goes on to hint at the possibility that Ugolino did in fact feed on his sons' corpses, for which reason he had been condemned by the Italian poet to end his miserable existence in hell. His fate—gnawing forever at the skull of the enemy who had him incarcerated—indicates how alien the rhetoric of filial cannibalism had been to medieval culture. Christian ethics did not require the familial sacrifice of the body. Unlike their Chinese counterparts, Italian children had not been burdened with the obligation of offering the flesh to an ailing parent.

Alien to European culture, filial cannibalism did exist in China. Hundreds of recorded cases attest that the medical sacrifice of the flesh had taken root at least in some segments of late imperial society. As Qiu Zhonglin has shown, the attraction of filial slicing lay in the combination of medical, ethical, and religious beliefs. Those who resorted to the self-sacrifice did so out of conviction in its therapeutic efficacy, coupled with a sense of filial duty and a hope of divine retribution. "Cutting the thigh" was premised upon the medical assumption that vitality could be transferred from one person to another, even as its moral underpinning was the filial obligation to repay parents the gift of the body.[33] The operation was often conducted in a temple, where divine epiphany was expected to heal the donor and his beneficiary, offspring and progenitor. "Cutting the thigh," furthermore, functioned as a ritual that strengthened family ties. Sacrificing her flesh for a mother-in-law, a bride would secure her position in her husband's family. The confluence of therapeutic practice, moral principle, and religious conviction proved irresistible across the generations. A source of pride, filial slicing became in some cases a family tradition. Lineages gained moral capital by the continuous sacrifice of the flesh, as a nineteenth-century Anhui gazetteer testifies:

> Hu Guang'min was a native of Xuxi [Anhui]. His brother was named Guang'zheng. Guang'min passed away at a young age. When their father was sick, Guang'min "cut the thigh" (*gegu*). When their mother was sick, Guangzheng's wife, née Cao, and Guang'ming's wife, née Wang, both "cut the thigh." When Madam Wang was sick, her son Daru "cut the thigh." When Madam Cao was sick her daughter in-law, also née Cao, "cut the thigh." When Guang'min was sick, his son Dalian "cut the thigh." Within the family, the practice of filial piety had been mutually continuous.[34]

The moral gesture of sacrificing one's flesh befitted a saint. Not surprisingly the hagiographies of several Chinese deities have them accomplishing the heroic deed. Composed by the automatic spirit writing technique, the Song period autobiography of Wenchang, the god of literature, extols his filial devotion. Séances conducted in 1181 revealed the depth of the god's devotion to his parents. Speaking in the first person, Wenchang told how he had saved his mother's life in a previous incarnation. The mother had suffered from a terrible abscess, a condition aggravated by the constant care for her single child. The god reciprocated by sucking her pus and blood, which filled his mouth. When the patient's condition stabilized, Wenchang proceeded to nourish her with his own flesh. Cutting the thigh, he fed his mother with a piece of his boiled flesh. A voice from heaven announced that his filial piety would be duly requited, whereupon she fully recovered.[35]

The extraordinary feats of filial cannibalism attracted storytellers and became a favorite topic of late imperial fiction. "Cutting the thigh" was so well known that in some cases it became the subject of comic reversal. A protagonist of a Li Yu (1610–1680) story, for example, slices a piece of his own flesh to cure a homosexual lover (instead of a parent).[36] Such fictional exemplars notwithstanding, there is solid evidence that filial cannibalism was historically practiced. Ongoing government concern reveals that slicing the thigh had become a social problem. Beginning in the eighth century and all through the nineteenth, officials debated how to treat the questionable filial custom: Should the government intervene to curb it, or should it reward its devout practitioners? Filial exemplars had been customarily rewarded by banners, memorial arches, and government subsidies. The question was whether those who sliced the flesh should be similarly awarded or, on the contrary, chastised.

As early as the Tang period, Han Yu (768–824) set the tone of the official discourse, arguing sternly against offspring sacrificing the flesh. The Confucian thinker noted that the ancients had never engaged in such extravagant activities, which could lead to the unfilial crime of terminating the family line. Leaving no issue had been declared by no lesser an authority than Mencius (fourth century BCE) as the most unfilial act. By injuring themselves to death, those who sliced the thigh might turn into unfilial—rather than filial—exemplars.[37] Following Han Yu, scholars derided the cooking of one's flesh as "ignorant filial piety" (*yu xiao*).

Relying on the *Classic of Filial Piety,* they stressed the sanctity of the body, which it was forbidden to violate, even for the sake of the parents who had endowed it. In 1728, the Yongzheng emperor instructed his officials to refrain from rewarding those who "cut the thigh." Even as he expressed sympathy to their misguided filial piety, the sovereign worried that encouraging them would be detrimental to the lives of his subjects.[38] The monarch was following in the footsteps of his Ming predecessor, Emperor Zhu Yuanzhang (1328–1398), who had similarly banned the government accolade of filial cannibalism. The language of the Ming edict alluded to the tale of the filial offspring who, seeking to satisfy his stepmother with fish, lay on the ice naked:

> As for lying on ice and cutting the thigh, the ancients did not practice it. Even though in later generations such cases have occurred, they have been rare. When one cuts the liver, the injury to the body is even greater. Furthermore, the parents may have one child only. Cutting his liver or slicing his thigh, the child might die. Lying on ice, he might freeze to death. Thus the parents will have no one to support them, and the family line will be terminated. Instead [of being filial], this will be the most unfilial act. . . . If cases of lying on ice or cutting the thigh become known, they should be excluded from the government roster of honors. Follow this order![39]

The edicts of Ming and Qing emperors notwithstanding, local officials continued to reward practitioners of filial cannibalism all through the nineteenth century. As Qiu Zhonglin has suggested, they disregarded their superiors' instructions partly because of the pressure exerted on them by local communities, which expected their filial exemplars being rewarded, and partly because of their own sympathy to the filial sacrifice. Even as they considered it uncouth, many officials were moved by what they considered as sincerity underlying the filial sacrifice. Ming and Qing essays on "cutting the thigh" employed such terms of approbation as "utmost sincerity" (*zhicheng*), "utmost feeling" (*zhiqing*), and "earnest love" (*du yu ai*). Similar approval of the medical procedure had been voiced as early as the eleventh century by Song Qi (998–1061): "Even though the vulgar people of the alleyways possess no learning of rites or righteousness, that they are willing to forgo their bodies for the sake of their parents is an expression of a sincere heart; this alone merits praise."[40]

To be sure, some Ming and Qing scholars persisted in opposing the filial sacrifice of the flesh. Considering it barbaric, a sixteenth-century editor excised all citations of "cutting the thigh" from the "filial exemplars" section of the gazetteer of Shaowu (in today's Fujian Province).[41] A century later, Pu Songling (1640–1715) likewise derided the feeding of one's flesh to one's parents. The biting satirist accused contemporary officials of encouraging the ignorant practice. Instead of pondering the true significance of filial piety, they were falling for the extravagant show of the sliced flesh. Pu Songling's comments attest the ongoing accolade of filial cannibalism, which contradicted imperial edicts:

> "Cutting the thigh" is something injurious to life. The superior person does not approve of it. Ignorant men and women, however, have no way of knowing that something injurious to life is unfilial. They simply follow those drives they cannot control. Surely there are real exemplars of filial piety in the world. The problem is the officials responsible for public mores are too overloaded with work to contemplate who deserves reward. Therefore they choose the easy way of praising obscure trifles, following the example of shallow people.[42]

The rhetoric of Nezha's suicide was identical to that of "cutting the thigh." Like the (ignorant) filial exemplars of the Ming and Qing periods, the child returned the body he had owed them to his parents. But his motivation differed. Whereas those who sliced the flesh used it as a medication for their parents, Nezha's sacrifice was not devoid of resentment. Even as his self-immolation saved his parents, the infant's sacrifice paved the way for his frontal attack upon them. Judging by what he said *after* the fact, Nezha had killed himself in order to haunt his father as a ghost. Adding the sin of disobeying his elder brother to the crime of rebelling against his father, Nezha explained to his sibling Muzha why he was free to kill their father: "Ripping open my belly, and pulling out my intestines, I have returned him my flesh and bones. We are no longer related. How could there be feelings of parent and child between us!"[43] Nezha's suicide functioned as protest, permitting him to attack his father, whom he no longer recognized as such.

The Chinese tradition of suicide as protest has ancient origins. As early as the third century BCE, the poet Qu Yuan (ca. 340–ca. 280 BCE) killed himself to express his grievance against the misguided king of the state of Chu. The honest official had been subject to slander and banishment, which led to his throwing himself into the Miluo River. His political protest has been celebrated ever since in elite and popular culture alike. The haunting lines of his farewell poem—"Enough. . . . Since none is worthy to work with in making good government, I shall go and join [the Immortal] Peng Xian"[44]—have been cherished as great literature, even as the common folk have dedicated to him a festival in which dragon boat races are held and offerings are thrown into the waterways. The self-immolation of the ancient poet-official reflected—and helped shape—a tradition of suicide as an accepted response to personal, social, and political injustices. Unlike the Judeo-Christian tradition, which prohibited suicide on theological grounds (even though exceptions were made for martyrdom), the Chinese had no religious sanction against self-immolation, which was considered an appropriate (if undesirable) solution to a wide array of intolerable situations. Officials were sometimes expected to kill themselves rather than switch alliance to a new regime; widows were cherished for choosing death over disloyalty to a deceased husband (especially during the late imperial period); and all through the present, some victims have relied on suicide for the public condemnation of their tormentors.

In her seminal essay "Women and Suicide in China," Margery Wolf contrasted the contemporary Western and traditional Chinese views of suicide: "In the West we ask of a suicide, 'Why?' In China the question is more commonly 'Who?' Who drove her to this? Who is responsible?"[45] Conducting fieldwork in rural Taiwan of the 1960s, Wolf explored the power of self-destruction as a tool of social and supernatural condemnation. Killing herself as an act of protest against her mother-in-law, a young bride could expect her natal family to exact revenge on her in-laws, just as her own ghost would hunt her erstwhile tormentor. She delighted in the knowledge that her husband's family would be publicly humiliated and would have to provide her with a sumptuous funeral, just as her brothers would wreak havoc on her in-laws, extorting financial compensation from them. Writing six centuries earlier, another Western observer provided an identical assessment of suicide as vengeance. The Venetian traveler Marco Polo (1254–1324) agreed with the American anthropologist that the Chinese rely on the social and religious repercussions of self-murder to avenge themselves:

> And so the men of the province of Mangi [South China] are more passionate than other people, and for anger and grief some very often kill themselves. For if it shall happen that some one of these shall give a blow to some other or pull out his hair or inflict some injury or harm upon him, and the offender may be so powerful and great that he is powerless to take vengeance; the sufferer of the injury will hang himself from excess of grief at the door of the offender by night and die, doing this to him for the greater blame and contempt; and so when the offender has been discovered by the witness of the neighbors they condemn him for compensation of the injury to be obliged at the burning of the corpse to honor him with instruments and servers and the other things, as has been said, according to their customs with active festivity. And this will be the greater reason why he hung himself, namely that this rich and powerful man should honor him at death in order that he may be likewise honored in the other world; so that they keep up this custom.[46]

The communal sense of guilt that follows self-murder is not unique to China. Rightly or more commonly wrongly, the relatives of a suicide feel responsible for the death. A growing body of psychological literature is dedicated to the "postvention" of suicide survivors; that is, healing the wounds of a suicide's family members. In China, however, where those related to the suicide were held by society accountable for his death, special mechanisms were created that could work both for and against them. The grand funerals that were held for the self-murderer humiliated those accountable for his demise, even as they served to expiate their guilt. Haunted by the spirit of a suicide, a family could hire the services of a religious specialist to exorcise it. If we consider the ghost an externalized reflection of internal remorse, the spirit medium who pacified it was acting as a psychologist alleviating the family's distress. The religious ceremonies that followed the suicide were at once punishment by the larger community and a means for the individuals involved to manage their psychological crisis.

The tendency to interpret suicide in social, rather than psychological, terms was reflected in the legal system that persecuted those responsible for it. Self-murder was considered a crime, for which another party—an instigator—was held accountable. The Ming and Qing criminal codes included a vast category titled "Pressuring a person to commit suicide" (*weibi ren zhisi*). Its twenty-five substatutes reserved different penalties to diverse forms of pressure resulting in self-murder: from robbery, sexual assault, blackmail, and theft to beating and public humiliation. In accordance with the morality of filial piety the severest punishments were reserved for those who had shamed their elders into killing themselves. Children whose unfilial behavior led parents or grandparents to commit suicide were beheaded.[47]

The legal concern with suicide as a crime (committed by another party) has enriched historians with a vast body of literature on self-murder in late imperial China. The Qing archives contain hundreds of tried suicide cases. These sometimes reveal a misery of existence, in which no more than a slight change for the worse could lead to self-murder. As Andrew Hsieh and Jonathan Spence have noted, the Qing records of suicide are tantalizing as much for what they tell as for what they do not. In many cases the historian would like to know more about the psychological makeup and family history of the suicide whose demise is laconically summarized in the legal records. What might have been, for example, the hidden background for peasant Yan's decision to take his own life? Did he kill himself merely because he had been robbed of his leather jacket?

> Because Yan Jingong's paternal uncle Yan Shouyu owed him wheat and beans, and didn't pay him back, [Yan Jingong] demanded that Shouyu take off his leather jacket and give it to him in payment. Because the weather grew cold, [Shouyu] demanded it back. Yan Jingong wouldn't give it back. Because Yan Shouyu had no leather jacket to get through the winter, he was in great distress and strangled himself.[48]

The legal records indicate that suicide was the weapon of the weak, resorted to by those otherwise powerless to avenge themselves. In a patriarchal society these were often women. A vast body of scholarship has demonstrated the tragic role of suicide in Chinese female lives.[49] Whereas global health care records show that in the modern era men commit suicide at a rate two to three times higher than women, in traditional China women were as liable as men—and sometimes more liable than men—to take their own lives. This is suggested not only by the plethora of Qing legal and historical references to female suicide, but also by the one Chinese province for which we have reliable census information and mortality data: Taiwan under Japanese colonial rule. From the 1900s through the 1940s, Taiwanese women committed suicide at a rate equal to or higher than that of Taiwanese men. The age profile is also telling: Chinese women were most exposed to the risk of self-murder at a young age (fifteen to twenty-five) when, leaving their natal families, they became subject to their in-laws. The gender inequality of the marriage system had the men sheltered in their paternal home, whereas their brides assumed a subservient position in a strange and often hostile environment. Upon her marriage, a young woman became subject to a host of people she had likely never met before: parents-in-law, brothers- and sisters-in-law, and husband. Forced to prove herself, unprotected and lonely, the burden was sometimes too hard to bear. Whereas global statistics for the modern period have the elderly committing suicide at a rate identical to or higher than the young, in traditional China young women were more prone to take their own lives.[50]

The social reality of female suicide was reflected in fiction. Scholars have noted the astonishing frequency of women killing themselves in Chinese literature.[51] Beginning in the Tang period and all through the nineteenth century, scores of stories, novels, plays, and poems lamented the sad fate of women who were driven to taking their own lives. No fewer than eight female suicides are elaborated upon in one Chinese novel alone. The women in Cao Xueqin's (1715?–1763) *Dream of the Red Chamber* kill themselves for a variety of reasons: A wronged maid throws herself into a well; a concubine who had been tortured by her husband's principal wife swallows gold; and a young woman whose fiancé walks away from the marriage slashes her throat with the precious sword that had been given to her as an engagement pledge. One of the novel's glamorous heroines hangs herself after a love affair with her father-in-law becomes known. Even though this last instance had been disguised by the author—under pressure from family members who might have been embarrassed by it—he did leave unmistakable hints of it in his masterpiece's opening poem: "Perfumed was the dust that fell, from painted beams where springtime ended. Her sportive heart and amorous looks the ruin of a mighty house portended."[52]

Dating from the same period as the Nezha legend, "The Courtesan's Jewel Box" illustrates the working of suicide in late imperial fiction. Among Feng Menglong's (1574–1646) best stories, it tells of the glamorous courtesan Du Shiniang whose true love for a fickle young man has been betrayed. Enamored of the young student Li Jia, the dashing courtesan lends him her own savings so he can purchase her from the procuress. The two set sail to his paternal home, meeting along the way a cunning merchant named Su. Bewitched by the courtesan's charms and sensing the student's fear of his father, Su convinces Li that it would be a fatal error to introduce the woman of low repute to his family. He offers mendaciously to buy her himself, and the spineless Li accepts. Learning of the transaction, the heroine comes on board and, clasping her jewel box, throws herself into the water, but not before showing the crowd of onlookers that it contained priceless treasures worth incomparably more than the paltry sum of a thousand taels for which she had been sold. The spectators curse Li for his faithlessness and condemn Su for his treachery. The two men escape their separate ways, both haunted by the ghost of the beautiful woman. Within a short period, Su dies of illness and Li, tormented by shame and remorse, goes insane.[53]

The legend of the defiant boy Nezha shares significant similarities with the story of the desperate courtesan. The two tales pivot upon a public act of self-murder, which brings shame upon those responsible for it. Nezha and Du Shiniang alike kill themselves in front of a crowd of onlookers (in the child's case his entire household, the dragon kings, and their retinues). The boy's ghost, like the dashing woman's spirit, haunts its tormentor (the father). Most tellingly, Nezha, like the purchased courtesan, is in a dependent position and therefore has no recourse but suicide to protest his fate. Nezha's self-immolation is shocking, for it is committed by a child. And yet it perfectly fits the paradigm—observed by Marco Polo—of suicide as the weapon of the weak. For no one is as dependent on another as a child on his parents.

The Nezha legend expressed grievances with the social order while at the same time succumbing to its hegemonic discourse. Its endurability hinged upon the ambiguity of the child's suicide, which could be interpreted as filial sacrifice even as it undermined the ethics of filial piety. Nezha killed himself to save his parents from the dragon king's wrath; at the same time his self-immolation was immediately recognizable as a dependent's protest against a superior. Their Confucian convictions mollified by his filial selflessness, readers were free to empathize with Nezha's enmity of his father.

The culture-specific interpretation of Nezha's self-immolation needs to be supplemented by a comparative perspective. Suicide should also be analyzed as a psychological phenomenon that transcends cultural boundaries. From a psychoanalytic perspective, Nezha's self-murder was self-punishment. It was inflicted upon him by his superego as a penalty for his tabooed fantasy of replacing his father as the mother's consort. Even though their temporal sequence has been reversed, the suicide was the self-inflicted retribution for patricide. Like Oedipus, who went into exile and blinded himself for killing his father, Nezha took his own life for the same unpardonable sin. This leads us to the myth's inevitable oedipal interpretation.

3

The Chinese Oedipus

The Oedipus complex is part of our language. Sigmund Freud's (1856–1939) notion that beneath the thin surface of our consciousness is hidden a forbidden sexual drive has changed the modern concept of the self. His theory of the oedipal drive—the infantile desire to possess the parent of the opposite sex while removing the other—has had a tremendous impact on the evolution of the twentieth-century arts and sciences. Freud's earliest formulation of his epoch-making discovery appeared in *The Interpretation of Dreams* (1900): "It is the fate of us all, perhaps, to direct our first sexual impulse towards our mother and our first hatred and first murderous wish against our father."[1] As Freud saw it, every boy passes through a phase in which he desires to kill his father and monopolize the mother's love. As he grows up, the child gradually suppresses the forbidden urge, channeling his sexual and aggressive energies into socially acceptable forms of work and love. Nonetheless, residues of his infantile fantasy remain hidden in the unconscious, finding expression in works of art the protagonists of which live them out. Literature echoes the hidden chords of repressed emotions. It is for this reason that heroes such as King Oedipus are gripping.

The Oedipus complex has been the subject of intense debate, in diverse disciplines from psychology and sociology to history and literary criticism. Many aspects of the Freudian theory—especially regarding the evolution of female sexuality—are nowadays considered outdated. Nevertheless the core of the male oedipal theory has been accepted by a vast number of thinkers and researchers as inherent in the biological and social makings of the family: "As soon as there was a family, there was the Oedipus complex; As long as there is a family, there will be an Oedipus complex," writes André Green. Melford Spiro concurs: "The only appropriate response to the question, 'Is the Oedipus complex universal?' is 'How could it possibly not be?' . . . If there were a human society in which mothers did not have male consorts—so that the son had no adult rival for the love of the mother—in such a society the Oedipus complex (by definition) would not exist. So far as we know, however, no human society of that type exists, or has ever existed."[2] In his *Freud for Historians*, Peter Gay likewise argues for the universality of the Freudian complex:

> The predominating evidence from experimental psychology, sociology, and anthropology strongly suggests, though it does not conclusively prove, a good fit between Freud's theory and human experience—everywhere. The oedipal triangle has made its appearance in all recorded cultures. . . . The Oedipus complex appears to be the lot of humans everywhere, and it has left its deposits both in expected and in exotic places: in politics and religion, education, and literature, even in the market place.[3]

Even as they claim its universality, scholars stress that the Oedipus complex varies in accordance with historical, social, and cultural circumstances. The dimensions and manifestations of the psychological phenomenon are culture-specific. Allen Johnson and Douglass Price-Williams, for example, have suggested that oedipal tales are subject to varying degrees of repression. The more complex a culture is, the greater the disguise applied to the sexual distress at its core. Whereas the myths of nonstratified societies blatantly display a child's oedipal drive, those of advanced cultures tend to camouflage it.[4] Significantly, Freud himself was fully aware that the suppression, and hence literary manifestations, of the oedipal triangle would vary across cultures and historical periods. Consider, for example, his comparison of the Greek complex (as reflected in *Oedipus Rex*) and the English complex (as mirrored in *Hamlet*):

> Another of the great creations of tragic poetry, Shakespeare's *Hamlet*, has its roots in the same soil as *Oedipus Rex*. But the changed treatment of the same material reveals the whole difference in the mental life of these two widely separated epochs of civilization: the secular advance of repression in the emotional life of mankind. In the *Oedipus* the child's wishful fantasy that underlies it is brought into the open and realized as it would be in a dream. In *Hamlet* it remains repressed; and—just as in the case of a neurosis—we only learn of its existence from its inhibiting consequences.[5]

Literature provided Freud with evidence of his theory. Art was for him proof of the hidden emotions it betrayed. In the very first intimation of his discovery, Freud alluded to *Oedipus Rex*. Writing to his confidant Wilhelm Fliess (1858–1928) on October 15, 1897, he associated the recollection of his childhood emotions with the reading of the Sophocles play: "A single idea of general value dawned on me. I have found, in my own case too, [the phenomenon of] being in love with my mother and jealous of my father, and I now consider it a universal event in early childhood. . . . If this is so, we can understand the gripping power of Oedipus Rex . . . the Greek legend seizes upon a compulsion which everyone recognizes because he senses its existence within himself."[6] Freud continued to ponder the literary manifestations of the oedipal triangle throughout his career, for example in a 1928 essay on Dostoevsky:

> It can scarcely be owing to chance that three of the masterpieces of the literature of all time—the *Oedipus Rex* of Sophocles, Shakespeare's *Hamlet* and Dostoevsky's *The Brothers Karamazov*—should all deal with the same subject, parricide. In all three, moreover, the motive for the deed, sexual rivalry for a woman, is laid bare.[7]

The suggestion that the Nezha myth should be read as an expression of the Oedipus complex has been made—independently of each other—by Fan Sheng and Steven Sangren. The Taiwanese physician and the American anthropologist concur that the legend is remarkable not only for the hostility of father and son, but also for the overt competition for the wife/mother's love, reaching its climax in the Nezha Temple episode. The dead child appears in his mother's dream, demanding that she dedicate a shrine to him. Waking in tears for her lost offspring, Lady Yin shares the apparition with her husband, only to be rebuked by him for fretting over the monster she had borne him. Following additional nightly visitations by her son, the mother ends up dedicating a shrine to him in secret. Attracting worshippers far and wide, the Nezha Temple is discovered by Li Jing, who razes it to the ground, but not before whipping to pieces the hateful image of his son. The unmistakable oedipal confrontation is considered by Sangren the source of the legend's attraction:

> The story's obvious oedipal overtones—the son's patricidal hatred, the father's murderous intentions towards his son, and the rivalry between them for the affection of the wife/mother—are particularly remarkable in China, where expression of such sentiments was largely inexpressible in other contexts. In other words, the story's longlasting and widespread popularity, and certainly its memorable qualities, may be attributed in part to the expression it provides for otherwise strongly suppressed emotions and sentiments.[8]

Fan Sheng goes further than Sangren, arguing for a Freudian interpretation of the Nezha Temple as a sexual symbol. The shrine, he suggests, stands for the mother's female organ, into which Nezha demands entry, insisting that his "Golden Statue" be placed inside. No wonder that the threatened father is enraged; no wonder too that he chooses to chastise his young competitor with a weapon of unmistakable phallic connotations. Fan points out that the word "whip" (*bian*) carries the additional meaning of "penis," especially in such compounds as "horse-whip" (*mabian*) and "dog-whip" (*goubian*). As he sees it, Li Jing intimidates the infant by a display of a mature male organ.[9]

Even if we shy away from Fan Sheng's overt sexual reading, we cannot but be struck by the myth's self-reference to the unconscious. As if anticipating a Freudian interpretation, Li Jing considers his wife's dream an expression of a hidden desire. "Dreams arise from the heart," he tells her. "It is only because you long for him [Nezha] that your dreaming-soul is confused" (14.119). Significantly, the Greek play likewise hints of repressed emotions by an allusion to the sleeping mind. As Freud has perspicaciously observed, "There is an unmistakable indication in the text of Sophocles' tragedy itself that the legend of Oedipus sprang from some primeval dream-material."[10] When Oedipus begins to be troubled by the recollections of the oracle, Jocasta consoles him, alluding to the common dreams of incestuous relations, which she thinks have no meaning:

> Many a man has shared his mother's bed
> in dreams, and living life is easiest
> for those who simply disregard the fact.[11]

The Nezha myth is not as sexually explicit as the Oedipus legend. Unlike the Greek hero (who does not know that Jocasta is his mother), Nezha is aware of his mother's identity, and he does not sleep with her. Whereas the Chinese child's animosity toward his father is laid bare, his erotic attraction to the mother is disguised. Nonetheless, the sexual drive underlying the riveting myth is indicated by Nezha's rivalry with his father for the affection of the mother/wife; by the legend's repeated allusions to the subconscious realm of dreams; and by specific symbols, such as the father's whip, that lend themselves to psychoanalytic interpretation.

Does the Nezha myth evince a Chinese Oedipus complex? Fan Sheng, Steven Sangren, and this author certainly think so, even though admittedly the Freudian theory is hard to prove. As Peter Rudnytsky has pithily observed, the acceptance of the Freudian insight ultimately depends upon self-realization. It is the evidence of the self that proves or disproves one's childhood attachment to his mother and animosity toward his father. What has been previously sensed within the self is validated by art or the example of another person. "I have found [it] in my own case too," declared Freud of his discovery, which, significantly, followed shortly upon his father's death. In the course of his self-analysis—which was to assume mythic proportions in the history of the psychoanalytic movement—Freud came to realize his long-repressed infatuation with his mother and jealousy of his father.[12] Having corroborated his own hidden emotions with those of patients and a work of art (*Oedipus Rex*), Freud was ready to claim the universality of a child's sexual attraction to the mother and animosity toward the father. "Whether it is 'the fate of us all' to experience the oedipal drama of incest and murder," writes Rudnytsky, "can only be judged by each individual on the basis of his or her own dreams."[13]

Oedipus in China

At least some Chinese critics found the Oedipus complex in themselves. Psychoanalysis (Chinese: *jingshen fenxi* or *xinli fenxi*) has had a significant impact on modern Chinese literature. Its influence has been felt in two waves: during the Republican Period (1911–1949), when a large number of works by Freud and on him were translated into Chinese (from Japanese and various European languages); and during the 1980s, when a new tide of translations (and republications of 1920s and 1930s materials) rekindled the interest of novelists and critics in the literary manifestations of the unconscious. One Freud scholar lived through both periods. In the 1930s, Gao Juefu (1896–1993) produced careful translations from the English of Freud's *Introductory Lectures on Psychoanalysis* and *New Introductory Lectures on Psychoanalysis.* In 1949, he saw them (like other works of bourgeois psychology) disappear from the bookshelves, only to supervise their republication in enormously popular editions, during his, and the century's, eighties.[14]

In this chapter we are concerned with psychoanalysis as a literary theory. It is noteworthy, however, that the two Freudian waves—of the 1930s and the 1980s—have had an impact on medical practice. The effect of the first had been modest: In 1935 the American-trained psychoanalyst Dr. Bingham Dai (Dai Bingyueng) opened a psychotherapy program at the prestigious Peking Union Medical University Hospital. He treated patients and trained medical students until the Japanese invasion of 1939 put an end to his intimate psychoanalytic group.[15] By contrast the Freud craze of the 1980s appears to have had a significant influence on the Chinese mental health profession. It triggered an enthusiasm for Freudian theory among psychiatrists and medical students, who have been attending psychoanalytic seminars in increasing numbers. The hunger for Freudian theory has led to the establishment (in the early 2000s) of the China American Psychoanalytic Alliance (CAPA), which offers psychoanalytic sessions via the Internet. The classic therapeutic configuration is now recreated via Skype: the Chinese patient lies on a couch, his image transmitted to the American therapist thousands of miles away. Psychoanalysis, the fortunes of which have been dwindling in the West, appears at the time of writing to have found a safe haven in China.[16]

The application of psychoanalysis to Chinese fiction originated with Zhao Jingshen's (1902–1985) "New Chinese literature and deviant sexual desires" ("Zhongguo xin wenyi yu biantai xingyu").[17] In this 1928 essay, Zhao examined the varieties of the Oedipus complex in contemporary works of Chinese fiction. The literary historian acknowledged Matsumura Takeo's (1883–1969) *Bungei to seiai* (Literature and sexuality) as one source of inspiration. Drawing upon Albert Mordell's *The Erotic Motive in Literature* (1919), Matsumura's study had been translated into Chinese in 1927. It introduced its Asian readers to some of Freud's most famous applications of psychoanalysis to literature and the arts, including his (and subsequently Ernest Jones's) oedipal interpretation of *Hamlet* and his explorations of the origins and artistic manifestations of Leonardo da Vinci's (1452–1519) presumed homosexuality. In his controversial *Leonardo da Vinci and a Memory of his Childhood,* Freud attempted to reconstruct the psychological profile of the Renaissance genius on the basis of his paintings and diaries and on the evidence of his contemporaries.[18]

Zhao rendered the Freudian concept as *Yedibusi cuozong* (Oedipus complex). Other Republican-period scholars variously transliterated the Greek hero's name, diversely translating the psychological cluster associated with it. In his elegant classical Chinese translation from the German of Freud's autobiography, Zhang Shizhao (1881–1973) chose *Etipu zarou* (Oedipus complex). Other translators rendered "complex" as *qingjie* ("emotional knot") or *niancong* ("thought cluster").[19] Most commonly used today, the terms *Edipusi qingjie* (Oedipus emotional knot) and *lianmu qingjie* ("attachment-to-the-mother emotional knot") gained currency during the 1980s.[20]

Several Republican-period novelists acknowledged their indebtedness to Freud. Guo Moruo (1892–1978), Qian Zhongshu (1910–1998), Shen Congwen (1902–1988), and most notably the "New Sensibilities" (Xin ganjue) authors of the 1930s noted their interest in psychoanalysis. In prefaces, essays, and sometimes within the body of the fictional work itself, they described the Freudian impact on their probe of dreams, sexuality, and the unconscious.[21] Particularly revealing are their explorations of desire and its repression within the family. In her *Psychoanalysis in China,* Zhang Jingyuan has convincingly argued that Freud's concern with sexuality and its suppression coincided with the modern writers' preoccupation with the family's repression of the individual. The struggle to liberate the young generation from the stifling influence of the old merged with the Freudian investigation of patricidal wishes. Hence "a great variety of fictional works deployed the oedipal pattern in literal and symbolic modes of representation."[22] Zhang goes on to demonstrate the oedipal triangle (whether father, mother, and son or father, mother, and daughter) in the works of Lu Xun (1881–1936), Ba Jin (1904–2005), Zhang Ailing (Eileen Chang) (1920–1995), and the playwright Yuan Changying (1894–1973). Other critics have similarly discerned oedipal frustrations in the novels of Yu Dafu (1896–1945) and, more recently, Liu Heng (born 1954).[23]

For our purpose here, the literature influenced by Freud is less relevant than the fiction and drama that preceded him. The Oedipus complex in traditional Chinese literature has not been extensively studied. Only a handful of essays have been dedicated to the Freudian cluster in classical literature, all stressing the high degree of suppression applied to it. Psychologists and literary critics have concurred that because of filial piety the Chinese oedipal urge had been muffled. The prudish and hierarchical Confucian society could not tolerate overt expression of sexual desire and/or violence of children toward their elders. Hence, to the extent that it was hinted at, the Oedipus complex was disfigured. Chinese literature did not feature the psychological cluster in its entirety. Disguising the disturbing oedipal drive, it implied isolated aspects of it only. Instead of a son's attachment to his mother *and* violence toward his father, Chinese authors described at the most a father-son conflict *or* a mother-son bond.

Gu Ming-Dong has noted that the weight of the Confucian ethics distorted the literary manifestations of the Freudian cluster. The critic's resentment of the culture's hegemonic ideology is readily apparent:

> Under the crushing pressure of overwhelming repression in Chinese culture and society, the Oedipus complex in Chinese literature disintegrates and is transformed from a nuclear complex to a multiplicity of individual complexes: the father complex, the mother complex, the son complex, and the daughter complex. All of them, growing out of different individuals' responses to different family situations in a morally repressive culture, are the twisted manifestations of the original Oedipus complex.[24]

The Nezha myth is possibly unique for its description of violence and sexual libido that are directed from the child toward his parents. In most Chinese tales the oedipal undercurrent is revealed by the father's murderous intentions toward his son or the mother's insane possessiveness of her male offspring. The jealous mother has been a favorite topic of Chinese literature for more than a millennium. As early as the fourth or fifth century CE "A Peacock Southeast Flew," mother Jiao tormented her faultless daughter-in-law, driving her away. Her venom led son and daughter-in-law to commit suicide. The ballad's hidden oedipal drive was brought to the surface fifteen hundred years later in Yuan Changying's (1894–1973) play of the same title. The first Chinese female to receive a PhD from a European university (Edinburgh), Yuan was likely influenced by Freudian theory. In her 1929 preface to the play, she alluded to Sophocles's *Oedipus Rex* (albeit in the context of tragedy rather than psychoanalysis), describing mother Jiao as "sexually jealous" (*chicu*). Yuan created intimate scenes disclosing the pathology of the mother's affection for her son. When he begs permission to leave home and find employment, she objects:

> Forget about a job. As long as you stay here by my side, allowing me always to stroke your shining hair, my heart will be satisfied enough. Ah! These past twenty years there was not one single day in which I did not caress your beautiful hair. I have created your beautiful hair with the essence of my very life.[25]

Whereas a son's violence toward his parent was for the most part inconceivable, classical literature did feature fathers savagely beating, killing, or even eating their male offspring. Psychoanalytically such tales may be interpreted as reflections of the father's fear of his son, of whom he feels obliged to dispose. They may equally be seen as expressing the child's terror of castration by his competitor for the mother's love. It could thus be argued that the weight of the Confucian ethics has transformed the literary manifestations of the Oedipus complex: The violence is directed from father to son rather than vice versa, with most tales culminating in child murder instead of patricide. The morality of filial piety entailed that the child would be victimized by the oedipal conflict, as Tseng Wen-Shing and Jing Hsu have suggested:

> The Chinese [oedipal] pattern acknowledges the life-long attachment between mother and son as a threat to the father, but, because of the great Chinese regard for older generations, any excess is more likely to result in the son rather than the father becoming the victim. This solution is more consistent with the stress on filial piety than the usual Western one would be.[26]

Examined in chapter 1, the tale of the Earl of the West (King Wen) illustrates the pattern of the son as prey to his father. Recall that the paragon of virtue knowingly consumed his filial offspring's flesh. Another example of a victimized child is provided by the well-known play *At the Bend of the Fen River* (*Fenhe wan*), which during the late imperial period enjoyed tremendous popularity in a wide range of regional dramas as well as in written fiction. The protagonist is the historical Tang general Xue Rengui (614–683), who returns to his home after years of absence in the battlefield. At the bend of the Fen River, the seasoned warrior meets a lad shooting geese and spearing fish. He ends up killing the boy (in some versions intentionally, for he could not tolerate the lad's superior marksmanship; in others by mistake, trying to save him from a menacing tiger). Arriving at his humble cottage, the general discovers a pair of men's shoes under his wife's bed. Enraged, he demands an explanation, and she replies that they belong to the son who had been born during his absence. Asking to see him, the wife explains that the boy is out hunting geese, whereupon the terrible truth dawns upon the grief-stricken father.[27]

The context of Chinese infanticide tales is often political. Whereas the biblical Abraham was willing to kill his son for the love of God, Chinese fathers made the sacrifice for the ruler's sake. Consider the above-mentioned story of Yue Yang (fl. 410 BCE) who did not flinch from eating a stew of his own son in order to accomplish the king's order that he conquer a neighboring state.[28] Another example is furnished by the Huizhou (Southeastern Anhui) lore of the local hero Wang Hua (587–649). Oral legend has it that the historical general murdered his nine offspring to win Emperor Li Shimin's (599–649) trust. Protecting Huizhou during the Sui Dynasty's collapse, the upright general switched his allegiance to the Tang, only to have its founder suspect his intentions: Would not a leader beloved of the people and father of nine potential rebels plot against him? Realizing the sovereign's concern, the loyal Wang Hua butchered his sons. As local lore has it, the gruesome sacrifice did not earn the steadfast general the trust he deserved, for the cruel Tang emperor forced him into suicide nonetheless. The father who victimized his kin was betrayed by the powers that be.[29]

Wang Hua has been worshiped for centuries as the Huizhou patron saint. Having secured the region's prosperity during the Sui-Tang dynastic upheaval, he has been venerated ever since as its tutelary divinity. Side by side with the fierce general, many villagers worshiped his unfortunate "princes" (*taizi*). Shrines were constructed for the murdered sons, who figured primarily in rituals of exorcism. Particular attention was given to the third of the nine infanticide victims. During the first month's Lantern Festival, the statue of the Third Prince (San Taizi) was brought out of its own shrine to his father's temple. Sitting side by side, offspring and progenitor enjoyed the spectacle together.[30] We will see in chapter 6 that the honorific Third Prince has been shared by the patricidal Nezha. To this day, the unruly child is commonly worshiped as the Third Prince. It is not impossible, therefore, that Huizhou villagers have conflated the son who had been victimized by his father with the one who rose in rebellion against his.

That the honorific Third Prince has become a catchword for an oedipal confrontation is suggested by yet another example, albeit ophidian rather than human. Chinese literature features an additional Third Prince who has been prey to paternal violence. The sixteenth-century novel *The Journey to the West* has the dragon king of the Western Ocean bring his third son to the heavenly court under charges of disobedience. The Jade Emperor sentences the Third Prince to death, and it is only Guanyin's intervention that saves the hapless child from the executioner's blade.[31] The goddess of mercy functions in the story much as a Chinese mother would in a similar situation. Rescuing sons from their father's wrath, Chinese female deities are—as Steven Sangren has suggested—the "embodiments of motherhood."[32] They intercede on their devotees' behalf much as a mother would in the traditional family setting.

That the son, rather than the father, should emerge as the victim of Chinese oedipal tales is the result of Confucian ethics. The primacy of filial piety dictated that the oedipal conflict lead to infanticide instead of the unthinkable patricide. From another angle, tales of fathers killing their male offspring mirror the former's jealousy, which might have been augmented by Chinese childbearing practices. It has been pointed out that Chinese boys enjoy physical intimacy with their mothers much longer than do Western children. Sons share the same bed with their mother—or sleep between their mother and father—at least until the next child is born. Even adolescents might lie on the same couch with their mother, helping her with her washing and enjoying her physical warmth. Such conditions might foster a father's resentment of the male offspring competing for the wife's/mother's intimacy. Nadine Tang and Bruce Smith have suggested that it is this extended physical bond of mother and son that accounts for the father's violence in Chinese tales such as General Xue's: "Whereas the prototypic Western son has been supplanted by his father (physically) long before he is aware of his oedipal strivings, in the East, it is the father who may feel the need to forcibly reclaim what is rightfully his (the mother's body)."[33]

The pattern of violence that is directed from father to son is not unique to China. It is apparent in the Greek myth of Cronus (who devoured his sons lest they depose him) as well as in the Persian legend of Rostam who, like Xue Rengui, killed in a duel a youth unknown to him, only to discover that it was his son Sohrab. The oedipal legend is masterfully narrated in Ferdowsi's (ca. 940–ca. 1020) epic *Shahname* (Book of kings), which, it has been speculated, might be related to Chinese literature.[34] The sympathy of the Persian poet lies with the victimized offspring rather than with his cruel progenitor. The gallant Sohrab had sensed an uncanny affinity with the aged warrior (his father) and had suggested that they cease fighting. Driven by jealousy of the handsome youth, however, Rostam declined his offer of truce. Blinded by "evil humor," he fought relentlessly, only to discover when it was too late the identity of the hero he had slain. When the dying Sohrab vowed that his father Rostam would avenge him, the latter realized that he was his own son. Only then did the monstrosity of his own crime dawn upon the grief-stricken father.[35]

Sons have been their father's victims in Nezha's (Nalakūbara's) county of origin as well. Scholars have pointed out that the Indian oedipal pattern is characterized by violence and sexual libido that are directed from the parents toward their offspring. In many—though by no means all—Indian tales of generational conflict, the father emerges as the triumphant aggressor. Śiva's relations with his incestuous sons are a case in point: He impaled one on his trident and beheaded the other. The former, Andhaka had been born blind, likely as a symbol of the unconscious desire he had harbored for his mother, Pārvatī. (Scholars have noted the intriguing similarity to the blind Oedipus).[36] The latter, Gaṇeśa, had been stationed by his mother as a guard at her door. Taking a bath, the voluptuous goddess instructed him to bar all intruders. The enraged Śiva broke in and beheaded the hapless child, supplying him later with an elephant head (hence the god's elephantine iconography). It is not hard to perceive the sexual drive behind the father's mutilation of his son, who was standing guard at the "threshold to Pārvatī's bath and bedroom, symbol of her shrine, womb, and point of sexual entry."[37] Indeed Śiva's beheading of his son has been interpreted as displaced castration. The emasculation is even clearer in versions of the myth that have Gaṇeśa with an elephant head to start with. Instead of decapitation, they have the furiously jealous father cut off his son's tusk in an unmistakable act of symbolic castration.[38]

The high degree of repression that is applied to the Chinese Oedipus accords with Allen Johnson and Douglass Price-Williams's observation that complex societies tend to disguise psychological frustration. In their *Oedipus Ubiquitous,* the two ethnographers have suggested that stratified societies camouflage the sexual distress at their core.[39] What is unique to the Chinese pattern is the enmeshment of the familial complex with the hegemonic discourse of filial piety. Gu Ming-Dong has observed that "oedipal themes in Chinese literature are restructured according to the dynamics of Confucian morality, taking the disguised forms of paternal demands for filial piety and children's fulfillment of filial duties."[40] He suggests, therefore, that the Chinese psychological cluster be termed "filial piety complex." Even though Gu alludes neither to the King Wen legend nor to the Nezha myth, his theory is applicable to both. Recall that it was filial piety that set Bo Yikao (King Wen's son) on the journey from which he was to emerge as a meat sauce, and that the same ethic determined Nezha's self-immolation.

Gu perceives an undercurrent of violence and repressed desire within the canonical tales of filial piety. One of the earliest and most famous Confucian paragons was the mythic emperor Shun, whose selfless devotion to his parents had earned him the empire. The filial emperor has been celebrated in literature and visual arts for twenty-five hundred years. He was hailed as a moral exemplar in Confucian classics such as the *Mencius* (fourth century BCE); his filial feats were elaborated upon in medieval hagiographies; and his legend was chosen to head *The Twenty-Four Filial Exemplars,* which enjoyed tremendous popularity throughout the late imperial period.[41] According to the legend, Shun reverently cared for his father and stepmother even though they repeatedly attempted to kill him. His exemplary devotion moved the reigning emperor, Yao, to abdicate in his favor. As Gu sees it, the tale pivots on the oedipal tension between the son and his father, who had been obsessed by fears of patricide: "The legend sets the pattern for the Chinese representation of oedipal desires: through mechanisms of repression and distortion, patricidal and incestuous desires are transformed into a hidden fear of patricide or sublimated into a blind demand for filial piety."[42]

The filial Shun legend shares the symbol of blindness with other oedipal tales worldwide. The father that torments Shun is described as sightless, indicating the unconscious aggression motivating him. Oblivious to his own hidden emotions, he is eventually healed by the devoted offspring who, licking the diseased eyes, miraculously restores their sight. The motif is shared by the Greek Oedipus and the Indian Andhaka, as well as by the Burmese Pauk Tyaing. The legend has Pauk Tyaing murdering his father, who is variously identified as a dragon or as a lion. He marries his mother, Queen of Tagaung, and has two sons by her. In some versions the Burmese Oedipus is punished by blindness, whereas in others his sons born of the incestuous liaison are cursed by sightlessness.[43]

One version of the filial Shun legend is noteworthy for the mother's sexual libido no less than for the father's violence. Discovered among the Dunhuang trove of medieval manuscripts, the *Transformation Text of the Son Shun* (*Shun zi bian*) has the stepmother try to seduce her adopted son. Thrusting a golden pin into her foot, she orders Shun to heal the wound. When the tending of the eroticized body part does not yield the expected intimacy, the stepmother's passion turns into venom. "Seeing my black hair and white face, his desire was aroused like a pig or a dog,"[44] she tells the blind father, accusing Shun of trying to rape her. Psychoanalytically, the stepmother is the thinly disguised biological parent. As in the majority of Chinese oedipal tales, desire and wrath alike are directed from progenitor to offspring, rather than vice versa.

The oedipal interpretation of the filial Shun could perhaps be extended to the tales of a son's attachment to his mother. The literature of filial piety might be underlined by the sublimated desire of the mother no less than by the hidden enmity of father and son. David Jordan has noted that the majority of late imperial tales concern the bond of a mother and her son (rather than a child's obedience to his father). In the successive versions of *The Twenty-Four Filial Exemplars,* the mother figures as the recipient of filial devotion approximately twice as often as the father.[45] To such an extent does the hagiographic genre embrace a woman's dependence on her male offspring that it could be read as expressing a hidden erotic drive. Jordan acknowledges as much, suggesting that the authors "tend to exemplify the filial piety of men and boys by means of the emotionally satisfying mother-son relationship".[46] Consider for example the following tale, celebrating the subconscious ties of mother and son:

> Zheng Shen of the Zhou Dynasty had the honorific name Ziyu. He served his mother with extreme filiality. One day when Shen was in the mountains gathering firewood a guest came to the house. His mother had made no preparations as she kept hoping that he would return, but he did not. Then she bit her finger, and at the same time Shen suddenly felt a pain in his heart. He shouldered his firewood and returned home; kneeling, he asked his mother what the matter was. His mother said, "A guest came unexpectedly and I bit my finger to make you aware of it."[47]

Dominating the Confucian tales of filial piety, the mother-son bond has been equally apparent in the writings of Chinese Buddhists. In his *Mother and Sons in Chinese Buddhism,* Alan Cole has argued that the love of the mother is the prevailing virtue in the Chinese Buddhist literature of the family, the father usually being absent. "The Buddhists in China developed a style of filial piety that was preoccupied with the mother," he writes. "A mother–son dyad came to headline Buddhist family values. . . . It would not be an exaggeration to say that the Buddhists became obsessed with writing about mothers and sons."[48]

Cole investigates a body of Buddhist sutras that have been authored in China, incorporating the Confucian virtue of filial piety into the ethics of the Indian faith. At the core of his study is the famous legend of the monk Mulian, whose sinful mother has been condemned to hell. The filial offspring employs his religious powers to save the miserable woman who gave birth to him. He takes upon himself a harrowing journey to the netherworld in order to repay her kindness in nurturing him. Securing the help of the Buddha, he finally smashes open the gates of the infernal regions, delivering her soul to heaven. Mulian's devotion to his mother is such that he risks going to the world of the dead for her sake. His filial example has left a deep impression on Chinese believers. Appearing for the first time during the Tang period (618–907), the story of Mulian's journey to the netherworld has served as a source for an enormous body of ritual opera. All through the twentieth century, the drama of Mulian's devotion has been ritually enacted in funerary ceremonies, in which it served to redeem the deceased. The legend of the filial offspring likewise became an integral aspect of the Ghost Festival (also known by its Buddhist name Yu-lan-pen) which, celebrated during the seventh lunar month, secured the salvation of childless spirits.[49]

A key aspect of the Mulian saga is the belief that only the son is capable of redeeming his mother. A woman's fate in this world, as well as in the next, depends upon her male offspring. Other family members, husband or daughters for instance, are irrelevant to the drama of love, gratitude, and indebtedness that binds a mother to her son. This is precisely what Mulian's mother declares when he finally gets to see her. Led in chains, emaciated and haggard, she addresses her son and savior as her Buddhist teacher: "My filial son, I cannot discard this sinful body by myself; If I am not favored by your exercise of filiality, oh Teacher, Who would be willing to exert themselves to save your mother?"[50] A woman cannot atone herself for her sins. It is the duty of her son to shoulder her guilt and expiate it for her.

Why has Mulian's mother been sentenced to hell? Which atrocious crime has she committed? Tang-period versions of the legend accuse her of diverse misdeeds including greed and the abuse of Buddhist monks (whom she refused alms). Even the earliest renditions, however, hint that the woman's crime is her very sexuality. The biological foundation of the mother's sin is clarified by the thirteenth or fourteenth century with the appearance of the *Blood Bowl Sutra* (*Xue pen jing*), which attributes a woman's sinful nature to her biological function. A mother is forever tainted by her bodily fluids, the blood that she discharges during menstruation and childbirth. Mulian is required to atone for the polluting substances by which he himself has been born. The male offspring is required to redeem his mother of her sexuality of which he himself is living evidence. As Alan Cole has pointedly observed, "In the *Blood Bowl Sutra*, reproduction produces sin and debt at the same moment. For the mother, Mu Lian's birth is her sin, and for him, his birth engenders a birth-debt. . . . Birth—the ultimate connection between mother and son—is the origin of sin, debt, and the obligation to repay."[51]

The *Blood Bowl Sutra* reflected, and generated, ritual practices that were intended to deliver a woman of her sinful biology. Beginning in the Southern Song period (1127–1279) and lasting in some regions of China all through the twentieth century, sons were required to purify their mothers of the polluting substance by which they themselves had been born. A bowl of rice or wheat spirits, dyed red, would be offered to the son to drink during his mother's funerary ceremonies. Wiping it clean, he would redeem the woman who had given him birth of her sinful sexuality. It would be hard to imagine a more poignant representation of the guilt and gratitude that tied late imperial women to their male offspring.[52]

Whereas the majority of Chinese filial piety tales mirror the psychological bond of mothers and sons, some might reflect the sexual libido of fathers and daughters. A case in point is the famed story of Cao E, who killed herself searching for her dad's corpse. Legend has it that the father of the second-century maiden drowned in a river. The fourteen-year-old Cao E wailed for him for seven days, finally throwing herself into the water. Five days later, the corpses of father and daughter surfaced together. Even though she died, Cao E did manage to rescue her father's remains.

That the devout daughter tale might mask a twisted sexual drive is suggested by a bitter critic of traditional Chinese culture. In his *Dawn Blossoms Plucked at Dusk*, Lu Xun (1881–1936) mentions the filial tale, which he considers typical of the perverse Confucian ethics. A native of Cao E's Shaoxing prefecture (in Zhejiang Province), the author was familiar with her story since his childhood. The region's principal river is named after the girl who drowned herself in its waters, and the locals have been worshiping her for centuries in an imperially sponsored temple, which survives to this day. Lu Xun recalls the version of the tale he has heard as a child:

> Official histories relate, and it is quite commonly known, that Cao E jumped into the river to look for her father, and after drowning herself still carried his corpse out. The problem is: *How* did she carry his corpse? When I was small, I heard elders in my home-town explain it this way: "At first, the dead Cao E and her father's corpse floated up to the surface with her clasping him, face to face. But passers-by seeing this laughed and said: 'Look, such a young girl with her arms round such an old man!' Then the two corpses sank back into the water. After a little while they floated up again, this time back to back."[53]

Lu Xun finds the tale's filial ethics as disturbing as its vision of propriety. Outraged by the morality that requires a daughter to commit suicide, he is equally troubled by the decorum dictating her saving her father with her back to him. For our purpose, however, his account is interesting as a revelation of the dim perception that filial tales might harbor incestuous desires. It appears that the Shaoxing natives were aware of the perverse, even necrophiliac, possibilities hidden in the moral tale. The perspicacious Lu Xun hints that filial stories might mask a forbidden sexual drive.

From Song Maocheng to Cao Xueqin

The logic of filial piety is brought to its oedipal extreme in a late Ming story by Song Maocheng (ca. 1570–ca. 1622). The protagonist of the "Filial Son from Wuzhong" (in southern Jiangsu) is a wine merchant whose wife and mother do not get along. When he is away on business, the wife deceitfully disposes of her mother-in-law. She sells her through a procuress into servitude. Telling the mother that her daughter has sent a boat to fetch her, she sends her instead to the prospective buyer a hundred miles south. Arriving at her destination and discovering that she has been duped, the mother attempts suicide. She is saved by her new employers, who treat her kindly. The mother ends up staying with them as their grandchildren's governess.

When her husband returns, the wife lies and tells him his mother has become a prostitute. He finds it hard to believe, but he has no evidence. A year later, when he is on a business trip, he sees a familiar figure pounding laundry by the roadside. It turns out to be the lost mother. Bursting into tears, the two hug each other, and he promises to be back within a month.

It is now time for the husband to treat his wife to the same trick she has played on his mother. "Let's go together on a pilgrimage to Mount Yu," he suggests, leading her instead to the very household into which she sold his mother. There he exchanges wife for mother. "I will give you a young and beautiful woman for this old one" he offers the buyers, who are delighted with the newly acquired female, who would presumably serve them as a concubine.[54]

The story illustrates the workings of *bao* (retribution). It is a perfect example of a person being punished in kind and in measure with her crime. Beyond the operation of justice, however, a more troubling dilemma emerges. As an ultimate value, filial piety entails that a dutiful son should sacrifice his wife for his mother, that is, exchange them. The Confucian virtue appears to be harboring—or sublimating—an oedipal drive. Tina Lu has rightly noted that the story is unsettling. She has suggested that one reason is the implicit monetary value placed on the two women's sexuality. In effect the husband traffics in women. Violating late imperial law, he profits from his wife's loss of chastity.[55] No less disturbing, however, is the hidden psychological scenario. Taken to the extreme, filial piety leads to an oedipal outcome.

The hegemonic Confucian ethics have made it exceedingly difficult to describe overt sexual attraction between mothers and sons. It is perhaps for this reason that in some Chinese works of fiction the incestuous drive is expressed by substitute figures that are linked by adoption or marriage. Stories of intramural lust might involve in-laws or stepmothers and their adopted offspring (as in the filial tale of Emperor Shun, whose stepmother tried to seduce him). Andrew Plaks has demonstrated that the late sixteenth-century *Plum in the Golden Vase* (*Jin ping mei*) weaves a skein of pseudo-incestuous relations between its licentious protagonists. The most obtrusive example involves three of the novel's principal protagonists: Ximen Qing, his pretty young wife Pan Jinglian, and his son-in-law (whom he adopted as an heir) Chen Jingji. The adulterous wife carries on a running affair with Chen Jingji, which reaches its climax after Ximen Qing's death (the father replaced, as it were, by his son). Even though the pretense of relations by marriage (rather than blood ties) is maintained, hints in the narrative indicate the possibility of a deeper familial conflict. Chen Jingji is, in some respects, his in-laws' offspring. He is referred to as "my son" by Ximen Qing, who functions as his mentor in nefarious activities.[56]

We conclude our brief survey of the Oedipus complex in Chinese literature with its greatest masterpiece. The protagonist of the *Dream of the Red Chamber* (ca. 1760) is locked throughout the novel's hundreds of pages in conflict with his father. Baoyu's oedipal rivalry with his father, Jia Zheng, reaches a climax of near infanticide. When a false accusation of rape is brought against his son, the father orders that Baoyu be beaten to death. Unsatisfied with his servants' execution of the order, he snatches the bamboo rod from them and mercilessly tears the boy's flesh himself. As Gu Ming-Dong has noted, the father's repressed fears of patricide are overtly expressed. Angrily retorting to those trying to save his son, Jia Zheng bellows, "Would you like me to wait until Baoyu commits patricide or regicide (*shifu shijun*). Would you still intercede for him then?"[57]

Baoyu's familial constellation is such that the competition with his father is not over the mother/wife but over the grandmother/mother. Jia Zheng's wife pales before his warm and assertive mother who, to her son's dismay, dotes upon her beloved grandchild. Baoyu's dominant grandmother, as well as his cold and distant father, might have been fashioned after figures from their creator's childhood. Cao Xueqin (ca. 1715–1763) grew up in a large household with complex relations within and across the generations. It has been suggested that an adopted son whose relations with the grandmother have been strained might have served as the model for Jia Zheng. The author's familial situation might have inspired, therefore, the fictional triangle of grandmother, son, and grandson.[58] From a psychoanalytic perspective, however, the novel suggests a pattern of an oedipal frustration that is perpetuated across the generations. Because *his* mother does not love him, Jia Zhang vents his frustration on his son. His emotional deprivation is expressed by violence toward an offspring. This becomes abundantly clear when Grandmother Jia arrives on the scene to save her grandson from his father's beating. Facing his mother, the cruel Jia Zheng regresses into a helpless child. Desperate for the love she never gave him, he breaks down in terror and shame. His agony comes out beautifully in David Hawkes's translation:

> Jia Zheng bowed down before her [his mother] and his face assumed the semblance of a smile.
>
> "Surely, Mother, in such hot weather as this there is no need for you to come here? If you have any instructions, you should call for *me* and let *me* come to *you*."
>
> Grandmother Jia had stopped when she heard this voice and now stood panting for some moments while she regained her breath. When she spoke, her voice had an unnatural shrillness in it.
>
> "Oh! Are you speaking to me?—Yes, as a matter of fact I have got 'instructions', as you put it; but as unfortunately I've never had a good son who cares for me, there's no one I can give them to."
>
> Wounded in his most sensitive spot, Jia Zheng fell on his knees before her. The voice in which he replied to her was broken with tears.
>
> "How can I bear it, Mother, if you speak to me like that?"[59]

Jia Zheng's helplessness demonstrates the merging of an individual psychology with a cultural pattern. His emotional deprivation is exacerbated by an internalized ethics that requires a son who has been denied motherly love to venerate her. Oedipal frustrations are compounded by a sense of moral failure, resulting in a loss of self-esteem. In this respect the *Dream of the Red Chamber* illustrates the inseparability of the Chinese oedipal drive from the hegemonic discourse of filial piety.

Sons and Mothers

Was Jia Zheng's sense of failure typical of Chinese men? Were other adult males similarly shamed by their mothers? The question could be rejected as meaningless; generalizations about the private sphere of familial relations are inherently hazardous. The relations of sons and mothers in China have been doubtless as infinitely varied as elsewhere. Surprisingly nonetheless, many scholars have argued that Chinese men have been inordinately burdened by a sense of guilt toward their mothers. Historians, anthropologists, and psychologists have concurred that to a greater extent than in other societies, Chinese mothers have nurtured their sons' indebtedness to them. Hsiung Ping-Chen, a historian of late imperial China, has noted that

> [I]n numerous instances, it was in fact the mother who tried to make good use of the intimate and emotional bonds between her and the boy to generate or to stimulate [a] sense of guilt. In so doing, she was to transform her own sadness or frustration into her son's lifelong sorrowful and seemingly unredeemable debt.[60]

The psychologist Walter Slote has marveled at the extraordinary "finesse" with which Asian American women employ martyrdom to manipulate their sons, and Margery Wolf has argued that neglected Taiwanese women turn to their male offspring for revenge.[61] The anthropologist of rural society has reproduced a typical sermon by a deserted wife, inculcating the sense of guilt in her ten-year-old child:

> You know that you are my only son, and that your father didn't take care of you. He ran away with a younger woman and left us all alone. You should know this. If you won't listen to me now, what will you be like when you are bigger? It must be that you want to make me mad so that I will die sooner, is that it? Why should I want to live so long when my life is so bitter? It is only because of you. If it weren't for you, I could just leave this world now. You won't listen to me, so perhaps I had best just go die. Then there will be no one to control you, and you will be happy.[62]

Historians and anthropologists alike have noted the primacy of the mother-son bond in the Chinese family. In her *A Tender Voyage,* Hsiung Ping-Chen has examined hundreds of autobiographies by Ming and Qing scholars that suggest the mother was the driving force behind her son's career. An astonishing number of leading statesmen and intellectuals have described their mothers as the most influential person in their lives.[63] Even though she does not allude to the Freudian hypothesis, Hsiung suggests a pattern of extraordinarily close relations between mothers and their male offspring:

> In the context of gender relations in traditional China, a man's mother, ironically, was too often the only woman he knew well and could openly and unabashedly love. For a woman, likewise, her male offspring were the only men she could both adore without any reservations and secure loyalty, affection, and gratitude. The emotional bond between a mother and her children was established in the intimate years of childhood. Out of this relationship a child not only recognized the details of his mother's fate, he was also made to identify with her grievances. The unique Confucian ethics of filial piety, moreover, allow, or really require, a son's absolute and permanent homage to his mother. The mother had good reason to put additional spiritual and material investment in her boys and to expect, or to demand, faithful return when they grow up. The peculiarly abundant memorial literature for women and mothers serves as an eloquent testimony to this psychological burden and social heritage.[64]

Drawing on clinical work rather than historical records, Walter Slote has similarly concluded that—at least until recently—the mother-son bond has been the most significant of Chinese familial relations. Case studies of Asian Americans, as well as Vietnamese and Koreans, have convinced him that in Confucian societies the son's emotional attachment to his mother supersedes his dependence on his wife. The psychologist goes as far as describing the oedipal configuration as normative in Chinese culture:

> The primary emotional tie in Confucian societies was between the mother and son, not husband and wife, a condition that perpetuated itself from one generation to the next. The mothers turned to the children, especially the sons and in particular the eldest son, for the comfort and devotion that they did not find in the husbands. In the early years of a child's life there was an empathic, symbiotic integration between mother and child, a blending into one another that I have rarely seen in any other setting. . . . Thus for the son the mother tended to remain the most significant woman throughout his life, a classically oedipal situation. The difference between East and West in this respect is that in the East Asian societies it is culturally supported, maintained, and reinforced; in the West it is not. The result has been that most males, particularly in the past, were not able to replace the mother with a contemporary woman of equivalent significance.[65]

Anthropologists and social historians have illuminated aspects of the Chinese family that contributed to the primacy of the mother-son bond. Within the extended family, a young wife learned early that she had only her son to rely upon, for her husband's loyalty rested usually with his brothers and parents. The ethic of filial piety tended to estrange spouses, contributing to the wife's dependence on her male offspring. Finally, the social custom that permitted a man to have several bedmates (whether concubines or prostitutes) while making divorce for women practically impossible, caused neglected wives to seek solace in their sons. Hsiung Ping-Chen has demonstrated furthermore that in elite families the mother was responsible for at least the primary stages of her son's education, for it was through his achievements that she established her worth. Traditional Chinese society left women hardly any avenue but their offspring's success to demonstrate their intellectual skills and moral virtue.[66] Hsiung's findings, like those of other historians and anthropologists, suggest that the dynamics of the Chinese family tended to enhance the mutual dependence of mothers and sons. Therefore, to the degree that the Oedipus complex is shaped by society, we should expect to find as much of it in China as elsewhere. If anything, the patriarchal Chinese society appears to have fostered the dimensions of the universal oedipal attachment.

If Chinese society tended to enhance a son's attachment to his mother, it might have equally distanced him from his father, whose authority over the family reigned supreme. The ideal of the extended family entailed that a father might control the family's resources long after his sons grew into maturity. So long as household division did not take place, the father remained at the least the nominal head of the extended family. "Chinese fathers possess strongly patriarchal authority, but also, in Marxist parlance, they control the means of production," writes Steven Sangren. "Under such circumstances, it is quite understandable that many sons might come to resent patriarchal authority and that fathers might come to view their sons' maturation as a sign of diminishing powers if not as a harbinger of their own deaths."[67] The father's economic clout, as much as his patriarchal authority, might have engendered the resentment of his male offspring.

In his *Sex and Repression in Savage Society,* Bronislaw Malinowski (1884–1942) has suggested that the Oedipus complex is characteristic of patriarchal and patrilineal societies.[68] Chinese civilization has been as patriarchal as any. By the first centuries BCE, Confucianism had equated the father's position in the family to the ruler's function in society, with obedience to the head of the family becoming the foundation of social and political education. The Confucian revival of the Song period (960–1279), and the concomitant decline in women's status, further embedded patriarchal authority in all strata of society. Hence it should not come as a surprise that late imperial literature evinces a bond between women and their male offspring, as much as their animosity toward the husband/father. In a patriarchal setting, the potentially oppressed mothers and sons are natural allies.

The estrangement of fathers and sons—no less than the latter's dependence on their mothers—has characterized not only the literati elite but also the uneducated. Just as the memoirs of leading intellectuals reveal their indebtedness to their mothers, so do gangsters confess the bondage to the women that nurtured them. Conflicts of fathers and sons coupled with love and remorse toward idealized mothers are a constant refrain in narratives of the "rivers and lake" (*jianghu*), by which term the outlaw community of drifters has been known. Avron Boretz's extensive study of manhood and masculinity in the Chinese underclass of "drifters, outlaws, con artists, thieves, bodyguards, loan sharks, debt collectors, vagabonds, [and] gamblers"[69] has revealed a repeated pattern of animosity toward the father mingled with sentimental attachment to the mother: "For the wanderers and prodigal sons of Taiwan's *jianghu,* fathers are an often problematic presence, a source of fear, [and] resentment. . . . The anger and frustration generated by (or at least articulated in) the father-son conflict stands in sharp contrast to the 'soft' emotions and unquestioned loyalty these same men expressed when speaking of their mothers."[70] The Chinese family appears to have fostered the dimensions of the oedipal drive across the social spectrum.

This is not to say, however, that the contours of the Chinese Oedipus complex were identical to the Western one. Some psychologists have argued that because in China the oedipal attachment to the mother was allowed to be vented, it rarely led to a confrontation between son and father (the latter accepting his spouse's bond with his offspring).[71] Even more noticeably, the psychology of the Chinese individual was influenced by the primacy of filial piety. The internalized value transformed and convoluted the manifestations of the oedipal drive, sexual libido and violence being expressed within the parameters of the hegemonic Confucian discourse. This book's protagonist had been forced to commit suicide before avenging himself on his father. The sacred ethics of filial piety dictated that self-immolation would precede the expression of Nezha's oedipal drive.

Even though the Nezha myth reflected an oedipal frustration, its intensity varied. Different renditions variously depicted the rebellious son's relations with his parents. We should turn to the diverse oral, dramatic, and cinematic adaptations that brought the legend to late imperial and contemporary audiences.

4

Teenage Delinquent or Revolutionary Martyr

Nezha figures in the greatest Chinese novel. The eighteenth-century *Dream of the Red Chamber* features a theatrical performance of *The Canonization of the Gods.* The aristocratic protagonists of Cao Xueqin's (1715?–1763) masterpiece while away their time watching plays, one of which is based upon the mythological epic. One spectator alludes specifically to the enfant terrible. The glamorous Xifeng exclaims of the bashful Qin Zhong: "Even if he is a Nezha [freak], bring him here at once!"[1]

Cao Xueqin's allusion to a Nezha play betrays the child's popularity in late imperial drama. Beginning in the seventeenth century and all through the present, the oedipal tale has been a favorite theatrical topic. *The Canonization of the Gods* has served as a source for an enormous body of late imperial and modern adaptations in oral literature, drama in a variety of styles, and, more recently, television serials and animated movies (in China and Japan alike). Some late imperial oral and theatrical renditions enacted the entire plot of the original novel, usually under the slightly different title of *Roster of the Gods* (*Fengshen bang*). Other ballads, operas, puppet plays, and cartoons focused on one or another of the novel's martial adventures, of which Nezha's confrontation with his father has been a favorite. Oral and dramatic versions of the oedipal child's exploits were known by various titles including *Chentang Pass* (*Chentang Guan*) (after his birthplace) and *Primordial Mountain* (*Qianyuan shan*) (after his master's residence). By the late nineteenth century, the name *Nezha Wreaks Havoc in the Ocean* (*Nezha nao hai*) gradually eclipsed all others. Alluding to the child's subjugation of the aquatic dragon kings, it hinted of his affinity with another beloved rebel. Dramatic adaptations of the impish Sun Wukong's adventures had been similarly titled *Wreaking Havoc in Heaven* (*Danao Tiangong*).[2]

How did storytellers, playwrights, and moviemakers handle the explosive Nezha legend? Did they elaborate upon, or conversely muffle, his animosity toward his father? A survey of the late imperial and contemporary Nezha ballads, plays, cartoons, and movies reveals more than one answer to the question. Whereas some artists have been preoccupied with the child's oedipal desire, others have completely ignored it, celebrating instead his victory over one or another pernicious adversary. Whereas some renditions center on the familial confrontation, others have carried the Nezha trope into the political sphere, transforming the child-hero into a revolutionary martyr. Influenced by American cinema, others still have placed the rebellious youth in an alienated urban environment, presenting him as a teenage delinquent à la James Dean.

This chapter surveys the Nezha legend in diverse late imperial and contemporary media: Oral literature in several regional styles, theater of different genres, print and broadcast animation (from China and Japan), a feature film, and a contemporary short story. The review is far from exhaustive; the scope of the regional lore celebrating the enfant terrible would have rendered any attempt at inclusivity impractical. But the renditions selected might illustrate the enduring vitality of the Nezha myth, which for centuries has been recreated by storytellers, playwrights, and filmmakers. Different tales, ballads, plays, and movies have variously told the legend in psychological, social, and political terms. In this chapter I will not analyze each version in its own stylistic terms. Rather than dwelling on the renditions' literary features and artistic merits, I will examine the light they throw on the malleable Nezha figure and the hidden chords his myth has struck.

Storytelling

In late imperial China, oral literature was the most widespread narrative art. As in other traditional societies, written fiction had been the privilege of the educated, whereas storytelling reached every segment of society, literate and illiterate alike. The art form had been highly developed and combined literary, theatrical, and musical accomplishments. Some oral genres were performed in prose only, others were sung, and many combined prose and verse, much like the prosimetric French *chantefables* (such as the medieval *Aucassin and Nicolette*). Different geographical regions had their own storytelling traditions that were performed in the local dialect, each with its unique melodies and linguistic traits. On street corners and in temple courtyards and teahouses, villagers and city folk, men, women, and children would gather to hear a male or female performer tell or sing a story, which often had been borrowed from one of the great historical or mythological novels. The complete performance of an epic tale such as *The Canonization of the Gods* could last several months, the listeners returning night after night to hear the gripping adventures unfold.

Beginning in the eighteenth century, some oral tales were recorded in writing. Drum ballads (*guci*), lute ballads (*tanci*) and other oral genres were sometimes transcribed, enjoying significant readership in both manuscript and print form. The degree to which the transcription was accurate—indeed whether it had been a recorded performance in the first place—doubtless varied. Transcriptions might be identified, for example, by the usage of characters for their phonetic, rather than semantic, significance (that is, by the writing of a word with a semantically wrong character that is identically pronounced). The aural emphasis indicates that the text might have been a record of an actual performance, even as it had served itself for chanting (in which case the amateur performer would require phonetic guidance rather than lexical accuracy). The writers and readers of such orthographically erroneous texts were likely only marginally educated. By contrast some texts were composed primarily for reading, even as they simulated the formal traits—such as the verse meter—of a given oral genre. This is the case with the so-called "literary lute ballads," which, rather than transcriptions of oral performance, were original and highly sophisticated compositions intended primarily for reading.[3]

In this section I examine three Nezha narratives that are presented as transcriptions of oral performances. Their regional and stylistic diversity indicates the spell that the child-warrior has held for audiences across China. The first is a mid-nineteenth-century drum ballad from Beijing titled *The Roster of the Gods,*[4] the second is an early twentieth-century Taiwanese *gezai* ballad titled *Song of Nezha Wreaking Havoc in the Eastern Ocean* (*Nezha nao donghai ge*),[5] and the third is an early twentieth-century Fuzhou (northern Fujian) *chantefable* similarly titled *Nezha Wreaks Havoc in the Ocean.*[6] The numerous orthographic errors in the Beijing drum ballad indicate that it is likely a transcription—or a near transcription—of an actual performance. Likewise, the rich Min'nan vocabulary of the Taiwanese song reveals that it is closely related to an oral tale. By contrast the elegant style of the Fuzhou *chantefable,* as well as its printed medium, might suggest that it has been initially composed for reading no less than for singing.

The oral tales closely follow the plot of *The Canonization of the Gods.* All three recapitulate the exact sequence of the accelerating conflict between Nezha and his father, indicating that ultimately they derive from the written novel. The Beijing drum ballad, the Taiwanese song, and the Fuzhou *chantefable* record an identical unfolding of the oedipal tragedy: From the birth of the flesh ball that the enraged father hacks in two, through the eventful childhood of the impetuous creature that emerges from it; Nezha's murder of the dragon prince and his courageous self-immolation that follows; the temple his loving mother dedicates to him and its demolition by the jealous father; the attempted patricide and the magic stupa that is bestowed upon the father to prevent it. The oral narratives reach the same uneasy compromise between father and son that is outlined in *The Canonization of the Gods.* The novel's convoluted mixture of filial piety and familial hatred, sacrifice, and murder is evident in the ballads it has inspired.

If the psychological configuration of the seventeenth-century novel is difficult enough, the oral tales further accentuate it. The three storytellers each highlight the animosity of father and son no less than the tender feelings of mother and child. They introduce changes to the plot that underscore Li Jing's cruelty, even as they elaborate in verse on his wife's compassion. The Taiwanese *gezai* ballad has the father himself try to kill his son. After he has been informed by the dragon king of Nezha's audacious crime, Li Jing pursues his offspring sword in hand. Whereas in the novel he merely vents his frustration wailing and moaning, in the ballad it is his wife who narrowly prevents him from committing infanticide.[7] The father's violence is more pronounced in the Taiwanese ballad than in the novel that served as its source.

In the rich Taiwanese variety of the Min'nan (Hokkien) dialect, the storyteller goes on to describe the tremendous efficacy of the Nezha Temple that has been destroyed by the father. In a text that is difficult to decipher (written not by reference to the characters' semantic value but by their Min'nan phonetic significance), he elaborates on the benefits that accrue to those worshiping the child-god. Humorous in tone, the list might indicate the kinds of health benefits, material gains, and spiritual rewards that early twentieth-century Taiwanese devotees sought from the divine infant. Those who beseeched Nezha for offspring were blessed by sons, even twins; the poor made a fortune; the dumb started singing; a cripple danced; a blind person regained his eyesight (so he could prognosticate by the temple's divination board); a crook-mouthed individual was healed (so that he could blow the fire); and a person whose urinary system had been clogged peed freely once more.[8]

Offering a possible hint of the pleasure-quarter environment in which the Taiwanese ballad was performed, the singer alludes to the god's clientele of prostitutes (Hokkien: *thàn-tsia̍h-tsa-bóo*). We are told that courtesans who supplicated Nezha for patrons were instantly rewarded. Two pimps who had invested in a new brothel worshiped at the Nezha Temple, and their profits increased to a windfall of four or five hundred silver per night. The jesting might have been intended by the performer (possibly herself a courtesan) as an aside to an appreciative audience of prostitutes and their clients.[9]

The Fuzhou *chantefable* elaborates on the pain of the mother who had lost her offspring. "Today my son has met a cruel death," she laments. "It cuts me inside. Now that he is no more, nothing is left for me. How could I possibly go on living?"[10] The mother's visceral grief is contraposed with her husband's spiteful indifference. Li Jing's hatred does not abate even after Nezha's self-immolation. In elegant standard Chinese (suggesting that the ballad might have been composed for reading), the author describes the mutual loathing of the father and his reincarnated offspring:

> Li Jing hasted outside as need,
> Nezha was standing at the gate indeed,
> His face looking just as it once did.
> The spear in his hand, blazed fire forth,

From the wheels underfoot, fire and wind rose.
Seeing him, Li Jing was awed inside,
"Stop playing tricks, you beast," he cried.
How dare your dead soul come back to this place?"
"Li Jing," Nezha retorted powerfully,
"My flesh and blood I have returned amicably.
No relation now exists between you and me.
How dare you ascend the sacred Taiping Peak,
My temple to burn, my golden statue to whip,
Today, I have come your life to take,
Thrusting my spear, straight into your face.[11]

Nezha of the Fuzhou *chantefable* does not merely threaten to kill his father; he vows to *eat* him. Approaching Li Jing's headquarters, he commands the gatekeeper, "Go quickly and report to the master. Tell him that Nezha is here. I have come to take his heart and liver with my wine (*yu qu ta xin gan chong jiu*)."[12] The cannibalistic language could be read as a metaphor of enmity. We have observed in chapter 1 the enduring power of man eating as a symbolic—and occasionally real—expression of hatred in Chinese culture. All through the twentieth century vengeance had been imagined, and in rare cases actually wreaked, by cannibalism. Instead of mutilating a hateful enemy's corpse, his humiliation would be brought about by the eating of his flesh. Nezha's vow to devour his father could be taken therefore as expressing the extremeness of his loathing.

The eating of one's father could be approached from yet another angle. From a Freudian perspective, it is an inherent reflection of the Oedipus complex that has governed the evolution of the human species. In his controversial *Totem and Taboo: Some Points of Agreement between the Mental Lives of Savages and Neurotics* (1913), Freud has suggested a correspondence between the ontogenetic oedipal stage of childhood and the phylogenetic oedipal phase of human evolution. He postulated that primeval society had been made of clans in each of which a dominating male sexually monopolized a group of females, driving away his contending sons. At one point the banished offspring gathered together and killed him, establishing the incest taboo that would guide human evolution thereafter. Freud hypothesized that the sons identified with the victimized father by eating him, at the same time that their guilt led them to worship him as a totem. "The violent primal father," he suggested, "had doubtless been the feared and envied model of each one of the company of brothers: and in the act of devouring him they accomplished their identification with him, and each one of them acquired a portion of his strength."[13] The eating of the father epitomizes therefore the twin aspects of the oedipal drive: the fear and hatred of the father as well as the admiration felt toward him as an object of emulation. Applying the psychoanalytic insight to

Nezha, it could be argued that his craving of his father's flesh is an inevitable manifestation of an unresolved oedipal drive.

The most elaborate retelling of the Nezha saga occurs in the nineteenth-century Beijing drum ballad. Titled *The Roster of the Gods,* it is an oral adaptation of the entire seventeenth-century novel, within which the oedipal child's adventures have been expanded as much as five times their length in the original *The Canonization of the Gods.*[14] The drum ballad is a prosimetric *chantefable,* so named after the role of the percussion instruments (small drum or clappers) in its performance. That *The Roster of the Gods* written text is a transcription or a near-transcription of such a performance is indicated by the numerous orthographic errors in its extant manuscripts. That the original performance took place in Beijing is indicated by the storyteller's allusion to local customs and famous sites. The drum ballad elaborates on the city's religious festivities, shedding light on its nineteenth-century lore. Thus, for example, the temple that Nezha's mother dedicates to him is an occasion for listing the famous Beijing pilgrimage sites:

> Dear friends: It has always been like that. When people are looking for excitement, one will say that the goddess of this mountain is efficacious, and another will claim that the buddha of that temple is miraculous. It is the same with us here in the capital. How many popular places do we have here: What Northern Peak, Eastern Peak, Western Peak, Central Peak, Miaofeng Mountain Golden Peak, Eastern Yaji Mountain Peak, Maju Bridge, Pantao Temple, Fengtai, and the third month festivities at the Temple of the Eastern Peak.[15]

One reason for the drum ballad's extraordinary span—several times that of the original novel—is the recapitulation of the story in both prose and verse. Climactic moments are sung as well as told, as if the performer was experimenting with the expressive potential of poetry versus plain language. Consider for example Nezha's suicide, which is repeated in both the metrical and the non-metrical idiom. As the Numinous Pearl (Nezha) arrives at his father's residence to discover he has been taken hostage by Ao Guang (the dragon king), the storyteller breaks into a song:

> Numinous Pearl loudly shouted:
> "Ao Guang! Stop blabbing senselessly;
> Listen to my every word carefully;
> A murderer pays for his crime dutifully.
> Besides:
> One person's crime is one person's guilt;
> A sharp blade in hand, I will carve open my built;
> The bones to my dad;

The flesh to my mom;[16]
And the debt paid to Ao Bing, your son.
The ancients have said: A murderer pays with his own life;
According to reason, leave my family safe and sound.
If you like this deal let me know right away;
Truthfully tell me, and I will do as you say."
The four dragon lords replied instantly:
"Brave Child!
Indeed, you are acting filially,
Sacrificing your body heroically;
You match the ideal perfectly;
Your name will be known to eternity.
Offering your life to save your father free;
Why on earth shouldn't we agree!"
Nezha said:
"If you all give your consent;
To the hall, let my daddy ascend."
Hearing his command, Ao Guang was not tardy;
Releasing the ropes, father was returned to his family.
Widely opening his eyes, Nezha exclaimed:
You eels, pay heed! Listen carefully:
"A hero's words are like black on white,
Once uttered, there is no way around!"
Having finished his speech, he quickly disrobed,
Taking off his shoes, barefoot he strode.
His red silk pants, he immediately stripped off,
Little tummy and white chest he fully exposed.
Ascending the grand terrace, Nezha cried:
You eels step back, stand to one side.
"Whoever tries to stop me in my deed,
Is nothing but a cowardly female indeed."
His speech concluded, he grasped with might,
The sacred sword glowing bright;
Pointed to his heart, and thrust inside.[17]

In terms of temporal development, the story should have ended right here with Nezha's suicide, and yet the prose narrative that follows retells it. The moment is so significant that chronology is ignored in order to re-examine the self-immolation. The storyteller revisits in prose his protagonist's final gesture to provide us with additional information: Awed by Nezha's powerful speech, the dragon kings have refused to hand him the sword to kill himself. By contrast, Li Jing does not hesitate to give his son the instrument of self-murder. It is the father who lands Nezha the coup de grace, driving him to suicide:

> We just told you of Nezha's proposal to the dragon lords that he kill himself. Having heard it they replied together: "In this case you are truly a filial son. Your proposal is most reasonable. We are willing to withdraw." "If you agree, you should immediately release my father," responded Nezha, whereupon the dragon lords quickly undid Li Jing's ropes. "A hero's words are like black on white," pronounced Nezha: "There is no way back." Removing his jacket, and pulling off socks and shoes, he took off his pants, revealing his white flesh. Standing on the ceremonial terrace, he said: "You need not trouble to kill me yourselves. Hand me a sword, and I will finish myself off." Hearing him, the dragon lords were so terrified that none dared step forward. Nezha flew into a rage: "Bah! You eel-scum deserve to die! You want your lord to kill himself, yet you refuse to hand him a sword. What's that supposed to mean!" The dragon generals and dragon kings were so scared that they hung their heads in silence. Seeing this, Commander Li hurriedly took the dragon king's Ao Ji's precious sword, and handed it to the prince. Spreading his arm to receive it, and facing the general, Nezha addressed him respectfully: "Implicating father and mother, your son has not been filial. Today he will sacrifice his life, repaying Mom and Dad's kindness." Then, grasping the precious sword, he threw himself on both knees.[18]

That Nezha's father has handed him the fatal sword is an addition to the plot that is not mentioned in the original novel. Evidently it has been made in order to accentuate Li Jing's cruelty. The drum ballad's implied author is as resentful of the father as he is fond of the child. His undivided sympathy is given to Nezha, Li Jing being portrayed as a brutal tyrant whose savagery affects everyone he encounters. Several episodes have been added to the narrative in order to illustrate Li Jing's cruelty. The storyteller has inserted into the tale an elderly couple whose pious veneration of Nezha is a foil to the father's spiteful infidelity. The childless Mr. and Mrs. Wang have volunteered to officiate at the Nezha Temple (which his mother has secretly established). Cleaning, mending, and toiling for the benefit of the temple's clientele, they fall prey to the vicious Li who happens upon it. The general orders that Mr. Wang be given forty strokes of the heavy bamboo, but not before cursing him for leading the people astray with his superstitious fabrications: "Ignorant rascal! How dare you mislead the masses with your evil lies, using this temple sham to commit crimes!"[19] An element of social (and religious) protest is perhaps evident in the depiction of the haughty Li. The storyteller might be expressing resentment against the officials' incredulous disdain of the lower classes' popular beliefs.

The principal victim of Li Jing's ire is his wife. Madam Yin is the natural ally of her son and as such the inevitable object of her husband's frustration. Tormenting spouse and child alike, Li Jing emerges from the Beijing drum ballad as a grotesque caricature of the traditional patriarch. When Madam Yin tells him that Nezha has appeared in her dream, her husband threatens her with divorce, and when (at the earlier stage of the suicide) she begs to collect her child's remains he does not hesitate to draw his sword and terrorize her with murder threats:

> When she heard that Nezha was carving out his flesh and bones, his mother felt as if sharp blades had been thrust through her heart. She wanted to rush forward and stop him, but how could she enter a hall full of [male] guests? She was well aware, moreover, of her husband's terrible temper. As much as she wanted to, there was nothing she could do.
>
> Having verified that Ao Guang had left, she rushed into the hall. Looking around she saw that its entire floor was red with blood. Nezha's severed left arm was still twitching, and his right arm was grasping the double-bladed sword. Barefoot and his hair disheveled, his eyes were wide open. He was facing upwards to the sky, his cut-off limbs pointing east and west. The breast and the abdomen had been carved open, and the entrails were strewn on the floor. "It kills me," screamed his mother, but her throat being chocked, she could say no more.
>
> Seeing his wife, Li Jing flew into a rage. Reaching to his waist, he drew the steel sword. "Wife, get out right now!" he shouted, frowning deeply. "If you stay here one minute longer, you will share his fate."[20]

Li Jing had repeatedly accused his son of unfilial behavior. Drawing upon the well-known example of the filial crow, which was believed to regurgitate and feed its elders, he had complained that Nezha did not rise to the level of birds and beasts: "Traitorous Son! . . . You are not the equal of a crow in filial piety. I knew right from the start that you would bring calamity upon our family. I should have killed you back then when you were just born."[21] His crude tirades contrast with the nobility of Nezha's self-immolation that follows. The child's adieu from his parents is a model of understated restraint. Even as he severs his familial relations, Nezha reiterates the culture's filial ideal:

> Numinous Pearl grasped the sword, falling on both knees,
> An adieu he bid his parents for their loving deeds.
> "Bearing and suckling a child is not easy,
> Such hopes you have had for me!
> Glorifying ancestors, honoring the clan, was my duty,
> Imperial honors to wife and children my responsibility.
> When the time came, my parents to heaven returning calmly,
> Who could have known?
> In midway I met with calamity.
> Today forced to separate abruptly,

No more a familial bond between you and me.
It was not I, who courted this calamity,
It was rather my star-crossed destiny.
Today, to Mom and Dad flesh and bones returning,
My coming and my going I am here recording.[22]

As he proceeds to mortify the flesh, the implied author's admiration of his protagonist is fully revealed. The storyteller sings the praises of the courageous child who does not flinch from killing himself. Even as he undergoes tremendous physical pain, Nezha neither wails nor cries:

> Nezha shouted: "Bah, old eels and misbegotten abortions! Watch me as I carve out my flesh and bones, and return them to my parents, atoning for Ao Bing's life." The dragon lords were so taken aback that they merely shook their heads, flicking their fingers. His eyes wide-opened, and possessed by Ao Bing's vengeful spirit, Nezha slashed open his breast. Swish, swish, swish, the loud sound of his carving was clearly audible, as he cut through to his ribs. His entire body was covered with blood, turning fully red. Those shrimp soldiers and crab generals were so terrified that their souls left them. Turning pale with fright, they stared dumbfounded. Nezha continued to cut down to his legs, turning up and down into a mess of blood. Gritting his teeth, he did not utter a sound. Nothing but the wild swishing of the sword could be heard. Alas, what a pity![23]

The Roster of the Gods drum ballad offers us a glimpse of values that might have been shared by a broad spectrum of late-imperial society. As a written text it was copied by people who had received only a modicum of education (hence the numerous orthographic errors), and as an oral narrative it had been available to an illiterate audience as much as a literate one. To the extent that the narrative reflects the worldview of the middle—or even lower—echelons of urban society, one might expect it to propagate conservative family values. Similar drum ballads dating from the late imperial period sometimes exhibit prudish sexual ethics even as they might protest against corrupt officialdom.[24] Indeed, Nezha's mother succumbs to the prevailing mores, being careful not to appear in male society. The storyteller explains that she has refrained from intervening with her son's suicide not only because of her husband's violence, but also because it took place in a room full of men. She has maintained Confucian decorum to the extent of sacrificing her son.

The conservative traits and broad social appeal of *The Roster of the Gods* make its open criticism of the father striking. The drum ballad does not require a psychoanalyst to unravel its repressed meaning. The oedipal and the marital frustrations are right there on the surface. The wife and the child—no less than the storyteller and his presumed audience—share an open hostility toward patriarchal authority. The animosity of father and son—no less than the resentment of husband and wife—are evident in dialogues and in monologues, in the authorial comments, and in the unfolding of the action. The Oedipus complex appears to be operating not only in the subconscious psychological sphere, but in the open realm of social action. The nineteenth-century oral myth might indicate therefore the degree to which the traditional family structure has fostered the conscious bond of mothers and their male offspring. In a patriarchal setting, the potentially oppressed wives and children are natural allies.

Drama

Much like the ballads celebrating him, Nezha plays have circulated either as part of *The Canonization of the Gods* or independently of it. Some dramatic renditions enacted the entire epic conflict between the Shang and the Zhou, including the Nezha sequel (even though the oedipal child's misadventures have been omitted from some versions).[25] By contrast, other plays focused on the Nezha figure, whose saga they narrated independently of *The Canonization of the Gods*. This is the case with the Qing-period play examined in this section, which has been titled after Nezha's birthplace *Chentang Pass* (*Chentang guan*).

Four fragmented Qing-period manuscripts of one and the same Kunqu-style play titled *Chentang Pass* (*Chentang guan*) survive in the Academia Sinica Folk Literature Collection. The libretto follows faithfully the seventeenth-century novel, the sequence of events being identical to the one in *The Canonization of the Gods*. The drama opens with Nezha's birth in a ball of flesh, followed by his father hacking it in two, the infant's murder of the dragon prince, his confrontation with the ogress Lady Rock, his self-immolation, the temple his loving mother has built him, its destruction by the jealous Li Jing, the attempted patricide, Nezha's subjugation under the magic stupa, and the uneasy truce with his father. Spared nothing of the tale's emotional intensity, the spectators are shown the acrimonious father-son saga in its entirety.

In the deadly confrontation of father and son, the playwright's undivided sympathy is reserved for the latter. Additions to the plot highlight Nezha's gallantry. The incarnated child refuses to fight his father as long as the latter is not ready for battle. "A hero (*haohan*) does not kill an unprepared warrior,"[26] declares Nezha, permitting his nemesis to saddle his horse and unsheathe his weapons. Compassion for the unfortunate child is further generated by his telling of the story. As the lead actor, the drama is presented from Nezha's point of view, his piteous voice dominating the play. Consider, for example, the following excerpt that covers the entire sequence of events from Nezha's decision to take his own life, through his parting from the Daoist Master, his confrontation with the dragon kings who have taken his father captive, his self-immolation, his taking residence at the temple atop Cuiping Mountain, and the enraged Li Jing's appearance on the scene. The entire sequence is narrated by Nezha, no voice other than his being heard:

> [Nezha says:] "I wish to pay for my crime. I would not dare implicate my parents. Where would I turn? Master, today we separate forever. Alas Master! Alas Master! This crime is my doing, and I should resolve it. Today I will return my body to my mother, who had harbored it in the womb. Alas my Master! Today, eyes wide-open, I head to the boiling oil and the axe's blade. My youthful body will be thrown in the gutter, entombed in a dirt-wall. Blood and tears streaming, how hard it is to part. Your kindness has been as deep as the ocean. Alas Master! Alas Master! I am afraid that your righteous and filial disciple has an unruly nature. O Master!"
>
> "Your disciple has left. Alas, such a calamity! Parting from my master, I am descending from the immortals' mountain. What is this ferocious wind? How can you be so insolent? You misbegotten scum, how dare you take my father captive. Stop right now! A hero will never involve his parents in his deeds. Today I will carve out my flesh for my mother, returning my bones to my father. Release them right now! The heavenly double-edged sword will cut three inches deep, severing forever the father-and-son bond. Let the people learn the example of the Numinous Pearl as he restores bones and flesh to his parents. Now I depart from this world, my soul fluttering far away to the Yellow Springs. The carved meat left behind, the spirit soaring. Alas! I have been destined to part from you."
>
> "Sinning against heaven, my crime as deep as the ocean, where can I turn? Let me stay for a while on this Cuiping Mountain, enjoying its beautiful surroundings. Let my incorporeal spirit dwell here temporarily. Alas! Who is this person coming?" His eyebrows knitted in fury, Nezha curses his father, venting his burning hatred. "I have already returned my bones to you. There is no more a father-son relation between us. How dare you come here to hurt me!"[27]

Literary critics have taught us that an inside view generates sympathy. The privileged access into a character's feelings engenders understanding of his motives.[28] The Kunqu playwright has chosen to provide such access to the toddler's mind rather than to his father's. Nezha's piteous voice is heard throughout the bulk of the play, whereas his father's has been muffled. Much like the nineteenth-century Beijing drum ballad, the Kunqu play betrays open hostility of patriarchal authority. The two texts evince sympathy toward those who have been oppressed by the traditional family values.

Animated Movies

Beginning in the 1970s, Nezha cartoons have enjoyed increasing popularity throughout East Asia. The adventures of the child-god have been celebrated in comic strips and animated movies in China and Japan alike. Some cartoons have been preoccupied with the infant's martial victories to the partial or complete neglect of his Oedipus complex. Instead of dwelling on Nezha's familial conflict, they have him battle wicked adversaries of all sorts. The fifty-two-sequels *Nezha Story* (*Nezha chuanqi*), for example, locks the infant-warrior in a series of life-and-death confrontations with the pernicious Lady Rock. Saving his parents from the ogress, the 2004 serial transforms the unruly child into a paragon of filial devotion. The painful familial hatred of the late imperial novel is transformed into a mushy harmony, as Nezha's father praises his selfless devotion: "Your father and mother will always be proud of you," he exclaims to the gratified Nezha.[29]

Whether printed or broadcast, Nezha cartoons have enjoyed as much popularity in Japan as in China. Pronounced Nataku in Japanese, the young warrior has been featured in some of the bestselling comics (manga) and their related animations (animé) from the 1990s onward. For the most part the Japanese cartoons are not related to the Nezha myth as narrated in *The Canonization of the Gods*. Instead of dwelling on the prodigy's hatred of his father, they incorporate him as a warrior into futuristic campaigns of extraterrestrial beings. In the immensely popular *X/1999* comics, movie, and television serial, Nezha (Nataku) is a superhuman endowed with extrasensory perception (esper). In the blockbuster television serial and computer game *Mobile Suit Gundam Wing*, he is a mega-robot who has been sent to Earth from an outer space colony to fight the secret and evil Organization of the Earth (OZ). Nataku is presented as a hybrid human-machine. Made of the futuristic alloy Gundanium, the ultimate warrior is equipped with spear-like beam glaives, which permit him to overcome human and alien adversaries alike.

Even though contemporary cartoons frequently ignore Nezha's oedipal confrontation, some do dwell upon it. Some comic strips and animated movies elaborate on *The Canonization of the Gods*' familial discord. This is the case with Fujisaki Ryū's (born 1971) cartoon serial *Hōshin engi* (Canonization of the gods), which is loosely based upon the novel's Japanese translation.[30] Featuring Nezha (Nataku) as one of its principal protagonists, the animation narrates his visceral myth in full. Fujisaki's cartoon was serialized from 1996 to 2000 in the *Weekly Shōnen Jump* magazine before being reissued in several book-form editions. It has inspired radio drama, video games, and a television serial, which has been distributed in North America under the title *Soul Hunter*. English-speaking audiences have been introduced to the Chinese legend through the medium of Japanese animation.

Fujisaki's animation largely follows the plot of the Nezha myth as narrated in the seventeenth-century novel. Nataku emerges from a ball of flesh that has been hacked by his father, and after killing the dragon, he commits suicide, only to have his tomb (as the cartoon has it) desecrated by Li Jing (Japanese pronunciation: Risei). One difference concerns the attempted patricide. In the original version it is thwarted by divine intervention, whereas in the animation the mother's sup-

Figure 3: Nataku (top) and his father (bottom right) as rendered by Fujisaki Ryū. Note Nataku's bracelets (which function as powerful projectiles) and his jet engine wheels.

plications prevent it; Lady Yin begs her son to desist from a murder that will pain her too much. In addition, the narrator suggests that his protagonist is incapable of the crime he has vowed to commit. Nataku is endowed with a hidden core of goodness that prevents him from killing his father. The implied author's fondness for the impetuous child is voiced by leading protagonists such as Jiang Ziya (Taikōbō), no less than by visual rendering. The sympathy toward Nataku—as well as the disapproval of Li Jing (Risei)—is graphically attested. Whereas Fujisaki designed the oedipal youth as a charming and valiant hero, he took pains to draw the father as a miserable, even repellent, person. The animated medium has enabled the artist to enhance the son's attraction no less than his progenitor's repulsion (figure 3).

Rather than drawing upon the Chinese iconographic tradition, Fujisaki has chosen to reinvent the child-warrior's emblematic weapons. Late imperial Chinese iconography usually has the child-warrior wield his cosmic ring in one hand and his fire-tipped spear in the other. The god is shown riding his wind-and-fire wheels, his celestial-confusion cloth floating delicately behind him. Dispensing with the spear, the contemporary manga artist reimagined the cosmic ring as two heavy bracelets worn on the wrists. Ejected as powerful projectiles, they home in on their targets with tremendous force. A similar technological twist has been given to the wind-and-fire wheels, which have been provided with jet engines. As for the celestial-confusion cloth, it has been redesigned as a cool skirt. The allure of twentieth-century fashion, along with the fascination of contemporary missile technology, has transformed the divine warrior's image.

The contemporary Japanese animation differs from the late imperial Chinese novel in its explicit familiarity with psychological theory. Fujisaki mentions Freud in the body of his artwork. Whereas the authors of the seventeenth-century novel had not heard of the Oedipus complex (to which they gave such powerful expression), Fujisaki has. The artist has two of his characters comment apropos Nataku that "some children attempt to kill their father in order to attain their mother. It's called an oedipal complex."[31] Like this writer, Fujisaki has perceived the legend's oedipal undercurrent and explicitly alluded to it in his adaptation.

The Nezha legend is given an entirely different interpretation in a classic animated movie produced in Shanghai in 1979. Titled *Nezha Wreaks Havoc in the Ocean* (*Nezha naohai*), it transforms the novel's psychological drama into an allegory of the communist struggle. Directed by Wang Shuchen (1931–1991), *Nezha Wreaks Havoc in the Ocean* is an animation masterpiece that combines a magnificent musical score with an exquisite graphic design. The music incorporates traditional Peking Opera melodies, whereas the gorgeous visual imagery is the work of the acclaimed artist Zhang Ding (1917–2010). After graduating from the Beijing (then Beiping) Academy of Art, Zhang journeyed in 1938 to the communist base of Yan'an, teaching painting at the legendary Lu Xun Art School. In the 1950s he played a major role in designing national emblems and stamps, and in the same year in which he drew the Nezha movie, he also created exquisite frescoes of the rebellious child for the (now) old Beijing airport (figure 4). *Nezha Wreaks Havoc in the Ocean* has been rightly lauded as an animation masterpiece. The internationally acclaimed movie has won awards in China, France, and the Philippines.[32]

Nezha Wreaks Havoc in the Ocean opens not with Nezha's birth but with the image of a helpless fishing boat that is tossed upon the waves in a cruel storm. Controlling the elements, the dragon kings laugh uproariously at its misery. The shift from the familial scene of childbirth to the larger picture of the ophidian gods tormenting the miserable fishermen is significant. As Cui Yunlan has rightly observed, the 1979 animation relegates the father-son conflict to a secondary position, with the struggle against the dragon kings occupying center stage.[33] Instead of an oedipal drama, the movie is a political allegory of a courageous youth protesting against the tyrannical abuse of power. Nezha is a revolutionary hero who leads the masses against their longtime oppressors. The dragon kings stand for the feudal lords of old, their demise ushering an era of peace, equality, and prosperity. In one scene a group of children upbraids a humiliated dragon king, listing one by one his crimes of old. The victims have turned into judges, much like the peasants during the 1950s landlord trials. The movie's ideological bent is unmistakable.

In his discussion of the original Nezha—the oedipal protagonist of the seventeenth-century novel—Steven Sangren has rightly observed a strong narcissistic

Figure 4: Nezha battling the four dragon kings. 1979 fresco by Zhang Ding at the (old) Beijing airport.

element. Nezha is the hero of our dreams because he lives what is impossible in real life. He manages to avoid the law of exchange, living into himself, in complete autonomy and disregard of those like the dragon kings that obstruct him, even sometimes removing them.[34] The narcissistic element is absent from the 1979 animation, in which revolutionary ideology has replaced the psychological want. The protagonist's wanton acts of violence are provided with ideological justification. Thus, Nezha murders the dragon prince not in an unbridled display of egotistic power, but because the creature has abducted an innocent child, whom it intends to devour. The dragons exact from the people human sacrifices, or else they punish them with a drought. It is for this reason that the courageous infant rises against them in rebellion.

The welfare of the people replaces desire as the primary motivation for Nezha's action. His two principal feats—the suicide and the rebirth—are equally guided by the commitment for social justice rather than by familial tension. The child kills himself following the dragon kings' threat of a cosmic flood that will cause innumerable sufferings. Indeed, it is the pitiable sight of a baby floundering in the waves that induces his self-sacrifice. Similarly, he is reborn not to avenge himself on his father but to save the people from their feudal tormentors. The most conspicuous difference between the animation and the novel is the absence of patricide. The father neither desecrates his son's temple nor does his offspring try to kill him. The courageous child is reborn instead to liberate the masses from their oppressors. As he vanquishes the dragon kings, the floods recede and an era of peace and prosperity dawns on the land. The movie culminates in a revolutionary victory.

In an essay titled "Rejecting Oedipus" ("Tichu Edipusi"), Luo Tongbing has rightly suggested that the 1979 animation has replaced the novel's psychological cluster with the vocabulary of the revolutionary struggle.[35] Even though the father's animosity is still there (at one point Li Jing disavows his son), it is relegated to a secondary position. The movie's principal concern is the individual's selfless sacrifice for the collective welfare. In this respect *Nezha Wreaks Havoc in the Ocean* illustrates the rebellious potential of the protean child. The familial discord could be carried into the social and the political spheres, with the oedipal child becoming a revolutionary martyr. Nezha could be used as a symbol of resistance, in this instance serving the socialist agenda.

From Animation to Opera

The modern media sometimes influence traditional art forms. The mainland animation *Nezha Wreaks Havoc in the Ocean* (1979) has surprisingly served as a source for regional drama across the Taiwan Straits. Within ten years of the socialist film's first screening, its plot line inspired a Taiwanese opera in the island's traditional *gezaixi* style. Performed by the Xinhexing theater company and directed by Jiang Qingliu (1935–2004), the play *Nezha Story* (*Nezha chuanqi*) has been widely acclaimed as a masterpiece *gezaixi*, being staged in such prestigious venues as the Taiwan National Theater (Guojia juyuan).[36]

The *gezaixi* play follows the animation's plot, borrowing from it elements that appear in no other written, oral, or dramatic version of the story. The *Nezha Story* opens, like *Nezha Wreaks Havoc in the Ocean,* with the cruelty of the dragon kings, who force the people to sacrifice them a "virgin boy" and a "virgin girl" (*tongnan tongnü*). The identical demand (and language) is followed in the opera, as in the animation, by the cruel *yakṣa* kidnapping an innocent child. Nezha's heroic rescue of the infant is the source of his skirmish with the water monster. The play culminates, like the cartoon, with the dragon kings' threat of a calamitous flood, which is averted by the child's self-immolation. Nezha's self-sacrifice saves the population at large, not only his family. That the animation has been the source of the *gezaixi* opera (rather than vice versa) is suggested by their respective dates (1979 and ca. 1990) as well as by their distribution. Whereas the opera has been performed in Taiwan only (and hence is not likely to have influenced a Shanghai production), the mainland animation has been screened with great success across East Asia.

In the mainland animation, the dragon kings' evil role has relegated the father's cruelty to a secondary position (even though he remains a threatening figure). By contrast, in the Taiwanese opera the oedipal conflict figures prominently (side by side with the battle against the ophidian monsters). Li Jing of the *gezaixi* play disavows his offspring: "He is no longer our son," he declares (in the Hokkien dialect, as the written text betrays by the usage of the third person pronoun *ī*). The father goes as far as an attempted infanticide, which is narrowly averted by his wife's piteous pleading. Much as in the Taiwanese oral ballad that predated it by almost a century, the Taiwanese play culminates in a near murder of the child by his outraged father. In both the *Song of Nezha Wreaking Havoc in the Eastern Ocean* and the *Nezha Story,* the mother protects her offspring from his father's wrath. In the ballad and the play alike, maternal compassion is an antidote to paternal cruelty.[37]

The father's wrath turns into admiration as his son volunteers to sacrifice his life. When Nezha declares his intention to kill himself to avert the calamitous flood, Li Jing realizes his son's worth. In a significant departure from all earlier versions (including the mainland animation), the Taiwanese opera has the child make his request of a temple *prior* to his death. Nezha's farewell wish is that after he commits suicide his parents dedicate a shrine to him. Whereas in the novel the request (which is made after the suicide) infuriates the father, in the *Nezha Story* he readily consents. The *gezaixi* play ends with the heroic child's tearful farewell from both parents. Mother *and* father lament the fate of their courageous offspring.

Unlike earlier renditions, the Taiwanese opera does not follow the suicide by rebirth and revenge. Whereas in other versions the self-murder is a prelude to the attempted patricide (or, in the mainland animation, vengeance upon the feudal dragon kings), the *Nezha Story* ends right there with the self-sacrifice. As Shi Guangsheng has noted, the modern *gezaixi* play does not follow the genre's traditional law of retribution, by which the "wicked should be punished for their crimes" (*e you e bao*).[38] Hence, the *Nezha Story* strikes a tragic note. The opera sings the sad tale of a courageous and filial youth, whose sacrifice remains unrequited.

Rebel without a Cause

The mainland cartoon *Nezha Wreaks Havoc in the Ocean* illustrates the god's potential for political resistance. The animation classic has transformed the oedipal child into a revolutionary martyr. A Taiwanese short story and a movie shed a different light on the malleability of the enfant terrible, presenting him as a trope of the adolescent quest. In Xi Song's (b. 1947) fiction, Nezha is portrayed as a sensitive youth possibly reminiscent of Goethe's Young Werther, whereas in a Tsai (Cai) Mingliang (b. 1957) film he is depicted as a rebellious teenager à la James Dean. The short story and movie alike illustrate the enduring attraction of the impetuous youngster, who has been incorporated into the contemporary Chinese discourse of adolescence and juvenile crime.

Xi Song (b. 1947) is a Taiwanese artist, known as a painter and a book illustrator no less than as a writer. His first story, "The Roster of the Gods' Nezha," was published in 1971 and then reissued in 1991 in the author's collected stories, which bore the same title. Xi has been especially fond of his earliest literary experiment, as he explains in the collection's preface:

> I still remember that evening twenty years ago, when my brush was running without a pause, writing the Nezha story: "Slicing the flesh for one's father, carving the bones for one's mother." As the blank space of white paper was miraculously filled with long slanting lines of characters, it seemed as if my brush's speed matched that of Nezha's fluttering sacrificed soul. I still remember the emotions that filled me as I reclined in solitude over my desk: Even as I shed tears for the piteous entreating of Nezha's spirit, I was madly elated, for this was the first time that I felt in control of the literary balance of form and content.[39]

Xi's Nezha is a poetic soul, too sensitive for the cruel world into which it has been born. Divinely beautiful and superhumanly strong, he is supplied with a foil in the person of the deformed servant Simang. The ugly-looking slave venerates his master's perfection, the latter reciprocating by a mixture of pity and disgust. Indeed, it is a combination of aesthetic revulsion and moral indignation that leads the young god to take his own life. Nezha confides in his Daoist master that he cannot abide the pain and the foulness of the mortal world:

> I know that on the eastern plains, war is about to break. My heroic brothers are about to lead their crack troops to the fields of slaughter. As I opened my red gauze sash, I could see in it the images of countless strewn bones, wailing women and children, and circling vultures—the foundations of tomorrow's world. But where would tomorrow's faith come from? I have seen young women selling their bodies. Wandering aimlessly in the back alleys, they are driven by hunger and desire. Had there been something to satisfy their thirst they would not have continued to prowl in filthy alleys, nurturing the insatiable desire of future generation. One day followed another—only when liberated from my vexations, did I perceive heaven's blue vault.[40]

Xi's Nezha does not get along with his parents, who fail to perceive his divine destiny. The oedipal frustration, however, is not the prime motivation for his separation from them (the scene of the attempted patricide is missing from the story). It is rather a general sense of isolation that leads the boy to abandon the world. The refrain of "no one understands me" runs through the story, as the despairing Nezha fails to find his place in a hostile environment. Alienated by his family, he finds something of a soul mate in the dragon prince, who is presented as his double: "I thought that he was my own reflection in the water," Nezha tells his Daoist master.[41] Hence, the slaughter of the water god is in one sense an act of self-murder, which prefigures the protagonist's suicide.

Wittingly or not, the Taiwanese author has rediscovered the original Buddhist significance of the lotus as the symbol of enlightenment. Medieval Buddhist art has fashioned the souls of the redeemed after the water lily. Painters and sculptors depicted step by step the gradual emergence of celestial beings from the sacred flower's petals, paradisiacal rebirth being imagined as horticultural regeneration (see chapter 7, figure 19).[42] Unlike the seventeenth-century novel in which his newly acquired lotus body serves Nezha to attack his father, Xi's story celebrates the holy plant as the goal of the religious quest. "The Roster of the Gods' Nezha" culminates with the divine child's rebirth as a "lotus in the pool of eternity."[43]

Like Xi Song, who explored Nezha in his first story, Tsai (Cai) Mingliang (b. 1957) used the rebellious child as an emblem in his first movie. Born in Malaysia, Tsai studied cinema in Taiwan, gradually emerging as one of the island's leading filmmakers. Produced in 1992, his *Teenage Nezha* (*Qing shaonian Nezha*) has been released in Europe and North America under the additional title *Rebels of the Neon God*. The movie does not tell the original Nezha legend. Instead it follows a group of disoriented teenagers along the shopping malls and game parlors of contemporary Taipei, which is depicted as a gray and depressing modern metropolis. Alienated from their families and from each other, the young delinquents spend their time playing video games and occasionally engaging in meaningless sex and petty crime.[44]

The movie's principal protagonist is a lonely and disoriented teenager named Xiaokang. His father (surnamed Li) being a humble cab driver and his mother an assistant cook, the confused youngster lacks a role model. He wastes his parents' hard-won money in cram schools (*buxiban*), studying nothing. Finally, he pockets the tuition money they gave him and, dropping out of class, goes wandering in the seedy Ximending district of Taipei. Concerned about her son's fate, the mother consults a female medium for the Celestial Maiden (Xiangu), who tells her that he is none other than the incarnated Nezha. It is for this reason, the goddess elaborates, that the teenager does not get along with his father (who shares Li Jing's surname). Xiaokang overhears his mother repeat the information to his father, whereupon he goes into a trance, declaring in a faltering voice that "I am the Third Prince Nezha."[45] The choreography of his possession has clearly been fashioned after that of Taiwanese spirit mediums, who flail their arms advancing in awkward dancing steps much as he does.

The movie's loose plot revolves around Xiaokang's attempt to avenge his father's humiliation at the hands of two delinquent youths who have smashed his cab's side mirror. Spotting the two at a pachinko parlor, Xiaokang follows one of them to a squalid love hotel. As the petty criminal—himself a disoriented and lonely teenager—makes love to an equally lost girlfriend, Xiaokang wreaks vengeance on his bright new motorbike. He slashes the tires and seat cushions, smashes the lights, breaks the bike's body, and tops it all by pouring liquid glue into the keyhole. Satisfied that his tormentor's pride of possession is past repair, he sprays the pavement in red with the words: "Nezha has been here."[46] The youthful delinquent enacts the vengeful role that Nezha devotees expect him to fulfill in society. We will see in chapter 6 that the Nezha cult has spread among Taiwanese gangsters precisely because of the furious god's uncontrollable violence.

Xiaokang's revenge does not earn him the father's gratitude. Cab driver Li does not know that his son has sought to avenge his lost honor, and when Xiaokang returns home after a night's absence, he shuts the door in his face. Much like *The Canonization of the Gods'* protagonist who has made Li Jing a belt of the dragon's sinews only to be rebuked by the horrified parent, Xiaokang's immature gesture is not reciprocated. The movie ends with the desperate youth roaming the gray and alienating Taipei landscape, as estranged as he has ever been from his parents.

Tsai Mingliang's movie draws upon an American source as well as a native Chinese inspiration. The *Teenage Nezha*'s (1992) delinquent protagonists have been partially fashioned after the emotionally confused characters of Nicholas Ray's (1911–1979) *Rebel Without a Cause* (1955). The American classic's generational conflict has been recreated in the Taiwanese film, the Taipei teenagers as disoriented and emotionally confused as their Los Angeles counterparts. Quoting from Ray's film, Tsai Mingliang pays homage to his American source: As he heads out of the game parlor in pursuit of his rivals, Xiaokang pauses to ponder a life-sized poster of the legendary James Dean (1931–1955) in his role of the troubled teenager Jim Stark. At least in one instance, the Chinese deity has been fused with a Western icon. Xiaokang has been modeled after Nezha *and* James Dean alike.

Conclusion

The enduring attraction of the Nezha myth suggests that it has struck deep chords in the Chinese psyche. Ever since its inclusion in *The Canonization of the Gods,* the legend of the oedipal child has been retold by novelists, storytellers, playwrights, and filmmakers. The seventeenth-century novel has served as a source for an enormous body of late imperial and modern written, oral, dramatic, and cinematic adaptations. Evidently, the figure of the patricidal infant has spoken to the repressed emotions of successive generations.

Nezha's modern appeal mirrors his adaptability to changing historical circumstances. Twentieth-century novelists, playwrights, and screenwriters have recreated the mischievous infant to reflect their own political, social, and psychological concerns. A mainland cartoon has depicted him as a revolutionary martyr, whereas a Taiwanese film has made him a symbol of adolescent confusion. Furnishing Nezha (Nataku) with cool accessories and snazzy weaponry, Japanese manga artists have fashioned a contemporary teenage icon. Modern playwrights have not hesitated to change the legend's original plot. The Taiwanese *Nezha Story* has dispensed altogether with the hero's rebirth and attempted patricide, the opera culminating in his tragic suicide instead.

Whereas modern authors have felt free to rewrite the Nezha myth, Qing-period (1644–1911) storytellers and playwrights have been loyal to the seventeenth-century version. The Kunqu play we have examined and the three oral narratives (Beijing drum ballad, Taiwanese *gezai* song, and Fuzhou *chantefable*) follow closely the oedipal confrontation as narrated in *The Canonization of the Gods*. It is striking that all four versions labor to highlight the father's cruelty no less than his wife's compassion. The ballads and play alike accentuate the animosity of father and son, their sympathies lying squarely with the latter. The open hostility of the father hints at the heavy emotional price that had been generated by patriarchal authority. Judging by the late imperial versions of the Nezha myth, the traditional Chinese family tended to foster the bond of mother and son, no less than their animosity toward the husband/father.

The oedipal confrontation is entirely missing, however, from some late imperial and modern narratives that portray Nezha as the gods' martial emissary. Instead of pondering the child's psychology, some storytellers, playwrights, and moviemakers have celebrated his victory over demonic adversaries. We will turn to the ancient literary tradition of Nezha the divine warrior.

5

Divine Warrior

Huang Feihu (Huang Flying-Tiger) is among the greatest warriors of the seventeenth-century novel. Like Nezha's, his story illustrates *The Canonization of the Gods*' concern with father-son relations. Driven to rebellion by the cruelty of the Shang, Huang finds himself locked in conflict with his father, who has been a loyal servant to the dynasty. The father insists that his son kill him; he would rather die than see his family's reputation of fidelity tarnished.[1] It is only by dint of a ruse that the son's colleagues manage to have the father join—against his will—the rebels' cause. Parent and offspring end up as warriors in the righteous Zhou camp. Reconciled, they fight hand in hand against the abusive Shang regime.

Nezha figures in the Huang Feihu story. At one point Huang senior and junior are taken captive by Shang troops. Their entire clan is loaded into prisoner carts and led in procession to the capital to await execution. Having lost all hope, the captives suddenly behold a golden boy descending from heaven. Nezha has been sent by his master to the rescue: Riding the wind-and-fire wheels that have been bestowed upon him by the Immortal Taiyi, he emerges from the clouds to halt the convicts' convoy. Armed with a fire-tipped spear and a pulverizing gold brick, the child-warrior single-handedly overcomes the guards, who flee in a panic. The prisoners' progress is halted. The Huangs are released, and father and son are led by the infant hero to a welcoming party of Zhou soldiers.[2]

His daring rescue of Huang Feihu evinces Nezha's extraordinary fighting skills. Following the uneasy compromise with his father, Nezha's principal function in the novel is that of divine warrior. Episode by episode, *The Canonization of the Gods* elaborates on the child-god's military exploits. Commissioned by his master Taiyi to join the campaign against the Shang, Nezha emerges as one of the Zhou's greatest heroes. Together with his elder brothers Jinzha and Muzha, he participates in scores of battles, in which his boundless courage and youthful energy play a decisive role. The child's heroic victories are glorified in prose and verse alike:

> The turban he wears shining resplendently,
> The ocean-woven garment tied by dragon and tiger veins.
> Nobody, anywhere, can resist his Golden Brick,
> The Cosmic Ring matching the Celestial-Confusion Cloth.
> In the West, he repeatedly wins victories on Qi Peaks,
> Protecting the Zhou dynasty for eight hundred years.
> In the East, he leads his armies through the Five Passes,
> His mighty spear and unfurled standard unsurpassed.
> Imperishable is the incarnated lotus body,
> Everywhere admired is the eight-armed Nezha![3]

The Canonization of the Gods expands on the child-warrior's extraordinary fighting techniques. Having been acquired in heaven, Nezha's martial arts are far superior to those of ordinary mortals: "Divinely transmitted, his subtle methods surpass all others." Nezha draws out his weapon "like a dragon stretching out its claws, as if riding on lightning, as if flying on the rainbow." The child-god manipulates his fire-tipped spear "like lightning traveling through empty space, like the wind howling through a forest of jades." No rival can withstand the divine warrior's martial arts, which resemble "a silver dragon churning the ocean, auspicious snowflakes filling the empty space."[4]

Nezha's invincibility largely depends upon the lotus body that has been fashioned for him by his master. Having forsaken his flesh-and-blood physique for a frame made of an immortal substance, Nezha has become invulnerable. Unlike ordinary bodies, the child's divine constitution is imperishable. Nezha is immune to injuries by spears and swords and to his foes' dark arts. Awesome magic weapons such as the soul-slaying banner (Luhun fan) can do no harm to the child who has returned his flesh and bones to his parents. Neither noxious columns of poisonous smoke nor bright rays of dazzling light can hurt the divine warrior, whose body has been fashioned of a paradisiacal flower. "Luckily, Nezha's body is not made of flesh and blood," explains a comrade in arms when a sorcerer's mirror fails to injure the delicate child.[5]

Nezha's role of divine warrior has been central to his figure in late imperial and modern drama. Theatrical adaptations of the child's myth are sometimes only tangentially related, if at all, to the oedipal conflict with his father. Instead of telling the story of his suicide and attempted patricide, they elaborate on one or another of the toddler's heroic exploits. Playwrights and moviemakers relish the image of the youthful—even delicate—warrior who fearlessly descends into the devils' midst, defeating them all. The element of surprise is provided by the infant's unexpected victory over dreadful monsters, their hideousness a foil to his fragile beauty. Replete with martial arts performances, the Nezha plays are classified as "military" (*wu*) rather than "romantic" or "literary" (*wen*). Ying Yukang elaborates on Nezha's martial role in the Peking Opera:

> In the Peking Opera martial plays (*wuda ju*) there is one unique character, courageous and dazzling, who is universally adored by audiences. He is Nezha. For the most part his repertoire includes martial plays of the spirits and demons type: The demons of the various quarters penetrate the human realm, endangering the people's livelihood. As the situation worsens, the Jade Emperor (or else the Bodhisattva Guanyin) orders the divine generals and their troops to subdue the demon hosts. Whether or not the Pagoda-Bearer, Heavenly King Li Jing, is appointed as the commanding general, the officer leading the vanguard is Nezha.
>
> In this type of spirits and demons show, the actors performing the demonic roles are painted with colorful facial masks—their appearance is savage and terrifying. Suddenly, in their ferocious midst, the vanguard, Nezha, makes his appearance. His face is powdered pure white, his body shining red. He wears a lotus-flower robe, wields the [Fire-Tip] Spear, carries across his shoulder the Cosmic Ring, and rides the Wind-and-Fire wheels. This god—the incarnated Numinous Pearl (Ling Zhuzi)—courageously descends into the demons' battle arrays to punish the wicked and reward the good. When, to the accelerating beat of gongs and drums, he makes his majestic appearance, there is no one in the audience who does not burst into applause.[6]

This chapter surveys Nezha's martial aspect in written texts and visual artworks from the Southern Song period (1127–1279) down to the present. It charts the evolution of his fighting career in fiction, drama, hagiography, and iconography from approximately the thirteenth century. A brief foray is necessary, however, into the warrior's earlier military exploits, which will be examined in greater detail below. In chapter 8 we will explore the Tantric origins of Nezha's military figure and show that his martial career had been launched in esoteric Buddhist scriptures that were translated from the Sanskrit during the medieval period. The child-god had contributed to the defense of the mighty Tang Dynasty (618–907), summoned by elaborate Tantric rituals that combined the recital of lengthy spells (*mantras*) with the manipulation of finger signs (*mudrās*) and the charting of mystical maps (*maṇḍalas*). His esoteric legacy has had a decisive impact on the imaginings of the young brave. The influence of Tantric Buddhism on the warrior's visual image needs to be briefly mentioned.

Tantric divinities usually appear in two forms: benign and wrathful. They each sport a benevolent mien side by side with a terrifying manifestation, which they

Figure 5: Three-headed and six-armed Nezha. Note the child-god's cosmic ring, gold brick, celestial-confusion cloth, and spear. Contemporary statue from King Wen's Temple, Youli, Henan. Photo by Ye Derong (A'de).

assume in order to force the sinful into the Buddhist path. Known in Sanskrit as *krodha,* and in Chinese as *fennu* (or *weinu*), the gods' ferocious manifestation has been fashioned after the voluptuous fantasies of the Indian supernatural. The awesome gods sport a multiplicity of bodily organs, bedecked by abundant accessories. Their numerous heads are adorned with diverse jewelry, and they wield assorted weaponry in each of their multiple arms.

As a proper Tantric divinity, Nezha featured a benign manifestation side by side with a wrathful apparition, which has had a decisive impact on his martial image. All through modern times, the child-god has been imagined with multiple arms, each embracing a different magic weapon. In late imperial novels such as *The Journey to the West* and *The Canonization of the Gods,* the young warrior usually sports six (or eight) arms, wielding respectively such fabulous implements as the magic gold brick, cosmic ring, fire-tipped spear, and celestial-confusion cloth (see figure 5). The warrior's temple iconography, no less than his portrayal in folk literature, betrays the legacy of the Tantric gods. Esoteric Buddhism determined Nezha's three-headed and six-armed fearful image.

Hagiography and Drama

A brief version of the Nezha legend is included in a Ming-period (1368–1644) encyclopedia of the supernatural, *The Grand Compendium of the Three Religions' Deities.*[7] Narrating the careers of more than a hundred divinities, the hagiographic collection has served as a source for scholars studying such prominent ones as Guanyin and Mazu.[8] The compendium's origins are a puzzle: fifty-five of its entries appear in a Yuan-period (1279–1368) antecedent, *The Extensive Record of the Gods.*[9] The question concerns the remaining seventy-five hagiographies (one of which is Nezha's). Missing from the Yuan-period source, these entries might have been added to *The Grand Compendium* during the Ming period. Alternatively, they might have belonged to an original, more complete, version of the Yuan-period work. It has been suggested that *The Extensive Record of the Gods* included chapters now missing from its only extant copy.[10]

Whether or not it derived from a Yuan-period antecedent, Nezha's Ming-period hagiography leaves no doubt as to his role of a demon queller. The young warrior has been sent down to earth by the Jade Emperor's express command that he subdue its evil spirits:

> Nezha was originally a great *arhat*-immortal in the service of the Jade Emperor. He was six feet tall, his head crowned by a golden disc. He had six heads, nine eyes, and eight arms. He puffed out dark clouds. He stood on a large rock. His hand wielded an instrument of the law (*falü*). He roared loudly, summoning clouds and rain, shaking Heaven and Earth. Because the world was full of demon-kings (*mowang*), the Jade Emperor ordered him incarnated on earth [to quell them] . . .
>
> The demons were all subdued by Nezha: The Bull Demon-King, the Lion Demon-King, the Elephant Demon-King, the Horse-Headed Demon-King, the World-Devouring Demon-King, the Mother-of-Demons Demon-King, the Nine-Headed Demon-King, the Tārā Demon-King, the Brahmā Demon-King, the five-hundred *yakṣas,* and the seventy-two Fire Crows all surrendered to him.[11]

The demons subdued by the young warrior are of native and foreign origin alike. Nezha quells creatures of the Chinese imagination such as the Fire Crow (Huoya), which carries burning embers in its beak, as well as imported monsters such as the Mother of Demons (Chinese: Guizi mu; Sanskrit: Hārītī), who began her career as a rapacious child-devouring ogress in India of the first centuries CE.[12] The creators of the Ming compendium (or its possible Yuan-period antecedent) were not clear on the attributes of the Indian mythological beings whose exotic transcribed names they recorded. Hindu and Buddhist gods such as Brahmā and Tārā are listed as demons in *The Grand Compendium of the Three Religions' Deities,* suggesting that by the time of its composition their divine attributes had been forgotten. Their awe-inspiring foreign names sufficed to rank the Indian deities as demonic creatures. The gods and ghosts of Sanskrit literature were equally incorporated into the vast Chinese pandemonium of evil creatures.

The role of demon queller allotted to him in the Ming encyclopedia (or in its Yuan-period source) is equally assigned to Nezha by Yuan- and Ming-period plays. Blurring the distinctions between edifying literature and entertainment, hagiography and drama present an identical image of the guardian deity. Beginning in the thirteenth century, playwrights portrayed Nezha as a martial god who leads his divine troops against a wide assortment of monstrous creatures. The plays sometimes differ in the identity of the supreme deity sending Nezha on his martial errand. The earliest extant (ca. 1300) drama has him performing his military feats on behalf of the Jade Emperor. As in the Ming-period encyclopedia, the young warrior's master is the paramount divinity of the Chinese popular religion. By contrast, a slightly later (ca. 1400) play has him accomplishing the same task by the Buddha's command. It describes Nezha as the devout acolyte of the World-Honored One, who assigns him the forceful conversion of the demonic hordes. The two plays are briefly examined in this section.

Dating from the Yuan period, the earliest extant Nezha play is titled *Third Prince [Nezha] Wreaks Havoc on Black-Wind Mountain; the God Erlang Drunkenly Shoots an Arrow at the Demon-Locking Mirror.*[13] The plot is simple enough: On his way to his military post, the god Erlang visits his colleague, the Third Prince Nezha, who serves as the commander of the Jade-Linked Chain-of-Fortresses. Feasting and drinking, the two martial gods entertain themselves by an archery contest. Whereas Nezha hits the mark, the drunken Erlang misses, shooting by mistake the Demon-Locking Mirror (Suomo jing). Serving as a heavenly prison, the looking-glass houses monstrous creatures, which are thereby released. Following the mishap, the play unfolds as a typical demon-quelling sequence. Nezha and his friend subdue the escaped monsters, the Nine-Headed-Bull-Demon King and the Hundred-Golden-Eyed Ghost, and lead them back to prison.

Appearing on stage in the first act, Nezha elaborates on his demon-quelling expertise. His military record has been such that he has been appointed by the Jade Emperor "Field Marshal for the Subjugation of Monsters in Command of Eight Hundred and Eighty-One Thousand Heavenly Troops." A long list of the toddler's defeated adversaries follows. Nezha has subdued the Ten Demon Lords, the Eight-Horned-Lion-Headed Ghost,[14] and the Iron-Headed-Azure-Heavens Ghost. He has also successfully battled four she-devils: The Celestial Harpy, the Terrestrial Harpy, the Wandering Harpy, and the Sexual Harpy. The female demons are referred to collectively as Māra's daughters (*Mo-nü*), which term has a Buddhist provenance. Sanskrit literature described Māra's (originally three) daughters as femmes fatales who lead men to their ruin. The three gained particular notoriety for their failed attempt to seduce Siddhārtha Gautama. When he was just about to attain enlightenment, they were sent by their father to stir the Buddha from his deep meditation. The Nezha play does not hint of the harpies' Buddhist pedigree. By the time of its composition, their Indian origins might have been forgotten. Following centuries of acculturation, the (now) four she-devils had been integrated into native demonology. By the thirteenth century, Māra's daughters had been safely ensconced in the vast Chinese pandemonium of devils, ghosts, ghouls, harpies, and the like.

The Field Marshal for the Subjugation of Monsters (Xiangyao Dayuanshuai) is attended by subordinate military divinities. Nezha is surrounded by a bevy of junior officials who obey his commands. Recalling the splendid processions of the gods in such early poems as *The Songs of Chu,* Nezha leads his heavenly troops in a triumphant parade. Here he is, singing in the first person:

> For subjugating monsters, I draw a perfect design,
> Exorcising demons, I gain eternal renown.
> Armed with long spear and broadsword,
> I wield light bow and arrows.
> Encircled by yellow banners and panther tails,
> I grasp the jade girdle of my royal white steed.
> In procession march the gods of north and south,
> White tiger and black dragon to my left and right.
> My messenger is the Yellow-Scarfed Stalwart,
> My attendant the Black Goblin of Heavenly Reeds.[15]
> On mountains and marshes, I triumph by water and fire,
> In heaven and earth, victorious by thunder and wind.[16]

The Yuan play overlaps with the one immediately following it. *The Third Prince Wreaks Havoc on Black-Wind Mountain* (ca. 1300) is separated by approximately a hundred years from *The Fierce Nezha's Three Transformations,* which has the young warrior battle many of the same monstrosities.[17] The early Ming *zaju*-style play opens with Nezha's subjugation of the Five Ghost Kings, residents of Flaming-Demon Mountain: The Creepy-Scaled Ghost, the Eight-Horned-Lion-Headed Ghost, the Iron-Headed-Azure-Heavens Ghost, the Blazing-Hundred-Eyed Ghost, and the Vast-Strength Ghost. The comedy culminates with his defeat of Māra's four daughters, who are described as denizens of the Nine-Yang Cave, atop the dreaded Yakṣa Mountain. In their despair the four harpies try to conceal themselves as inanimate stones (*wanshi*). But they are instantly identified by Nezha's divine eye (*tianyan*) and taken captive. The play ends with the young warrior leading the subdued demons and ogresses to his master, the Buddha.

Nezha's adversaries are vicious cannibals. The Five Ghost Kings feed on the local population, "devouring the people as staple grain."[18] The demons are endowed with tremendous magic powers, spitting out poisonous vapors, sending forth hailstorms, emanating blazing fires, and conjuring up terrifying beasts of prey. All of these, however, are no match for the Tantric warrior. Assuming his multiheaded and multiarmed manifestation, Nezha defeats the Five Ghost Kings and the four harpies alike. Interestingly, a gradation is apparent in his deployment of the esoteric magic. The child-warrior appears two-headed and four-armed when fighting the ghost kings, and three-headed and six-armed when facing Māra's daughters. Evidently, the subjugation of the she-devils required greater strength than the suppression of their male counterparts.

As Xu Xinyi has pointed out, the difference between the Yuan play and the early Ming one lies in the latter's Buddhist orientation. Whereas Nezha of *The Third Prince Wreaks Havoc* is a general in the service of the Jade Emperor, in *The Fierce Nezha's Three Transformations* he is the Buddha's Victorious Acolyte (Shansheng tongzi). The different masters entail varying ideologies. Whereas in the Yuan play the goal is the demons' forceful subjugation, the early Ming one has them converted to the Buddhist faith. As he sends Nezha on his martial errand, the Buddha reminds him of the faith's prohibition of killing. Rather than annihilating the subjugated demons, they should be made aware of their moral transgressions and led to enlightenment. The lesson is well learned by the devout warrior, who pronounces to the captive Māra daughters, "You and I shall leave this mountain, crossing over to Paradise. Each one of us shall be released from the wheel of suffering and rebirth. Listening to the Buddha's Dharma, we will be reborn in Heaven. Renouncing the demons' way, we will become gods."[19]

The Buddhist orientation of the early Ming play is evident in Nezha's weaponry. Subjugating the Five Ghosts Kings, the young warrior employs rays of golden light.[20] The pyrotechnic has an ancient Buddhist pedigree, originating with the Tathāgata himself. In a vast number of Mahāyāna scriptures the World-Honored One emits rays of golden light from his forehead, topknot, fingers, toes, and every pore of skin. The divine beams, trillions of them, reach the highest heavens and the lowest hells in each and every world system. A prime example of "skillful means" (*upāya*), they serve to coerce, convert, and lead to salvation each and every kind of being, from sinful souls trapped in purgatory, to restive ghouls and harpies.[21] Just as the Buddha has employed divine light to deliver *nāga* snakes and *rākṣasa* demons, his martial acolyte has relied upon the luminous energy to convert the Five Ghost Kings.

Nezha's martial fame was mirrored in Ming-period fiction. Novelists described their protagonists' military skills by reference to the invincible child. *The Historical Romance of the Declining Tang and the Five Dynasties* compared two of its martial protagonists with Nezha. The brutal founder of the Later Liang Dynasty, Zhu Wen (852–912), was described as an "Eight-Armed Nezha," whereas General Shi Jiantang's (857–921) skills were likened to those of a Nezha actor: "Is he the

Third Prince Nezha, or is he a powdered performer of his," wondered the late Ming author.[22] By the sixteenth and seventeenth centuries, the child's martial arts became the yardstick by which other warriors were measured.

Fighting the Monkey King

Despite his renown, the young warrior was not invariably victorious. Plays that feature Nezha as a secondary character sometimes have him defeated. Nezha is vanquished, for example, in Zhu Youdun's (1379–1439) *The Bodhisattva Mañjuśri Subjugates the Lion.* The play provides an etiological explanation for the ancient iconography of the bodhisattva riding the beast. The big cat had to be tamed, a mission that was entrusted to Nezha. The infant, however, proved unequal to the task. The lion defeated Nezha, overcoming even his fearful three-headed and six-armed Tantric manifestation. Hence, the bodhisattva himself was forced to tackle the feline. Stronger than Nezha, Mañjuśri subjugated the lion, making it his mount.[23]

Nezha's greatest rival has doubtless been Sun Wukong. Beginning in the Ming period (1368–1644), the monkey king has defeated the young warrior in the successive written, oral, and dramatic versions of *The Journey to the West.*[24] Declaring himself the Great Sage Equal to Heaven, the audacious monkey rebels against the Jade Emperor, who commissions Nezha to fight him. The toddler's appearance on the battlefield amuses the clever simian: "Little Prince," said Sun Wukong laughing, "Your baby teeth haven't even fallen out, and your natal hair is still damp!"[25] Nevertheless the fight with the fearless child proves much harder than the mighty Sun Wukong had imagined. The duel between the baby knight and the monkey warrior lasts for dozens of rounds, as the fighters pursue and dodge each other across the heavens. It is only by resorting to the magic of cloning—duplicating himself and attacking the unsuspecting Nezha from behind—that Sun Wukong is finally able to overcome him.

The duel between the mighty simian and the fearless toddler has been a favorite topic of late imperial and modern drama, cinema, and visual arts (see figure 6). Like Nezha, Sun Wukong is capable of the magic of multiplication. He transforms his iconic weapon, the compliant iron staff, into tens of thousands of staffs that fight on his behalf. Nezha, for his part, wields in each of his six arms a different weapon, which he transforms into zillions of arms. The sixteenth-century *The Journey to the West* elaborates on the battle in prose and verse alike. Here is a brief excerpt in Anthony Yu's translation:

> The six-armed Prince Nezha
> The heaven-born Handsome Stone Monkey King.
> One was consigned to come down to earth,
> The other in guile disturbed the universe . . .

Figure 6: Nezha battling Sun Wukong. Qing-period illustration of *The Journey to the West.* From *Qing caihui quanben xiyouji* (Beijing: Zhongguo shudian, 2008).

A few rounds of bitter contest revealed no victor,
But the prince's mind would not so easily rest.
He ordered the six kinds of weapon to change
Into hundreds and thousands of millions, aiming for the head.
The Monkey King, undaunted, roared with laughter loud,
And wielded his iron staff with artful ease:
One turned to a thousand, a thousand to ten thousand,
Filling the sky as a swarm of dancing dragons.[26]

His formidable foe shares significant similarities with Nezha. Sun Wukong is the prototypical rebel. Inquisitive and arrogant, he questions divine and earthly authority alike. The difference between the defiant simian and the mischievous toddler lies in the powers they challenge: Nezha disobeys paternal rule, whereas Sun Wukong rebels against political authority. "Many are the turns of kingship, and next year the turn will be mine,"[27] declares the audacious monkey as he tries to overthrow the Jade Emperor. Undaunted by the divine armies facing him, Sun Wukong challenges heaven itself.

Sun Wukong does not defy his parents for the simple reason that he has none. The fabulous monkey has emerged from a magical stone, which has been miraculously impregnated by the sweet essence of heaven and earth. In this respect Sun Wukong embodies—to a fuller extent than Nezha—the desire for self-production. Steven Sangren has suggested that the Nezha myth betrays the fancy of complete autonomy. The cultural anthropologist has interpreted the child's regeneration from a lotus flower as a fantasy of independent coming into being: "In sum, the Nezha story posits a desire for radical autonomy—that is, to be one's own transcendent producer."[28] Having no parents, the monkey has certainly realized the dream of complete independence. Like Sholem Aleichem's (1859–1916) *Mottel the Cantor's Son,* he is a "lucky orphan." Lacking kin, he is obligated to none.

Lady Rock

The superhuman strength of mythic warriors is evident from their infancy. Like the baby Heracles who strangles snakes in his cradle, the toddler Nezha vanquishes such awesome adversaries as the dragon kings. At the tender age of seven, the infant draws a mighty bow that generations of warriors have been unable to bend. Known as the cosmic bow (Qiankun Gong), the weapon has been left behind at the Chentang Mountain pass (of which Nezha's father is the commander) by the legendary Yellow Emperor. Even though no one but the mythic ruler has been able to lift it, the child effortlessly shoots one of its heaven-shaking arrows. Whizzing through space, the shaft flies miles away, penetrating the White-Bones Cavern atop the dreadful Skull Mountain, lair of the ogress Lady Rock (Shiji niangniang). Its force is such that it kills her acolyte the Azure-Clouds Lad, thereby embroiling the mischievous infant in one of his favorite exploits: the narrow escape from the harpy.[29]

Much like the dragon king (whose son Nezha has killed), Lady Rock vents her anger on the father of the astonishing infant. She orders Li Jing to summon the culprit for punishment or else he himself will be executed. Showing complete disregard for his son's fate, Li Jing slavishly obeys the ogress's command. Leading Nezha to her ghastly abode, he obsequiously announces, "My traitorous son has shot the arrow. Your disciple would not dare disobey you. I have brought him along, and he is awaiting your command."[30] Contrary to his and the harpy's expectations, though, Nezha has no inclination to submit. The fearless infant strikes the ogress's other acolyte, the Colorful-Clouds Lad, and as the latter wriggles in pain, Nezha attacks the demon herself. Having been trained in Daoist magic for hundreds of years, Lady Rock proves stronger than the child-warrior. When she captures his magic weapons, the cosmic ring and the celestial-confusion cloth, he has no choice but to seek his master's help on the Primordial Mountain (Qianyuan shan). Nezha's master, the Immortal Taiyi, captures the ogress inside his Nine Dragons Net of Spiritual Fire. As she burns to death, she reverts to her original form of a senseless stone (*wanshi*). Like other Chinese demons, Lady Rock's true form is revealed upon her demise.

Elaborated over an entire chapter of the seventeenth-century novel, the Lady Rock episode shares significant similarities with the dragon king story. As narrated in *The Canonization of the Gods,* the two share an identical structure, in which Nezha's confrontation with the awesome adversary is preceded by his killing of its underling (Lady Rock's acolyte in the former; the dragon king's son in the latter). The plots unfold according to the familiar pattern of parents fighting their children's cause, as the ogress and the ophidian monarch seek reparations from Nezha's father. In this respect, the two stories are an essential component of the divine child's myth. If it were not for Lady Rock and/or the dragon king, Nezha would not have fallen out with his father, and the legend would not have reached its oedipal climax. The Lady Rock and dragon king episodes are the necessary prelude to Nezha's defiance of paternal authority.

The Lady Rock and the dragon king episodes predate the seventeenth-century novel. A terse version of both is included in the above-mentioned Ming-period encyclopedia, *The Grand Compendium of the Three Religions' Deities.* The encyclopedia's brief summary of the two stories shares significant similarities (and differences) with the elaborate version narrated in *The Canonization of the Gods:*

> When he was five days old, Nezha went bathing in the Eastern Ocean. He trampled over the [dragon king's] Crystal Palace. He somersaulted straight to the top of the Precious Pagoda. Because he had trampled over his palace, the infuriated dragon king challenged him to a fight. By then, Nezha was already seven days old, and he

could overcome the nine dragons. The old dragon had no choice, except complaining to the [Jade] Emperor. The General [Nezha] knew of his intention. Intercepting him by Heaven's Gate, he killed the dragon.

Mounting the Jade Emperor's altar, Nezha took the Buddha's bow and arrows. He shot an arrow, unintentionally killing Lady Rock's (Shiji niangniang) son. Lady Rock raised an army to fight him. The General [Nezha] took the Demon-Felling Club from his father's altar and, fighting his way Westwards, slew her.

Considering that Lady Rock had been the demons' chief, Nezha's father was infuriated. He worried lest his son's killing her would provoke the demon hordes to war. Therefore, the General [Nezha] sliced off his flesh and bones, returning them to his father. Holding fast to his inner soul (*zhen ling*), he hastened to the Buddha's side, pleading that the World-Honored One make him complete once more. Considering that Nezha could subdue the demons, the Buddha snapped a lotus flower. He fashioned its stem into bones, its roots into flesh, its fiber into tendons, and its leaves into clothes, giving life to Nezha once more.[31]

The Grand Compendium's version of the legend differs from *The Canonization of the Gods*' in several respects. In the former, Nezha is seven *days* old when performing his astonishing feats, whereas in the latter he is seven *years* old. The encyclopedia describes the bow drawn by the infant as the Buddha's, whereas the novel attributes the mighty weapon to the Yellow Emperor. Most significantly, the earlier source has Nezha resurrected by the Buddha's grace, whereas the later one has him saved by the Immortal Taiyi. The transformation from Buddhist to Daoist soteriology will be explored in chapter 7. Here suffice it to note that it reflects the growing Daoist impact upon the originally Buddhist legend. Prior to the seventeenth century, the child's savior had been invariably identified as the World-Honored One. His appearance as a Daoist immortal in *The Canonization of the Gods* capped a long process by which the child-god and his teacher were gradually cloaked in Daoist garb.

Another discrepancy between *The Grand Compendium* and *The Canonization of the Gods* is the incident that prompts the child's suicide. The encyclopedia has his slaughter of Lady Rock lead to Nezha's conflict with his father, whereas the novel has his subjugation of the dragon king prompt the familial discord. The difference might serve to highlight the similarity, and interchangeability, of the two episodes. In the Lady Rock and the dragon king stories alike, the child's misdeed results in the injured party seeking reparations from the father. Whether it is the female demon's humiliation or the dragon king's disgrace, Nezha's father is incensed by his child's disregard for social hierarchy.

As mentioned earlier, Nezha's hagiography in the Ming-period *Grand Compendium of the Three Religions' Deities* might have derived from a Yuan-period antecedent. If so, the Lady Rock and dragon king stories might have been known as early as the thirteenth century. Support for this hypothesis might be provided by visual art. I will argue that the two stories have been pictorially rendered upon the famed Quanzhou pagodas, which were constructed between 1228 and 1250. Covered with a total of 160 Buddhist images, the two stone monuments are an important source for the Buddhist lore of the Southern Song period (1127–1279). They feature, for example, one of the earliest representations of Nezha's rival, the monkey king Sun Wukong.[32] If the child-god figures on the Quanzhou pagodas, it might furnish evidence for the popularity of his legend during the last decades of the Southern Song Dynasty.

Situated on the grounds of the renowned Kaiyuan Temple in the port city of Quanzhou (Fujian Province), the twin pagodas (*ta*) are covered each with eighty life-size images of buddhas and bodhisattvas, saints and guardian divinities. The ground floor of each pagoda features fierce martial gods, such as the vajra-wielder Vajrapāṇi. The warrior divinities protect the stupa's gates, and it is in this appropriately martial role that the Nezha images appear. On the southeastern corner of the Eastern Pagoda's ground level, flanking the two sides of an ornamental gate, are twin images of—I suggest—the benign and wrathful Nezha (see figures 7, 8). The benevolent aspect is represented by a childish figure, clad in armor and wearing a helmet. Nezha is shown riding the dragon he has subdued. In his left hand he holds the belt he has made from the creature's sinews, and in his right hand he wields the bow that no one but the Yellow Emperor (or the Buddha) has been able to draw. The god's malevolent aspect is rendered by the stern three-headed and six-armed figure opposite. Sporting flaming hair and bulging eyes, the wrathful Nezha is terrifying indeed. In a manner typical of many Tantric divinities, he wields not only a sword, but also the sun and the moon, each in one hand.[33]

It should be emphasized that the Quanzhou pagodas bear no cartouches. My identification of the Nezha image may be either accepted or rejected. If he *is* Nezha, the Quanzhou images evince the Southern Song popularity of the child-god. By the early thirteenth century, Nezha's battles with Lady Rock and the dragon king were celebrated in visual art. It is noteworthy that an echo of the former victory might be discernible in the above-mentioned play *The Fierce Nezha's Three Transformations.* The early Ming (ca. 1400) comedy has the child-god adversaries, Māra's daughters, conceal themselves as rocks. The four harpies appear as "senseless stones" (*wanshi*), the same form Lady Rock assumes upon her demise.[34] In the early Ming play, the Ming encyclopedia, and the seventeenth-century novel alike, Nezha's female foes are identified as stone spirits.

That the child-god was particularly effective against rocky adversaries is attested by anecdotal literature. In his *Record of Hearsay* (*Yijian zhi*), Hong Mai (1123–1202) tells of a Jiangxi ritual master (*fashi*) who had been attacked at midnight by a stone spirit (*shijing*). Trained in the Daoist exorcistic techniques, the master proceeded to recite the "Spell of Nezha's Fireball" to subdue the pernicious

Figure 7: (Benevolent) Nezha on the thirteenth-century Quanzhou pagoda. Note the vanquished dragon underfoot, the belt made from its sinews (in the child-god's left hand), and the divine bow (in the child-god's right hand). Photo by Meir Shahar.

Figure 8: (Wrathful) Three-headed and six-armed Nezha on the thirteenth-century Quanzhou pagoda. Photo by Meir Shahar.

monster.[35] Hong Mai's story reveals that as early as the twelfth century the child-god was summoned to battle "stone spirits." Providing the ritual context for the Lady Rock legend, the anecdote betrays an uncanny affinity between entertainment literature and rites of exorcism. Novelists, playwrights, and ritual masters alike conceived of Nezha as an expert in the subjugation of rocky creatures.

The Lady Rock episode has remained a popular subject of drama all through late imperial and modern times. *The Canonization of the Gods*' version of the adventure has served as a source for a significant number of Kunqu-style plays, which date from the Qing period (1644–1911). As in the seventeenth-century novel, the Immortal Taiyi subdues the demon, for which reason the plays are titled after his residence *Primordial Mountain* (*Qianyuan shan*).[36] The battle with Lady Rock has provided ample opportunities for the display of martial skills, and by the early twentieth century the Kunqu drama had been adapted into Peking Opera. Renowned "martial actors" (*wusheng*) such as Gai Jiaotian (1888–1970), Li Lanting (1888–1955), and Zhang Yunxi (b. 1919) vied with each other in creating elaborate juggling and acrobatics for it. In 1919, the daring Gai even experimented with roller skates for Nezha's "Wind and Fire Wheels," demonstrating the rapid pace with which Western inventions were put into unexpected use in Republican-period China.[37]

Traditional dramatic renditions of the Lady Rock adventure inspired modern cinematic adaptations. In 2004, the Chinese Central Television aired the fifty-two-sequels *Nezha Story* (*Nezha chuanqi*), which was simultaneously issued as a ten-volume comic strip. The serial pictured the entire Zhou rebellion against the Shang in terms of the child's struggle with the harpy. The ogress figures in the animation as the principal force behind the wicked Shang regime, whereas the fearless toddler leads the valiant Zhou forces. Following countless confrontations in which she fails to subdue the infant, the serial culminates with the harpy penetrating Nezha's body in order to accomplish her evil designs through him. Conscious that his tremendous strength will enable the harpy to perform great evil, the brave Nezha chooses to commit suicide under his father's magic stupa. He is then reborn by grace of the Goddess Nüwa (who had figured in *The Canonization of the Gods* as the object of the Shang king's lecherous designs). The serial culminates amid the cheers of the grateful Zhou people, whose adored hero has been restored to them.[38]

Magic Weaponry

Chinese martial gods are often associated with an emblematic weapon, symbol of their innate power.[39] The heroic Lord Guan (Guangong) is identified by his mighty halberd, whereas Sun Wukong's iconic tool is the magic ring-staff that changes its dimensions according to his will. Nezha's symbolic weaponry has accompanied him since the moment of his birth. Recall that he emerged from the ball of flesh that his father hacked, wrapped in the celestial-confusion cloth (Huntian ling) and armed with the cosmic ring (Qiankun quan). The former he uses to churn the ocean, tumbling down the dragon king's palace, whereas the latter he uses as a boomerang, smashing his enemies' brains. As the conflict with his father accelerates, the child warrior is equipped by his celestial master with additional magic arms. Fashioning for Nezha a new body made of a lotus flower, the Immortal Taiyi bestows upon him the fire-tipped spear (Huojian qiang), the magic gold brick (Jinzhuan), and the wind-and-fire wheels (Fenghuo lun), with which the infant-god roams the heavens.[40]

The martial emblems that are attributed to Nezha in the seventeenth-century *The Canonization of the Gods* have informed his iconography down to the present. Contemporary statues and paintings of the child-god match his depiction in late imperial fiction. Wrapped in the (usually red) celestial-confusion cloth, Nezha is shown riding his wind-and-fire wheels. The young warrior brandishes the fire-tipped spear in one hand and the cosmic ring in the other. When equipped with additional limbs—in the manner of the Tantric divinities—he wields his magic gold brick as well (compare figures 5 and 9).

Figure 9: Nezha brandishing the fire-tipped spear and cosmic ring. Wrapped in the celestial-confusion cloth, he is riding the wind-and-fire wheels. The Nezha Temple, Xixia County, Henan. Photo by Ye Derong (A'de).

The weapons that are attributed to Nezha in *The Canonization of the Gods* have accrued to him in a gradual process that lasted several centuries. Written sources and visual artworks that predate the seventeenth-century novel ascribe to him different emblems. A historical survey reveals an intimate connection between the evolution of the child's myth and the transformation of his iconic weaponry. It also attests to the varied religious influences on the imagination of the god's attributes. Whereas some of Nezha's weapons are of Buddhist origin, others derive from the arsenal of Daoist exorcism.

We begin our survey of the god's martial iconography with the Buddhist pagodas of Quanzhou. The thirteenth-century stone monuments depict a young warrior clad in armor and wearing an elegant crest-ornamented helmet (see figure 7). The floating sash behind him is likely none other than the celestial-confusion cloth, which is apparent in the contemporary iconography. Other than this magic attribute, however, Nezha bears none of the insignia familiar today. Instead of the cosmic ring, magic brick, fire-tipped spear, and wind-and-fire wheels, he wields the awesome bow that no one but the mythic Yellow Emperor has been able to wield, as well as the belt he has made of the dragon prince's sinews.

Beginning in the Song and all through the Ming period, diverse literary and religious texts have associated Nezha with a fire-emanating wheel and/or a fire-emanating ball. Possibly related to the wind-and-fire wheels that he rides in *The Canonization of the Gods*, they differed in function. Whereas in the seventeenth-century novel the wheels are means of transportation, in the earlier sources they are tossed by the invincible child against his hapless adversaries.

The earliest account of Nezha's fireball occurs in Hong Mai's *Record of Hearsay*. The twelfth-century record reveals the adoption of the unruly infant by Daoist exorcists. It tells of a Jiangxi ritual master (*fashi*) named Cheng who is attacked by a mighty stone spirit. Reciting the "Spell of Nezha's Fireball," Cheng summons the mighty infant, who employs the magic weapon to vanquish the demonic creature:

> Cheng reached the Sun-Family Hill. When the moon's color revealed a weak luminescence, a black, bell-shaped prodigy emerged directly out of the trees in front of him. It circled and turned, producing a noise as if it intended to attack him. Cheng anxiously recited a spell and walked the Big Dipper Outline (*bugang*). The prodigy showed not the slightest fear and gradually pressed in upon his body. Cheng realized that this was a "stone spirit" (*shi jing*). Consequently he recited the "Spell of Nezha's Fireball" (Nezha huoqiu zhou) and, forming a *mudrā*, recited: "Divine General! Can you tolerate a *wangliang* demon obstructing my way? Expel him forthwith!"
>
> Suddenly a fireball emerged from behind Cheng's body and struggled with the black lump. After a while a noise burst out, like clashing metal, and the black lump disappeared. The fireball made several revolutions around Cheng's body and also vanished.[41]

Figure 10:
The Buddhist Dharma wheel as a fire-emitting weapon (top right). Detail of a fifteenth-century mural from the Fahai Temple, Beijing. From Wang Shufang, *Fahai si bihua* (Shijiazhuang: Hebei meishu, 2007).

Ming-period fiction, drama, and hagiographic literature variously identified Nezha's fiery weapon as a Dharma wheel (*falun*), a fire wheel (*huolun*), or a golden wheel (*jinlun*). In *The Grand Compendium of the Three Religions' Deities,* the child vanquishes the demonic hordes by means of a Dharma wheel; in Zhu Youdun's (1379–1439) play he battles the lion with a golden wheel; and the 1592 edition of *The Journey to the West* describes his "lightning-propelled fire wheel."[42] The term Dharma wheel indicates a connection between the fire-emitting weapon and the Buddhist symbol. That the ancient emblem of the Buddhist law has been imagined as a fiery armament is attested by Ming-period visual art. Established in 1439, the Beijing Fahai Temple features a beautiful mural of a (likely female) Tantric divinity. The goddess wields an assortment of weapons in each of her multiple arms: a saber, a hatchet, a bow, an arrow, and a flaming Dharma wheel. The image suggests that

Figure 11:
Nezha wielding (in his left hand) the mysterious embroidered ball. The deity's tender age is attested by his childish hairdo. Ming-period woodblock illustration from *The Grand Compendium of the Three Religions' Deities* (*Sanjiao yuanliu shengdi fozu sou shen Daquan*).

the symbol of the Buddhist teachings has been conceived of as a weapon, the one Nezha employs in contemporaneous written sources (figure 10).

As intriguing as his flaming Dharma wheel, Nezha is equipped with an embroidered ball (*xiuqiu*), which he tosses at his helpless enemies. The magic implement is attributed to the child-god in all the above-mentioned Ming sources: *The Grand Compendium*, Zhu Youdun's play, and *The Journey to the West*, the latter describing its operation together with the Dharma wheel: "The lightning-propelled fire-wheel was like darting flame; Hither and thither the embroidered ball rotated."[43] *The Grand Compendium*'s hagiography of Nezha is accompanied by a woodblock print in which the mysterious weapon might be discernible (see figure 11). The warrior's youthful age is rendered by his childish hairdo, which is dressed in tufts. In his right hand Nezha embraces a spear, and in his left hand he wields what appears to be a ball tied by a rope. This might be the embroidered ball that is mentioned in the accompanying text as well as in other Ming-period sources.

If Nezha's weaponry is related to Buddhist symbolism, it is equally indebted to

Daoist liturgy. Whereas his flaming Dharma wheel drew upon the Buddhist emblem, the young warrior's magic brick derived from Daoist ritual. Mark Meulenbeld has convincingly argued that the gold brick employed by Nezha in *The Canonization of the Gods* evolved from the gold bricks that are described in early Ming Daoist scriptures. The ritual compendium *Daoist Methods United in Principle,* for example, prescribes gold bricks for locking demons in bottles.[44] Dating from the early fifteenth century (and drawing upon earlier sources), the manual predates *The Canonization of the Gods* by at least two centuries. There can be no doubt that the ritual treatise served as the novel's source (rather than vice versa). Nezha's iconic gold brick derived from the magic armories of Daoist priests.

Nezha's wind-and-fire wheels and his fire-tipped spear might have similarly drawn upon the arsenal of Daoist exorcism. The Thunderbolt Angel (Pili shizhe) is summoned by Daoist priests to battle the demons of disease. In the fifteenth century *Daoist Methods United in Principle,* he wields a gold brick and a golden spear, even as he rides fire wheels.[45] It is likely, therefore, that Nezha's gold brick, fire-tipped spear, and wind-and-fire wheels have been borrowed from the armories of the Daoist gods. The child-god's iconic weapons have accrued to him in part from Daoist ritual. We will see in the next chapter that the native faith has played a significant role in shaping the cult of the originally Buddhist god. Daoism has contributed to the late imperial proliferation of the Nezha cult.

6

The Child-God

The contours of the Nezha faith have been shaped by the god's extraordinary myth of familial strife. Nezha's unique attributes have determined his religious clientele no less than the stubborn detractors that struggled to uproot his cult. As an invincible warrior, Nezha became the tutelary divinity of armed militias and street gangs as well as a favorite of Daoist priests and ritual masters, who harnessed his extraordinary powers to fight the demonic hordes. As the prime violator of the Confucian ethics, he was despised by the literati elite, which pushed his believers away from the empire's hubs of administration. At once attractive to teenagers and repellent to their teachers, the Nezha cult has assumed forms whose popularity is hard to gauge.

The Nezha myth negotiated oedipal tensions inherent in the patriarchal Chinese family. By definition such tensions have had to remain unconscious and could not be officially condoned. Hence the Nezha cult could never aspire to imperial patronage. Unlike such respectable deities as Guangong or Mazu, whose temples were adorned by government certificates in the emperor's own hand, the child-warrior was never listed in the state's rosters of the gods. Confucian educators could not possibly endorse the worship of a patricidal infant whose myth threatened the empire's ideological foundations. As much as it could, the bureaucracy actively marginalized the veneration of the child who sought to wreak vengeance on his father.

At once enticing and subversive, the Nezha cult has mushroomed under the radar of government officials. Even as the number of shrines dedicated to him has been limited, the enfant terrible has made his presence felt in other gods' temples. Nezha has figured as an ancillary divinity on other gods' altars and, as the General of the Middle Altar (Zhongtan Yuanshuai), has served as the protector of temples (regardless of the principal divinity worshiped therein). The military exploits of the child warrior have graced temple murals, and his visceral plays have been performed in their courtyards. Furthermore, the child whose cult has been marginalized by the elite has become a spirit mediums' favorite. Nezha has been among the most frequently called upon divinities in rituals of possession.

The cult of the defiant infant has shared significant similarities with that of the rebellious simian who declared himself "Great Sage Equal to Heaven." Temples for Nezha and the monkey king (Sun Wukong) have been similarly situated in outlying areas, removed from the empire's educational and administrative hubs. Even when they do figure in cities, shrines for the subversive and mischievous divinities have been erased from the official records. Equally ignored by the literati elite, Sun Wukong and Nezha have flourished in rituals of possession. Across China, and throughout Southeast Asia, the monkey and the enfant terrible have been among the most popular divinities in spirit-mediums' séances.

Nezha differed from Sun Wukong in his Daoist role. As early as the Song period (960–1279), the child-warrior had been summoned by Daoist ritual masters to battle evil spirits. In the ensuing Yuan (1279–1368) and Ming (1368–1644) periods, Nezha figured in the Thunder Rituals performed for the subjugation of demons. His significance in the Daoist rites of exorcism has had a decisive impact upon the child-god's presence in the temples of the popular religion. Under the influence of the Lüshan ritual tradition, Nezha has been appointed General of the Middle Altar. In parts of Fujian, and throughout much of Taiwan, he has been worshiped as the commander of the Five Armies of spirit soldiers. As such, his image is placed in temples, regardless of the principal deity venerated therein. From his elevated position on the shrine's offering table, the General of the Middle Altar leads his divine troops in defense of the local community.

Nezha's flourishing Taiwanese cult has attracted growing attention in recent years. Historians and anthropologists have studied several of his temples on the island. Zeng Guodong has explored the largest one (Taizi Gong in Xinying), and Xu Bingkun has written on the Dongyao Temple in Xinzhu. In Tainan County, Xu Xianping has surveyed 320 temples that feature Nezha either as a principal or as an ancillary divinity, and Yang Tianhou and Lin Likuan have examined the rebellious god's cult on Jinmen Island (off the Fujian coast).[1] Across the Taiwan Straits, Christina Cheng and Chen Xuelin (Hok-Lam Chan), independently of each other, have studied the Nezha temples in the former Portuguese colony of Macau.[2]

Studies of the child-god's temples have been supplemented by surveys of his role in spirit-medium cults. As early as 1955, Allan Elliott noted that in Singapore, Nezha's popularity among spirit mediums was rivaled only by Sun Wukong's. Three decades later, Hock Tong Cheu examined the child-god's centrality in rituals of possession across peninsular Southeast Asia: Thailand, Singapore, and Malaysia.[3] Several studies have demonstrated Nezha's significance in Taiwanese spirit possession: David Jordan has described the religious functions of the child-god's spokespersons in the 1960s, and Charles Stafford has examined their social roles in the late 1980s. Hong Shuling has written on Nezha and female possession, Hu Taili has noted the assistance rendered by the naughty child's mediums to illegal gamblers, and Avron Boretz has associated possession by the defiant god with the construction of masculinity among the Taiwanese underclass.[4]

This chapter draws upon recent scholarship as well as upon my own fieldwork. It integrates the findings of anthropologists and historians with the information I have gathered during visits to Nezha temples and interviews with his mediums. In October 2008, I participated in the child-god's birthday festivities at the Xinying Taizi Gong (Taiwan), and on the following day I visited another of his temples in Xinzhu; in July 2010, I traveled to a remote Nezha temple in southwestern Henan, as well as to two shrines of his in Fujian Province; in October 2011 I conducted fieldwork and interviewed Nezha spirit mediums on Jinmen Island; and in June 2012 I visited several of the child-god's temples in Northern Taiwan, participating in a ritual of possession at the Taibei suburb of Beitou.

The chapter is divided into three sections: The first surveys selected Nezha temples, in Henan, in Macau, on Jinmen Island, and in Taiwan (where they are most numerous); the second is dedicated to Nezha's martial functions as the General of the Middle Altar, exploring in this context the impact of Daoist ritual traditions on his thriving contemporary cult; the third section examines spirit possession, which is the most widespread form of the Nezha cult. The contradictory social functions of Nezha mediums and the role of spirit possession in the negotiation of familial tensions are explored.

Temples

The location of several Nezha temples is shown on map number 1. Far from exhaustive, it displays only shrines that have either been visited by the author, have been described in the scholarly literature, or have been mentioned on the Internet. No more than a tentative effort to delineate the geographical scope of the Nezha cult, the map will doubtless be altered by future research that will bring to light numerous other centers of worship.

As tentative as the map might be, the absence of Nezha shrines in North China is striking. With the exception of the now defunct Nezha temple in Beijing, the map features no shrines for the child-god north of southern Henan. Phrased differently, it shows no Nezha temples throughout the North China plains. It might be argued that the absence is due to a scholarly bias: Because the fieldwork of recent decades has been conducted primarily in Taiwan, Hong Kong, and Macau, it has yielded Nezha shrines in South China. Had the surveys been carried out in the north the picture would have been different. Fieldwork conducted in the 1940s, however, as well as recent explorations of specific localities, strengthens the case for the (at least relative) lack of Nezha temples in the north. It is instructive, for example, that Nezha does not figure in Willem Grootaers's extensive records of popular religion in Republican-period Chahar Province (present-day

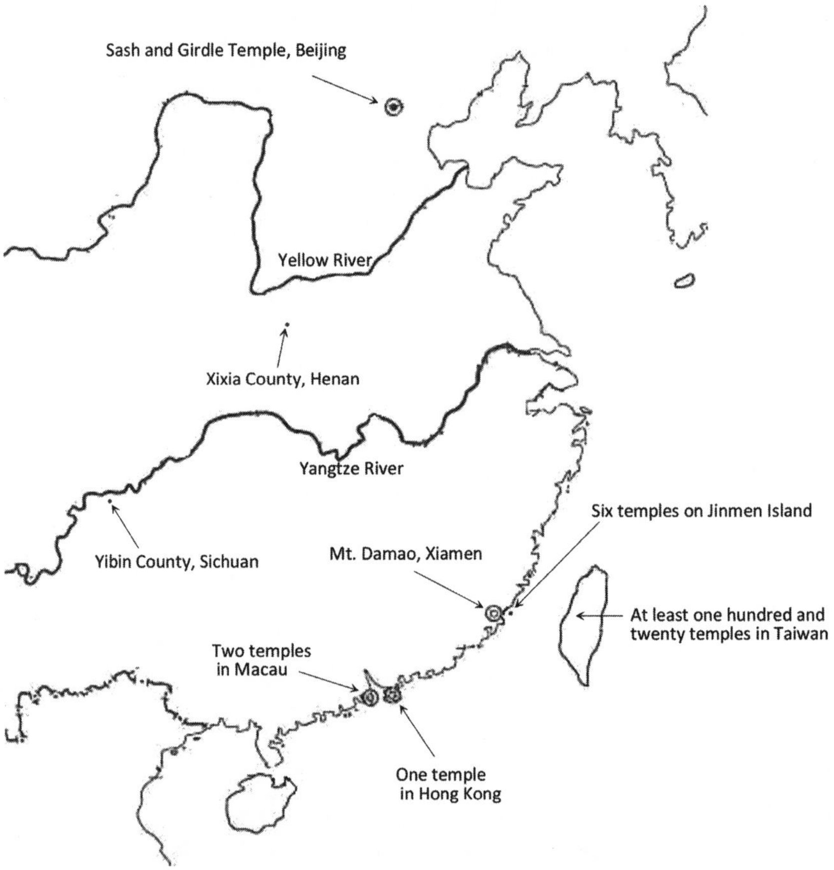

Map 1: Location of some temples dedicated to Nezha as the principal deity.

northern Hebei and northern Shaanxi). On the eve of the communist takeover, the Belgian scholar and his Chinese associates surveyed hundreds of village temples, not one of which had been dedicated to Nezha.[5] Even though they likely existed, Nezha shrines in North China were evidently few and far between.

The prevalence of the Nezha cult in South China (and its relative absence from the north) was pointed out to me in July 2010 during a visit to the child-god's temple in the remote Xixia County, southern Henan. The temple's manager volunteered to comment on the lack of his divine patron's temples in North China. "Nezha is a sea-god," he told me. "He battles aquatic creatures such as the dragon kings. Therefore the people of South China's coastal regions venerate him. The people of the North are not familiar with him." The explanation is not necessarily convincing, if for no other reason than because the cult of the dragon kings themselves has been widespread throughout the North China plains. It is nonetheless revealing as an indication of the Nezha devotees' awareness that their tutelary divinity is not widely venerated in North China.

The modest Nezha shrine in old Beijing was an exception to the absence of his northern temples. A small shrine of one hall only, it had been situated next to the Black Dragon Pool (Heilong tan) not far from the Yongding Gate, in the city's south. Established during the Qianlong reign (1736–1795), it survived through 1952, when the site was transformed into a public garden. The temple revealed the surprising economic associations of the rebellious child's myth. Because he had made a magically potent belt from an awesome dragon's sinews, Nezha became the tutelary divinity of the Sash and Girdle Guild (Taodai hang). His temple had been dedicated by belt makers, who conducted their commercial and social activities within it. Even as the temple was situated in the capital city, it illustrated the elite's contempt of the unfilial infant. The Beijing Nezha shrine was not mentioned in Qing-period gazetteers. No earlier than the Republican period was it first mentioned in folkloric accounts of the capital as well as in Japanese studies of its guilds.[6]

Henan

The relative absence of Nezha temples in North China might be subsumed under a more refined delineation of his cult's geographical spread. The child-god's temples have been situated for the most part on the empire's margins. They were located either in border regions (such as Taiwan), or in outlying areas within central provinces. Shrines for the unfilial child would usually be found in a province's remote and poor hinterland, far from the seats of government and the centers of Confucian education. Like other eccentric gods such as Jigong and Sun Wukong, Nezha's cult flourished on the fringes of the Chinese state.[7]

The Nezha temple in Xixia County, Henan, illustrates the geographic marginality of the unfilial child's cult. Likely dating from the Qing period (1644–1911), it is situated in the province's remote southwest. Bordering the adjacent Shaanxi and Hubei Provinces, the poor and mountainous region is far removed from Henan's administrative hubs. Some 250 miles of tortuous mountain roads separate Xixia County from the current and former provincial capitals of Zhengzhou and Kaifeng respectively. The local town Dinghe and its surrounding villages rarely made it into the prefectural-level, not to mention the provincial-level, gazetteers. The Nezha hamlet shrine was never mentioned in Qing-period publications. The earliest written reference to it dates from 1990, when the *Xixia County Gazetteer* made the unlikely claim for its late Yuan or early Ming founding.[8]

As humble as its origins might be, the Xixia Nezha shrine stakes claims of considerable economic ramifications for the entire county. Beginning in the 1990s, it has been competing (primarily with the Nezha temple in Yibin, Sichuan) for the position of the god's ancestral temple, which would bring in flocks of pilgrims from across Southeast Asia. Realizing the potential windfall of a thriving

Nezha temple, county officials have joined its publicity campaign. Government-sponsored publications assert that the child-god was born in Xixia County, where his first temple had been situated. The fantastic geography outlined in the *The Canonization of the Gods* is identified with the local topography, the sites of the child-god's feats becoming tourist sites: Nezha's birthplace (Chentang Guan) is spotted in the local village Kuiwen (where his current temple is located); the nearby Dinghe Stream is said to be the fabulous Nine-Bends River, in which the infant-god washed his girdle (causing the dragon king's palace to tumble down); and the peaks towering above it are recognized as the Cuiping Mountain, where Nezha's mother dedicated his first shrine to him.

The child-god's battle with Lady Rock has been tied to local geography as well. According to the Xixia version of her myth, the harpy had been equipped with wings (interpreting her name *shiji* (stone cliff) as the identically pronounced *shiji* (stone chicken)). After trying unsuccessfully to seduce Nezha's father (a novel addition to the legend), and after being defeated by the infant-god, the chicken-demon hid in a mountain ravine some six miles off Kuiwen village. The local villagers beseeched the Jade Emperor to expel the ogress, which preyed upon their children. Following the divine sovereign's command, the City God rounded up a posse including an assortment of native divinities who, together with the local hunters, exorcised the chicken-shaped harpy. The local ravine has henceforth been known as the "Expelling Chicken Canal" (Gan ji gou).[9]

The Xixia lore of the child-god, as well as the story of his temple's resurrection, is recorded in a government-sponsored publication. Dating from 2004, *Nezha's Native Place* has been issued by the Xixia County historical committee. Trumpeting the case for Kuiwen village being Nezha's birthplace, it elaborates the proofs of the temple's ancestral position. The pamphlet documents the significant role played by overseas pilgrims in the restoration of Nezha's shrine. During the 1980s, Taiwanese devotees began trickling to Xixia in search of the god's native shrine, to which they would henceforth conduct yearly pilgrimages. The decisive moment came in 1996, when a delegation from the island's Zhanghua County chose the exact spot in which to situate the newly restored temple. *Nezha's Native Place* records the dramatic role played by a possessed ritual master in determining the divinely ordained site. (Even though the pamphlet identifies him as a *fashi* (ritual master), his possession indicates that he might have been a spirit medium.)

> In 1996, Mr. Ke Ciqing, head of the Shunxing'gong temple [Zhanghua County, Taiwan], led a delegation of several dozen people to offer incense and worship at the Xixia Nezha ancestral temple. In order to verify the exact location of Nezha's birthplace, the delegation brought along a ritual master (*fashi*). His task was to conduct a ritual at the temple's courtyard, ascertaining the god's birthplace. Barefoot, his pants rolled up and his chest exposed, the ritual master wielded an incense burner. Drawing charms and

> reciting spells, he declaimed with authority. The incense burner's flames scorched his skin, so much so that his entire body was covered by blazing scars. The entire audience was dumbfounded. They all said: "He must be possessed by the god Nezha, who is displaying his divinity" (*fushen xianling*). Approaching the ritual master, they asked: "Would it be appropriate to build here the great hall of Nezha's ancestral temple?" "Sure," he answered, "no problem."[10]

The 1990s restoration of the Nezha Temple is related to world-shaking events that took place five decades earlier. In the spring of 1945, the Japanese launched one of their last war efforts in what came to be known as the Battle of Western Henan and Northern Hubei. The campaign raged in part through Xixia County, with the invading army trying to push its way to neighboring Shaanxi. The defending Forty-Second Division included a young platoon commander named Fan Mingpan, who had been a firm Nezha devotee. Supplicating the divine warrior's help, he scored a local victory by repelling the enemy troops. In 1949, Mr. Fan relocated with the remnants of Chiang Kaishek's army to Taiwan. Suffering in his old age from illness, he was cured by his divine patron, whereupon he vowed to restore his temple. Leading a delegation to Xixia County, Mr. Fan initiated the contemporary flood of Taiwanese pilgrims to the Nezha Temple.[11]

In July 2010, I visited Xixia County with my friend Ye Derong (A'de), discovering that it currently houses two Nezha temples. The first is the plush marble structure that was constructed in 2001–2002.[12] Donated by Taiwanese pilgrims, it is situated in the Dinghe riverbed, inside Kuiwen village. Easily accessible by the newly constructed Nanyang-Xi'an highway, it attracts worshipers from hundreds of miles away. The second (and older) shrine is a modest red brick building situated atop the Cuiping Mountain peak, at the very place where Nezha's mother was said to have dedicated a sanctuary to him. A narrow mountain trail leads to a one-room red brick structure that, albeit reconstructed in 1995, has clearly maintained the original shape of a hamlet shrine. It features a homely papier-mâché icon of Nezha that has been fashioned by the local villagers. The touching image is noteworthy for the child-god's bright red underpants.

On New Year's Eve, and during the ensuing Lantern Festival, the local people climb the winding path to the upper Nezha shrine atop Cuiping Mountain. Offering oblations for a year of health and plenty, they begin their steep ascent at midnight, returning near dawn. During the night, the narrow trail, which is overgrown with vegetation, is full of worshipers carrying lights, lanterns, and fireworks. The commotion, we have been told, lasts all through the following morning.

Macau

At least in one instance, Nezha has been worshiped in a Christian environment. The former Portuguese colony of Macau features two shrines dedicated to the child-god: the Old Nezha Temple (Nezha Gu Miao), halfway up Persimmon Hill on Traversa de Sancho Pança, which likely dates from the eighteenth century; and the New Nezha Temple, which is known as the Big Saint Paul Nezha Temple (Da Sanba Nezha Miao), after the adjacent ruins of the imposing Saint Paul Cathedral. Dating from 1898, it has been the latter's fortune to be included (in 2005) in the World Heritage Site of Macau's Historic Center. The minuscule shrine for the Chinese child-god figures in the UNESCO-recognized site alongside such formidable Catholic monuments as the eighteenth-century Saint Joseph's Seminary Church, which has coordinated the Jesuit missionary activities in China, Japan, and Southeast Asia.[13]

The two Macanese temples for the child-god reveal his prophylactic role as the queller of the demonic hordes. In their independently conducted studies, Christina Cheng and Chen Xuelin have shown that the old temple's renovation in 1897—like the new one's establishment the following year—coincided with the outbreak of an epidemic along China's southern coast. The plague that threatened the Portuguese colony ravaged as well the neighboring British one, the residents of which called upon the same god for rescue. The Hong Kong Nezha temple in Sham Shui Po, Kowloon, was established in the 1890s, when a statue of the divine warrior was invited to the colony from Huizhou, Guangdong. Like its Macau counterparts, it evinced Nezha's efficacy in battling the demons of disease. The child-warrior has been called upon to ward off invading pestilence as much as marauding enemy troops.[14]

The toddler-divinity is particularly effective in protecting infants. Christina Cheng's fieldwork suggests that at least some Macanese consider him the patron deity of children. The Old Nezha Temple features a ritual (unattested elsewhere) for safeguarding infants' health. On the occasion of the god's birthday (which is celebrated in Macau on the eighteenth day of the fifth lunar month), children are brought to his temple to be stamped by his protective seal. The Precious Seal of Prince Nezha of the Thirty-Third Heaven is dipped in red ink and is impressed upon the toddler's navel, protecting the toddler against all manner of harm and disease. The divine inoculation is effective for a year, until Nezha's birthday is celebrated anew, and his young clientele is once again stamped by his mighty charm.[15]

Nezha's predisposition toward children is not universally acknowledged. In the Taiwanese and mainland temples I visited, informants insisted that the child-god is equally effective in handling adults' problems as he is in protecting their offspring. Downplaying the centrality of infants in the Nezha cult, temple administrators and spirit mediums stressed its appeal across age differences. Be that as it may, child-related issues do figure prominently at the Old Nezha Temple. Fretful Macanese mothers arrive there not only to heal their young, but also to educate them. Christina Cheng notes the irony that the mischievous god is called upon to discipline naughty infants. "If their children are unruly, [mothers] would tie a divine bonding with Nezha, so that he becomes [the child's] god-father."[16] The disobedient god expounds filial piety to misbehaving infants.

Nezha's special connection with children and mothers might be interpreted as subversive of patriarchal authority. Charles Stafford has made the suggestion apropos the god's naughty spirit mediums in Taiwan. We will return to his intriguing hypothesis below. Here suffice it to note his observation that all mediums—not only Nezha's—are by definition unfilial, for they mortify the flesh endowed by their parents. Conceived of as infants, the Chinese spokespersons of the gods are known as "divining children" (*jitong*). Their efficacy depends upon violation of the Confucian dictum: "Our bodies—to every hair and bit of skin—are received by us from our parents, and we must not presume to injure or wound them: This is the beginning of filial piety."[17] Even though they mutilate their parents' sacred gift, spirit mediums are sought after by mothers to protect their offspring. Stafford concludes that the possessed spokespersons for the gods provide an alternative to the male-dominated patrilineal family. The spirit mediums "are patronized mostly by women, and are part of a private religious sphere which might teach children loyalty to their mothers, possibly to a matrifocal ideal."[18]

Confucian ethics considers filial piety the foundation of virtue and its lack the source of wrongdoings. A god who rebels against paternal authority is likely to engage in a variety of misdemeanors. Nezha has been called upon to assist in diverse misdeeds in which dignified divinities would not deign take part. In the Las Vegas of the East, his dubious engagements have been related to gambling. In the early twenty-first century, Macau has emerged as one of the world's biggest gaming territories, its glittering casinos bringing in revenues of more than ten billion U.S. dollars annually.[19] Whereas august gods such as Guangong and Mazu would not get involved in the lucrative action, the naughty Nezha has been sympathetic to his clientele's greediness. Gamblers flock to the child-god's shrines, supplicating his divine assistance in hitting the jackpot. The Old Nezha Temple on Traversa de Sancho Pança features two honorary plaques that have been donated by grateful players: "Just ask and win" reads one; "He made me rich," concurs the other.[20]

Nezha's assistance to gamblers has not been limited to Macau. The unruly god has been helping Taiwanese bettors as well. During the mid-1980s, the island was swept by a wave of illegal gambling known by the wishful euphemism Everybody's Happy (Dajiale). A system of shadow gambling, Everybody's Happy depended upon the national lottery, except that bettors were required to guess only two of the six winning numbers, thereby increasing their chances. At the height of the gambling craze, players turned to the gods for help, choosing to supplicate those—like Nezha—who have been known for their criminal (or at least mischievous) streak. Spirit mediums for the unfilial child were beseeched to provide hints of the winning numbers, and their shrines were crowded by bettors. The gambling wave sparked an increase in the number of Nezha temples and the popularity of his possessed spokespersons. Other audacious divinities similarly benefited from the Everybody's Happy fad. Bettors venerated Nezha side by side with the impish Sun Wukong and the clownish Jigong. Much as the Macanese New Nezha Temple features a statue of a somersaulting Sun Wukong, icons of the fearless monkey were placed in the Taiwanese gambling dens side by side with the unruly infant's (figure 12).[21]

Nezha and the monkey king (Sun Wukong) have engaged in a variety of misdeeds besides gambling. Gangsters have long noticed the illicit proclivities of the patricidal infant and the audacious simian. Avron Boretz's extensive study of the Chinese criminal underclass has revealed its symbolic manipulation of the two defiant deities. Nezha and Sun Wukong, he writes, "have particular meaning for (and enormous popularity among) the 'brothers of the dark path,'" a term designating a "hard-core underworld of professional criminals, organized rackets, shady businesses, and crooked politicians."[22] A god who rebelled against his father might be harnessed for each and every illegal enterprise.

Nezha's potential for resistance might be exploited for social, cultural, and political causes no less than for organized crime. In the case of a colonial settlement, his figure might be rallied against the hegemonic power of foreign rulers. Nezha's popularity in Macau might have been partially due to his subversion

Figure 12: Nezha (front row center) and the monkey king Sun Wukong (front row left) in a Taiwanese gambling shrine (spring 1987). Photo by Meir Shahar.

of Portuguese authority. Christina Cheng suggests that the New Nezha Temple at the heart of the Macau historic center challenged the cultural hegemony of the surrounding colonial monuments. The rebellious god's tiny shrine defied the dominance of the adjacent Catholic churches: "The Nezha Temple of the Ruins of St. Paul's symbolizes an 'architectural subversion.' The humble structure is an architectural metaphor ridiculing the looming, magnificent façade of the Ruins of St. Paul's [Cathedral]."[23]

Even as Nezha has served as the tutelary divinity of gamblers, the custodians of his cult struggle to clear it of moral suspicions. The figure of the child-god is simultaneously drawn in opposite directions. Whereas gamblers and gangsters have perceived the unfilial divinity's potential to subvert law and order, his temple administrators present an immaculate image of a self-sacrificing hero. Members of temple committees, as well as at least some spirit mediums, deny their god's involvement in illegal or semilegal activities. Nezha's connection to gambling is rejected at the very Macanese temple that boasts the bettors' grateful plaques. Informants at the Old Nezha Temple condemn the association of the child-god with the sinful practice.[24]

Nezha apologetics are as evident in Taiwan as they are in Macau. Whereas dignified deities such as Guanyin or the Jade Emperor enjoy untarnished reputations, the mischievous child's needs pleading for. The director of his Danshui shrine at the northern tip of the island told me that Nezha would never acquiesce in immoral propositions. Chinese gods, he explained, are either "proper" (*zheng*) or "dark" (*yin*). Belonging in the former category, the brave child would never assist gamblers.[25] Steven Sangren reports similar claims by other informants in Taiwanese Nezha temples. Rejecting the allegations of his improper behavior, the devotees of the playful god aim to place him on an equal moral footing with the august members of the Chinese pantheon.[26]

Nezha figures prominently on the Macanese holiday calendar. His birthday is the occasion of boisterous festivities that attract large crowds. Unlike Hong Kong and Taiwan that mark the child's birthday on the ninth day of the ninth lunar month, in Macau it is celebrated on the eighteenth day of the fifth lunar month. The old and the new Nezha temples vie with each other staging elaborate parades. Macanese dignitaries mix with members of overseas delegations from Nezha temples in Hong Kong, Taiwan, and Malaysia. Processions of lion dancing and fairy spirits march down the streets of the modern city and through the cobbled alleys of its historic center. Toddlers impersonate the infant-god, brandishing his iconic weapons, the cosmic ring and the fire-tipped spear.[27]

Jinmen Island

The little island of Jinmen illustrates the dramatic transformation of a landscape from the ravages of war to the ensuing peace. Known in European languages as

Quemoy (from the Portuguese transcription of the Hokkien pronunciation), it is situated within swimming distance (three miles) from Xiamen City in mainland China, even though it belongs to the Republic of China (Taiwan), a hundred miles eastward. During the late 1950s, Jinmen was devastated by constant shelling and repeated incursions by PRC guerrilla troops. The fifty-square-mile bone-shaped isle—narrow in the middle and bulging at both ends—was crisscrossed by trenches, underground tunnels, and bunkers. As a symbol of Cold War resistance to communism, the island's beautiful beaches were strewn with mines and fenced by barbed wire.

Fifty years later, Jinmen demonstrates the thaw in hostilities across the Taiwan Straits. The locals head to Xiamen for shopping and the movies, even as their island has become a tourist attraction for mainlanders and Taiwanese alike. Jinmen is a bird-watching haven, home to a wide variety of sea fowls, and a station on the migration routes of many others. It is also a perfect laboratory for the student of Chinese religion; the tiny territory boasts more than two hundred temples and shrines.[28] When I visited him on the island in October 2011, the ethnographer Wang Ch'iu-Kuei noted that with so many temples dedicated to such a rich assortment of divinities, one is likely to witness the celebration of a god's birthday or a Daoist *jiao* ceremony practically every day.

Nezha's presence in Jinmen is multifaceted: The Lüshan tradition that considers him as the General of the Middle Altar (Zhongtan Yuanshuai) has a strong hold on the island, for which reason the child warrior serves as the protector of its temples, regardless of the principal deity worshiped therein. As such, the statue of Nezha is placed on the shrine's offering table, from where he leads his divine troops in defense of the local community. In addition, Nezha figures as an ancillary divinity in forty-three temples, in which his statue graces the main altar side by side with the main deity.[29] Finally, at least six of the island's temples are dedicated to the child-warrior as the principal object of worship.[30] I will only comment on one of these: the so-called Five-Villages Prince (Wuxiang Taizi), which unique traits suggest a lengthy period of independent growth. Located on the island's eastern shore, this Nezha cult displays idiosyncrasies that reflect an indigenous tradition, possibly dating as far back as the seventeenth or eighteenth century.

If Jinmen has been situated on the margins of the Chinese empire, its eastern coast has been its own backwater. The isle's population is mostly concentrated in the relatively sheltered western waterfront, facing Xiamen City across the bay. The eastern seaboard, subject to the mighty winds from the Pacific Ocean, is only thinly settled. The subcounty of the Golden Sands (Jinsha zhen) is exposed to regular sandstorms, bearing in addition the brunt of the seasonal typhoons. Along its windswept shores seven tiny villages have joined together in the cult of the tutelary god Nezha. Sharing between them no more than five humble shrines, the seven hamlets have created the network of the Five-Villages Prince. It is a

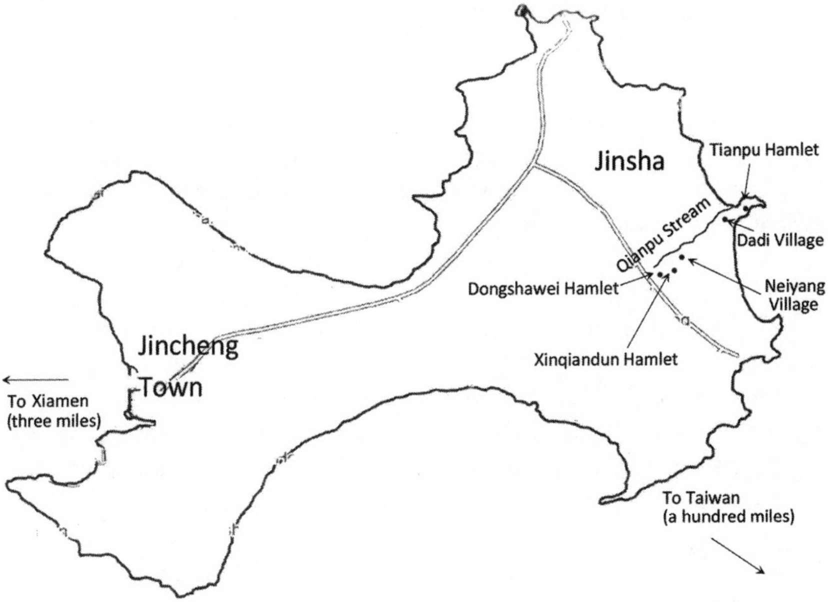

Map 2: The rotating Nezha cult on the eastern shores of Jinmen Island. The child-god sojourns two years at a time at Neiyang Village; two years at Dadi Village; and one year each at Dongshawei, Xinqiandun, and Tianpu hamlets.

rotating cult, by which the protecting god moves according to a regular scheme between the five temples that serve the seven villages. Nezha sojourns two years at a time at the Neiyang Village temple (which cares as well for the neighboring hamlets of Dongshan and Dongxi); two years at a time at the relatively large Dadi Village shrine; and one year each in the humble shrines of Dongshawei, Xinqiandun, and Tianpu hamlets (map 2). The complete cycle lasts seven years.[31]

Its myth of origins traces the rotating cult to the appearance of the god himself on Jinmen's windblown shores. The community elders repeat a story their grandparents told them in the early Republican period. Once upon a time a white-clad knight was seen riding a white steed along the Qianpu Stream, which connects the seven hamlets. He was spotted day after day making the exact same route. When the villagers consulted their temple oracles, they were informed that he was none other than the god Nezha, wishing to take up residence among them. As his route covered all seven hamlets, it was decided that a rotating cult would be most fitting, the newcomer being hosted in turn by the local divinities in their own temples. Ever since then, Nezha has been a guest in the five temples, entertained in each by a different deity.[32]

The idiosyncrasies of the Five-Villages Prince betray an indigenous tradition that likely evolved over a long time. The cult's iconography differs from that of other Nezha temples. The five shrines share a statue of the child-god mounted on horseback. Elsewhere, Nezha is usually shown atop the wind-and-fire wheels, which originated in the seventeenth-century *The Canonization of the Gods*. In contrast to this common perception of him, the rotating cult's myth of origins has him riding a white steed. The Nezha of eastern Jinmen Island has dispensed with the magic means of transportation. His distinctive myth and singular iconography portray a mounted knight.

Nezha's birthday is another unique feature of his Five Villages' cult. Whereas throughout Taiwan (as well as in other Jinmen temples) it is held on the ninth day of the ninth lunar month, the rotating cult marks it on the twenty-first day of the tenth lunar month. The birthday festivities are intimately related to the god's passage from one shrine to another. On the second day of the eleventh lunar month—ten days after his birthday—the god is carried in a colorful procession to the new temple that will host him for another year (or two). The parade heads on its way not before a formal invitation is extended to Nezha, requesting his consent to take up residence at his new quarters. A delegation of village elders addresses the petition to the god's icon, as well as to his incense burner, both of which are displayed in the festive procession.[33]

The rotating Nezha cult has provided a social network of communication to the seven isolated hamlets. Its role in mediating intervillage disputes might date back several centuries. Cai Rongying suggested to me that the unified cult of the child-god had served to negotiate issues of landownership as early as the 1680s, when the villagers returned to their homes following twenty-years of forced evacuation.[34] (The Qing Dynasty had attempted to starve out the Zheng Chenggong regime in Taiwan by removing the entire population from the Fujian coast, including Jinmen.) Whereas the lack of written documents makes it hard to ascertain the claim, there can be little doubt that by the late Qing period, Nezha played a significant role in unifying the settlers on Jinmen's eastern coast against weather hazards and bandit raids alike. In a region tormented by storms and warfare, the fearless infant has served as a rallying symbol. The cult of the young warrior has provided its scattered devotees with the means of coordinating their economic, social, and military efforts.

Taiwan

Visual art no less than fiction and drama attests to the popularity of the Nezha myth. The legend that has spread by means of fiction and drama has also been graphically disseminated. Scenes from the oedipal god's career have been among the most frequently depicted in Taiwanese temples, rendered in colorful frescoes and painted on horizontal beams, carved in latticed windows and engraved on stone pillars, the so-called "dragon columns" (*long zhu*) that support temple roofs.[35] Chen Yiyuan and his associates have conducted a comprehensive survey of Jiayi County shrines and have discovered that regardless of the deities worshiped therein, Nezha figures prominently on their walls. The child-god's martial feats have been a favorite topic of temple murals, the two most popular ones being his subjugation of the dragon king and his battle with the stone harpy Lady Rock (both of which had been rendered in stone as early as the thirteenth-century Quanzhou pagodas). Whoever the Taiwanese shrine's principal deity, the fearless infant is likely to figure in its murals.[36]

Nezha is not the only *The Canonization of the Gods*' hero who is featured in Taiwanese temple frescoes. Zhou warriors such as Jiang Ziya and Huang Feihu are also commonly depicted, as is the pathetic Bo Yikao, whose sad tale of cannibalization we have examined in chapter 1.[37] Recall that the filial infant has been rendered into a meat sauce by the vicious Shang king, only to be eaten by his own father. Nezha differs from his fellow protagonists in that his figure is inserted into visual narratives from which in the original novel he is absent. The attraction of the child-god has been such that painters choose to include him even where he plays no role in *The Canonization of the Gods*' plot. Chen Yiyuan points out that the visual renditions of the Golden Light Battle Array often feature Nezha, even though he does not appear in the corresponding chapter 46 of the seventeenth-century novel.[38]

Nezha's prominence in temple murals is matched by his ubiquity in temple parades. Impersonated by masked and unmasked performers alike, the toddler divinity figures in practically every Taiwanese religious festival, regardless of the deity in whose honor it is celebrated. In some cases, young children embody their hero, carrying his iconic weapons and riding his wind-and-fire wheels (figure 13). At others, he is revealed as a larger-than-life puppet. Worn by trained performers, the Nezha facial masks are marked by dimpled cheeks and a broad grin as befitting a child-god (figure 14). Wielding his emblematic weaponry—the cosmic ring and the fire-tipped spear—the endearing toddler marches down the streets, sometimes accompanied by the figures of his elder brothers. Fellow warriors in *The Canonization of the Gods*'—Nezha, Jinzha, and Muzha—appear together in the processions of the Taiwanese gods.

Instead of being outrivaled by the modern media, the traditional Nezha pageantries have been revitalized by contemporary technology. Recent years have witnessed the emergence of a new performance art—the so-called Electronic Music Prince (Dianyin taizi)—in which Nezha puppets dance to the beat of ear-splitting techno music. Enjoying tremendous popularity, the performances take place in traditional and contemporary venues alike. Even as they accompany the birthday festivities of the gods, the electronic Nezha dances have been featured in such high-profile events as the Kaohsiung 2009 World Games and the Shanghai 2010 World Expo. Betraying the child-god's connection to Taiwanese identity, the electronic Nezha has figured in the island's national holiday. On the occasion of the Republic of China's one hundredth anniversary, one hundred

Figure 13 *(above)*:
Wielding his iconic spear and riding his wind-and-fire wheels, a young girl impersonates Nezha. The goddess Mazu's birthday festivities, Jiayi County, Taiwan (Spring 1987). Photo by Meir Shahar.

Figure 14 *(left)*:
A masked Nezha performer, wielding the deity's iconic cosmic ring and fire-tipped spear. Jinmen Island (October 2011). Photo by Meir Shahar.

Nezha performers danced in the streets of Jiayi City. News clips reported that the youthful Third Princes had practiced for more than a month the complex choreography involving a hundred larger-than-life puppets waving the national flags.[39]

The child-god's attraction has been partially due to his divine means of locomotion. The rider of the wind-and-fire wheels is venerated by the drivers of wheeled vehicles: Cyclists and roller surfers, cab drivers and teamsters. Functioning as the tutelary deity of the transportation trade, images of the wheeled Nezha are placed on the vehicle's dashboard. From his exalted position by the driver's side, the child-god guarantees the journey's smooth progress. At least one cyclist has named his sturdy mountain bike after the indefatigable warrior Nezha.[40]

Nezha's prominence in temple murals, his popularity in festive parades, and his ubiquitous dashboard icons are all indications of his Taiwanese renown. The best illustration of his omnipresence in the island is provided by the temples that feature Nezha as an object of worship. As in the case of the smaller Jinmen isle, we might distinguish between three tiers of Taiwanese temples displaying the child-god's icons. The widest circle is that of shrines in which, as the General of the Middle Altar, Nezha functions as the temple's guardian. In these, his image is placed on the offering table, from where he leads his battalions of spirit soldiers. The second circle is that of shrines that feature the child-god as an ancillary divinity, his image situated on the main altar to the side of the principal deity. The innermost circle is made of shrines that are dedicated to the toddler as the main divinity. Nezha's role of General of the Middle Altar being discussed below, I will provide here some statistics of the second and third types of temples only.

The most detailed survey of Nezha's presence in Taiwanese temples has been conducted in the island's southwest. In the summer of 2002, Xu Xianping visited 553 townships and villages in Tainan County. He counted 60 shrines dedicated to Nezha as the principal deity and 260 temples that figure him as an ancillary divinity, more than four times as many.[41] Based upon careful fieldwork, the survey has placed Nezha among the most popular deities in the county in terms of both temples dedicated to the toddler and those featuring him as a secondary deity. Xu Xianping's research suggests that the overwhelming majority of Tainan temple-goers must be familiar with the divine child-warrior.

Admittedly, Nezha's popularity in Tainan County likely exceeds his fame elsewhere in the island. Tainan is home to the largest Taiwanese Nezha temple, the Taizi Gong in the town of Xinying. We will discuss this major center of the child-god's cult, which serves as a pilgrimage center for Nezha devotees from across the island. Xu Xianping has noted that within Tainan County the largest concentration of Nezha shrines is in the Taizi Gong's immediate vicinity. It is probable that the temple's network of affiliated shrines is similarly denser inside the southern Taiwanese county than outside of it. Hence the number of Nezha shrines in Tainan is probably larger than in other Taiwanese counties.[42]

For counties other than Tainan we do not possess surveys as detailed as Xu Xianping's. His is the only study of temples that feature Nezha either as a principal god *or* as an ancillary divinity. Elsewhere in the island, we have only lists of shrines that are dedicated to the child-god as the main object of worship, and these, based upon the government registries rather than upon fieldwork, are incomplete. In 1979, for example, Qiu Dezai counted a total of 114 Nezha temples in the island; two years later the *Taiwan Provincial Gazetteer* arrived at the number of 115.[43] More information might be gleaned from the publications of associations for the promotion of the toddler's cult. In 2008, at a Nezha temple in the town of Xinzhu, I was given a small booklet issued by the Chinese Daoist General of the Middle Altar Association for the Promotion of the Way. It listed the addresses and contact information of ninety-three Taiwanese Nezha shrines.[44]

As incomplete as they doubtless are, the varying statistics of Nezha temples in Taiwan might be compared to the equally partial numbers of other deities' shrines. Scholars have attempted to rank the popularity of the child-god, measuring the number of his registered temples against those of other Taiwanese divinities. According to Liu Zhiwan's calculations, in 1983 Nezha was the tenth most widely venerated god on the island. The registered shrines dedicated to him numbered 120, far fewer than the most popular Wangye Plague Gods (874 temples) and the Bodhisattva Guanyin (595 temples), but far more numerous than those of many other divinities. Liu Zhiwan's estimates indicate a respectable standing for the child-god as one of the most well-known deities in Taiwan, not nearly as popular as the top-ranking ones but nonetheless widely recognized.[45]

In his Taiwanese temples, Nezha is worshiped under diverse appellations and titles ranging from his surname and first name (Li Nezha), through Prince (Taizi), Lord Prince (Taizi ye), and Third Prince (San Taizi) to his Daoist appointment as the General of the Middle Altar (Zhongtan Yuanshuai). I will comment briefly on two of the toddler's temples: the Prince Palace in the town of Xinying (Xinying Taizi Gong) and the Eastern Kiln Prince Palace (Dongyao Taizi Gong) in Xinzhu City.

The Xinying Prince Palace It is not uncommon for Taiwanese villages to be named after the temple that serves as the locus of their communal life. This denominational practice enables us to date the Prince Palace (Taizi Gong) in Xinying to the first decades of the Han Chinese settlement in Taiwan. The temple gave its name to the village Taizi Gong (now part of Xinying Town), and whereas the former was not deemed worthy of mention in historical sources, the latter was. A provincial gazetteer dated 1717 alludes to the hamlet of "Taizi Gong zhuang," which likely existed for several decades prior to this *terminus ante quem*. Hence we are able to confirm the local tradition that dates the Nezha temple to the second half of the seventeenth century. The Taizi Gong's own records have it established in the 1660s by families that emigrated from Quanzhou prefecture (Fujian Province) in the wake of Zheng Chenggong's conquest of the island.[46]

Its history extending more than three hundred years, the Xinying Taizi Gong has been renovated numerous times. It underwent thorough restoration in 1728 and again in 1883, at which time it was given its present shape of a red brick, three-hall building covered by a classical boat-shaped roof. Following the Taiwanese maxim "build a temple, plant a banyan," the reconstruction was accompanied by the sowing of the remarkable tree. Now more than a hundred years old, the Taizi Gong's banyan casts its enormous shadow over the Nezha temple's entrance. Its countless branches have sent down shoots that, turning into roots, support its ever-extending parasol.[47]

By the 1970s, the increasingly prosperous villagers felt it was time to renovate their local source of pride. Members of the Nezha temple committee debated whether to dismantle the 1883 shrine and build a new one in its stead or construct a modern temple side by side with the old one. After consulting with the god by means of divination blocks (*jiao*), the second option was chosen. In 1980 work began on what was to become the largest Nezha temple structure in Taiwan. An imposing three-story edifice, it is topped by a huge statue of the child-god weighing no less than twenty thousand pounds (figure 15). Presently, the Taizi Gong is made of two shrines, the old banyan-shaded one and the new icon-topped one. The former is sometimes referred to as the "front temple" and the latter as the "back temple."[48]

The largest and one of the oldest Nezha temples in Taiwan, the Xinying Prince Palace stands at the core of the toddler's network of shrines. Most Taiwanese Nezha temples consider themselves offshoots of the Xinying Taizi Gong, to which they conduct the yearly *jinxiang* pilgrimage. On the occasion of the child-god's birthday (the ninth day of the ninth lunar month), hundreds of thousands gather to celebrate.[49] They bring along their icons of the divine warrior to be charged by his superior power as manifested in the parent temple. Most pilgrim congregations are headed by a spirit medium who mortifies the flesh in front of the violent god's altar, and many delegations, especially troupes of female devotees, perform choreographed dances at the temple's gates. At the Prince Palace, the pilgrims are treated to the customary temple fair, with opera performances, game booths, and food stalls. During the 2008 Nezha birthday celebrations, I counted at the Taizi Gong no fewer than five makeshift stages in which simultaneous shows were taking place: three puppet theater stages, one Taiwanese opera (*gezaixi*) stage, and an enormous platform, equipped with elaborate audio-visual devices, on which scantily dressed female performers were singing and dancing.

Nezha devotees make him offerings that befit his age. They bring toys to the Taizi Gong for the child-god to play with. In this respect, the Prince Palace is no different from other Nezha temples, whether in Taiwan or on the mainland. In all

Figure 15: The huge Nezha statue atop the Taizi Gong (Xinying, Taiwan). Photo by Meir Shahar.

the Nezha shrines I have visited, the offering tables have been strewn with marbles, balls, toy trucks, flying saucers, and the like (figure 16). The knickknacks betray an endearing aspect of the child-god's cult: Nezha is venerated not only for his fearsome martial qualities but also for his adorable babyish traits. The toddler's cult allows for the expression of parental love. No wonder the child-god's temples are overflowing with toys, which are sometimes distributed to local children. The custodian of the Xinzhu Eastern Kiln Prince Palace (discussed below) told me that the donated knickknacks are stored in a large box, the contents of which are periodically divided among visiting infants.[50]

Nezha is conceived of either as a child or as a newborn, for which reason he is sometimes offered babyish things. At a Nezha temple on the outskirts of Xiamen (Fujian Province) I spotted a pacifier hanging from the toddler's icon.[51] The same accessory has been the subject of an elaborate story featured in the Taiwanese press. In October 2011, on the eve of his birthday, the child-god appeared in a female devotee's dream, demanding that she offer him a pacifier. The lady had been blessed with children due to Nezha's help, for which reason he had a claim upon her. She forgot the vow that she had made him years before, whereupon he was revealed to her, making his request. Appropriately titled "Forgetting her vow if blessed with a child; the Third Prince appearing in her dream," the Taiwanese news clip featured interviews not only with the grateful devotee—who scurried to fulfill the god's demand—but also with the fertility clinic physician who had treated her some twenty years earlier.[52]

The child-god's love of playthings is matched by his penchant for sweets. His devotees hold that, like most children, Nezha is addicted to candy, for which reason his food offerings are inclined toward sugary things: chocolates, jelly-

Figure 16: Toy tractor and candies on the Nezha altar, the Taizi Gong (Xinying, Taiwan) (October 2008). Photo by Meir Shahar.

beans, toffees, and other confectioneries. The same sweets are consumed by the Nezha spirit mediums when, in a state of possession, they act out the child-god. Attending a Nezha séance on Jinmen Island, I had been instructed to bring along chocolates to satisfy the god's craving. The medium specialized in spirit writing, tracing revelatory characters on a drawing table. In the course of his trance, his hands on the drawing board, I stuffed his mouth with Ferrero Rocher bonbons. The god expressed his satisfaction by a broad grin, to the delight of the surrounding audience.[53]

The largest Nezha temple in Taiwan and the center of a dense pilgrimage network, the Xinying Taizi Gong wields considerable political and economic clout. It is a required stop on the campaign trail of aspiring politicians such as the former Republic of China president Chen Shuibian (b. 1950), and it contributes to a range of social welfare activities such as the 1998 establishment of a local community center and a public library.[54] The temple's standing is further elevated by its elegant publications. An elaborate Daoist *jiao* ritual held at the Prince Palace has been commemorated in a glossy volume titled *Times of Offering: Commemorative Album of the 1994 Seven-Day Yuan-jiao Ritual for Blessings and State-Protection.* The thick volume features dozens of photos documenting step by step the 1994 ritual, which has involved hundreds of Daoist priests, puppeteers, and actors, as well as thousands of lay devotees. Striking images reveal ritual arenas the size of football fields, covered with slaughtered pigs and paper money offerings.[55]

Potentially of great interest to the folklorist, the Xinying Taizi Gong has published an elegant volume of its written divinatory slips (*qian*). Like most Chinese temples, the Prince Palace features an oracular procedure that combines numbered sticks and written prophecies. The questioner shakes a bundle of sticks until one falls out. The number on it directs him or her to a printed verse that, in the classical idiom (itself requiring interpretation), furnishes an answer to his query. Scholars have pointed out that the oracles in question—halfway between elite and popular culture—are often related to famous stories and plays. Chen Yichuan, the editor of the Taizi Gong divinatory volume, has correlated each of the temple's prophetic verses to a famous legend. An oracle reading "the truth can't be obscured forever; ghosts and spirits recognize one's evil deeds," has been tied, for example, to a story of the clairvoyant Judge Bao meting out justice to the guilty.[56]

The Xinying Taizi Gong has been involved in scholarly activities as well. In collaboration with Zhongshan University in Gaoxiong, it has sponsored an academic conference on the history, lore, and cult of its tutelary deity. The conference brought together leading historians and anthropologists to discuss various aspects of the Nezha phenomenon. The resulting volume—*Proceedings of the First Academic Conference on Nezha*—has been of great help to this author. Among various excellent essays, it features Zeng Guodong's scholarly history of the Taizi Gong itself.[57]

The Eastern Kiln Prince Palace The founding of temples is often linked to divine revelations. We have seen that the rotating cult of the Five-Villages Prince has followed the appearance of the mounted god on Jinmen's windblown shores. The Macanese Nezha cult has been similarly traced to the child-god's epiphany. According to the legend, one night a Portuguese lady spotted an unknown child on Persimmon Hill. Barefoot, wrapped in a red sash, and his hair dressed in childish buns, he was playing all by himself. Worried about the unknown toddler who was wandering outside at midnight, the good woman urged him to return home, whereupon he vanished. The following morning, when she told the story to her Chinese neighbors, they realized he was none other than the god Nezha. His temple was thereupon established, halfway up Persimmon Hill, on Traversa de Sancho Pança.[58]

The 1986 founding of the Eastern Kiln Prince Palace (Dongyao Taizi Gong) has followed not the god's epiphany but that of his statue. The legend goes that laborers were felling acacia trees on the eastern hills of Xinzhu City (in northwestern Taiwan). The cut trees were fed to a large kiln and burnt into charcoal. While the fire was raging inside the oven, the woodcutters heard the pitiable cries of a baby. The wailing lasted night after night all through the work's completion. When they cleared the kiln, the laborers discovered inside it a small golden-lacquered icon of the infant-god, which had miraculously survived the blazing flames. The divine statue's revelation prompted the establishment of a temple. The sacred icon—approximately six inches tall—is enshrined on the main altar of the Eastern Kiln Prince Palace.[59]

Situated among the green hills of Xinzhu's eastern suburbs, the Eastern Kiln Prince Palace serves a large clientele. When I visited the temple in October 2008, I was told that its followers number ten thousand. Even though the figure might have been exaggerated, the Nezha temple does play a significant role in Xinzhu's religious life. Xu Bingkun has shown that the Eastern Kiln Prince Palace functions as the social hub of the local Dongxiang neighborhood.[60]

As in many of his Taiwanese shrines, Nezha is worshiped in the Eastern Kiln Prince Palace side by side with his brothers. His icon on the main altar is flanked by those of the eldest one (Jinzha) on his left and the second eldest (Muzha) on his right. The wall behind him is painted with a pattern of writhing dragons, recalling the infant-god's victory over the aquatic monsters.

The General of the Middle Altar

It is tempting to interpret Nezha's popularity in Taiwan in political terms. Might not his flourishing cult mirror the island's search for freedom? The precarious relations between the precocious infant and his authoritarian father might have served as a metaphor for the fragile truce between Taiwan and the mainland.

China appears eager to swallow its mutinous offspring much as Cronus did in the Greek myth, even as the island is seeking an independent path in the shadow of its mighty progenitor. The unruly child might have appealed to the Taiwanese precisely because of his defiant traits. Although admittedly hard to prove, the interpretation of the Taiwanese Nezha phenomenon as political allegory should not be offhandedly dismissed.

Its possible political connotations notwithstanding, Nezha's Taiwanese fad has ancient origins. The child-god's cult has been rooted in the island's religious history. His role of General of the Middle Altar has been instrumental in the rise of the Taiwanese Nezha. This martial role has been assigned him by Daoist ritual, attesting to the native faith's contribution to the foreign god's cult. We will turn now to the Daoist facet of the originally Buddhist deity.

The Five Armies

Taiwanese villages are protected by invisible armies. Battalions of spirit soldiers guard the community against malignant ghosts ranging from the demons of disease to rapacious enemy troops. In accordance with Chinese cosmology, the Shadow Soldiers (Yinbing) are arrayed in Five Armies (Wuying), which are stationed at the five cardinal points: north, south, east, west, and center. "The Five Armies," writes John Lagerwey, "are to the village what the five sacred peaks are to China as a whole, and what the five organs are to an individual."[61]

In Taiwan, Nezha is considered the Five Armies' supreme commander. The overwhelming majority of the island's temples recognize the child-god as the field marshal of the central army, who acts as the commander-in-chief of all five. The headquarters of the invincible infant are located within the temple, his icon placed on its offering table. From this elevated position, the General of the Middle Altar commands his own central (or middle) regiment, even as he coordinates the operations of the other four. The locations of the northern, southern, eastern, and western armies are indicated by "bamboo talismans" (*zhufu*), which the uninitiated would be hard-pressed to spot. A short bamboo slip inserted into a pot and placed at a crossroad suffices to mark the station of the heavenly hosts. Usually it is marked by a short inscription describing the Shadow Soldiers' commission to expel malignant intruders.[62]

The commander-in-chief of the Five Armies is referred to by diverse titles, sometimes incorporating his surname. Nezha is worshiped as the General of the Middle Altar, as the General of the Middle Altar Li, and as the Field Marshal of the Thirty-Three Heavens (Sanshisan Tian Duyuanshuai), an honorific that mirrors Daoist and Buddhist cosmologies alike. The Daoist heavens number thirty-three, and they might have been fashioned after the identical number of paradises that surround the Buddhist Mount Sumeru.[63] Significantly, the General of the Middle Altar holds a central position in the three dimensions of space alike. In the horizontal sphere, Nezha commands the middle army, and in the vertical one he is situated above the General of the Lower Altar, whose icon is situated on the temple's floor, under the offering table. Albeit painted in the predator's typical orange stripes, the latter is identified as the Black Tiger. In this instance, Daoist ritual has been curiously unsystematic; even though it features a General of the Middle Altar (Nezha) and a General of the Lower Altar (Black Tiger), it recognizes no General of the Upper Altar.

The Five Armies figure prominently in the Daoist rites that are conducted by the so-called barefoot "ritual masters" (*fashi*). The first stage of each and every ritual consists of the summoning of Nezha's heavenly troops who are stationed around the altar to protect it. At the ceremony's conclusion, the spirit soldiers are dutifully thanked for their efforts. They are feasted and are awarded prizes before being sent back to their barracks. These two stages, the gathering of troops and their dispersal, occur in every ritual regardless of its purpose, which might vary according to the occasion, from the salvation of the dead to the healing of the living; from the expulsion of disease demons to the bestowal of offspring and good harvests.[64]

Nezha's spirit soldiers are summoned by means of rhyming incantations that, as Kristofer Schipper has noted, are written in the vernacular.[65] The spells vary from temple to temple and from one ritual lineage to another. Xu Yucheng has collected a significant number of the General of the Middle Altar incantations. The following brief excerpt is from a spell employed by a ritual master on Penghu Islands (the Pescadores). It is remarkable for its frank display of what Steven Sangren considers the key to the oedipal child's myth—the desire for autonomy and self-creation:

> Respectfully inviting the Third Prince Nezha,
> Aged seven, displaying his magic powers.
> Mighty indeed, mighty indeed,
> The Prince Nezha's one million troops.
> A million troops arrayed together,
> Horses and footsoldiers coming to the altar.
> He has no father, he has no mother,
> Creating himself (*du zicheng*), and reared by Heaven.
> Upon the water, fashioned from a lotus flower,
> This Third Prince has no elder brother.
> . . .
> This disciple devotedly begs to invite you:
> General of the Middle Altar descend here please.
> Heavenly Troops come quickly as ordered by law!
> (*shenbing huoji ru lü ling*)[66]

In October 2011, I participated on Jinmen Island in a ritual for the summoning of Nezha's heavenly troops. Conducted by a barefoot master of the Lüshan sect, it was part of an elaborate Daoist *jiao* ceremony, which was held at the local Paragon of Virtue from Suiyang Temple. The title Paragon of Virtue from Suiyang (Suiyang Zhujie) alludes to General Zhang Xun (709–757), whose morals had been the subject of a heated debate as early as the Tang period. During the An Lushan rebellion, the loyal Zhang Xun defended the besieged town of Suiyang. His heroic defense had been carried out at the terrible price of cannibalism; the general had fed his own concubine to the starving troops, going on to butcher all the other women (and the elderly) in the hunger-driven city. Following his death at the rebel's hands, the general had been cited for heroism by the emperor. Nonetheless, some officials wondered whether it would not have been better for him to evacuate the besieged city than to have eaten the people entrusted to his care.[67]

The Jinmen barefoot master conducted the ceremony according to a handwritten manual titled "The Ritual of [Heavenly] Troops Deployment" ("Fangbing keyi"). The icons of the General of the Middle Altar (Nezha) and the General of the Lower Altar (Black Tiger) were taken out of the temple and placed on a makeshift altar in the courtyard (figure 17). They were proffered meat and noodle offerings, even as stacks of hay and buckets of water were laid out for the coming heavenly cavalry. Blowing his horn to summon the spirit soldiers, the Lüshan master performed a ritual dance, at the height of which—to the deafening accompaniment of pipes and drums—he slashed his tongue with a sword. Four yellow-colored flags were smeared with his blood and placed at the four corners of the village (north, south, east, and west) identifying the location of the four surrounding armies. (Situated inside the temple, the location of the central army needed no marking.)

More than one person's blood was spilled in the ceremony. Even as the barefoot master was slashing his tongue with a sword and dabbing the armies' banners in his gore, a spirit medium was piercing his flesh with skewers. The Temple of the Paragon of Virtue from Suiyang is equipped with a set of five needles topped each with the head of a general (of whom Nezha is one). Known as the skewers of the Five Armies' Commanders (Wuying tou), they are thrust into the body of a possessed medium, who carries them around throughout the ritual of heavenly troops' deployment. Inserted into the hands and cheeks of the porcupine-resembling medium, the spikes are held in place by transparent adhesive tape, the kind used for sealing envelopes and the like.[68]

Kenneth Dean has suggested that the mortification of the flesh functions as an offering to the gods. "The spirit medium is in fact a sacrifice," he writes.[69] His interpretation might be applicable to the Jinmen rites of the Five Armies. The magically potent blood of ritual masters and spirit mediums is employed to summon Nezha's spirit soldiers.

Figure 17: Nezha as the General of the Middle Altar (right). Note the meat and noodle offerings, as well as the ritual master's paraphernalia, which includes a horn, a woodblock, a bell, a dragon-headed whip, and a manual titled "The Ritual of [Heavenly] Troops Deployment." Jinmen Island (October 2011). Photo by Meir Shahar.

Daoism

The rituals of the Five Armies are both ancient and geographically widespread. Instructions for the summoning of the armies of the five quarters figure in Daoist scriptures of the Zhengyi School from as early as the fourth century CE.[70] By the late imperial period, the five generals and their divine hosts have penetrated local religion in vast regions of central and southern China. Ethnographic fieldwork has revealed the significance of spirit soldiers in the protection of villages from Sichuan and Guizhou in the west, through Jiangxi and Zhejiang in the lower Yangtze basin, to Fujian and Taiwan in the southeast.

The individual identities of the generals in command of the Five Armies have differed from one locality to another. Diverse divinities and/or local heroes have been chosen to head the battalions of spirit soldiers in different regions. Whereas in Fujian and in Taiwan, the General of the Central Army is usually identified as Nezha, in Sichuan and in Guizhou the child does not figure as the leader of spirit soldiers.[71] In some areas, furthermore, the commanders of the heavenly hosts are not individually named. The Five Armies are summoned with no reference to the personal identities of their commanding officers.

Nezha figures as the General of the Middle Altar primarily in Fujian and in Taiwan, (even though, occasionally, he might be appointed to the post elsewhere). Li Fengmao has suggested that the child's rise to the elevated rank has been related to his adoption by the Daoist lineages of Fujian Province.[72] As early as the Southern Song period (1127–1279), Fujian Daoists harnessed the powers of the Buddhist warrior to exorcise demons. They incorporated Nezha into their ritual manuals, which have served as the source for the late imperial Fujian lineages of Lüshan, San'nai, and Pu'an. Theses lineages of barefoot masters have secured Nezha's position as General of the Middle Altar in Fujian and its neighboring Taiwan. The young warrior's contemporary prominence in Taiwan derives in part from his Song-period attraction to the Daoist priests of Fujian Province.

The earliest reference to Nezha in Daoist scriptures is by a Fujian priest. In his *Recorded Sayings*, the renowned master Bai Yuchan (1194?–1229) is asked about esoteric Buddhism (which he refers to as the School of Yoga (Yujia)). In reply, he enumerates the names of several Tantric divinities, whose cult was apparently prevalent in Song-period Fujian. As Edward Davis has noted, the exotic names of these originally Indian and Central Asian gods must have been one reason for their attraction. In addition to Prince Nezha, the Daoist priest mentions the Medicine King Dragon Tree (who is none other than the Buddhist philosopher Nāgārjuna); the Two Great Lords Incense Mountain and Snowy Mountain; the female Swine Head and the male Elephant Trunk (both deriving from Śiva's elephantine infant Gaṇeśa); the Diamond Stalwart (Jin'gang lishi) and the skull-bearing Spirit of the Deep Sands (Shensha shen) (who, converted by Xuanzang, functions as his escort in the sixteenth-century novel *The Journey to the West*).[73]

Bai Yuchan had been among the creators of the exorcistic Thunder Rituals that feature Nezha as a divine warrior. His Fujianese lineage incorporated the originally Buddhist divinity into the Daoist rituals that were intended to bring rain in times of drought and expel the demons of disease. The Thunder Rituals of Bai Yuchan and his disciples have been preserved in a vast compendium of rites, the fifteenth-century *Daoist Methods United in Principle*. They include incantations for the summoning of the invincible child, who is variously referred to as "fierce general," "prince," and "king." Some magic recipes associate Nezha with the brave general Zhao Gongming, whom he battles in the seventeenth-century *The Canonization of the Gods*. Others pay homage to his Tantric image, depicting a "three-headed and nine-armed" divinity, "emanating dark fog from its [three] noses."[74]

His significance in Fujian Daoism need not obscure Nezha's attraction to Daoists elsewhere. We have mentioned in chapter 5 the Song-period story of a ritual master (*fashi*) from Jiangxi Province who drafted the child warrior to battle a stone harpy. According to Hong Mai (1123–1202), Master Cheng of Zhang village (in northeastern Jiangxi) had received Daoist training in the Maoshan lineage. Even though he himself had not been ordained, he practiced such orthodox Daoist techniques as the ceremonial dance of the Big Dipper. When attacked at midnight by the rocky prodigy, he summoned the invincible child to the rescue. Reciting the "Spell of Nezha's Fireball," he exorcized the monster.[75]

Nezha's skills as a demon queller have been equally recognized in other provinces. Patrice Fava has discovered in Central Hunan an exorcistic mask of the child warrior mounted atop the fearful image of General Han Xin (230–196 BCE) (figure 18). The remarkably expressive mask originated in Shigong Village, which is home to some fifty practicing Daoists, thirty identified as "Daoist masters" (*daoshi*) and the remaining twenty as "[ritual] masters" (*shigong*). Said to be three hundred years old, the mask was discovered among the paraphernalia of a "ritual master," whose exorcistic implements featured, in addition, a serpent-headed baton to which a whip (*mabian*) was attached.[76]

The Nezha mask has been used in *nuo* ritual drama. Its tremendous power derived from the combined grievances of the two spirits it featured. Nezha and Han Xin alike have experienced premature deaths. Both have been victims of tyrannical power, Nezha by his father and Han Xin by Emperor Liu Bang. The historical general Han Xin had faithfully served the Han Dynasty founder Liu Bang (256–195 BCE), only to be unjustly suspected by him of intended rebellion. Trumped-up charges were brought against the brave soldier, who was executed forthwith.[77] Han Xin's wronged spirit had been placated by his appointment to the position of divine exorcist. Much like other Chinese demon quellers (Zhong Kui is a notable example) it was fear of his ruthless vengeance that led to his apotheosis.[78]

His role of Daoist exorcist has had a decisive impact upon the imaginings of Nezha. We have seen in chapter 5 that at least some of his martial emblems have accrued to the young brave from Daoist ritual. The very scripture that incorporates Nezha into the ranks of the thunder gods is also the first to mention his iconic weapons. The ritual manual *Daoist Methods United in Principle* features a Thunderbolt Angel (Pili Shizhe), who brandishes a gold brick and a golden spear, even as he rides fire wheels.[79] It is likely that Nezha's gold brick, fire-tipped spear, and wind-and-fire wheels have been equally adapted from this comrade-in-arms. The fifteenth-century manual has served as a source for *The Canonization of the Gods*. The iconic weapons celebrated in the seventeenth-century novel have derived from the armories of *Daoist Methods*. Nezha's martial emblems have been borrowed from the arsenal of Daoist exorcism.

Figure 18: Nezha mounted atop General Han Xin. Ritual mask dating from the early Qing period. Shigong Village, Central Hunan. Photo courtesy Patrice Fava.

Possession

Chinese spirit mediums are conceived of as children. This is not to say that they are necessarily young, even though many do embark upon their religious vocation in their late teens.[80] It means, rather, that whatever their biological age, they are supposed to maintain the childish qualities necessary for communion with the divine. Mediums are expected to be genuine. Acquired adult skills would be detrimental to the gods' spokespersons, whose divine message must be devoid of artifice and deceit. The medium's knowledge is believed to be as intuitive as an infant's. The contemporary social reality of most mediums not being highly educated is ideologically justified by their need for spontaneity. What the prophet knows has not been taught him. Like a child, his clairvoyance is inborn rather than learned.[81]

There is also a darker aspect to the medium's association with children. Communicating with the spirit world, infants are susceptible to its hazards. An illness suffered in infancy might be the first symptom of divine revelation. Spirit mediums often claim they have been forced into the oracular vocation by a malady that has been inflicted upon them in childhood. The god has consented to their recovery on condition that they serve as his mouthpiece. In this respect the spokespersons for the gods are living on borrowed time. They should have died in infancy, but their lives have been extended. As Charles Stafford has noted, they "were not meant to survive but were allowed to do so, for a special purpose, namely being a medium for communication with the gods."[82]

The terminology applied to them articulates the perception of the mediums as infants. In South China and throughout Southeast Asia they are known as "child diviners" (*tongji;* Hokkien: *tâng-ki*) or as "divining children" (*jitong*).[83] Alternative names such "child heart" (*tongxin*) equally impart the significance of the innocent gaze for the oracular message. The juvenile nomenclature is matched by infantile dress. As Kristopher Schipper has noted, the mediums are dressed—or more accurately undressed—as toddlers. Barefoot with their shoulders exposed, they wear no more than pants (or underpants) and a small diamond-shaped cloth. Partially covering their naked chest and belly, the red cloth is a child's and a woman's intimate article of clothing.[84]

Their childish identity is likely one reason for the mediums' fondness for Nezha. The infant-god is among the most frequently encountered divinities in rituals of possession. Fieldwork conducted in Fujian, in Taiwan, and across peninsular Southeast Asia (Thailand, Singapore, and Malaysia) has revealed his prominence in spirit-medium cults.[85] Nezha's attraction to the "divining children" should likely be attributed to their identical age. The child-god is a natural choice for the gods' juvenile spokespersons. Because he is an infant, Nezha is a medium's divinity par excellence.

Impersonating the Child-God

In June 2012, I participated in a possession ritual at the lush Beitou suburb of Taipei City. The séance took place at a Nezha temple that was ideally situated among green hills and running streams. Established in the 1980s, the Yongxing Gong is adjacent to a majestic waterfall, by the side of which is a handsome relic of the Japanese colonial rule: an elegant shrine dedicated to Fudō Myōō, the fierce god of Buddhist Tantric origin.

The séance opened with the (not yet possessed) medium sitting in an imposing chair opposite the Nezha statue on the main altar. Facing the god who would soon take hold of him, the medium inhaled from an incense burner held for him by an assistant. Breathing heavily, he belched loudly several times. Suddenly, he jumped to his feet, his voice rising to a squeal. Thumping the altar table with both fists, he screamed in a high-pitched voice. The childish tantrum signified the infant-god's presence. Nezha had taken control of his spokesperson.

The high-pitched squeak, coupled with a halting baby talk, is typical of the Nezha séances.[86] The mediums for the infant-god act out his childish persona: They might laugh or play, and they are easily distracted. In order to gain the medium's attention, it is sometimes necessary to tempt him with toys and sweets. Before answering his patrons' queries, the Beitou medium demanded that they provide him with candy. In this he resembled the Nezha medium I interviewed in October 2011 on Jinmen Island, who had me feed him Ferrero Rocher chocolates during the séance.

Nezha's spokeswomen perform the same childish role as his male mouthpieces. Hong Shuling has studied the renowned female medium Liao Lindian (1914–1988), who has established a thriving Nezha temple in Yunlin County, Central Taiwan. Hong comments on the god's babyish traits as revealed through female possession:

> Popular fiction describes Nezha as a child. Hence, when embodied by a spirit medium, he displays childish characteristics. . . . He speaks in an infant's voice, he writes with difficulty, and in general he prefers talking to writing. He plays with marbles, spinning tops and similar toys, and he enjoys cakes and candies. He employs childish figures of speech, etc. When I visited the Nezha Temple . . . I noticed on the altar numerous playthings, such as toy cars, marbles, *wangzi* figurines[87] and the like. Liao Lindian's daughter told me that they were all offerings by devotees to Nezha. When Liao Lindian would go into a trance, she would express her liking for these playthings. Hence the devotees would make offerings of them.[88]

The god's childish traits might be amusing or irritating, depending on the situation. A member of the Wan'an Tang temple committee (on Jinmen Island) shared with me his frustration over the Nezha mediums' unreliability. In the midst of a séance, a *jiao* ceremony, or a religious parade, they might lose interest in the proceedings and head off to play. Even when they are physically present, their spirit might roam elsewhere. Moreover, the infant-god is occasionally moody and, for no apparent reason, refuses to communicate with his devotees.[89] A similar pattern of erratic behavior emerges from Charles Stafford's account of a Nezha medium in southeastern Taiwan:

> During the session, children were playing outside on the streets of the village, setting off fireworks. Each time a firework exploded outside, the *tâng-ki* [medium] would become very agitated. I was told that the Third Prince [Nezha] loved to play with children, and when he heard the fireworks he wanted to end the grown-up discussions and run off to play.[90]

Their capriciousness notwithstanding, the Nezha mediums provide the same range of services as spokespersons for the other gods. They engage in exorcism and healing, writing protective charms, which may be dabbed in their own blood for extra measure.[91] Most commonly, they function as oracles, addressing questions as diverse as their clientele's concerns, from intimate marital problems to communal decision making. The patrons of the Beitou Nezha temple are requested to fill a rubricated form, checking the category in which they require counsel. Attesting the medium's scope, it includes no fewer than the following nine boxes: "Health," "marriage," "luck," "business," "dates" (auspicious and inauspicious), "family," "ancestors," "baby pacification," and "education." The bureaucratically inevitable "other" category is added in a tenth box.

Summoning the Child-God

Two modes of possession are evident in contemporary Chinese religion. One has the medium going into a trance by himself, with no support from another religious functionary, and the other has a Daoist priest or a ritual master command the deity's descent into the medium's body. The priest assumes a deified position that, in the latter case, is superior to the medium's. Kristofer Schipper compares him to a puppeteer, who works the medium like a marionette on strings. From his august post as the Jade Emperor or as the venerable Laozi, the priest summons a subordinate divinity into the medium's body. He orders the junior deity to do his bidding through the medium's person.[92]

The origins of the second mode of possession are a puzzle. Michel Strickmann has suggested that esoteric Buddhism introduced the roles of the divine priest and his child-medium into Chinese religion. Tantric Buddhist scriptures that were translated into Chinese during the Tang period (618–907) provide detailed guidelines for the summoning of deities (or ghosts) into the bodies of possessed children. The Tantric master bids the spirit tell future events through its infant mouthpiece. Another procedure has him transfer a demon of disease from a patient's body into the person of a child. Interrogated and forced to acknowledge its identity, the inflicting demon is henceforth exorcised.[93] Even though similar techniques might have evolved independently in Daoist circles, it appears likely that esoteric Buddhism did contribute to the Chinese mode of possession by command of a deified priest.[94]

I have encountered the second mode of possession—that of Nezha being summoned by priestly order—in a small fishing community on Meizhou Island, off the Fujian coast. In July 2010, I visited the local Lianchi Gong Temple, which is dedicated to the sea goddess Mazu. As in several of her Fujianese temples, the goddess's altar is flanked by another dedicated to Nezha. The invincible child serves as Mazu's bodyguard.[95]

The Lianchi Gong is home to a Nezha medium whom I have not met. Carrying passengers on his motorbike taxi, he was away when I visited. I did however meet a sixty-three-year-old gentleman who functions as his ritual master (even though he declines to describe himself as such). The latter volunteered to write in my field notebook the formula by which the child-god is summoned. Sipping tea and smoking, he recorded in his gnarled fisherman's hand the incantation that had been taught him by his uncle:

> Respectfully, we invite the Third Prince Nezha of Chentang Pass.
> When seven years old, displaying his divinity,
> Wearing a turban, wrapped in a sash,
> He wields a golden spear, tossing an embroidered ball.
> Atop the hundred-flower bridge, he leads a million men.
> Mastering the necessary rituals, he saves the multitude.
> From as far as a thousand miles he instantly comes,
> Whoever calls him, he immediately responds.
> Inviting the great person here, to the incense burner
> I the august Taishang Laojun (Laozi) order you:
> Instantly, by order of the law, reveal yourself for [the people's] protection (*jiji rulü ling, xiafan jiuhu*).

The formula has been orally transmitted in the fisherman's family for generations. A possible hint of its antiquity is suggested by the reference to the "embroidered ball." We have seen in chapter 5 that Ming-period sources had attributed the magic weapon to the child warrior. By the seventeenth century, however, the "embroidered ball" had disappeared from the Nezha arsenal, being replaced by such Daoist implements as his gold brick. It is possible, therefore, that the Meizhou Island incantation derives from Ming-period sources.

In October 2011, I witnessed Nezha being summoned by means of another incantation. The séance took place once again off the Fujian coast, this time on Jinmen Island. The local Wan'an Tang Temple specializes in spirit writing. The large temple employs no fewer than eleven mediums, who serve a total of eight different deities. (The mediums' names, photos, and contact information are listed in one of the temple's handsome publications.[96]) In a state of trance the medium traces characters, either with a stick or with his fingers, on a wooden table. One or two interpreters follow the stick and/or finger movements, reading the inscribed words out loud. A fourth person transcribes the oral pronouncements, which are sometimes published.

At the appointed evening hour, a bench was set by the altar for the Nezha medium to sit upon. Several people, including the interpreters and temple director, began chanting the god's incantation. Apparently familiar with the tune, others present joined in the singing. While they were chanting in beautiful melodious Hokkien, the medium gradually started trembling. As his shaking grew violent, the interpreters grabbed the bench to prevent it from capsizing. Slowly rising to his feet, the medium stretched his limbs. Suddenly he hit the altar table with his open palms. The dramatic gesture signified the presence of the god. Nezha was available for consultation by his devotees.

Chanted in the Hokkien dialect, the Wan'an Tang incantation is available in print in one of the temple's volumes of spirit writing. It is a standard formula used at the temple for the summoning of all gods, regardless of personal identity. The wording does not change from one divinity to another; rather a blank space is left to be filled by its name. The incantation lists the divine powers that are manipulated by the ritual master. In the following excerpt, I have enclosed in parentheses its changeable part, in this instance filled by Nezha's name:

> We respectfully invite this temple's (Nezha) of a thousand years.
> The victorious and resplendent King Nāgārjuna
> And the True Warrior Great General of the North
> In five steps, they are revealed together like clouds.
> . . .
> The Eight Diamond [Stalwarts] and the Six Heavenly Kings
> [The Lords] of Incense Mountain and Snowy Mountain incarnated at once.
> . . .
> All the Buddhas of the Three Worlds descending together
> The ten generations of Yoga masters incarnated at once.
> This disciple sincerely and earnestly prays and invites:
> (Nezha) descend to this temple of a thousand years!
> Heavenly troops come quickly as ordered by the law!
> Heavenly troops come quickly as ordered by the law![97]

The incantation brings us back to the thirteenth-century Daoist priest Bai Yuchan. Its resonance with his writings attests to the historical continuity of Fujian religion. The spell that has been recorded in twenty-first-century Jinmen shares significant similarities with the records of the Southern Song priest. Both allude to esoteric Buddhism, to which they identically refer as the School of Yoga (Yujia), and both depict a largely similar pantheon of esoteric Buddhist divinities: The Buddhist philosopher Nāgārjuna (whose religious cult was introduced to China by the Tantric School, and whose Chinese name—Dragon Tree—is a literal translation of the Sanskrit *nāga* (snake/dragon) and *arjuna* (tree)); the [Eight] Diamond Stalwarts (Sanskrit: Vajrapāṇi); the Two Lords Incense Mountain and Snowy Mountain, and of course, this book's protagonist, Nezha.[98] In this respect the Jinmen incantation evinces the long-term impact that esoteric Buddhism has wielded—through the vehicle of the Daoist religion—on the local religion of southeast China. Incorporated into Daoist ritual, esoteric Buddhist divinities found their way into the popular religion of Fujian Province, becoming objects of lay worship.

Unfilial Infants

Nezha is a spirit-medium deity par excellence not only because he is a child, but because he is an unfilial one. The infant-god shares with his childish spokespersons a disregard for paternal authority. Charles Stafford has noted that all mediums—not only Nezha's—are by definition unfilial, for they mortify the paternal gift of the body. The self-laceration might take various forms: heads are smashed against stone altars; skewers are thrust into cheeks; spike balls are hurled against foreheads; swords slash tongues; and firecrackers burn the skin. The diverse forms of self-torture equally violate the sacrality of the ancestral flesh. The mediums' mortification flies in the face of the Confucian dictum: "Our bodies—to every hair and bit of skin—are received by us from our parents, and we must not presume to injure or wound them: This is the beginning of filial piety."[99]

His mortification of the flesh evinces the medium's authenticity. Informants usually explain that only a plaything in the hands of the gods would subject his body to torture. The unnatural spectacle of self-laceration proves the deity's presence. Charles Stafford is likely correct in asserting that their unfilial behavior is the very source of the mediums' power. "What the mediums profess to know," he writes, "is accepted as the truth precisely because of their violence. It might even be suggested that their efficacy actually comes from their unfilial self-laceration."[100]

Stafford has conducted his 1980s fieldwork in southeastern Taiwan. In the village he has studied, Nezha mediums are patronized primarily by women. The unfilial infant is sought after by mothers for their children's sake. Women beseech the patricidal deity's help in healing and educating their young. Stafford has concluded that the god's spokespersons offer an alternative to the patriarchal social order. Mediums challenge paternal authority by spilling the patrilineal flow of blood. The unfilial "child-diviners" are the locus of a matriarchal religious sphere, subverting patriarchal authority. Rebellious infants such as Nezha offer women the symbolic means for resisting male domination:

> [The mediums'] everyday practice is relatively private and dominated by the concerns of women. In this way, and through the symbolism I have described, they are linked to what might be called the sphere of women and children in Chinese religious life. . . . To the extent that spirit mediums are represented as children, they embody both the danger and the power of their namesakes. They are children who have symbolically broken the patrilineal flow of blood, and their own flowing blood is powerful. In Angang [the fictitious name given by Stafford to the village he has studied] these "unfilial children" are patronized mostly by women, and are part of a private religious sphere which might teach children loyalty to their mothers, possibly to a matrifocal ideal.[101]

Stafford has demonstrated the role of Nezha mediums in the creation of an independent female sphere. His illuminating research indicates the ways in which the oedipal god's cult might have served women seeking to resist patriarchal authority. Other anthropologists have emphasized the role of the Nezha myth in the negotiation of masculinity. Avron Boretz considers Nezha a metaphor for Chinese possession at large. The violence of the child's myth is equaled by the virulence of the spirit medium's performance. The tantrums, madness, and self-laceration of the "divining children" allow the release of familial frustration. Identifying with rebellious figures such as Nezha, Chinese males are able to work out their oedipal frustration. Through the patricidal Nezha myth, and by the medium's violence, they are purged from excess anger and desire. The medium's performance objectifies the Oedipus complex, permitting Chinese men to assume their proper familial roles as sons and fathers:

> [The medium's] regressive outbursts relive the primal frustration of desire and violently assert, in the idiom of a child tantrum, an autonomous male self that transcends the constraints of assigned social roles—be they demanding father or obedient son. . . . The actors oscillate between two extremes of martial masculinity, austere and restrained at one end, feral, capricious, and uncontrollable at the other. What we see, then, is the ritual objectification of the defining emotional struggle of Chinese male subjectivity, rooted in the conflicted relations between fathers and sons in the patrilineal family.[102]

Charles Stafford and Avron Boretz reveal each in his own way the roles of the Nezha figure in the negotiation of familial tensions. The former discovers the patricidal god's function as a symbol for female resistance; the latter interprets the medium's violence as an outlet for male desire. Both studies unravel the cathartic significance of the oedipal god's myth and of its frenzied expression in the idiom of possession.[103] Just as Sophocles's play has enabled its Greek audience to vent their hidden desires, the dramatic performance of the Nezha medium has released the unspoken frustrations of the Chinese family. Venting suppressed emotions, the oedipal god's cult has mitigated Chinese familial tensions.

Nezha's cathartic impact notwithstanding, some mediums downplay his transgressive traits. Much like the Macanese temple functionaries discussed above, they struggle to present an immaculate image of the child-deity. I have encountered at least one medium who—in a state of trance—rejected the accusation of the god's unfilial behavior. In October 2011, I interviewed at the Wan'an Temple on Jinmen Island a spirit medium who specializes in automatic writing. My first question threw the incarnated Nezha into confusion: I asked him who he loves more, his mother or father? Guessing where I was heading, the possessed medium refused to answer. Changing the topic of discussion, I asked several other questions (including whether or not I will finish the book about him), before returning to my original query about his familial circumstances. This time around, Nezha was well prepared. Tracing bold characters on the drawing board, he flatly denied the patricidal tendencies that are attributed to him in popular lore: "*The Canonization of the Gods* is nothing but fiction," he stated. "A god must adhere to the principles of loyalty and filial piety (*zhong xiao jieyi*)."

Apologetics might be at work even in the course of possession. The Jinmen medium's response reveals the degree to which some of his clerics struggle to clear Nezha of immoral suspicions. The patricidal god's cult is simultaneously drawn in opposite directions. Whereas it has served some as a symbol of resistance, others have muffled its controversial traits. Even as his myth has expressed hidden familial tensions, the custodians of the Nezha cult struggle to draw an image of the god that conforms to the hegemonic Confucian discourse.

The Nezha apologetics take us back to the oedipal conflict that lies at the core of his myth. What might have been the textual source of the patricidal legend? The next chapter explores the origins of the god's familial discord in Chinese Buddhist scriptures.

7

Biological and Spiritual Fathers

A significant figure has been omitted from our discussion of the Nezha myth. The preceding chapters have not alluded to the prodigy's master, the Immortal Taiyi. *The Canonization of the Gods* assigns the Daoist sage pivotal roles in his disciple's earthly and heavenly careers. He is the Immortal Taiyi who appears on the scene shortly after the hero's birth and names him; he is the immortal who protects the mischievous infant from the wrath of the harpy Lady Rock; and it is to the immortal's abode that the child's disembodied soul flutters after his suicide. Finally, he is the immortal who resurrects Nezha, fashioning for him a divine body made of a lotus flower.

In many respects, the Daoist immortal awards Nezha everything the biological father has begrudged him: love, protection, and a new lease on life. It would not be an exaggeration to consider him a substitute father, one who has been chosen by Nezha over his flesh-and-blood one. Considering the immortal's role, we might gain an additional perspective on the rebellious infant's myth. Rather than an oedipal tale of a murderous father-and-son conflict, the legend might mirror a young person's search for spiritual guidance. Instead of a brutal competition over the mother/wife's love, the myth might betray the difficult choice between a familial authority and an otherworldly mentor. If the fatal triangle of a son, a father, and a mother dominates the contemporary myth, that of a son, a biological father, and a spiritual one might have prefigured it in earlier versions.

As early as the first centuries CE, the Daoist faith had circumvented Confucian ethics, postulating spiritual progenitors over biological parents. Kunio Mugitani has demonstrated the significance of the Original Father (Yuanfu) and the Mysterious Mother (Xuanmu) in early Daoist scriptures. The filial piety that is addressed to these divine progenitors supersedes the devotion to one's flesh-and-blood parents. "To realize spiritual enlightenment and Daoist immortality, a person must rely on the divine authentic parents. . . . This implies that in the pursuit of the Dao, one must also leave behind one's biological parents."[1] The origins of Nezha's choice lie not in the native Daoist faith, however, but in the imported

Buddhist religion, which has been the source of his legend. Prior to the seventeenth century, the prodigy had been drawn to the Buddha Śākyamuni rather than to the Immortal Taiyi. His myth's early versions betrayed a conflict between Confucian ideology and Buddhist—instead of Daoist—salvation. The story's antecedents reflected a tension between Chinese family values and Buddhist monasticism.

Between Father and Buddha

We begin our search for the myth's Buddhist origins with the 1592 edition of *The Journey to the West.* The story of Monk Xuanzang's westward journey in search of the scriptures includes a complete—albeit brief—version of the Nezha legend. Predating *The Canonization of the Gods* by some thirty years only, its religious context differs. Whereas the former's action takes place amid the heavenly grottoes of Daoist immortals and sorcerers, the latter's unfolds to the cheers of enlightened Buddhist beings. Nezha of *The Journey to the West* seeks refuge at the western paradise where the Tathāgata Buddha preaches the Dharma to the bodhisattva hosts:

> When the Prince [Nezha] was three-days old, he went bathing in the ocean, causing a disaster: He trampled upon the Water-Crystal Palace; he captured a dragon; and he wanted to tear off its tendon to make a belt. Having learned of this, his father, the Heavenly King, became fearful of the consequences. Therefore, he sought to kill his son, whereupon Nezha became enraged: A sword in hand, he cut off his own flesh, and returned it to his mother. He scraped the bones, and returned them to his father. The father's semen and the mother's blood were given back to them.
>
> Nezha's soul, meanwhile, headed straight to complain to the Buddha at his Blissful Realm of the West. The Buddha was in the midst of expounding the scriptures to the Bodhisattva hosts. He heard the cries for help from across the Divine Pennants and the Precious Canopy. Gazing with his Eye of Wisdom, he instantly realized that this was Nezha's spirit. He fashioned for him bones made of the divine-lotus' roots, and a garment made of the lotus' leaves. Reciting the mantra that revives the dead, he brought Nezha back to life.
>
> Endowed with divine strength, Nezha subdued the demons of the ninety-six caves to the Dharma. Later, his magic powers further increased, and he tried to kill [his father] the Heavenly King, in revenge for his scraped bones. The helpless Heavenly King had no choice but to beg the Buddha Tathāgata to save him. As he valued harmony, the Buddha bestowed upon him an exquisitely translucent golden magic stupa [pagoda], which stored sacred *śarīra* relics. On each level, the stupa contained a splendidly radiant image of the Buddha, reminding Nezha that he should consider the Buddha his father. Hence, his enmity [toward his biological one] was resolved.
>
> This is why Nezha's father is known as the Pagoda-Bearer Heavenly King Li.[2]

The legend's religious import couldn't have been clearer. Nezha's defiance of paternal authority results in the substitution of a spiritual father (the Buddha) for the biological one (the Heavenly King Li). The familial conflict leads him from the confines of his natal household to the embrace of the Buddhist community. In this respect, the legend of the patricidal infant might mirror the fundamental conflict between Buddhist monasticism and the Confucian social order. Historians have elaborated upon the tremendous difficulties that accompanied the introduction of the Buddhist *sangha* to China. By joining the Buddhist order, a Chinese individual violated the hegemonic ethics of filial piety.[3] The conflict was particularly severe in the case of male offspring, who were expected to reside with and care for their elderly parents, even as they were held responsible for the survival of the agnatic lineage by reproduction. The legend of the feral child offered a radical solution to the conflict. The Buddhist symbol of the stupa (pagoda) served "to remind Nezha that he should consider the Buddha his father." Spiritual power and paternal authority were united in the person of the Buddhist savior.

The legend's implications for the biological parent are ambiguous. *The Journey to the West* version does not elaborate upon the ensuing relations between Nezha and his father. On the one hand, the Buddha has intervened to save the Heavenly King Li from his son's wrath, in which sense the story might be interpreted as buttressing Confucian ideology. On the other hand, having usurped the biological parent's authority, the Buddha's position is far superior. There can be no doubt that Nezha's principal obligation is to his religious savior. Inasmuch as the child pays his dues to the flesh-and-blood father, it is only because he obeys the Tathāgata's command. The foreign faith might have accommodated native family values, but its supremacy has remained unchallenged. The Buddha is the ultimate source of both religious and familial ethics.

The legend's Buddhist setting is attested by the person of the savior and the manner of salvation alike. The Buddha resurrects Nezha from a lotus flower. The blossom has been chosen for the divine incarnation not only because of its ancient connotations of purity, but more specifically because of its role in Buddhist soteriology. As early as the first centuries CE, Buddhist devotees conceived of paradisiacal rebirth in horticultural terms. Those fortunate enough to be reborn in the Buddha's presence emerged from lotus buds, as the influential *Lotus Sutra* explained: "And in whatsoever Buddha-field he shall be reborn, there on a self-originated lotus made of the seven jewels he shall be reborn in the presence of the Tathāgata."[4]

The Buddha Amitabha's Pure Land has been among the most coveted paradises. The hope of rebirth in his Pure Land has been a prominent feature of Buddhist religiosity across Asia. The faithful who devoutly recite Amitabha's name are redeemed by his divine grace, being reborn into his western paradise. As early as the first centuries CE, redemption in Amitabha's Pure Land has been imagined in floral terms. Those who trust in the Buddha's grace are resurrected from divine lotus blooms. Flower-like beings, they emerge from the sacred lotus blossoms into a realm of purity and happiness:

> When beings of this [superior] type are about to die, the Buddha of Measureless Light [Amitabha] appears before them, accompanied by a great crowd of attendants. Then, these beings follow this Buddha and go to be reborn in his land. They are reborn naturally and miraculously in the center of a lotus made of the seven precious substances, and they dwell in the state from which there is no falling back. They come to possess wisdom and courage, supernormal powers and spiritual mastery.[5]

Floral regeneration became a favorite topic of Buddhist art across Asia. Redeemed souls were visually rendered as newborns wrapped in lotus blooms. Some artists faithfully followed a given Pure Land text. The ca. fifth-century *Amitabha Visualization Sutra* enumerated nine ranks of rebirth in the paradise of the west, from "the upper birth of the upper rank," through "the middle birth of the upper rank," downward to the "lower birth of the lower rank." A seventh-century Dunhuang mural depicted them all in the form of babies emanating from nine lotus blossoms.[6] Other artists focused on the process by which the flower is transformed into a divine being. They created a series of images recording the mysterious metamorphosis of the lotus. Dating from as early as the fifth century CE, the Yungang and Longmen caves include numerous examples of these pictorial narratives, showing first a newborn's head peeping from inside the corolla, then the gradual transformation of the petals into the limbs, and finally the release of a full-blown ethereal being, the divinity of which is indicated by a hallow (figure 19).[7] There can be little doubt that these images of horticultural redemption served as the ultimate source for Nezha's floral incarnation. The child's lotus body had been fashioned after the paradisiacal dreams of medieval Buddhism.

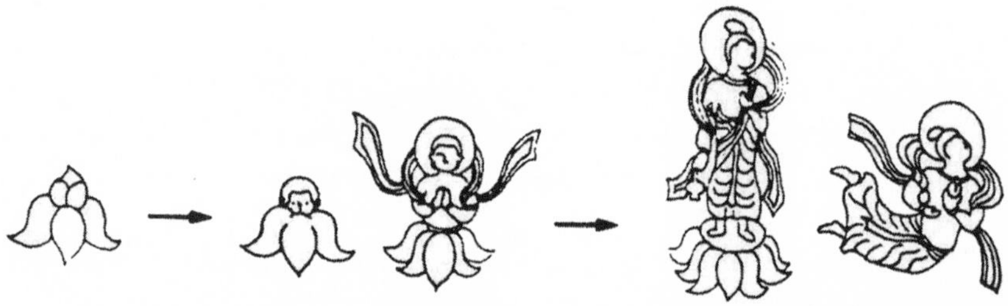

Figure 19: Lotus rebirth as rendered at the fifth-century Yun'gang Caves. From Yoshimura Rei, *Tianren dansheng tu* (Shanghai: Shanghai guji, 2009), p. 23.

Nezha and Miaoshan

The Song period (960–1279) did not leave us a complete version of the Nezha (then "Nazha") legend. Not infrequent references to the disobedient infant, however, indicate that by the eleventh century his story was well known. They suggest, furthermore, that the legend's contours were likely similar to those recorded in *The Journey to the West.* The Song-period story celebrated a child who, returning to his parents the body he owes them, seeks refuge with the Buddha.

We begin with a poem by the scholar official Su Zhe (1039–1112), brother of the renowned literatus Su Shi (1037–1101). Titled "Nazha," it describes the infant as an enlightened Buddhist being. As Su Zhe has it, Nezha's familial sacrifice has won him release from the relentless wheel of life and death. The poem encapsulates the legend's principal features that are familiar from later versions. It summarizes in a nutshell the child's contempt for his biological father, his veneration of the Buddha, and the stupa (pagoda) that the latter has fashioned to discipline him:

> The Northern Heavenly King had a son who was mad:
> He only venerated the Buddha—not his dad.
> The Buddha, knowing he was crazy and hard to be told,
> Ordered the father a magic stupa in his left hand to hold.
>
> Approaching the Buddha, the child bowed his head,
> Not unlike revering his dad.
> The Buddha is as hard to spot as the Uḍumbara Flower,[8]
> Those who meet him, from Samsara released by his power.
>
> Oh, why did you [Nazha] alone get such a chance?
> The barriers of karma are hard to surpass.
> The decline of the dharma eons upon us,
> Amidst rivers and lakes our skiff passes.[9]

Nezha was not the only questionable creature to be disciplined by a pagoda (stupa). The Buddhist emblem had served to quell the White Snake succubus of the Hangzhou legend. The snake transformed herself into an alluring female, preying upon the sex-starved Hangzhou men. She was eventually captured by the Buddhist monk Fahai, who had the ophidian femme fatale imprisoned underneath the Thunder-Peak Pagoda on the shores of the scenic West Lake: "When the West Lake dries up," he intoned. "When rivers and seas are no more; when the Thunder-Peak Pagoda crumbles down; the White Snake will be released."[10] The legend enjoyed great popularity in Hangzhou oral and written fiction. Its earliest record postdating Su Zhe's poem by some three centuries, it might have been influenced by the Nezha legend.[11] The Buddhist stupa's disciplinary function might have been incorporated into the lore of the Hangzhou succubus from the myth of the unruly infant.

Su Zhe was a member of the literati elite, and his poem evinces the laity's familiarity with Nezha (Nazha). Most references to the rebellious infant, however, occur in Song-period monastic writings. Buddhist monks were fascinated by the child who was willing to pay the highest price (suicide) for his spiritual freedom. Allusions to his extraordinary example occur in the *recorded sayings* of several late Tang and early Song Chan masters. The following example is taken from the public dialogues (*gong'an*) of Datong (819–914) as recorded in the *Jingde Records of the Lamp Transmission* (which was completed in 1004). Note the speaker's assumption that the listener (and reader) is acquainted with the story:

> *Question:* "Prince Nazha cut off his bones and returned them to his father. He cut off his flesh and returned it to his mother. Where was Nazha's original self (*benlai shen*)?"
>
> In reply, the master put down his staff.[12]

The dialogue appears to employ the Nezha story to ponder the meaning of the self. In the absence of a physical body, is there an inner entity that obtains enlightenment? For our purpose, the philosophical query is less relevant than the legend that serves to illustrate it. The framework of the fearless child's myth is discernible through the short dialogue: his parting from his parents, his suicide, and his religious awakening. A similar example is provided by the dialogues of the early Song master Deshao (891–972), likewise recorded in the *Jingde Records of the Lamp Transmission:*

> *Question:* "Prince Nazha cut off his flesh and returned it to his mother. He cut off his bones and returned them to his father. Thereupon, he sat on the Lotus Throne, preaching the Dharma to his parents. We wonder, however, how the Prince could have had a self."
>
> The Master replied: "You should all look at the Head Monk."[13]

The Chan masters Datong and Deshao are in accord that Nezha returned his flesh to his mother and his bones to his father. Later versions of the legend similarly note that the bones he handed his father had been scraped of all meat by the courageous infant.[14] Flesh and blood were given back to the mother, whereas the cleansed bones were bequeathed to the father. Chinese cosmology considers the flesh a manifestation of female *yin* power, whereas the bones are regarded as a male *yang* force. Hence the child was expected to repay his flesh to his mother and his bones to his father. In this respect, the legend mirrors Chinese mortuary practices: Double burial is widely practiced in South China. First the corpse is interred in a temporary grave and, after several years, the bones are exhumed for a secondary, permanent, burial. As James Watson has shown, women absorb the pollution of the (flesh-endowed) corpse in the first stage, whereas the men manipulate the bones in the secondary one.[15]

Deshao's brief dialogue introduces yet another element to the story. Following his suicide and religious awakening, Nezha led his parents to enlightenment: "He sat on the Lotus Throne, preaching the Dharma to his parents." The child who had disobeyed his father and mother was apparently recognized as their teacher. It is this further aspect that leads us to consider the similarities between the Nezha myth and another legend that gained currency during the Song period, that of Princess Miaoshan. The two stories revolve around the same tension between filial piety and Buddhist celibacy. Their protagonists defy their parents, only to become their ultimate saviors. Dating from ca. 1100, the legend of Miaoshan may be summarized as follows:

> Miaoshan was a king's youngest daughter. From childhood she displayed Buddhist aspirations, adhering to a vegetarian diet and discoursing on the Dharma. When she came of age, her father decreed her marriage, but she refused, declaring her intention to become a nun. The king sent Miaoshan to a nunnery, ordering the abbess to assign her the hardest chores so as to shake her resolve. However, divine beings assisted her, and the princess remained steadfast. Disavowing his daughter, the enraged father ordered her execution. (In some versions she is miraculously removed from the execution grounds, in others she is burnt to death, but is reincarnated shortly thereafter.)
>
> Years later the king was afflicted by a terrible disease. A prophecy informed him that a remedy made from the eyes and hands of a person with no anger would cure him. A mysterious monk residing in seclusion atop a sacred mountain gouged out his own eyes and severed his own hands to prepare the medicine. The monk turned out to be none other than Miaoshan. Restored to his health, the king came to offer his thanks, whereupon she was revealed to him as the Goddess Guanyin (Avalokiteśvara) of a thousand arms and a thousand eyes. Converting to the Buddhist faith, the king became her devotee.[16]

The similarities between the Miaoshan and the Nezha legends are manifold. From the perspective of art history, the two myths serve an identical etiological function, accounting for their protagonists' iconographic traits. Established centuries earlier, the heroes' visual images are embedded within new mythic frameworks. The Heavenly King, Vaiśravaṇa, had carried a stupa (pagoda) in his left hand from as early as the Tang period. The Nezha myth furnished the reliquary with a disciplinary function, the stupa enabling the father to control his unruly toddler. As for Miaoshan, her myth supplied an etiological explanation for the goddess Avalokiteśvara's Tantric representation with a thousand hands and a thousand eyes (one in each palm). Her ultimate sacrifice of the gouged eyes and the severed limbs won Miaoshan the divine compensation of countless hands and eyes. The stories of the defiant princess and the unruly prince weave long-established iconographies into novel narratives of familial strife.

More pertinent to our discussion is the two myths' identical subject matter. The stories of Miaoshan and Nezha pivot upon the conflict between paternal authority and individual salvation. Their plots unfold according to a similar narrative pattern of defiance (by the child toward his or her parent), death (of the child, by suicide or execution), and finally redemption (of the parent by the child). The offspring disobeys his father and mother only to become their spiritual mentor. Realizing their child's sanctity, the parents' wrath is transformed into reverence. Miaoshan's father becomes her firm devotee, making offerings to her image of a thousand arms and a thousand eyes, whereas Nezha "sits on the Lotus Throne, preaching the Dharma to his parents." Judging by Deshao's *Recorded Sayings,* the Song-period version of the Nezha myth ended, like Miaoshan's, on a note of religious reconciliation.

Their role of apologies for Buddhist monasticism does not diminish the myths' oedipal significance, either in Nezha's or in Miaoshan's case. Wilt Idema has convincingly argued for an incestuous drive underneath the legend of the chaste princess. The king's hatred of his daughter is a reflection of frustrated desire, and his tyranny borders on rape. The sexual undertones are especially clear in versions of the Miaoshan legend that have her disrobed and paraded in front of a jeering audience. The defiant princess is led naked to the execution ground, her female body an object of her father's male gaze. A nineteenth-century rendition has the princess locked in a prison, where she is shackled naked to the wall. Visiting her in the middle of the night, the father tries to tempt her with vivid descriptions of conjugal bliss. Even though his professed intention is to have her marry someone else, his daughter doesn't fail to notice the impropriety of his advances. Disrobed and humiliated, Miaoshan berates her father in terms that leave no doubt as to his deviant drive:

> My father the emperor, dead daddy, you are misled and deluded and unenlightened, and your perverse heart is all ablaze. This is not the behavior of a lord and emperor in possession of the Way! Daddy, you are the ruler of the myriads of people, the lord of the whole nation. If you cannot control your family, how can you control the nation? It you are a Son of Heaven and an emperor of men, in possession of the Way, how would you, a father, ever think of entering this side palace at midnight, in the third watch, and urge your daughter to marry a husband? How would it look if the world came to know of this?[17]

The resemblance of Nezha and Miaoshan extends to their position as siblings. He is the third son, and she is the third daughter. He is preceded by two brothers, she by two sisters. The four elder siblings equally conform to familial norms and social hierarchies. They obey their father and mother, and they exhort their young siblings to be respectful of paternal authority. In the familial conflict between the youngest child and his parents, they side with the latter. All four are filial, but none performs an extraordinary feat of piety as their youngest siblings do. The extremes of defiance and of loyalty alike are reserved for the third child.

The position of the third sibling has been shared by other saints and divinities. Chinese hagiographic literature often attributes spiritual aspirations to a third son or a third daughter, especially if they are of royal blood. The accolade Third Prince or Third Princess turns out to have been bestowed upon quite a few holy persons. The semi-legendary Bodhidharma (fl. ca. 500), reputed founder of the Chan school, has been described as the "third son" of a South Indian king since as early as the eighth century,[18] whereas the Fujianese god of the theater Lei Haiqing (also known as Tiangong Yuanshuai) is considered the Third Prince of no less a parentage than the Jade Emperor's. The honorific has been extended to divine beings of the animal world as well. The fearless horse that Xuanzang rides in his sacred mission to India is an incarnation of the dragon king's Third Prince.[19]

The association of a third sibling with sanctity might have been introduced to China from India. One of the most famous tales of the Buddha's former lives tells how he fed his own body to a starving tigress that, maddened by hunger, was about to devour its own cubs. Canonized in written scriptures and embellished in visual art, the story identified its saintly protagonist as the Third Prince Mahāsattva, son of King Mahāratha.[20] The Indian connection leads us to a consideration of the universal motif. The exceptional third child is a common subject of world folklore. To the readers of English literature the example of King Lear would come to mind. As pointed by Glen Dudbridge, the Shakespeare tragedy shares important motifs with the Miaoshan legend. A father's trust in his elder daughters is in both tales betrayed, and it is the third one—whom he has disavowed—who turns out to be the most loyal. Chinese and English literature appear to celebrate in this instance the common motif of the rejected third offspring who proves worthier than her elder siblings.[21]

Tang-Period Antecedents

Among the thousands of documents discovered a century ago in Chinese Central Asia is a short manuscript commemorating the completion of a Dunhuang cave. Dating from the first half of the tenth century, the handwritten document describes the murals in the newly dedicated grotto:

> As one exits the cave there is on both sides a painting of the Eight Dragon Kings and of the God Vaiśravaṇa attending the Nazha assembly. . . . The Dragon Kings are shown in the ocean. They constantly inspect the water supply. They sprinkle sweet dew in due

> times. They bring forth wind and rain according to the seasons. Vaiśravaṇa brought along the Buddha Amitabha to attend Nazha's assembly. [They] did not arrive on time, whereupon Nazha drew his sword, getting ready to kill. Realizing that Amitabha was coming, Nazha's heart was joyful.[22]

The tenth-century description of the Dunhuang mural rings familiar to those acquainted with the Nezha myth of later periods. The cast of characters is largely identical: the hot-tempered infant, his father (the Heavenly King Vaiśravaṇa), the dragon kings, and the Buddha (even though he is identified not as Śākyamuni or Tathāgata, but rather as the Buddha Amitabha). Particularly tantalizing is the reference to the child's murderous intentions. Why did he draw his sword, and whom did he intend to kill? Guo Junye, who has studied the manuscript in conjunction with other Dunhuang documents, suggests that he was planning to kill his father. Relying upon visual representations and their accompanying cartouches, she has reconstructed the following Tang tale, which might have been related to the Nezha myth of later periods: The child prepared a Dharma assembly. When no guest arrived for the religious feast, he suspected his father was to blame, and he prepared to kill him. The father, however, did appear eventually, bringing with him—inside his pagoda—no lesser a guest than the Buddha Amitabha. Nazha's anger was transformed into delight, and the violent confrontation was suspended.[23]

Guo Junye draws upon several Dunhuang cartouches that mention the tale's protagonists. The following two date from the late Tang (ca. ninth century): "The Great Saint of the North, the Heavenly King Vaiśravaṇa, invited the Buddha Amitabha of the Western Paradise to enter the stupa and attend the Nazha assembly"; and "The Buddha Amitabha of the Western Paradise entered the stupa and attended Nazha's Dharma assembly."[24] In addition, she has identified forty-six extant Dunhuang murals and drawings that accord with the written traces of the tale. In various configurations, the paintings appear to render the story of the child's Dharma assembly. Some murals show the Heavenly King holding in both hands the pagoda, to which a young person (presumably Nezha) is paying homage. Floating on the clouds above them is a heavenly retinue, likely of the Buddha Amitabha, who is heading toward the pagoda. Other paintings are more explicit still, showing a small Buddha figure (presumably Amitabha) within the Heavenly King's stupa.

The written evidence for Guo's reconstructed tale is limited. It includes no more than the above-mentioned traces. It might be argued, therefore, that she has read back the pattern of the later Nezha myth into the Tang-period excerpts. Nevertheless, the brief passages she has unearthed are intriguing, not only because they feature the same protagonists as the legend of later periods, but also because they elaborate upon the same ritual emblem. We have seen that in *The*

Journey to the West, the pagoda serves to remind Nezha of his obligation to the Buddha. It is by means of the sacred reliquary that the unruly infant is controlled in all known versions of the myth. Similarly the Dunhuang cartouches (and paintings) give the stupa central stage as the object that negotiates the triangular relations between the child, the father, and the Buddha. Amitabha is revealed to the child within the very pagoda that the father wields, as the ninth-century inscription specifies: "The Great Saint of the North, the Heavenly King Vaiśravaṇa, invited the Buddha Amitabha of the Western Paradise to enter the stupa and attend the Nazha assembly." The resonance with the Nezha legend of later periods is unmistakable.

The tale of Nezha's Dharma assembly has been reconstructed on the basis of late Tang materials. Guo Junye relies upon written documents that are traceable to the ninth and tenth centuries. The paintings she has examined likewise date from the ninth century onward. Their significant number (more than forty murals and drawings) indicate that the story they render must have been well known, at least in the Dunhuang region of northwest China. It is not impossible, therefore, that the triangle of the child, the biological father, and the spiritual progenitor originated in the story of the child who invited the Buddha to his Dharma assembly. The late imperial legend of the unruly Nezha might be related to the Tang-period tale, the traces of which have been unearthed at Dunhuang.

We have traced the troubled history of Nezha's familial relations to the late Tang period. How, in the first place, did he and his father come to figure in the Chinese imagination? What might have been the reasons for the fervent medieval belief in Vaiśravaṇa and his rebellious infant? The next chapter examines the role of esoteric Buddhism in shaping the Asian cult of the oedipal pair.

8

Esoteric Buddhism

Nezha made his debut on the Chinese stage in ritual scriptures that were translated from the Sanskrit during the Tang period (618–907). Even though he had occasionally been mentioned in earlier Buddhist writings, these were seventh- and eighth-century masters such as Vajrabodhi (Jin'gangzhi) (671–741) and Amoghavajra (Bukong jingang) (704–774) who first equipped the young god with the rounded personality that was to shape his Chinese cult for future generations. Their massive ritual compendiums mirrored a new phase in Buddhist history, which is commonly referred to as "Tantric" or "esoteric." (I employ the two terms interchangeably.)[1]

Tantric ritual harnesses the powers of the gods for the practitioner's service. Esoteric Buddhist scriptures feature a vast panoply of deities, many originating like Nezha in pre-Buddhist India. The gods grant the devotee enlightenment and superhuman strength. They guide him toward religious salvation, even as they cater to his mundane needs. The skilled adept might manipulate the gods to combat enemy troops and the demons of disease, as well as to increase his sexual prowess and worldly riches. Handling the Tantric divinities requires familiarity with their iconographic attributes. In order to activate their divine might, the practitioner must be able to visualize the gods in meditation. Hence, Tantric scriptures are replete with iconographic data. The precise likeness of the gods is rendered in writing and in drawing alike. The earliest Chinese descriptions of Nezha's visual image occur in esoteric Buddhist scriptures.

Tantric literature details the ritual tools that are appropriate for summoning a given deity. In order to enlist the god's services, the adept must be familiar with his or her individual *mudrā, mantra,* and *maṇḍala*. The *mudrās* (of which there are hundreds) are symbolic gestures that are made with the fingers (of one or both hands). The *maṇḍala* is a mystical map of the divine realm, which determines the layout of the god's altar. Finally, the *mantra* is an oral spell by means of which the practitioner summons the deity, making its divine powers manifest. The term *mantra* is usually reserved for short charms of several syllables only, whereas the term *dhāraṇī* designates long spells, which sometimes amount to hundreds or even thousands of syllables. Often devoid of semantic meaning, the charm's power lies in its phonetic value. Hence Tang-period masters were careful to transcribe rather than translate the Tantric spells. Many of the esoteric scriptures that feature Nezha are nothing but spells for summoning him. Known as *dhāraṇī* sutras, the bulk of the text is made up of a Sanskrit charm. A Chinese-language preface elaborates upon the merit that will accrue to the practitioner by its proper recital.

Nezha appeared in early esoteric scriptures not in his own right but as his father's messenger. The Tantric masters were interested in him in the first place as one who would intervene on their behalf with the Heavenly King of the North. Hence we commence our discussion of the Tantric Nezha with the god of which he was an offspring angel—Vaiśravaṇa.

The Father

Among the most prominent pan-Asian divinities, Vaiśravaṇa's cult originated three thousand years ago in Vedic India. By the time the great epics were composed—in the middle of the first millennium BCE—his position as a god of wealth and of war had been firmly established. The Indian deity was adopted by the Buddhist faith, and during the first centuries CE his cult spread to East Asia. Originally known as Kubera, Buddhist authors usually referred to him by the name Vaiśravaṇa (Pāli: Vessavaṇa), a patronymic meaning "son of Viśravaṇa." Its etymology related to "sharp of hearing" (from the Sanskrit verb *vi-śru*), the name was translated into Chinese as Duowen Tian (Much-Hearing Deva). It was usually transliterated as Pishamen (Japanese: Bishamon).

In the *Rāmāyana* and *Mahābhārata,* Vaiśravaṇa is the Lord of and Giver of Wealth (Dhanapati, Dhaneśvara, or Dhanada). The god of riches resides in the sumptuous Ālaka Palace, which is appointed with all luxuries. He relaxes in the fabulous Caitraratha gardens, the trees of which are covered with jewels, and he rides the magnificent Puṣpaka aerial chariot, which is drawn by geese as swift as thought. In addition to his legendary wealth, Vaiśravaṇa possesses great strength. He is the mighty lord of the awesome *yakṣa* spirits, which inhabit the waters.[2] The semidivine, semidemonic creatures have held a spell upon the Asian imagination. Their Sanskrit name transcribed into Chinese as *yaocha* or *yecha,* they have been celebrated in Chinese lore all through modern times. The renowned fighting monks of the Shaolin Monastery, for example, named two of their martial techniques Big Yakṣa and Small Yakṣa.[3]

Vaiśravaṇa leads his mighty *yakṣa* troops from the north. The Sanskrit epics had him reside on the northern slopes of the mythic Mount Meru, the location of which was inherited by Buddhist authors. Vaiśravaṇa became the Heavenly King of the North, one of the four Buddhist Lokapālas (World Rulers) associated respectively with the cardinal points. His northern connection was likely one reason for the god's appeal to Chinese warriors. As early as the first centuries BCE, the north had been associated in the Chinese imagination with fighting skills. The Daoist martial god Zhenwu (True Warrior) had been known as the Emperor of the North (Beidi). His spatial connection according with the native conception of martial heroism, Vaiśravaṇa was incorporated into the Chinese pantheon as a god of war.[4]

Buddhist scriptures highlighted Vaiśravaṇa's role as state protector. Translated into Chinese in the early fifth century, the *Sutra of Golden Light* has the Heavenly King of the North declare in the first person his commitment to the kingdom's safety and its ruler's well-being. The Four Heavenly Kings, he explains, follow incognito the sacred scripture, and in whichever kingdom it is recited, they stand guard by the king, averting calamities both natural and human-made. Thus, the *Sutra of Golden Light* guarantees the king's personal fortunes no less than his kingdom's affluence. Enemy troops, Vaiśravaṇa vouchsafes, would be destroyed even before their arrival at the country's borders.[5]

War looms large in the Tantric imagination of divinity. As Michel Strickmann has shown, the rhetoric of esoteric Buddhism is replete with violence.[6] The Tantric practitioner summons warrior deities to battle demons ranging from enemy troops to the agents of disease. Hence the fearful Vaiśravaṇa rose to prominence in the Tantric pantheon. Esoteric scriptures detail the recipes for enlisting the Heavenly King's military aid. As indicated by its title, *The Mantra of the Heavenly King of the North Vaiśravaṇa Who Follows the Army* divulges the oral spell that, if recited a hundred thousand times, would annihilate enemy forces. Translated by the eighth-century Amoghavajra, the esoteric scripture enumerates the ritual steps that would ensure the god's assistance in battle. These include guidelines for painting the golden-armored divinity, as well as instructions for the kinds of foodstuffs and perfumes (frankincense) that should be offered him.[7]

The Tantric claims for Vaiśravaṇa's military efficacy were readily embraced by medieval Asian rulers. The locations of his ubiquitous shrines were one indication of the Heavenly King's protective function. Beginning in the eighth century, Vaiśravaṇa icons were placed on Chinese city walls, warding off enemy troops and marauding bandits. His shrines were commonly established in military barracks and government compounds, usually at their northwest corner.[8] The martial god offered similar protection to Japanese cities. During the early tenth-century Tengyō rebellion, a Vaiśravaṇa statue was placed at the southern main gate of the capital city Kyoto. It was later moved to the Dharma King's Temple of State Protection (Kyō-ō gokokuji), currently known as the Tōji Temple.[9]

The cult of the martial god penetrated all layers of medieval Chinese society, his attraction leaving its mark on the very bodies of his sturdy clientele. Wrestlers and criminals bore Vaiśravaṇa tattoos, hoping to be empowered by his divine might. Duan Chengshi (ca. 803–863) tells of his servant "who had the image of the

Heavenly King tattooed on his back, saying that it gives him divine strength. . . . On the first and the fifteenth of the lunar month, he would prepare milk-porridge. Sitting bare-chested, he would instruct his wife and children to make offerings and worship his back." The Tang author adds that "the riffraff of Shu (Sichuan) liked to brag and fight, often being thrown into jail. Their entire backs were covered with tattoos of the Heavenly King Vaiśravaṇa. Seeing his image, the guards would not dare cane their backs."[10]

Vaiśravaṇa's twin aspects of wealth and war shaped his iconography. As a god of wealth, he sported a corpulent physique. Bedecked with jewels, he was shown holding (in his left hand) a moneybag, a purse, or a gem-spitting mongoose. The small carnivore became a symbol of riches because in ancient India its fur had been used to make purses.[11] In China, the god's mongoose was sometimes conceived of as a mouse (the Sanskrit *nakula* [mongoose] being translated into Chinese as *shu* [mouse]). The mousy symbol of riches was attached to other deities as well. Iyanaga Nobumi has shown that the Japanese Mahākāla (Daikokuten) is associated—like Vaiśravaṇa—with mice. The god of fortune is surrounded by the little rodents, who serve as his harbingers of prosperity.[12]

The ultimate Buddhist treasure is a relic of Śakyamuni's body (bone, tooth, hair, or ashes), which is commonly stored in a stupa (pagoda). It is perhaps for this reason that the Buddhist reliquary has been added to the iconography of the god of riches. Beginning in the Tang Dynasty (618–907), Vaiśravaṇa was often shown holding a stupa, his gem-spitting mongoose (or mouse) being relegated for one of his attendants to carry (figure 20). We have seen in preceding chapters that the Nezha myth sought retroactively to explain the Buddhist emblem. Assigned a disciplinary function, the pagoda allows the father to control his unruly infant.

The Heavenly King's iconography highlights his military prowess as much as his fabulous wealth. In the Dunhuang grottoes, Vaiśravaṇa usually figures as a warrior divinity that stands guard at the cave's entrance. Frescoes, paintings on silk, and prints—dozens of which were discovered at the Central Asian oasis—have him clad in armor and wielding a sword, a spear, or a trident. Many icons combine the emblems of wealth and of war, with the mighty god carrying them both. The ferocious-looking Vaiśravaṇa might hold the stupa in his left hand and the sword or spear in his right, or the weapon might be suspended from his belt, visible under his armor (see chapter 2, figure 2).[13]

Vaiśravaṇa's Chinese cult had been localized through the identification of the Indian god with a historical Chinese warrior. Li Jing (571–649) was a renowned general who had led the Tang armies to numerous victories in China and Central Asia. Shortly after his death, the heroic warrior became the object of a religious cult, which flourished into the Song period (960–1279). The general's military exploits were celebrated in a large body of oral and written fiction, which gradually

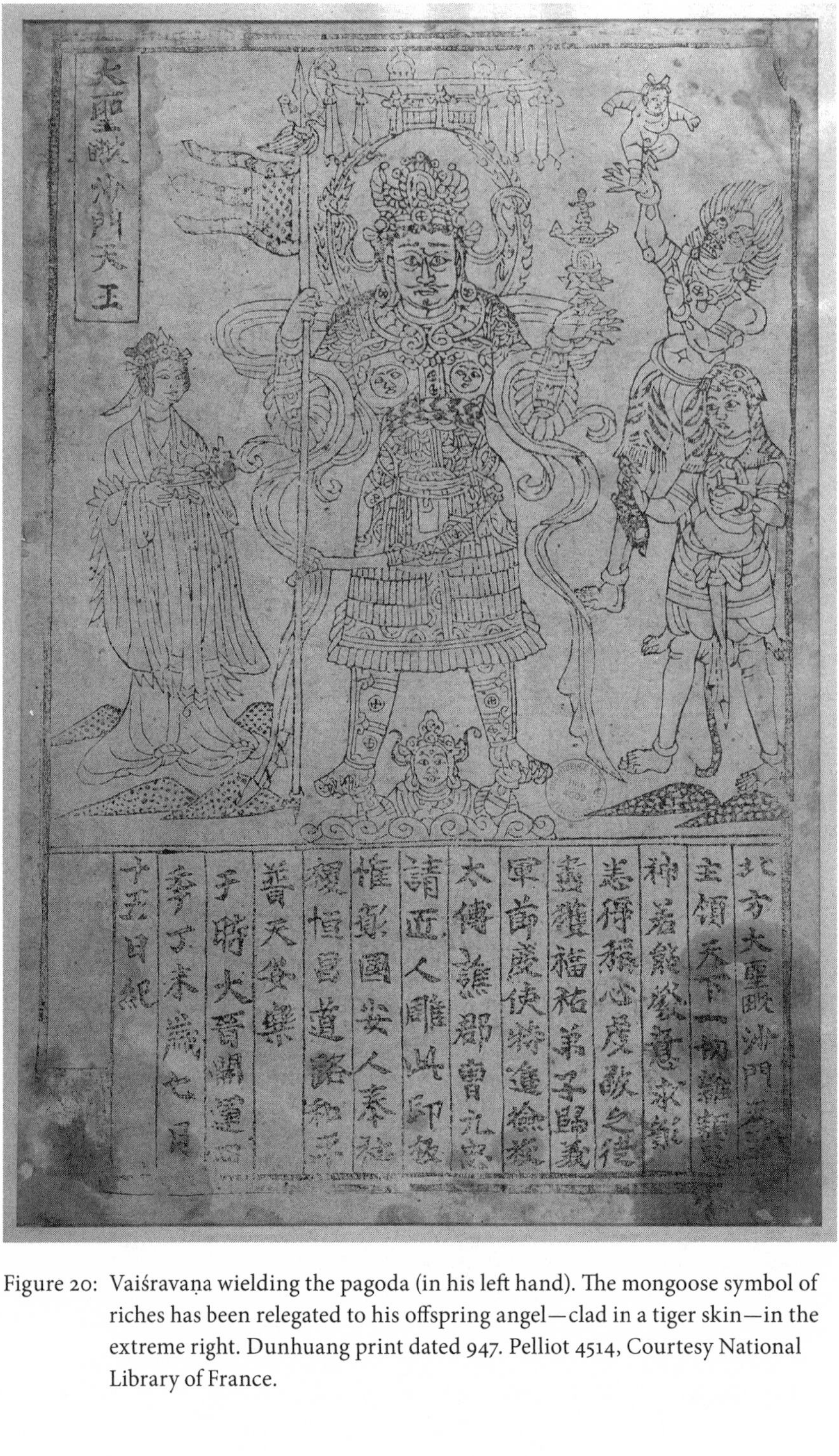

Figure 20: Vaiśravaṇa wielding the pagoda (in his left hand). The mongoose symbol of riches has been relegated to his offspring angel—clad in a tiger skin—in the extreme right. Dunhuang print dated 947. Pelliot 4514, Courtesy National Library of France.

associated him with the Indian god. Storytellers and playwrights merged the Tang general with the martial Heavenly King.[14] Thus, the historical general—who might well have been a Vaiśravaṇa devotee—was identified with the object of his cult. The emergence of the composite figure of the Heavenly King Li Jing might be interpreted within the framework of the Chinese naturalization of Buddhism. Tansen Sen has demonstrated the significance of sacred geography in the transformation of China into a Buddhist paradise. Chinese monks identified within their own borders the holy dwelling places of the Indian gods. Vaiśravaṇa's history demonstrates that the foreign gods themselves were recognized as Chinese.[15]

The formidable Vaiśravaṇa had served as the tutelary deity of Khotan (Chinese: Hetian) (in today's western Xinjiang), whose kings considered themselves his descendants. The founding myth of the Khotanese royal house survives in Chinese and Tibetan records alike. According to the former, the ancestor of the Khotanese kings had prayed to the martial god for an offspring, whereupon—like Athena springing out of Zeus's head—Vaiśravaṇa's statue broke open and a baby emerged from its forehead. The king took the baby home to the great delight of his subjects. He was obliged, however, to return to the temple, as the divine infant refused to feed on mortal milk. Responding to his supplications, the earth underneath the god's statue bulged in the form of a nipple, suckling the child.[16]

Tibetan records of the Khotanese myth provide the same etiological explanation for the kingdom's Sanskrit name Ku-Stana (literally, "earth nipple"), but their version of the preceding events differs. The Indian king Dharmāśoka, they have it, traveled to Khotan and camped at the site of its future capital. Taking a bath in a lotus pond, his chief consort beheld the Heavenly King leading his triumphant procession across the sky. Pondering the image of the handsome god, she conceived, giving birth to a beautiful son. Fearing that he would depose him, King Dharmāśoka had the baby cast in the desert, whereupon the earth broke open and a teat emerged to suckle the infant.[17]

His Khotanese offspring was one of many. Diverse Buddhist authors had attributed to Vaiśravaṇa dozens of sons. The Pāli *Dīgha Nikāya*, for instance, had him sire no fewer than ninety-one (the number was occasionally reduced in later sources to five).[18] Some of the Heavenly King's princes had been identified in Sanskrit literature (and in its Chinese translation) by name: Janeśa, Maṇibhadra, and this book's protagonist Nalakūbara (Chinese: Nezha) are examples. Others were referred to more generically as a Vaiśravaṇa "son" or "heir apparent" (Sanskrit: *kumāra;* Chinese: *tongzi* or *taizi*). A medieval manuscript discovered at the Central Asian Dunhuang grottoes divulges the "Mantra of the Vaiśravaṇa Clever Heir-Apparent." The spell activates the awesome powers of the Heavenly King's offspring, who is not identified by name.[19]

A heart-rending tale of an unnamed Vaiśravaṇa offspring is included in a twelfth-century Chinese anthology. In his *Record of Hearsay,* Hong Mai (1123–

1202) tells of young girl who fell in love with a handsome stranger. The uninvited youth settled in her house, bestowing mind-boggling riches upon her parents. Suspecting his daughter's wooer to be a ghost, the father invited a Daoist to exorcize him. The Daoist reminded the gallant youth of the unsurpassable gap that must separate mortals from immortals. He ordered him to leave, not before mentioning that had it not been for the latter's father, the Heavenly King of the North, he would have petitioned his arrest. The girl is left to lament her divine lover, whose first name is not disclosed.[20]

Tantric scriptures assigned his offspring the role of messengers for the Heavenly King. Vaiśravaṇa communicates with his devotees by means of his children. His sons distribute the Heavenly King's wealth to the faithful, even as they assist his devotees in the battlefield. The following section outlines the functions of his offspring in the Vaiśravaṇa cult before turning to the one who was to achieve the greatest Chinese fame: Nezha.

The Tantric Angels

Angels figure prominently in the Western monotheistic faiths. God being occupied and important, the winged cherubs take care of his faithful's daily concerns. The etymology of the term (from the Greek *angelos* [messenger]) betrays its significance of dispatch bearer. In the Jewish, the Christian, and the Islamic traditions alike, the angels serve to communicate the devotees' needs to the almighty. In much the same way, Tantric Buddhism has assigned its principal divinities a bevy of young envoys, who are often identified as their offspring.[21] Vaiśravaṇa is a case in point. The Heavenly King's twin aspects of wealth and war are administered by his sons, who act as his angels. We begin with the former.

Vaiśravaṇa's wealth is dispensed by his offspring angels. The god's children function as his messengers, bestowing riches upon the Tantric practitioner. Esoteric scriptures dating from the Tang period provide detailed instructions for summoning Vaiśravaṇa's familial deputies. Those who recite the proper spell, draw the correct ritual diagram (*maṇḍala*), and execute the appropriate hand gesture (*mudrā*) are blessed by the apparition of Vaiśravaṇa's sons, who distribute their father's wealth. A detailed description is provided in Amoghavajra's (704–774) *Sutra of the Heavenly King Vaiśravaṇa*, which is careful to note that the riches thus obtained should be used in a proper Buddhist fashion:

> If the practitioner recites the [Vaiśravaṇa] mantra often and without interruption, the son of the Heavenly King Vaiśravaṇa will come to him. Named She'ni'suo, the son will assume the appearance of a youth (*tongzi*). He will address the practitioner: "Why are you calling for my father?" The practitioner should reply: "I need the riches to make offerings to the Three Jewels [the Buddha, the Dharma, and the Sangha]." The youth

> She'ni'suo will immediately hasten back to his father, reporting to the Heavenly King Vaiśravaṇa: "The practitioner requires riches to make offerings, thereby benefitting all sentient beings." The Heavenly King will instruct the youth She'ni'suo: "Until the rest of his days, you should bestow upon him one hundred gold coins daily." Hence, the child She'ni'suo will each day place a hundred gold coins by the practitioner's head. The coins emit a wondrous aroma.[22]

An identical procedure for summoning Vaiśravaṇa's angel of fortune is outlined in the writings of the Tantric master Vajrabodhi (671–741), except that the messenger's name differs slightly. Whereas Amoghavajra identifies the Heavenly King's son as She'ni'suo, Vajrabodhi has Chan'ni'shi.[23] That both appellations allude to the same Vaiśravaṇa offspring had been pointed out as early as the eighth century by the Buddhist lexicographer Huilin (737–820).[24] She'ni'suo, Chan'ni'shi, and the additional variant She'ni'sha are alike transcriptions of the Sanskrit Janeśa (Pāli: Janavasabha), who is mentioned as his father's envoy in early Buddhist scriptures. In the *Longer Āgama Sutra* (*Dīrgha Āgama*) the Heavenly King of the North Vaiśravaṇa dispatches his son Janeśa as a messenger to his counterpart, the Heavenly King of the South Virūḍhaka. The Heavenly King's angel is described as exceedingly strong, his name taken as an expression of his might: The Pāli Janavasabha means "Bull of the People."[25]

The significance of his offspring angels is reflected in the arrangement of the Vaiśravaṇa altar. The mandalas of the Heavenly King often have him flanked by his familial envoys. An example is furnished by the Japanese priest Shōchō's (1205–1281) *Asaba shō* (Anthology of A, Sa, and Va). Reflective of the Tantric tradition as practiced by the Tendai School, the anthology reproduces a Vaiśravaṇa mandala, which is followed by instructions for the worship of the Heavenly King and his kin. Vaiśravaṇa is surrounded (in the back row) by his colleagues, the Heavenly Kings of the South, East, and West, and (in the front row) by his family members, including (from right to left) his mother-in-law Hārītī, his wife Śrīdevī, and his offspring messengers, identified as the "child Chan'ni'[shi] and the rest."[26] Recall that the transcription Chan'ni'shi (Japanese: Zennishi) was chosen by Vajrabodhi for Vaiśravaṇa's son Janeśa.

Shōchō's mandala offers a key for the interpretation of a recurrent motif in medieval Buddhist art. The Tantric configuration of the Heavenly King and family is mirrored in numerous artworks from Central Asia, China, and Japan. Beginning in the Tang period, Vaiśravaṇa was often shown flanked by his consort Śrīdevī and a youth, whom we are now permitted to identify as his offspring angel. Some icons featured as well the mother-in-law Hārītī, as proscribed by Shōchō. This is the case with a print discovered at Dunhuang and dated 947 (Pelliot 4514) (see above, figure 20). Donning armor and bearing his iconic stupa (pagoda) and spear, the Heavenly King is supported by the goddess of the earth, Pṛthivī. He is flanked (on his left) by his consort Śrīdevī (Chinese: Jixiang tiannü) and (on his right) by his child messenger. Farther back is Śrīdevī's mother, the demonic Hārītī (Chinese: Helidi).[27] The "Mother of Demons" (Chinese: Guizi mu), as she was nicknamed, used to feed on the children of Rājagṛha, who turned to the Buddha for help. The World-Honored One taught the ogress a lesson, kidnapping her youngest and most beloved infant. Hiding him under his begging bowl, he had the ogress repent for her sins. Hārītī ceased to devour other people's children, converting to the faith instead. The female fiend was incorporated into the Buddhist pantheon, illustrating its indebtedness to Indian mythology. It was not uncommon for rehabilitated Hindu demons to become Buddhist guardian divinities.[28]

Vaiśravaṇa's familial configuration had been a favorite topic of Central Asian Buddhist art. Dunhuang murals, paintings on silk, and prints feature the Heavenly King's kin. Dating from the eighth century onward, the artworks betray the role of the Vaiśravaṇa offspring as his father's angel of wealth (compare figures 20 and 21). The youth is shown holding the gem-spitting mongoose, which as early as the first centuries CE had served as the Heavenly King's emblem of riches. (Recall that the Sanskrit term for the purse, *nakulaka,* derived from the *nakula* [mongoose] fur of which it had been made.) The Heavenly King's paintings could be taken as visual representations of the rituals for the summoning of his offspring angels. Carrying his father's icon of riches, the offspring messenger is about to deliver it to the faithful. Awaiting Vaiśravaṇa's command, he will distribute the Heavenly King's wealth to the pious practitioners. Tang-period murals, paintings, and prints attest to Vaiśravaṇa's reliance on his angels of fortune.

Scholars have noted the unique tiger gear that is worn by the Vaiśravaṇa angel. The Heavenly King's messenger is draped in the beast's pelt, its head serving as his helmet. The tiger's ears, eyes, and fangs protrude above the messenger's head. Its paws are crossed under his chin, and its tail is visible between the angel's legs (see figures 20 and 21). The outfit has been the subject of a scholarly dispute. Some art historians believe that it originated in the Tibetan custom of awarding heroes a tiger pelt. The Tibetans ruled Dunhuang from 781 through 848 and their tiger-skin trophies had been extensively recorded in contemporaneous Chinese sources. The motif might therefore reflect the impact of Tibetan culture on Tang-period Chinese art.[29] In contrast, some historians have sought its origins further afield. Hsing I-Tien has argued that the tiger-clad messenger had been fashioned after the lion-draped Heracles, whose image had been brought to Central Asia by Alexander the Great (356–323 BCE). The Greek hero is similarly draped in the beast's skin, its head serving as his helmet. The paws are likewise tied under the warrior's chin, the tail protruding between his legs. Even though the feline differs (lion rather than tiger), Hsing believes that the quintessential outfit made of its pelt might have influenced Central Asian, Tibetan, and Chinese art.[30]

Figure 21:
Vaiśravaṇa, attendant, and mongoose, line drawing by Hsing I-Tien, after Tang-period painting (Stein painting 38). From Hsing I-Tien, "Heracles in the East: The Diffusion and Transformation of His Image in the Arts of Central Asia, India, and Medieval China," *Asia Major,* Third Series 18, no. 2 (2005): p. 141.

The trinity of Vaiśravaṇa, consort, and offspring angel spread from the Dunhuang grottoes eastward. It is apparent in the ninth-century rock carvings from Dazu (Sichuan) and in the famed *Scroll of Buddhist Images* (*Hua fan xiang juan*), which was painted during the late twelfth century at the Dali Kingdom of Yun'nan.[31] Farther to the east, the Heavenly King's family became a favorite topic of Japanese art. Beginning in the late Heian period, statues of Vaiśravaṇa (Japanese: Bishamon), his wife Śrīdevī (Japanese: Kichijōten), and his son (identified as Zennishi) had graced numerous Buddhist, and even Shinto, shrines. Among the finest surviving examples are the eleventh-century statues at the famed Kurama-dera Temple in the northern outskirts of Kyoto (figure 22). Shading his eyes, the imposing Heavenly King gazes southward at the capital city, of which he has been considered the guardian divinity. Clad in armor and wielding a

Figure 22: Vaiśravaṇa, Śrīdevī, and offspring. Eleventh-century statues from the Kurama-dera Monastery, Kyoto. From *Kurama-dera no meihō* (Kyoto: Kurama-dera, 1986).

mighty spear, he is flanked on his left by his consort and on his right by his offspring messenger. Śrīdevī (Kichijōten) is holding a wish-granting jewel (Sanskrit: *cintā-maṇi*), as she forms the *mudrā* of charity (Sanskrit: *varada*). Her son carries a small box containing, presumably, his father's riches.[32]

The Japanese temples that feature him identify Vaiśravaṇa's son as the "child Zennishi" (Zennishi Dōji). We have noted that in his thirteenth-century mandala, the Tendai priest Shōchō alluded to the Heavenly King's offspring by the same name. It appears that of the various appellations associated with Vaiśravaṇa's angels the one that caught the Japanese fancy was Janeśa, transcribed into Chinese as Chan'ni'shi and pronounced in Japanese Zennishi. Heian- and Kamakura-period representations of Janeśa (Zennishi) differ from their Central Asian prototypes in their rendition of his emblem of wealth. Whereas in Dunhuang art the Vaiśravaṇa offspring wields a gem-spitting mongoose (or mouse), in Japanese art he carries a small box, which we might presume is full of hidden treasures.

Angels of War

Much as his financial affairs have been entrusted to them, Vaiśravaṇa relies upon his offspring to command his armies. His numerous sons lead the Heavenly King's *yakṣa* troops to battle. The most detailed account is the *Rituals of Vaiśravaṇa,* which, although attributed to Amoghavajra (704–774), was likely authored by his disciples. The text records an attack on China's borders, which supposedly took place during the master's lifetime. Summoned to court, Amoghavajra conducted in the emperor's presence an esoteric ritual, in response to which Vaiśravaṇa dispatched his son to battle. The Heavenly King's offspring was put in command of the divine troops that repelled the foreign aggressors:

> During the first year of the Tang Dynasty's Tianbao reign (742), the town of Anxi (in today's Xinjiang) was attacked by five foreign states, including Arabia and Samarkand. On the eleventh of the second lunar month an envoy arrived at the capital, asking for military support. The emperor informed the Chan Master Yixing, "Monk! Arabia, Samarkand and the other states are besieging Anxi. An envoy has arrived asking for military support. However, Anxi is twelve thousand miles away. The troops would require eight months to reach it. I have no way of helping them." Yixing replied, "Why does not Your Highness request reinforcement by the divine troops of the Heavenly King of the North, Pishamen [Vaiśravaṇa]?" The emperor asked, "How can I summon them?" Yixing replied, "You should call for the foreign monk Amoghavajra to summon them." Amoghavajra was promptly called for. When he entered the Inner Palace he said, "Hasn't the emperor summoned me because of the armies of the rebellious five states, who are besieging Anxi?" "Yes," replied the emperor. Amoghavajra said, "Your highness should hold an incense burner and enter the mandala (*daochang*). I will summon the Heavenly King's divine troops to help you."
>
> Having entered the mandala, and before Amoghavajra had repeated the mantra twenty-seven times, the emperor suddenly beheld two or three hundred divine beings (*shenren*). Bearing armor, they entered the mandala. "Who are these people?" the emperor asked Amoghavajra. "This is Dujian, the second son of the Heavenly King of the North Vaiśravaṇa," replied Amoghavajra. "Leading his divine troops, he came to bid you farewell before heading for Anxi." The emperor made him offerings, and sent him on his way. Later, on the [first day] of the fourth month, an envoy arrived from Anxi, reporting, "On the eleventh of the second month, during the morning hours, dark clouds and mists appeared some thirty miles northeast of Anxi. A ten-foot-tall person emerged from the clouds, leading between three to five hundred soldiers, all clad in golden armor. By evening, the blasts of horns and drums sounded. The din was heard three hundred miles away. The earth shook and the mountains trembled for three days. The five invading armies were terrified and retreated. Their camps col-

> lapsed. . . . In addition golden mice bit asunder the strings of their bows and crossbows. The enemy's weapons were all damaged beyond repair.[33]

The *Rituals of Vaiśravaṇa* identifies the offspring who repelled the western barbarians as the Heavenly King's second son Dujian (the Sanskrit origins of whose name are uncertain).[34] The latter is recognized as his father's angel of war in another Amoghavajra scripture, *The Mantra of the Heavenly King of the North, Vaiśravaṇa, Who Follows the Army, Protecting the Dharma*. Its very title betrays the scripture's warlike spirit, which might be taken as emblematic of esoteric Buddhism. Paul Demiéville has noted that the *Mantra of the Heavenly King*'s martial protagonists resemble the Homeric gods in their military engagements.[35] The chief warrior in the esoteric scripture is Vaiśravaṇa's heir apparent Dujian. Amoghavajra guarantees that the prince will assist his devotees in battle: "If the practitioner is capable of reciting [Vaiśravaṇ's] mantra day and night without interruption, the Heavenly King will dispatch his Heir Apparent Dujian. Leading one thousand heavenly troops, Dujian will protect the practitioner, staying by his side. If he wishes anything, the practitioner should just say so, for [Dujian] to obtain it."[36]

The story of Dujian's defeat of the western barbarians has enjoyed great popularity in Buddhist circles. Retold by Chinese and Japanese authors alike, it contributed to the military renown of the Vaiśravaṇa offspring.[37] Nonetheless, the story is historically unfounded. Scholars have pointed out the numerous inconsistencies that belie the possibility of Amoghavajra displaying—on that occasion—the might of his divine patrons. There is no historical evidence of a foreign attack on Anxi in 742; Amoghavajra was at the time in Ceylon, so he could not summon the Heavenly King; and Yixing (683–727) was long dead, so he could not recommend the Tantric master to the emperor.[38] In all likelihood the legend was created by Amoghavajra's disciples, who were striving to enhance the reputation of their deceased master no less than the prestige of the magic techniques he had bequeathed them.

The role of mice in Dujian's victory is noteworthy. His father's mousy emblem of riches has acquired a military function, with the enemy weapons being destroyed by the mysterious rodents: "Golden mice bit asunder the strings of their bows and crossbows. The enemy's weapons were all damaged beyond repair." Recall that the Heavenly King's symbol of wealth—the Indian gem-spitting mongoose—has been conceived of in China as a gem-spitting mouse (*tubao shu*), which in this instance has been drafted to assist its lord in battle. The belief in the military efficacy of the Vaiśravaṇa mice is similarly attested by Xuanzang's (602–664) account of their role in Khotan's defense. The king of Khotan (himself a Vaiśravaṇa descendant) made offerings to the awesome desert rats that defeated an invading Xiongnu army: "[The enemy soldiers] hastened to harness their horses and equip their chariots, but they found that the leather of their armor, and their horses' gear, and their bow strings, and all the fastenings of their clothes, had been gnawed by the rats."[39]

The Heavenly King's sons battle the demons of disease as much as they battle enemy troops. When the Japanese emperor Daigo (reigned 893–930) fell gravely ill, he was healed by Vaiśravaṇa's child emissary. The story is handsomely illustrated in a twelfth-century painted scroll, *The Legends of Mount Shigi* (*Shigisan-engi*). The dying emperor sought the help of the Shingon monk Myōren at his shrine atop Mount Shigi. Conducting an esoteric ritual, Myōren summoned the Heavenly King, whereupon a child dressed in armor—presumably Vaiśravaṇa's son—appeared in the sickroom. Identified as the Sword-Protector of the Dharma (Ken no gohō), the child cured the emperor. The elegant scroll has the infant war-

Figure 23: Vaiśravaṇa's angel, the Sword-Protector of the Dharma, from the twelfth-century *Shigisanengi*. From Komatsu Shigemi, ed., *Shigisanengi emaki* (Tokyo: Chuuoukouronsha, 1987).

rior roll the “wheel of the Dharma” of which he is the protector. The child is depicted wearing, like a hedgehog, a garment of swords. In the manner of another esoteric martial god, Acala Vidyārāja (Japanese: Fudō Myōō), he wields a sword and a noose (figure 23).[40]

Nalakūbara (Nezha)

Of all his angels, the Vaiśravaṇa offspring that caught the Chinese fancy was Nalakūbara, whose Chinese name Nezha attests to the significance of esoteric Buddhism in his history. The name was given to the unruly infant by the Tantric master Amoghavajra, who transcribed the Sanskrit Nalakūbara as Nazhajuwaluo 那吒矩韈囉.[41] In other writings of his, the prolific author dispensed with the ending *juwaluo*, giving Vaiśravaṇa's son the Chinese name Nazha 那吒.[42] The latter was only slightly altered—some seven centuries later—by the addition of the mouth radical, producing the modern pronunciation Nezha 哪吒.

Amoghavajra's Nazhajuwaluo (followed by the shortened Nazha) might seem far removed from Nalakūbara, but it might have derived from one of the latter's original variants. Different Sanskrit and Prakrit texts variously give the divine child's name as Nalakūvara, Nalakūvala, Narakuvera, and Naṭakuvera (for which Nazhajuwaluo would be an accurate transcription, as the Sanskrit retroflex *ṭa* had been transliterated in medieval Chinese as *zha*).[43] Another possible variant, Narta-kavara (literally, “the best of dancers”) is suggested by the Tibetan translation of the infant's name: Gar-mkhan-mchog.[44]

Nalakūbara (Nezha) has been entrusted with his father's financial and military affairs alike. His role as his father's treasurer is attested by the priceless gifts he bestowed upon his favorites. Tang period Chang'an boasted a Buddha tooth, which was the object of a fervent religious cult. Legend had it that the sacred relic had been bestowed upon the eminent monk Daoxuan (596–667) by none other than the Vaiśravaṇa heir apparent, Nezha. The legend of the sacred gift enjoyed great popularity in the Tang capital. Grand Councilor Zheng Qing (?–899) recorded the nightly circumstances under which Nezha (Nazha) made his donation to the renowned cleric:

> The *vinaya* master Daoxuan was extremely steadfast, often observing his religious duties at night. Once he stumbled down the stairs, only to discover that a hand was stretched from midair to support him. He turned to look and saw that it was a young man. “Novice, what are you doing here in the middle of the night?” he asked. “I am no mortal,” the young man replied. “I am Prince Nazha, King Vaiśravaṇa's son. Protecting the Dharma, I have been looking after you for a long time.”
>
> “Poor monk that I am,” Daoxuan said, “I do nothing but cultivate the way. Could I trouble you, O Prince, Mighty Spirit, and Lord? If in the western regions there be

something that could promote the Buddha's worship, I would be grateful if you could bring it here.

"I have a sacred relic of the Buddha tooth," replied the prince. "Even though it is old, it is still worth sacrificing one's life for. Could I dare begrudge it?"

Thus Daoxuan obtained it. This is the Buddha tooth now stored at the Chongsheng Monastery.[45]

Nezha's sacred gift was the occasion of an annual festival that was celebrated during the third lunar month. Tied as it was to the capital's religious calendar, the story of his Buddha tooth was told to native and foreign visitors alike. The Japanese monk Ennin (793–864) recorded it in his travel diary:

Third Moon: 25th day [April 20, 841]. I went to the Chongsheng Monastery and worshiped at the festival of the tooth of the Buddha Śākyamuni. I was repeatedly told that [Daoxuan], the Priest of the Zhongnan Mountains, obtained it from the Vaiśravaṇa Deva's Heir Apparent, Prince Nazha, who brought it from heaven and gave it to the Priest. At present it is placed in the monastery where offerings are made to it.[46]

The legend reverberated in later Japanese lore, which transformed its protagonist's divine identity. Japanese drama had the sacred relic bestowed upon Daoxuan by Śiva's heir Skanda (Japanese: Idaten), rather than by Vaiśravaṇa's son Nezha. The Buddha tooth, furthermore, found its way to Japan, currently being stored at the Sennyūji Temple in Kyoto.[47]

Nezha's military engagements are recorded in the same scriptures that celebrate his brothers' martial skills. The *Rituals of Vaiśravaṇa,* which has Dujian defeating the western barbarians, notes that on previous occasions his younger sibling accompanied their father to battle. It turns out that Nezha—identified as the Heavenly King's third prince—was assigned the role of carrying the Heavenly King's pagoda: "Previously Vaiśravaṇa had defended the kingdom's borders, following the Buddha's order. His third son Nazha was instructed to accompany the Heavenly King, holding his stupa (pagoda)."[48] The brothers' respective roles are further elaborated upon, as Dujian is assigned inspection tours of his father's domain, whereas Nazha carries the Buddhist emblem:

Amoghavajra said: On the first of each month, the Heavenly King meets with all the gods (*devas*), ghosts, and spirits; on the fifteenth, his second son Dujian bids him farewell, leaving for a world inspection tour; on the fifteenth Vaiśravaṇa meets with his fellow Heavenly Kings [of the East, South, and West], and on the twenty-first Nazha hands him the stupa [which he regularly carries on his father's behalf]. On that day offerings of milk porridge should be made. If milk is unavailable, the Heavenly King should be offered purple-mint (perilla) and honey porridge.[49]

Contrary to the later Nezha myth (which invariably has the father manipulate the pagoda to discipline his offspring), the Tang-period esoteric scripture has the latter wield it. That Nezha had at one time been conceived of as the bearer of his father's emblem is attested by visual art. A Tang-period drawing of Nezha—the earliest extant—has him carrying the pagoda. Preserved at the Kyoto Ninna Temple, the drawing leaves no doubt as to the young prince's martial heroism. Bearded and mustachioed, Nezha is heavily armed. His head protected by a magnificent helmet and his body covered with thick mail, the third prince wields a sharp sword in addition to the Buddhist reliquary (figure 24).[50]

Nezha's military functions are elaborated upon in another Amoghavajra scripture: *The Tantric Rituals of the Heavenly King of the North Vaiśravaṇa, Who Follows the Army Protecting the Dharma*. The scripture differs from Amoghavajra's other writings in identifying the young warrior as the Heavenly King's grandson (rather than his third son). It has Nezha declare in the first person his role of state protector:

> At that time Prince Nazha, his hand holding a halberd and his eyes giving a stern look to all around, said to the Buddha, "I am the grandson, the second son of the third prince of Vaiśravaṇa, the Heavenly King of the North. . . . I enforce the Buddha's Dharma, wishing to subdue the hateful people and snuff out the evil mind. I would day and night stand guard protecting the king, the grand ministers, and the hundred officials. I would kill the devils and the like; I, Nazha, would use the *vajra* staff to stab their eyes and heart." . . . At that time Vaiśravaṇa's grandson Nazha also told the World-Honored One, "I would in the future subdue and destroy to ashes all the evil humans, and would protect the kingdom's borders."[51]

The military renown of the valiant Vaiśravaṇa offspring spread beyond monastic circles. Tang-Dynasty soldiers beseeched the Heavenly King and his son Nezha to assist them in the battlefield. An eighth-century inscription from a garrison town in Wenchuan County (in today's Sichuan) reveals that the local commanders worshiped the father and son precisely because of their proven efficacy in the dynasty's defense. The border region was a hotbed of conflicts with the expanding Tibetan empire, and the local troops needed the divine support of Vaiśravaṇa and his heroic offspring. The inscription alludes to the Heavenly King's victory over the western barbarians, confirming Nezha's role of pagoda bearer:

> Praise Him! The splendid virtue of the Heavenly King! Parching the ocean into dry land; blowing Mt. Sumeru into fine dust; healing the masses; and destroying the *asura* demons, this is the awesome Heavenly King displaying his divine might. Residing in the Water-Crystal Palace, he protects the Jambu-dvīpa Continent. Bearing the pagoda, Nazha stands erect. Wielding flowers, Śrī-mahā-devī (Tian'nü) gazes shyly . . .

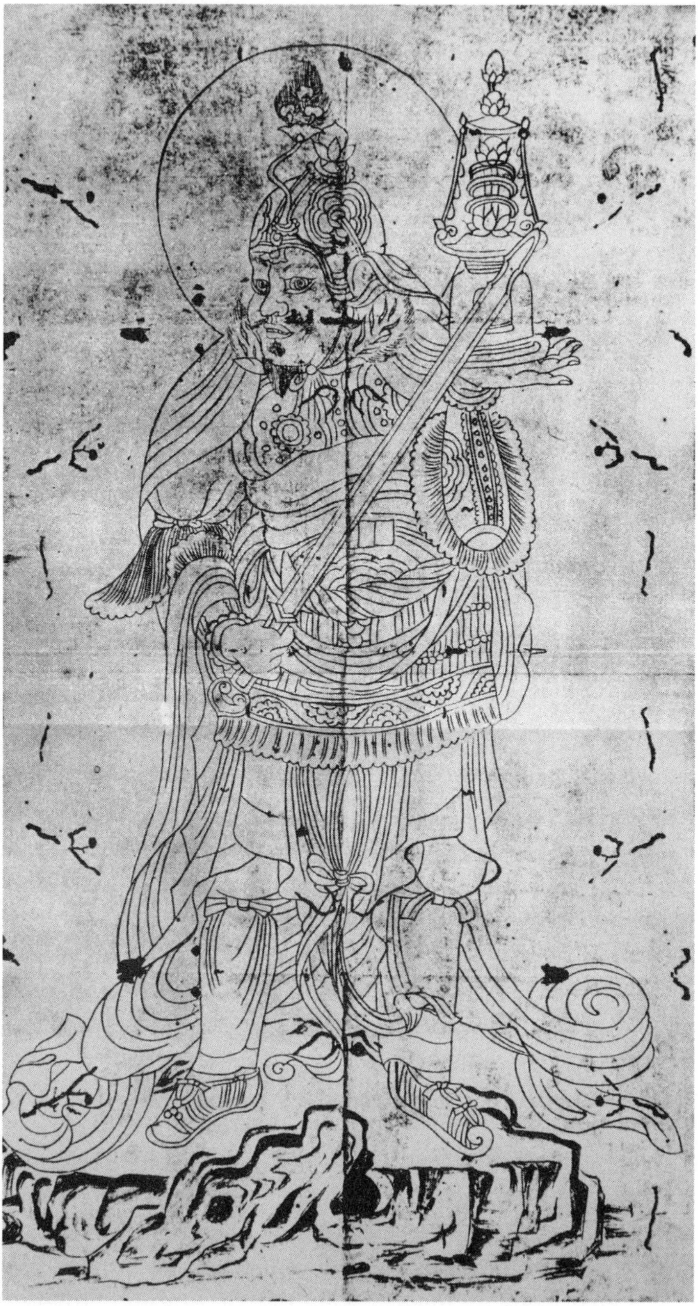

Figure 24: Nezha holding his father's stupa. Tang-period drawing preserved at the Ninna Monastery, Kyoto. *Taishō shinshū daizōkyō zuzōbu,* vol. 7, pp. 566–567.

> During the Tianbao reign (742–755), he manifested his divine might. Protecting our Tang Empire, he was revealed at the Kingdom of Khotan. Against a thousand odes, he broke the enemy's spirit. Thus our sovereign needed not worry about enemies, and the army was saved the calamity of warfare. The ancient fort at Wenchuan is a military site: mountain defenses and jade walls; brave soldiers and mighty arms. It is a fitting place for protecting the nation. Congealed emerald peaks pile up. Sweet cool springs gush forward. Here a Heavenly King hall was established.[52]

The veneration enjoyed by the Heavenly King's third offspring is attested by ritual manuals dedicated to him. Nezha had figured not only in his father's scriptures but also as the subject of his own *dhāraṇī* sutras. Huilin's (737–820) bibliographic dictionary lists two (now lost) Tantric manuals that featured Nezha as their principal protagonist: *Prince Nazha's Dhāraṇī Sūtra of Seeking Accomplishments* and *The Sūtra of Nalakūbara's* [*Nazha's*] *Seeking Accomplishments*.[53] The texts' esoteric orientation is attested by their titles; the term "accomplishment" (Chinese: *chengjiu;* Sanskrit: *siddhi*) alludes to the magic powers that are obtained by the Tantric practitioner. Similar texts dedicated to the child's esoteric cult made it also to Japan, for they are listed in the fourteenth-century Tantric encyclopedia *Byakuhō kushō* (Selections from the oral transmission of white treasures).[54]

Were the now-lost Nezha sutras compiled in China, or were they translated from the Sanskrit? A likely answer is provided by corresponding Tibetan texts. The *Dergé Kanjur* canon includes two esoteric manuals of the rebellious child's cult: *The Yakṣa Nartakavara* [*Nalakūbara*] *Tantra* and *The Text of the Great Yakṣa General Nartakavara* [*Nalakūbara*].[55] The Tibetan texts describe Nalakūbara as the commander of his father's awesome *yakṣa* army.[56] Complete with elaborate *dhāraṇī* spells, they had been translated from the Sanskrit, showing that Nalakūbara's esoteric cult had been well established in medieval India. The Chinese Nezha sutras—like the Tibetan ones—were most likely rendered from the Sanskrit. The Tantric cult of Vaiśravaṇa's martial son originated in medieval India, from where it spread throughout Asia.

The Nalakūbara *tantras* are preceded in the Tibetan canon by ritual texts dedicated to another *yakṣa* general, his brother Maṇibhadra (or Maṇigrīva).[57] The two siblings, Ananda Coomaraswamy suggests, had served as the commanders of their father's army as early as Vedic times.[58] The esoteric literature dedicated to the "Great-*Yakṣa* Maṇibhadra" had enjoyed tremendous popularity throughout Asia. Manuscript fragments of his Sanskrit spells—dating from the first centuries CE—have been found along the Silk Road in today's Xinjiang Province. Unlike Nalakūbara's Chinese sutras (which are now lost), a Maṇibhadra ritual manual is extant in the Chinese canon. The numerous Maṇibhadra texts sometimes identify the "Great Yakṣa" as Vaiśravaṇa's son (and Nalakūbara's brother) and sometimes celebrate him independently of them.[59]

The Three-Headed Prodigy

Nezha's esoteric heritage is visually attested. We have noted in preceding chapters that the Tantric divinities subdue their adversaries by means of a wrathful manifestation (Sanskrit: *krodha;* Chinese: *fennu*). In the manner of the Indian gods, their wrathful apparitions are multiheaded and multiarmed. Bedecked with abundant jewelry, the awesome Tantric divinities wield assorted weaponry in each of their numerous arms. As a proper esoteric god, Nezha is equipped with three heads and between six and sixteen arms. His terrifying Tantric iconography has been rendered in Tibetan and Chinese art alike. Here are the Tibetan guidelines for the drawing of the fearful god:

> *Sras Gar-mkhan-mchog* "The [Vaiśravaṇa] Son, the excellent dancer [Nalakūbara]". He has three faces—a yellow, a blue, and a white one—all bearing a fierce expression, and the colour of his body is red. He has sixteen hands, the right ones holding the following attributes: thunderbolt, wheel, jewel, lotus, sword, snare, arrow, and battle axe; the attributes held by the left hands are: a bell, trident, mongoose, an ornament of flowers (*me tog gi phur ma*), a *ba dan* [streamer with pendants of silk], skull-cup, bow, and a whisk. The deity wears a garment of silk, a loincloth of tiger skin, snakes and jewels.[60]

Fashioned after the Indian fantasies of the divine, Nezha's Tantric iconography has held a spell upon his Chinese believers. Beginning in the tenth century and all through modern times, his three-headed and six-armed apparition has been repeatedly depicted in Buddhist and non-Buddhist literature alike. Song-period Chan literature abounds with allusions to the multilimbed "Wrathful Nezha [Nazha]." Shanzhao's (947–1024) recorded sayings describe, for example, the "Wrathful Nazha striking the emperor's bell; Three-headed and Six-armed he shakes heaven and earth."[61] The twelfth-century *Blue-Cliff Records* uses the well-known image of the formidable Nazha to describe a prototypical eccentric saint:

> At times, idly sitting in a grass-strewn hut atop a lonely peak,
> At others, barefoot roaming the bustling city centers.
> One minute, like a Wrathful Nazha, displaying three heads
> and six arms,
> Another, like the moon's or the sun's face, beaming rays
> of universal compassion.[62]

Casual references in popular literature reveal the attraction of the wrathful Nazha to a lay clientele. The early Ming novel *Water Margin* (ca. 1400) has its martial protagonist Wu Song display his courage by reference to the esoteric Buddhist warrior. When challenged by an unworthy adversary, Wu Song contrasts him with the multiheaded and multiarmed Nezha: "If he was three-headed, six-armed, and as powerful as Nezha, I would have been afraid of him. . . . As it is, he is only one-headed and two-armed. Clearly he is no Nezha. Why should I be afraid of him?"[63] Roughly contemporaneous with the *Water Margin,* the *Quelling the Demons' Revolt* has a Tantric icon of the child-god come to life. The historically renowned Xiang'guo Temple in Kaifeng houses a Nezha statue, "its three heads like three dark mountains; its six arms like six steep ridges."[64] The icon comes to life assisting the famed Judge Bao Zheng (Baogong) to capture an evil sorcerer disguised as a Buddhist monk.

The formidable Nazha has held such a grip upon the Chinese imagination that they envisioned their capital in his image. According to a fourteenth-century legend, Beijing (then Dadu) had been fashioned in the Tantric warrior's shape. The city's designers had been graced by the divine epiphany of the child warrior, whereupon they drew its walls in his likeness. Beijing's eleven gates corresponded to the fearful god's three heads, six arms, and two feet. Hence, the capital of the Yuan Dynasty (1279–1368) was referred to in popular lore as Nezha City (Nazha Cheng). That the sacred metropolis has been named after the Tantric warrior is as succinct an indication as any of the impact that esoteric Buddhism has had upon the Chinese imaginings of divinity.[65]

Nezha's role of dragon tamer likely contributed to his significance in Beijing lore. Hok-Lam Chan has convincingly argued that the child's expertise in battling the aquatic monster had been the key for his appointment as the capital's tutelary deity. Yuan-period Dadu (like present-day Beijing) had suffered from alternating floods and water shortages, which were equally attributed to the dragon king. It was Nezha's ability to control the watery creature—and thereby the weather—that had earned him the role of the capital's heavenly protector. Thus, Nezha's birthday in the second month coincided with the festivities of the Dragon-Raising-Its-Head, when the capital's residents beseeched timely rains from the ophidian king.[66]

His identity of dragon tamer brings us back to the Nezha legend. Let us briefly recall the child-god's principal feats, which have been celebrated in Chinese fiction, drama, and visual art since the thirteenth century at the latest: When he was seven years old, Nezha killed the dragon king's heir and made a belt from its sinews. Shortly thereafter the invincible toddler came upon a divine bow that no one but the mythic Yellow Emperor of old had been able to bend. The child effortlessly drew the bowstring and shot an arrow that killed the acolyte of the ogress Lady Rock. The dragon king and the harpy sought reparations from Nezha's father. A familial conflict issued, at the height of which Nezha committed suicide, returning to his parents the body he had owed them. Reincarnated in a lotus body, he attempted to avenge his suicide by patricide. His father was narrowly rescued by divine intervention.

What might have been the sources of the child's heroic feats? Where did his legend's dragon and bow motifs come from? In order to answer these questions we need reach further back to the Indian lore of Nezha's predecessor, Nalakūbara.

9

Nezha, Nalakūbara, and Kṛṣṇa

By the mid-thirteenth century, the principal features of the Chinese Nezha had been established. Written and visual evidence attest to his childish persona, his oedipal confrontation with his father, and his superhuman strength, manifested in the subjugation of a dragon and the drawing of a mighty bow that only gods had been able to bend. Are these features related to the child's original manifestation as Nalakūbara? Does his myth derive from his predecessor's Sanskrit lore? We begin our investigation of the legend's Indian background with Nalakūbara's dubious identity as a semidivine, semidemonic, *yakṣa* spirit.

Those who enforce the law and those who violate it sometimes come from the same background. We are told that in certain families one brother may become a police officer and another a criminal. Whether this folklore reflects social reality or not, it does describe the Indian gods, who often transcend judicial categories.[1] Take the *yakṣas* for example. In the *Rāmāyaṇa* the water spirits fight along with the gods against the cannibalistic *rākṣasas*, who are none other than their cousins, for the *yakṣa* king and the protector of the gods' wealth Vaiśravaṇa is the half-brother of the arch-evil Rāvaṇa, leader of the *rākṣasa* hordes.

The portrayal of Nalakūbara in Sanskrit literature should begin therefore with his troubled family background. The *yakṣa* was incorporated as a guardian deity into the Buddhist pantheon precisely because of his personal familiarity with the powers of evil. His very uncle was the vicious Rāvaṇa who had kidnapped the most beloved Indian heroine Sītā. Indeed, the earliest extant Nalakūbara episode concerns his sexual and generational competition with his uncle. In Vālmīki's *Rāmāyaṇa*, the evil *rākṣasa* rapes his nephew's lover, the attractive courtesan Rambhā. As a consequence of his sexual crime, Rāvaṇa is unable to force himself upon Sītā, for he had been cursed by Nalakūbara never to lie with a woman against her will. The story might have been added to the epic as an afterthought, explaining Sītā's emergence unblemished from her captivity in Rāvaṇa's hands.[2]

In the *Rāmāyaṇa*, Nalakūbara is defeated by his evil uncle, who rapes his lover.

In a Buddhist Jātaka tale, he emerges victorious from a sexual competition with a Garuḍa bird. The beautiful Queen Kākātī, wife of the king of Benares, had been kidnapped by the divine bird. The king informs his court musician Naṭakuvera (Nalakūbara) of her disappearance. Naṭakuvera hides within the rich plumage of the Garuḍa King, who carries him to his love nest. There, Naṭakuvera himself copulates with the kidnapped woman. When the Garuḍa King realizes he has been duped, he sends Kākātī in disgust to her lawful husband. The bird is left to lament his own role in bringing Naṭakuvera to its sweetheart:

> Out upon the foolish blunder,
> What a booby I have been!
> Lovers best were kept asunder,
> Lo! I've served as go-between.[3]

The best-known Nalakūbara tale similarly portrays him as a sexual trickster. Belonging to the celebrated Kṛṣṇa story cycle, the episode has enjoyed tremendous popularity in oral and written fiction as well as in visual art. Nalakūbara and his brother Maṇigrīva (Maṇibhadra), it goes, were frolicking with naked women in the waters of the Ganges, unmindful of the approaching sage Nārada. Enraged by their impropriety, the sage cursed the *yakṣa* brothers, transforming them into twin Arjuna trees. After a hundred celestial years, the baby Kṛṣṇa, who had been tied by his mother to a mortar as punishment for childish mischief, crawled between the two trees. Easily uprooting them, he brought the two brothers back to life. The story concludes with the twin *yakṣas'* hymns of praise to the baby-god.[4]

The three episodes each portray Nalakūbara as a lover, a role he continued to play in Indian regional literatures and visual arts. In Piṅgaḷi Sūranna's Telugu novel *The Sound of the Kiss* (*Kaḷāpūrṇodayamu*) (ca. 1600), for instance, Nalakūbara is not only the most handsome man in the world, but also the richest (being the son of the god of wealth Vaiśravaṇa). Dating from roughly the same period (the sixteenth century), the image of the splendid youth—intertwined with his consort, the ravishing Rambhā—is rendered on a sculpted pillar at the Lepākṣi temple in Andhra-Pradesh.[5] Does the amorous figure of the Indian Nalakūbara accord with his portrayal in Chinese fiction? Is the image of the Indian *yakṣa* related to the Chinese deity Nezha?

On the most general level the demonic aspects of the Chinese enfant terrible derive from his *yakṣa* origins. Nezha's violence is rooted in his dubious identity as god *and* demon. His outrageous behavior echoes his familial ties with the arch-evil *rākṣasa* ghouls. Furthermore, the child's conflict with his father might have been prefigured in Nalakūbara's generational conflicts with his uncle Rāvaṇa and the sage Nārada respectively. Nevertheless, key elements of the Chinese myth are missing from the Indian legend. Nalakūbara neither kills a dragon nor lifts a magic bow. His family discords notwithstanding, he does not attempt to murder his father as his Chinese incarnation does. Even if Nezha's personality is indebted to Nalakūbara's, it is impossible to trace the plot of his Chinese story to the latter's. Nezha's Chinese adventures seem to have been fashioned after a different model.

There is also an age difference. Whereas Nalakūbara is invariably portrayed as a young man, his Chinese descendant is a child, even a baby. We have seen in chapter 6 that his tender age has defined the contours of the Chinese Nezha cult. The endearing infant is made offerings that befit his age—marbles, balls, toy trucks, and the like—and his mediums are tempted with candies. Possessed by the toddler divinity, spirit mediums act out his childish persona, talking in a high-pitched voice and occasionally throwing tantrums. Whereas his Indian predecessor has been imagined in his middle or late teens, Nezha has been usually conceived of as an infant.

Kṛṣṇa

The story of Nalakūbara's punishment by the sage Nārada does feature an infant. This is of course the great god Viṣṇu, incarnated as the baby Kṛṣṇa. Turning our attention from the tale's secondary protagonist (the *yakṣa* Nalakūbara) to its principal one (the divine savior Kṛṣṇa), we are struck by the similarities to the Chinese Nezha myth. Kṛṣṇa, like Nezha, is first and foremost a baby. His story pivots upon the concealment of a great god under a child's fragile appearance. The infant Kṛṣṇa, like the baby Nezha, kills a dragon (Sanskrit: *nāga*). Kṛṣṇa's childhood, like Nezha's, is marked by oedipal tensions, culminating in the murder of a surrogate father-figure (King Kaṃsa). Furthermore, Kṛṣṇa foreshadows Nezha's martial feat of drawing a divine bow that no one has been able to bend.

The child Kṛṣṇa (Bāla-Kṛṣṇa) is among the most important Indian gods. Viṣṇu's babyish incarnation, as a central figure of the *bhakti* devotional movement, has been the subject of countless literary and visual works of art. The baby Kṛṣṇa cycle had originated—likely independently of the Viṣṇu figure—during the first millennium BCE. By the first centuries CE, however, their legends were firmly intertwined. The *Harivaṃśa* supplement to the *Mahābhārata* contains the principal feats of the divine infant, including the subjugation of the dragon Kāliya and the defeat of the ogress Pūtanā. His story cycle was subsequently enlarged in the *Viṣṇu Purāṇa* (ca. fifth century) and the *Brahma Purāṇa* and received its canonical Sanskrit form in the ninth- or early tenth-century *Bhāgavata Purāṇa* (which reflected the influence of the South Indian *bhakti* movement). The latter had served as a source for an enormous body of drama and song in regional languages. To this day, the pranks of the playful Kṛṣṇa are lovingly sung throughout the subcontinent. His divine exploits have been similarly celebrated in visual art; from Gupta-period sculpture through early-modern court painting, down to contemporary gaudy posters, the baby-god has been among the most widely portrayed in Indian art.[6]

Kṛṣṇa, like Nezha, is first and foremost a baby. The delight of his literature derives from the suspense of concealment, the might of the great god being hidden in a baby's fragrant body. Mother Yaśodā's futile attempts to discipline her mischievous Kṛṣṇa result in displays of his supernatural strength. Indeed, it is as an illustration of the divine child's might that the protagonist of this book—Nalakūbara (Nezha)—makes his appearance in the Kṛṣṇa cycle. Unable to control her playful son, Yaśodā ties him to a heavy mortar. The infant effortlessly carries it around and, rubbing it against the twin Arjuna trees, releases the *yakṣa* brothers Nalakūbara and Maṇigrīva, who become his devotees.

The child Kṛṣṇa is a butter thief. His innovative pilfering methods are the subject of numerous stories in which he breaks into his mother's (and her neighbors') pantries. His butter-theft exploits have made the child-god a favorite figure of contemporary dairy advertisements. They also occasion an enchanting episode in which the god as the totality of the universe is revealed to his mother. Suspecting her son of stealing butter yet again, Yaśodā orders him to open his mouth, only to behold within it the entire cosmos—including her native Braj County, her own village, and she herself—as she gazes into Kṛṣṇa's mouth:

> She then saw in his mouth the whole eternal universe, and heaven, and the regions of the sky, and the orb of the earth with its mountains, islands, and oceans; she saw the wind, and lightning, and the moon and stars, and the zodiac; and water and fire and air and space itself; she saw the vacillating senses, the mind, the elements, and the three strands of matter, She saw within the body of her son, in his gaping mouth, the whole universe in all its variety, with all the forms of life and time and nature and action and hopes, and her own village, and herself.[7]

Following such epiphanies, Kṛṣṇa is quick to erase them from his mother's memory. Out of compassion for her limited comprehension, he wishes to save her the pains of cognitive dissonance. There is, then, a degree of alienation inherent in the Kṛṣṇa cycle. The god is forever a stranger to his human parents. Indeed, Kṛṣṇa was miraculously transferred into Yaśodā's womb from the womb of another woman (Devakī). Divine children have a destiny that transcends their parents. Those who raise them are by definition no more than foster parents. This is the case with Nezha, whose real (spiritual) father is the Buddha (or, in later versions, the Daoist Immortal Taiyi), as well as with the immensely popular Harry

Potter, who is raised by the "muggle" Dursley family even though he belongs to the wizards' realm.

The god's inherent alienation from his parents may assume oedipal overtones. It has been pointed out that Kṛṣṇa is among the most overtly oedipal figures in Sanskrit literature. His childhood is marked by an accelerating conflict with his maternal uncle King Kaṃsa, who functions in the myth as a surrogate father figure. Scholars have pointed out that in most Indian oedipal stories aggression and sexual libido are directed from the father's generation to the son's. (This is the case with the above-mentioned Nalakūbara episode, where an uncle rapes his nephew's lover). By contrast, the Kṛṣṇa episode is almost unique in the son's victory over his father figure. Bāla-Kṛṣṇa (the "Child-Kṛṣṇa") murders his wicked uncle and inherits his throne. The "symbol of the aggressive and eroticized child" vanquishes his father. Robert Goldman has noted that "in killing Kaṃsa, the demonic king who has been seeking to destroy him since his birth, the boy Kṛṣṇa more closely approximates the Western oedipal hero than perhaps any other figure of Indian myth or legend."[8]

Sharing the same age and same oedipal tendencies, Nezha and Kṛṣṇa also perform the identical feat of subduing a water monster. In Nezha's case it is the dragon king; in Kṛṣṇa's it is the *nāga* Kāliya, inhabiting the Yamunā Pool. The Sanskrit term *nāga* denotes the entire ophidian class, which is why it is sometimes rendered into English as "serpent," or "snake" (or "water-serpent" or "water-snake"). Significantly, it has been translated into Chinese as *long,* which is the name of the mythical animal subjugated by Nezha. Thus, the two child-gods vanquish the same aquatic monster, which I will refer to as a dragon (following the common Western rendition of the Chinese term).[9]

The Chinese and the Indian infant-divinities achieve their cosmic victories over the dragon at the identical tender age of seven (given for Kṛṣṇa in the *Harivaṃśa* and the *Viṣṇu Purāṇa* and for Nezha in *The Canonization of the Gods*).[10] In addition, it might be argued that their respective myths betray the same obsession with the child-god's loincloth, belt, or girdle. The article of clothing figures in Kṛṣṇa's subjugation of Kāliya no less than in Nezha's defeat of the dragon king. The *Bhāgavata Purāṇa* specifies that before jumping into the dragon's poisoned pool, Kṛṣṇa tightened his loincloth (or girdle) (Sanskrit: *raśanā*), and Nezha's conflict with the dragon followed the child-god's dipping of his magic sash in the river. In the Chinese myth the article of clothing figures yet again as Nezha prepares a belt from the dragon prince's sinews. Recall that the formidable accessory had won Nezha the everlasting esteem of Chinese belt makers, who appointed him the tutelary deity of their Sash and Girdle Guild.[11]

Chinese and Indian authors alike highlighted the delicacy of the infant faced by the dreadful dragon. The beauty of the Nezha and Kṛṣṇa narratives depended upon the contrast between the handsome child and the hideous monster. Here is the *Bhāgavata Purāṇa* description of the horrendous dragon Kāliya coiling himself around the flower-like Kṛṣṇa:

> Biting him in all tender parts, twisting himself, he enclosed completely in his coils the Lord who looked extremely beautiful, delicate, and effulgent like a cloud; who was adorned with Śrīvatsa mark and was dressed in raiment of bright golden hue; who, with a bewitching, smiling, face and with feet tender like the pericap of a lotus, was sporting in the water with absolute fearlessness.[12]

By the fifth century CE, Kṛṣṇa's subjugation of the water monster became a favorite topic of visual art. His battle with the dragon has been among the child-god's most celebrated exploits (figure 25). Dancing over the subdued *nāga,* the child-god's iconography is related to the great god Viṣṇu's, of whom he is considered an avatar. Viṣṇu's couch is made of a water monster. The recumbent god sleeps on the dragon of eternity Ananta or Śeṣa, "who is the good *alter ego* of the evil Kāliya."[13] Ananta and Kāliya each sport five hoods, which serve as Viṣṇu's canopy. Thus the iconography of the three Asian deities features a similar water monster. Viṣṇu and Kṛṣṇa, like their Chinese counterpart Nezha, are shown atop a tamed dragon.

Overcoming a similar water monster, Nezha and Kṛṣṇa display their divine might by another identical feat. The two youthful gods draw a mighty bow that no one else has been able to bend. In Nezha's case, it is the mythic weapon that had belonged to the Yellow Emperor, and the infant uses it to kill the acolyte of the rock spirit Shiji Niangniang. In Kṛṣṇa's case, it is the treasured possession of his nemesis, King Kaṃsa. Not even the gods have been able to bend the sacred bow, yet Kṛṣṇa effortlessly draws it, snapping it in two.[14] Interestingly, the *Rāmāyaṇa* has the same exploit performed by Viṣṇu's other avatar, Rāma. King Janaka has promised his daughter to the man capable of bending Śiva's bow. No one but the mighty god has been able to draw the awesome weapon, yet Prince Rāma easily bends it to the breaking point.[15] Thus, the three divinities that have tamed a similar water monster also wield an identical instrument. Kṛṣṇa, Viṣṇu (Rāma), and Nezha each successfully draw a magic bow.

Legends of divine bows appear to have been common in Indo-European literatures. It is striking that Odysseus, like Rāma, regains his wife Penelope after drawing a great bow that he alone is capable of stringing. The motif had entered at least some versions of the Buddha's life, as Prince Siddhārtha himself is similarly said to have obtained his consort Yaśodharā.[16] From Kṛṣṇa and Rāma to the Buddha Śākyamuni and the Chinese Nezha, the topos of the mighty bow illustrates the fluidity of mythic thought. Iyanga Nobumi has likened Buddhist mythology to a vast stream, the mighty flow of which has mythic motifs forever interacting in novel narratives.[17] The divine weapon that is drawn by diverse heroes in multifarious legends is a case in point.

Figure 25:
Kṛṣṇa atop the subdued Kāliya. Bronze statue. Pallava-Chola, ninth century. From Calambur Sivaramamurti, *The Art of India* (New York: Harry N. Abrams, 1977) illustration 63.

The *Supreme Secrets of Naṇa Deva*

Kṛṣṇa is among the most important Indian gods, and evidence of his renown comes from as far as China. The thirteenth century witnessed the construction of one or possibly two Brahmanical temples in the southern Chinese port of Quanzhou (Fujian Province). Fashioned by Tamil merchants in the South Indian Chola Style, their remains have survived to this day.[18] They include two votive pillars decorated with images from Viṣṇu's life. Two scenes are particularly relevant to our discussion. They show the child-god playing the flute atop the conquered Kāliya dragon (recognizable by his five hoods), and his uprooting of the Arjuna tree, releasing the imprisoned Nalakūbara and his brother (Figures 26, 27).[19]

The Quanzhou images of the Indian child-god evince his Asian renown. The Kṛṣṇa legend had spread along the maritime trade routes throughout South Asia. (Recent archeological finds indicate that the antics of the Indian deity might have reached China by the Central Asian Silk Road as well.[20]) Even though the extant images likely played no role in the emergence of the Chinese Nezha—they were carved too late for that—it is not impossible that the creators of the Chinese myth were familiar with the antics of the Indian dragon tamer Kṛṣṇa. It is noteworthy that the southern Chinese port of Quanzhou has yielded one of the earliest surviving Nezha icons. Recall the thirteenth-century Quanzhou pagoda featuring the mighty infant atop the vanquished dragon (see chapter 5, figure 7).

We possess a textual hint—it is no more than that—of a possible connection between the two Asian child-gods. A Chinese esoteric text features a deity called Naṇa, whose name and attributes appear to be a hybrid of **Na**lakūbara and Kṛṣ**ṇa**. The *Scripture of the Supreme Secrets of Naṇa Deva* (*Zuishang mimi Nana tian jing*) suggests the possibility that Tantric masters have colored Nalakūbara in the hues of his divine savior Kṛṣṇa. The scripture might support the hypothesis that the Chinese Nezha was created by the merging of the Indian Nalakūbara with Kṛṣṇa.

The *Scripture of the Supreme Secrets of Naṇa Deva* belongs to what might be described as the second wave of Chinese Tantric translations. Considering Amoghavajra and his eighth-century colleagues as representatives of the first stage, the second phase includes translations that were conducted under the patronage of the Northern Song (960–1127). Some of the most important Tantric *sūtras*—including the *Guhyasamāja* and the *Hevajra*—were rendered into Chinese during this latter phase. The *Supreme Secrets of Naṇa Deva* was translated by the prolific Kashmiri monk Tianxizai (Devaśāntika?) (?–1000) who, after arriving in China in 980, worked for twenty years in the imperially sponsored Institute for the Translation of the Sūtras. Devaśāntika was responsible for rendering some of the most outrageous sexual, even necrophilic, Tantric manuals. His *Rituals of the God Vināyaka Explicated by Vajrasattva* guides the practitioner in the production

Figure 26: Kṛṣṇa atop the subdued Kāliya. Quanzhou remains of a thirteenth-century Hindu temple. Photo by Meir Shahar.

of zombie sexual slaves. More pertinently for our purpose, he had translated a *dhāraṇī sūtra* of Nalakūbara's brother Maṇibhadra (Maṇigrīva).[21]

Like other *dhāraṇī* sutras of its kind, the *Supreme Secrets of Naṇa Deva* opens with a great gathering of Indian divinities headed by the Buddha. The congregation has assembled at Vaiśravaṇa's Palace, where a charming youth named Naṇa makes his appearance.[22] After being empowered by the Buddha, the young god reveals the supreme secret spell that occupies the bulk of the text. Naṇa is described as follows:

Figure 27: Drawing the mortar, Kṛṣṇa releases Nalakūbara from underneath the Arjuna tree. Quanzhou remains of a thirteenth-century Hindu temple. Photo by Meir Shahar.

At that time there was a Deva called Naṇa. His appearance was exceptionally handsome, and his face beamed with a gentle smile. He was holding the sun, the moon, and various weapons. His numerous treasures and abundant jewelry shone more brightly than the sun and the moon. He made himself a *luoye* robe[23] from the dragons Nanda (Nantuo) and Upananda (Wuponantuo), and a belt from the dragon Takṣaka (Dechajia).[24] He possessed the same immense strength as Nārāyaṇa (Naluoyan) [i.e., Viṣṇu]. He too came to the assembly and sat down facing the Buddha . . .

At that time the Buddha emanated great light from his dharma-body of meditation. The light covered the entire Buddha Universe, reaching all the great evil *yakṣas*, the various types of *rākṣasas* (*luocha*) and *piśācas* (*pishezuo*),[25] and all the evil dragons (*nāgas*) (*long*) as far as the heavenly constellations. When the Buddha's light shone upon them they all awoke to the truth.

The Buddha's light returned to him and, after encircling him three times, entered his head. It then reissued in seven colors from his brow, entering Naṇa-Deva's head.

When the Buddha light penetrated his head, Naṇa Deva displayed an enormous body like Mt. Sumeru. His facial expression alternated between terrifying anger and a

> broad smile. He had a thousand arms, and he was holding a skull (kapāla [*geboluo*])[26] and numerous weapons. He was handsomely adorned with a tiger-skin robe and skulls. [Mightily strong] He emanated blazing light and terrifying strength. When Naṇa Deva displayed this [divine] body, the great earth shook, and all who beheld him were terrified.[27]

The mysterious Naṇa's connection to the Chinese Nazha (Nezha) is unmistakable. The two young divinities share similar names and an identical residence (Vaiśravaṇa's Palace). They are also equally adept in the subjugation of dragons, which Naṇa, like Nezha, uses as a belt. Recall that the Chinese god has become the patron deity of the Sash and Girdle Guild because of his expert fabrication of a dragon-sinews belt. Furthermore, the *Supreme Secrets of Naṇa Deva* predates all extant Nezha sources associating the child-god with a dragon. Thus, the Tantric sutra might have been the textual source of the legend portraying Nezha as a dragon tamer.

At the same time Naṇa differs from Nazha. Their names are not identical and, more significantly, their titles differ. Whereas Tantric literature has invariably identified Nazha as a *yakṣa,* the *Supreme Secrets of Naṇa Deva* describes him as a god (*deva*). Naṇa's divine standing is therefore higher than Nazha's. Significantly, even as he makes his appearance in Vaiśravaṇa's palace, Naṇa is not identified as his son. Indeed, his position is much more elevated than the Heavenly King's, so much so that at least one scholar has considered the *Supreme Secrets of Naṇa Deva* irrelevant to the Nazha (Nezha) saga.[28]

From another angle, the charming Naṇa is perhaps reminiscent of an Indian *deva*, the mighty Viṣṇu incarnated as the bewitching child Kṛṣṇa. First, he is as powerful. We are told that Naṇa "possessed the same immense strength as Nārāyaṇa," the latter being a common appellation of Viṣṇu.[29] It is noteworthy that as an incarnation of Viṣṇu, Kṛṣṇa himself is sometimes referred to in Sanskrit literature as Nārāyaṇa,[30] in which sense the text might be interpreted as alluding to the child-god. The Naṇa Deva Sutra might be hinting of its mysterious protagonist's association with Kṛṣṇa.

Second, the mighty Naṇa is as charming as the Indian butter thief. The scripture highlights the allure of its divine protagonist: "His appearance was exceptionally handsome, and his face beamed with a gentle smile." Even when assuming his fearful form, Naṇa's "facial expression alternates between terrifying anger and a broad smile." Thus it is not impossible that Tianxizai (Devaśāntika)—or his Indian sources—had an impression of the beloved Kṛṣṇa in mind when they created the enchanting dragon tamer Naṇa (who was to influence the Chinese Nazha). Kṛṣṇa might have played a role in the eventual emergence of the Chinese Nezha.

Conclusion

Nezha and the Kṛṣṇa incarnation of Viṣṇu share significant similarities. The two gods are toddlers, and their respective myths pivot upon the concealment of divine might under a misleadingly fragile appearance. The two child-gods are motivated by similar oedipal urges and perform identical heroic feats. At the tender age of seven, Nezha and Kṛṣṇa alike subdue a dragon. Furthermore, the two youthful gods equally draw a divine bow that no one else has been able to bend.

The Nezha legend and the Kṛṣṇa myth are related. Nezha is none other than Nalakūbara, who figures as a secondary character in the lore of the Indian child-god. It is not impossible that Nalakūbara has acquired some traits of his story's principal protagonist. The Tantric masters that brought the *yakṣa* to China might have colored him in the hues of his savior, the divine child Kṛṣṇa. Support for this hypothesis is furnished by the *Scripture of the Supreme Secrets of Naṇa Deva*, which appears to celebrate a fusion of the two divinities. The Tantric scripture indicates that two of the greatest Asian story cycles might be related. The legends of the Chinese child-god Nezha might have been influenced by the myths of his Indian counterpart Kṛṣṇa.

Epilogue

Esoteric Buddhism and the Chinese Supernatural

Nezha is a Chinese god. Following fourteen hundred years of acculturation, his figure has evolved to accommodate native values and tastes. The Indian infant has been clothed in Chinese toddlers' dress, his hair done in tufts like theirs. Daoist priests equipped him with their exorcistic weaponry, and his modes of worship—from spirit possession to pilgrimage—have been adapted to local religious practices. Most important, the myth of the rebellious child has been shaped by the confessed ideologies and suppressed desires that weigh upon Chinese individuals. The legend of the rebellious infant has evolved to express the universal oedipal urge within the culture-specific idiom of Confucian filial piety. Responding to changing social and political circumstances, the figure of the malleable infant has been variously rendered. His late imperial legend has been informed by the hegemonic discourse of filial sacrifice, whereas the People's Republic of China has hailed him as a revolutionary martyr. In a different vein, Taiwanese filmmakers have portrayed Nezha as a disoriented teenager in an alienated urban environment.

Do Nezha's distant origins as an Indian *yakṣa* matter? Does his descent from Nalakūbara (and his possible association with Kṛṣṇa) have any significance? This author believes it does, because the child-god is not the only one introduced to China by esoteric Buddhism. Recent scholarship has revealed the scope of the Tantric impact upon the Chinese imagination of divinity. Tantric ritual masters harnessed the powers of each and every Indian mythological being, from the *deva* gods to the *asura* demons, from the *nāga* dragons to the *rākṣasa* ghouls. Their ritual tracts have acquainted Chinese religious practitioners with a vast array of divine and demonic creatures that have been adopted by Daoism and the popular religion alike. Recall the motley crowd of esoteric divinities that are invoked along with Nezha on Jinmen Island: from the philosopher turned Tantric divinity Nāgārjuna, through the Two Lords of Incense Mountain and Snowy Mountain, to the Diamond Stalwart Vajrapāṇi.[1]

Far from being the prerogative of Buddhist clerics, the Tantric divinities have been called upon by Daoist priests and village ritual masters. Their riveting myths have been celebrated in Chinese fiction and drama, and their voluptuous iconographies have been rendered in native painting and sculpture. Avalokiteśvara's Tantric manifestations are a case in point. The Thousand-Armed Guanyin has been a favorite topic of the Chinese visual arts all through modern times, even as the popular legend of Miaoshan has sought to explain the esoteric iconography retroactively (see chapter 6). Avalokiteśvara's other Tantric incarnations have been equally influential. The Horse-Headed Guanyin (Hayagrīva) has served as a conduit by which the Sanskrit lore of the fire-emanating mare has penetrated Chinese fiction. Furthermore, traces of the equine bodhisattva are discernible in the widespread Chinese cult of the Horse King (Mawang) who, all through the modern period, has been referred to by the Tantric epithet "King of Spells" (Sanskrit: Vidyārāja; Chinese: Mingwang).[2]

Other creatures of the Indian (and the Central Asian) imagination have been similarly introduced to China by esoteric Buddhism. To cite just a few examples: The Mighty Golden-Wing Bird Garuḍa has merged with the Daoist God of Thunder (Leigong). Protagonist of a vast body of Tantric scriptures, Viṣṇu's avian mount shares striking similarities with the Daoist divinity that range from their iconography (part human, part bird) to their principal functions of rainmaking and the healing of snakebites. Furthermore, Chinese fiction has associated the awesome Indian bird with the patriotic Chinese hero Yue Fei (1103–1142), who is considered his avatar[3]; bearing his Tantric necklace of skulls, the God of the Deep Sands (Shensha shen) has similarly figured in Chinese lore. Assigned the role of Xuanzang's guardian in the sixteenth-century *The Journey to the West,* his iconic skulls season the novel's plot. They belong to Buddhist pilgrims whom the awesome divinity devours[4]; finally, Vajrapāṇi—wielder of the quintessential Tantric emblem of the diamond (*vajra*)—has captured the imagination of Chinese artists and warriors alike. His muscular physique has been rendered in painting and sculpture even as martial artists have sought to obtain his invulnerable "diamond body" (Sanskrit: *vajra-kāya;* Chinese: *jin'gang shen*).[5]

To be sure, Indian divinities had made it to China long before the mature Tantric movement arrived there in the seventh century. Heathen gods and demons had lauded the Buddha's teachings in the writings of earlier Buddhist schools. Nonetheless, the Tantric movement likely played a greater role than either the Theravada or the Mahāyāna in the introduction to China of non-Buddhist deities (which are nowadays referred to as Hindu). There are two principal reasons. First, esoteric Buddhism was willing to embrace Indian gods that—perhaps because of their enormous popularity—other Buddhist schools had been reluctant to endorse. Śiva's queer family is a case in point. His elephantine offspring Gaṇeśa, his alluring wife (in her ferocious manifestation of Kālī), and the outrageous snake-wrapped god himself all figure in Tantric ritual.[6] Second, esoteric Buddhism assigned these Hindu deities a central role in its program of worldly empowerment and enlightenment. It is by means of worshiping the Indian gods—and becoming one with them—that the practitioner attains wealth and power no less than release from the relentless cycle of life and death.

This book's protagonist might illustrate the difference between the Tantric movement and earlier Buddhist schools in their treatment of Indian mythology. Nezha had been mentioned in Buddhist writings as early as Aśvaghoṣa's *Acts of the Buddha* (ca. second century CE), which was translated into Chinese in the early fifth century. But the passing reference to the delight at his birth—used as a metaphor to the universal joy upon the Buddha's nativity—had had no impact whatsoever on the Nezha cult.[7] Only when he was summoned to lead his father's armies and distribute the Heavenly King's fabulous wealth did Nezha catch the attention of Chinese devotees. Phrased differently, the ritual function assigned him by esoteric Buddhism played a major role in the emergence of the Chinese Nezha devotion. The Tantric program of worship, coupled with the inevitable emphasis upon the correct rendering of the deities' images, fostered the East Asian cult of the Indian divinities. The centrality of ritual and iconography in Tantric Buddhism was the key to the pan-Asian dissemination of the Indian gods.

The scholarly study of Chinese esoteric Buddhism has been neglected for many decades, principally because of the lack of a recognized lineage associated with it. Unlike Japan, where the Tantric movement has found an institutional expression in the Shingon and the Tendai sects, Chinese esoteric Buddhism never existed as an independent school, which is why its significance has been hard to gauge. This book joins recent scholarship in showing that despite the lack of religious establishment, the Tantric movement has exerted a significant impact upon the Chinese religious landscape.[8] Scholars such as Michel Strickmann have rightly surmised that the proper way of appreciating Chinese esoteric Buddhism is through its influence upon native religion.[9] If to this day Daoist priests and village ritual masters make use of *mudrā* hand symbolism and *mantra* incantations, this is due to the contribution of medieval Tantric Buddhism. Their methods of summoning a deity into a child's body have been (at least partially) fashioned after the Indian techniques of *āveśa* possession, and the gods they call upon—such as this book's protagonist—attest to the enduring attraction of the Tantric supernatural. Nezha illustrates the role of esoteric Buddhism in bringing Indian mythology to bear upon the Chinese imagination of divinity.

Beginning in the first centuries CE, Buddhism has served as a vehicle for the Indian influence upon Chinese culture. Buddhism brought to China the styles and the techniques of the South Asian visual arts. It introduced to China the sophisticated modes of Indian philosophical discourse and the literary gems of

Sanskrit poetry. The Buddhist contribution to China has ranged from the religious to the material spheres, from fiction and poetry to the culinary arts.[10] Indian civilization has had a decisive impact upon Chinese culture through the medium of the Buddhist faith. The history of the oedipal god Nezha might furnish a footnote to the encounter between the two civilizations.

Abbreviations

DZ	Kristofer Schipper and Franciscus Verellen, eds. *The Taoist Canon: A Historical Companion to the Daozang.*
FSYY	*Fengshen yanyi.* Author given as Xu Zhonglin. Edited by Li Guoqing.
SE	The Standard Edition of the Complete Psychological Works of Sigmund Freud
SKQS	*Wenyuange siku quanshu*
T.	*Taishō shinshū daizōkyō*
Tôh.	*A Complete Catalogue of the Tibetan Buddhist Canons*
T. Zuzō	*Taishō shinshū daizōkyō zuzōbu*
X.	*Wan xu zangjing*

NOTES

Introduction

1. Lévi-Strauss, *Tristes Tropiques,* p. 61, where he applies the statement to the three methodologies that inspired him: Marxism, psychoanalysis, and geology.

1 Sons and Fathers

1. *Fengshen yanyi,* author given as Xu Zhonglin, edited by Li Guoqing (Beijing: Beijing tushuguan, 2001) (hereafter *FSYY*), 12.101–14.128; at least three English translations are available: Stephen Owen, "Romance of the Gods," in his *An Anthology of Chinese Literature,* pp. 771–806; Gary Seaman and Victor Mair, "Romance of the Investiture of the Gods"; and Gu Zhizong, *Creation of the Gods,* 1:131–167; compare also Wilhelm Grube's German translation, *Die Metamorphosen der Goetter,* 1:156–195.

2. *FSYY,* 14.127.

3. On *The Canonization of the Gods* and Taiwanese temples, see Zeng Qinliang, *Taiwan minjian xinyang yu "fengshen yanyi" zhi bijiao yanjiu;* on the late Ming fiction of the supernatural, see Shahar, *Crazy Ji;* Dudbridge, *Legend of Miaoshan;* Liu Ts'un-Yan, *Buddhist and Taoist Influences on Chinese Novels;* Seaman, *The Journey to the North;* Durand-Dastès, *La conversion de l'orient;* and Philip Clart's introduction to his translation of Yang Erzeng, *Story of Han Xiangzi.*

4. Meulenbeld, "Civilized Demons," pp. 2–43, 271–282.

5. The earliest edition is *Xinke Zhong Bojing xiansheng piping Fengshen yanyi* (The newly printed, Zhong Bojing annotated, Canonization of the Gods). A copy is available at the Naikaku Bunko Library; see the photographic reprint in *Guben xiaoshuo jicheng* (Shanghai: Shanghai guji, 1994).

6. Zhang Peiheng's preface to *Fengshen yanyi: Xin zhengli ben* (Nanjing: Jiangsu guji, 1991), pp. 1–13; compare the editors' preface to the *Guben xiaoshuo jicheng* photographic reprint edition, 1:1. They concur that Zhong Bojing's (1574–1624) name has been falsely added to the novel for marketing purposes. Zhang compares the *Pingyao zhuan*'s 1620 preface (which does not mention the *Fengshen yanyi*) with its Chongzhen (1628–1644) revision (to which it has been added); on the novel's indebtedness to *The Journey to the West,* see Nicholas Koss, "The Relationship of the *Hsi-yu chi* and *Feng-shenyan-yi,*" and Sheng Fang, "Zailun *Fengshen yanyi* yinxi *Xiyou ji:* yu Xu Shuofang tongzhi shangque."

7. See Zhang Peiheng's preface to *Fengshen yanyi: Xin zhengli ben,* and the editors' preface to the *Guben xiaoshuo jicheng* photographic reprint edition; see also Li Guoqing's preface to *FSYY,* 1–5.

Liu Ts'un-yan (*Buddhist and Taoist Influences,* pp. 118–124) has advanced the hypothesis of Lu Xixing's (style: Chang'geng) (1520–ca. 1601) authorship. His evidence has been an eighteenth-century catalogue of plays that ascribed the novel to the Daoist priest. However, neither contemporary sources on Lu nor any of the numerous *Fengshen yanyi* editions associate him with it. Variously titled *Chuanqi hui kao* and *Yuefu kao lüe,* the drama catalogue was itself unclear about Lu Xixing's identity, erroneously dating him to the Yuan period. Its author, furthermore, voiced his own uncertainty about the attribution of the novel to the Daoist priest. For a thorough refutation of the Lu Xixing hypothesis, see Zhang Peiheng, "*Fengshen yanyi* zuozhe bukao." I might add that the *Fengshen yanyi* indebtedness to the *Xiyou ji* (The Journey to the West) creates a further difficulty in dating it to the sixteenth century.

8. *FSYY,* preface, p. 2.

9. The *Popular Tale of King Wu Punishing King Zhou* belongs in a group of five short novels that bear the title "popular tale" (*pinghua*). All five were published in or around the Yuan Zhizhi period (1321–1323) by the Yu publishing house of Jian'an (Fujian). Copies are preserved at the Naikaku Bunko Library, Tokyo; see the modern reprint edition *Wu wang fa Zhou pinghua* (Shanghai: Zhongguo gudian wenxue, 1957), and Liu Ts'un-yan's translation in his *Buddhist and Taoist Influences,* pp. 8–75. Like the other *pinghua, King Wu Punishing King Zhou* is an uneasy hybrid of official histories and oral lore; on its written sources, see Zhou Yibai, "Wu wang fa zhou pinghua de lishi genju"; see also Lu Shihua, *Yuan dai pinghua yanjiu,* pp. 113–123, and Hanan, *Chinese Vernacular Story,* p. 8.

10. *FSYY,* 16.309.

11. The historical novel survives in several successive versions; see for example the 1606 *Chunqiu wuba qixiong lieguo zhizhuan* and the 1615 *Chunqiu lieguo zhizhuan.*

12. D. C. Lau, trans., *Confucius: The Analects,* 1.2, p. 59.

13. Legge, trans., *Sacred Books of China, Texts of Confucianism, Part 1: The Hsiao King,* 7.473.

14. Legge, trans., *Sacred Books of China, Texts of Confucianism, Part 1: The Hsiao King,* 14.483. On the Confucian concepts of filial piety and loyalty, see Liu Zehua, *Zhong'guo zhengzhi sixiang shi: Qin, Han, Wei, Jin Nanbei chao juan,* 161–176; Knapp, "The Ru Reinterpretation of Xiao"; Lee, "The Dichotomy of Loyalty and Filial Piety"; and Pines, *Everlasting Empire,* 126–129.

15. Luo Guanzhong, *Three Kingdoms,* trans. Moss Roberts, 37.281.

16. "Cong er bu jian, fei xiao ye; jian er bu cong, yi fei xiao ye," *Da Dai li ji hui jiao jijie,* "Zengzi shi fu mu," p. 517; see also Liu Zehua, *Zhong'guo zhengzhi sixiang shi,* p. 166.

17. *Zizhi tongjian,* 291.9511.

18. Lau, trans., *Confucius: The Analects,* 18.1, p. 149, discussed by Liu Zehua, *Zhong'guo zhengzhi sixiang shi,* p. 167.

19. *Yi jing,* Kun hexagram.

20. Cao Xueqin and Gao E, *Honglou meng,* 33.341.

21. Su Huanzhong et al. distinguish between King Wen's propriety and Nezha's idealism; see their preface to *Chewangfu quben Fengshen bang,* 1:5.

22. Narrated in chapters 33 and 59 through 66, the two stories are discussed by Ho Kin-chung, "Nezha: Figure de l'enfant rebelle," pp. 21–23.

23. Sima Qian, *Shiji,* basic annals of Zhou, 4.19.

24. *FSYY,* 20.169.

25. *FSYY,* 20.170.

26. I follow Jiang Liangfu, who takes *zi* 兹 as the equivalent of *zi* 孳, meaning in this

context *zi* 子 "child" (hence "his *son's* flesh"); see his *Qu Yuan fu jin yi,* p. 174. Wen Yiduo and David Hawkes (whose translation I otherwise follow) understand *zi* as "that" (hence their reading: "When [King] Zhou bestowed *that* flesh on him."). The latter reading raises the question of whose flesh is it. The two scholars believe it is Mei Bo's, who is mentioned elsewhere in the text as pickled by King Zhou; see Wen Yiduo, *Tianwen shu zheng,* pp. 107, 101, and David Hawkes, *Songs of the South,* pp. 133, 148. I am grateful to Ye Derong (A'de) for pointing Jiang's reading to me.

27. Huangfu Mi, *Di wang shi ji,* pp. 26–27; compare *Yiwen leiju,* 12.7b, and *Taiping yulan,* 642.10a, 861.4b.

28. Compare *Chunqiu wuba qixiong lieguo zhizhuan* (1606 edition), 1.19b, *Chunqiu lieguo zhizhuan* (1615 edition), 1.22b, and *FSYY,* 20.169; see also Liu Ts'un-yan, *Buddhist and Taoist Influences,* p. 94

29. *Wu wang fa Zhou pinghua,* p. 41.

30. As Confucius's disciple Zigong is quoted saying; see Lau, trans., *Confucius: The Analects,* XIX, 20.155.

31. Lewis, *Sanctioned Violence,* p. 174.

32. See Lewis, *Sanctioned Violence,* 28, 79, 206–209; On Chinese cannibalism, see Des Rotours, "Quelques notes sur l'anthropophagie en Chine," and his "Encore quelques notes"; see also Chong, *Cannibalism in China.*

33. Sima Qian, *Shiji,* basic annals, Xiang Yu, 7.328.

34. *Han Fei zi,* "Shuolin," 22; see also *Zhanguo ce,* "Wei ce."

35. "Qiuran ke," translated by Cyril Birch as the "Curly-Bearded Hero," p. 1060.

36. *Shuihu quanzhuan,* 27.427–431, Sidney Shapiro's translation, 2:446–452.

37. On *gegu,* see Qiu Zhonglin, "Bu xiao zhi xiao," and his "Renyao yu Xueqi"; Yu, *Sanctity and Self-Inflicted Violence,* pp. 62–88; Chong, *Cannibalism in China,* pp. 93–103, 115–123; and Sutton's enlightening comments, "Consuming Counterrevolutionaries," pp. 151–152.

38. Lu Hsun, *Selected Works,* 1:20.

39. Sutton, "Consuming Counterrevolutionaries," p. 155.

40. The events are documented in Zheng Yi, *Scarlet Memorial;* they are analyzed by Sutton, "Consuming Counterrevolutionaries."

41. See Levenson, *Death and Resurrection.* Extensive scholarship has been dedicated to Canaanite and Phoenician child sacrifice; see, for example, Day, *Molech;* and Brown, *Late Carthaginian Child Sacrifice.*

42. Mozi, *Mozi jiaozhu,* "Lu wen," p. 719; compare *Mozi jiaozhu,* "Jie zang xia," p. 263. In his "Beasts or Humans," Yuri Pines emphasizes that Mozi considered the practice alien.

43. Qiu Xigui, "Sha shouzi jie," p. 48; the story of Yiya is mentioned in the *Han Feizi jijie,* "erbing," p. 42, and "shiguo," p. 74.

44. "*Wei chang bu shi xin,*" in *Li ji jijie,* "Shaoyi," p. 937; on the Hebrew offerings of the first fruits (*bikurim*), see, for example, Exod. 23:19, Exod. 24:26, Deut. 26:1–11.

45. On the division of the *zuo,* see Wang Ningsheng, *Gu su xin yan,* pp. 172–173.

46. Katz, "Banner Worship and Human Sacrifice."

47. Herodotus, *Persian Wars,* book I, chapter 119, trans. George Rawlinson.

48. See Rundin, "Pozo Moro," pp. 436–447.

49. Bassett, "Exposure of Oedipus."

50. *FSYY,* 22.189–190.

51. *Wu wang fa Zhou pinghua,* pp. 41–42.

52. *Bo wu zhi,* 4.1a.

53. Naxin, *Heshuo fang'gu ji,* 2.29–30; the tomb is also mentioned in the fourteenth-century *Wu wang fa Zhou pinghua,* p. 42.

54. On the Youli King Wen temple, see *Tangyin xianzhi,* 3.3a–4b, 9.18b; and *Youli cheng zhi.*

55. See Daoyuan, *Jingde chuandeng lu, T.* no. 2076, 51:220b.

2 Patricide and Suicide

1. See Hsieh Yu-Wei, "Filial Piety and Chinese Society"; and Knapp, *Selfless Offspring,* p. 3.

2. Knapp, *Selfless Offspring,* p. 3; anthropological studies reveal that all through the late twentieth century local societies throughout East Asia continued to regard filial piety as a primary virtue; see Jordan, "Folk Filial Piety in Taiwan," and the essays in Ikels, *Filial Piety.*

3. Ikels, *Filial Piety,* p. 5.

4. See David Jordan's translation of the *Twenty-Four Filial Exemplars* in his "Folk Filial Piety in Taiwan." The collection is available in various modern editions such as *Xiao jing, ershisi xiao zhuyi;* some add to it contemporary examples of filial piety; see, for example, *Gu jin ershisi xiao.*

5. See Knapp, *Selfless Offspring,* pp. 6–7.

6. Knapp, *Selfless Offspring,* p. 130.

7. Knapp, *Selfless Offspring,* pp. 126–127.

8. Lu Hsun, *Dawn Blossoms Plucked at Dusk,* p. 35; and Knapp, *Selfless Offspring,* p. 1. The tale had been criticized by such Ming scholars as He Mengchun (1474–1536); see Qiu Zhonglin, "Bu xiao zhi xiao," p. 84.

9. David Johnson, trans., "Selections from the Twenty-Four Exemplars," p. 141; compare David Jordan's translation, "Folk Filial Piety," p. 89, and the original in *Xiao jing, ershisi xiao zhuyi,* 75–76. Presumably because it is considered offensive, the tale has been omitted from modern editions such as *Gu jin ershisi xiao.*

10. See Knapp, *Selfless Offspring,* p. 7; compare Holzman, "Place of Filial Piety," p. 198.

11. See Hsiung Ping-Chen, *Tender Voyage,* pp. 21–22.

12. Ikels, *Filial Piety,* p. 4.

13. See Ōtsuka Hidetaka, *Zōho Chūgoku tsūzoku shōsetsu shomoku,* pp. 139–142, and Li Guoqing's preface to *FSYY,* p. 3.

14. *FSYY,* 14.128; the Immortal Taiyi (14.125) explained that it was necessary to vent Nezha's murderous inclinations.

15. On the God of Thunder and the Garuḍa bird, see Mark Meulenbeld, "Civilized Demons," pp. 74–90.

16. *Fengshen yanyi,* 1695 Sixuecao Tang edition (copies at the Beijing University Library and the Beijing National Library), preface, pp. 3b–4a.

17. *FSYY,* 12.109.

18. *FSYY,* 13.117.

19. Bakhtin, *Rabelais and His World,* p. 11.

20. *FSYY,* 14.122–123.

21. Wu Cheng'en, *Xiyou ji,* 14.164–165; and Anthony Yu's translation, *The Journey to the West,* 1:312–314.

22. Su Zhe, "Nazha," in *Luancheng ji, sanji,* 1.12b.

23. *FSYY,* 14.127.

24. Brook, Bourgon, and Blue, *Death by a Thousand Cuts,* p. 56.

25. Doolittle, *Social Life of the Chinese,* p. 140.
26. Gabbiani, "Insanity and Parricide."
27. Ho Kin-chung, "Nezha: Figure de l'enfant rebelle," pp. 17–19.
28. *FSYY,* 13.117.
29. Todorov, *The Fantastic,* p. 159.
30. Legge, trans., *Sacred Books of China, Texts of Confucianism, Part 1: The Hsiao King,* 1.466.
31. Yu, *Sanctity and Self-Inflicted Violence,* p. 62.
32. Alighieri, "Divine Comedy," *Inferno,* Canto 33, p. 178; discussed by Shulamith Shahar, *Childhood in the Middle Ages,* pp. 135–136.
33. See Qiu, "Bu xiao zhi xiao"; Qiu, "Renyao yu Xueqi"; and Jimmy Yu, *Sanctity and Self-Inflicted Violence,* pp. 62–88.
34. *Anhui tonghzi* (Guangxu Period (1875–1908)), quoted in Qiu, "Bu xiao zhi xiao," p. 58.
35. Kleeman, *A God's Own Tale,* pp. 97–98. The story of Miaoshan (Avalokiteśvara) who sacrificed her eyes and arms for her father is discussed in chapter 7.
36. Li Yu, "A Male Mencius's Mother Raises Her Son Properly by Moving House Three Times," in his *Silent Operas,* p. 126; on *gegu* in fiction, see also Lu, *Accidental Incest,* pp. 145–156.
37. Han Yu is quoted in Qiu, "Bu xiao zhi xiao," pp. 81–82. According to the *Mencius* (book 4, part 1, chapter 26), "There are three things which are unfilial, and to have no posterity is the greatest of them" (*Bu xiao you san, wu hou wei da*); See Legge's translation, *Works of Mencius,* p. 313.
38. Qiu, "Bu xiao zhi xiao," pp. 78–80.
39. *Ming shi lu,* Ming Taizu shi lu, 234.3419–3420.
40. Quoted in Qiu, "Bu xiao zhi xiao," p. 82.
41. See Qiu, "Bu xiao zhi xiao," p. 84.
42. Pu Songling, "Xiaozi" in his *Liaozhai zhiyi,* 5.656.
43. *FSSY,* 14.123.
44. Titled "Li Sao" ("On Encountering Trouble"), the poem has been translated by Hawkes, *Songs of the South,* p. 78.
45. Wolf, "Women and Suicide in China," p. 112; on suicide as protest in ancient China, see Lin Yüan-huei, *Weight of Mt. T'ai,* pp. 318–323, 329–345.
46. *Marco Polo: The Description of the World,* 1:337.
47. Hsieh and Spence, "Suicide and the Family," p. 36.
48. Translated by Hsieh and Spence, "Suicide and the Family," p. 39.
49. See Wolf, "Women and Suicide in China"; the essays collected in Ropp, *Passionate Women;* and Ropp's extended bibliography on female suicide in pp. 143–156 of that volume.
50. See Wolf ("Women and Suicide in China"), who notes the impact of modernization on the age profile of Chinese suicides. As the young become less dependent on their elders, the number of young suicides decreases, whereas that of elderly women increases; on this modern transformation see also Ikels, *Filial Piety,* p. 7, 14–15; on the emerging patterns of suicide in contemporary China, see also Phillips et al., "Suicide and Social Change in China."
51. See Hsieh and Spence, "Suicide and the Family," pp. 39–45; and Zamperini, "Untamed Hearts."
52. This is David Hawkes's translation of Cao Xueqin, *Story of the Stone,* 1:144; see also Hsieh and Spence, "Suicide and the Family," pp. 43–44.

53. Yang Xianyi and Gladys Yang, trans., *Courtesan's Jewel Box*, pp. 246–271; and Zamperini, "Untamed Hearts," p. 89.

3 The Chinese Oedipus

1. Freud, *Interpretation of Dreams*, p. 261.
2. Green, *Tragic Effect*, p. 232; and Spiro, *Oedipus in the Trobriands*, p. 162.
3. Gay, *Freud for Historians*, pp. 98–99.
4. Johnson and Price-Williams, *Oedipus Ubiquitous*, p. 7. On the varieties of the oedipal theme in world folklore, see also Edmunds and Dundes, *Oedipus: A Folklore Casebook*.
5. Freud, *Interpretation of Dreams*, p. 263. The Freudian reading of Hamlet was elaborated by Ernest Jones, *Hamlet and Oedipus*.
6. Freud, *Complete Letters of Sigmund Freud to Wilhelm Fliess*, p. 272.
7. Freud, "Dostoevsky and Parricide," 21:188.
8. Sangren, *Chinese Sociologies*, pp. 198–199; Sangren began exploring the Nezha myth in his "Myths, Gods, and Family Relations."
9. Fan Sheng, "Yidipasi yu Nezha," pp. 59–60.
10. Freud, *Interpretation of Dreams*, p. 262.
11. Sophocles, *Oedipus Rex*, trans. David Mulroy, p. 60.
12. On Freud's discovery of the Oedipus complex, see Rudnytsky, *Freud and Oedipus;* Jones, *Life and Work of Sigmund Freud*, 1:319–327; Gay, *Freud: A Life for Our Time*, p. 100; and James Strachey's preface to his translation of *The Interpretation of Dreams*, pp. xvii–xix, and note 2 to page 262.
13. Rudnytsky, *Freud and Oedipus*, p. 17; see also pp. 64–65, 358–359.
14. See Gao Juefu's translations of Freud [Fuluoyide] *Jingshen fenxi yinlun* and *Jingshen fenxi yinlun xinbian;* see also Zhang, *Psychoanalysis in China;* Wang Ning, "Reception of Freudianism in Modern Chinese literature"; Larson, *From Ah Q to Lei Feng*, pp. 49–54; and Jiang and Ivanhoe, *Reception and Rendition of Freud in China*.
15. See Blowers, "Bingham Dai, Adolf Storfer, and the Tentative Beginnings of Psychoanalytic Culture in China: 1935–1941."
16. See Kirsner and Snyder, "Psychoanalysis in China"; and Wan, "Fundamentals of Freud."
17. Zhao Jingshen, "Zhongguo xin wenyi yu biantai xingyu."
18. See Matsumura Takeo, *Wenyi yu xing'yu*, which drew for its part on Albert Mordell, *The Erotic Motive in Literature* (1919); see also Zhang, *Psychoanalysis in China*, pp. 139–141.
19. See Zhang Shizhao, *Fuluoyide xuzhuan*, p. 31; see also Zhang, *Psychoanalysis in China*, p. 45.
20. Missing from the 1936 edition of Gao Juefu's *Jingshen fenxi yinlun xinbian*, both terms appear in the revised 1987 edition.
21. See Zhang, *Psychoanalysis in China;* and Wang Ning, "Reception of Freudianism."
22. Zhang, *Psychoanalysis in China*, p. 101.
23. See Zhang, *Psychoanalysis in China;* Wang Ning, "Reception of Freudianism"; Gu Ming-Dong, "Filial Piety Complex," pp. 177–178; and Gu Ming-Dong, "Chinese Oedipus in Exile." As early as 1922 Zhou Zuoren alluded to psychoanalysis in his discussion of Yu Dafu's story "Sinking" ("*Chenlun*"); see his *Ziji de yuandi*, p. 55.
24. Gu Ming-Dong, "Filial Piety Complex," pp. 167–168.
25. Yuan Changying, *Kongque dongnan fei*, p. 8. Mother Jiao is described as "sexually jealous" in the preface (p. 1); see also Zhang, *Psychoanalysis in China*, pp. 79–81; and Liu

Xiongping, "Edipusi qingjie yu xiandai wenxue," p. 47. The original ballad has been translated by Anne Birrell, "A Peacock Southward Flew."

26. Tseng Wen-Shing and Jing Hsu, "Chinese Attitude," p. 34; compare Zhang, *Psychoanalysis in China*, p. 70; Tang and Smith, "The Eternal Triangle Across Cultures: Oedipus, Hsueh, and Ganesa," p. 568.

27. Compare "Fenhe wan" in *Jingju congkan* (vol. 39, pp. 45–67), in which the arrow that hit the boy had been aimed at a menacing tiger, with the version translated by L. C. Arlington and Harold Acton (*Famous Chinese Plays*, p. 218), in which the general intentionally killed the boy. The eighteenth-century novel *Shuo Tang hou zhuan* (53.32b) concurs with the former version of the general killing the boy as he tries to save him from the beast; see also Zhang, *Psychoanalysis in China*, pp. 69–70.

28. *Han Fei zi*, "Shuolin," 22 (see chapter 1).

29. The legend has been commemorated at the Killing-the-Sons Embankment (Sha'er Tang) in Jixi County; see Cheng Guangxian, "Wang'gong de jibai and yiwen."

30. This was the case at Jincun Village; see Lagerwey, "Village Religion in Huizhou," p. 347.

31. Wu Cheng'en, *Xiyou ji*, 8.86, 15.170–171; and Anthony Yu's translation, 1:193–194, 1:321–322.

32. Sangren, "Female Gender in Chinese Religious Symbols."

33. Tang and Smith ("Eternal Triangle Across Cultures," p. 570) apply this explanation to the Śiva and Gaṇeśa myth as well, contrasting the Chinese and Indian patterns with the Western one.

34. The shared oedipal theme of the Nezha and the Sohrab legends has led J. C. Coyajee to speculate that they derive from a common source. Intriguing as his thesis might be, I find no evidence of a connection between the Persian epic and the *Fengshen yanyi;* see Coyajee, *Cults and Legends of Ancient Iran & China*, pp. 99–134; and Mair, "Medieval, Central Asian Buddhist Theme," pp. 12–13.

35. Compare Jerome Clinton's verse translation of Ferdowsi, *Tragedy of Sohrab and Rostam*, pp. 139–153, with Reuben Levy's prose version, Ferdowsi, *Epic of Kings*, pp. 75–80.

36. See O'Flaherty, *Śiva*, p. 192; On the Andhaka myth, see also Handelman and Shulman, *God Inside Out*, pp. 113–158.

37. Courtright, *Gaṇeśa*, p. 117.

38. See Courtright, *Gaṇeśa*, pp. 114–122, and Ramanujan, "Indian 'Oedipus,'" p. 130. In his "Fathers, Sons and Gurus," Goldman argues that in Indian tales of the "positive" Oedipus (in which the violence is directed from the child toward his elder), the father is often represented by a substitute such as a guru or an uncle. On the Indian oedipal paradigm, see also Silk, *Riven by Lust*, pp. 164–170.

39. Johnson and Price-Williams, *Oedipus Ubiquitous*, p. 7.

40. Gu Ming-Dong, "Filial-Piety Complex," p. 168.

41. See *Mencius*, book 5, part 1, chapter 2 (Legge's translation pp. 342–343); *Xiao jing, ershisi xiao*, pp. 43–47; and Jordan's translation "Folk Filial Piety," p. 83. For a structural analysis of the legend's earliest manifestations, see Lai, "Unmasking the Filial Sage-King"; on its Han and medieval evolution, consult Knapp, *Selfless Offspring*, esp. pp. 49–53.

42. Gu Ming-Dong, "Filial-Piety Complex," p. 170.

43. See Brown, "Dragon of Tagaung"; Spiro, "Oedipus Complex in Burma"; and Edmunds, "Oedipus in Burma."

44. My translation follows Wilt Idema's in his *Personal Salvation and Filial Piety*, p. 201 note 98. The original is included in Xiang Chu, *Dunhuang bianwen xuanzhu*,

p. 1:328. Gu Ming-Dong was unaware of this version, which is illuminatingly discussed by Idema.

45. In the earliest Yuan period version, the mother is the recipient of devotion in 46 percent of the tales, as compared with 17 percent for the father and 25 percent for the two of them combined. In the remaining stories the filial devotion is directed toward step-parents or grandparents; see Jordan, "Folk Filial Piety," pp. 70–71.

46. Jordan, "Folk Filial Piety," p. 72.

47. David Johnson, trans., "Selections," p. 139; compare David Jordan's translation, "Folk Filial Piety," p. 84; and the original in *Xiao jing, ershisi xiao zhuyi*, pp. 59–60.

48. Cole, *Mothers and Sons*, p. 41.

49. See, among others, Johnson, *Ritual Opera, Operatic Ritual.*

50. This is Victor Mair's translation of the ninth- or tenth-century Dunhuang *bianwen* version; see his *Tun-Huang Popular Narratives*, p. 118; The original is *Damuqianlian mingjian jiumu bianwen bing tu*, in Xiang Chu, *Dunhuang bianwen xuanzhu*, p. 1:937.

51. Cole, *Mothers and Sons*, p. 207.

52. See Cole, *Mothers and Sons*, pp. 197–217; Seaman, "Sexual Politics of Karmic Retribution," and Idema, *Personal Salvation and Filial Piety*, pp. 23–26.

53. Lu Hsun, *Dawn Blossoms Plucked at Dusk*, postscript, p. 106 (amending the transliterated Tsao Ngo into Cao E). I am grateful to Shang Wei for pointing out this passage to me.

54. Song Maocheng, *Jiu yue ji, bieji*, 2.268–270.

55. Lu, *Accidental Incest*, pp. 144–145.

56. Plaks, "Problem of Incest," pp. 128–131.

57. Cao Xueqin and Gao E, *Honglou meng*, 33.341; see Gu Ming-Dong, "Filial-Piety Complex," pp. 170–174.

58. On the possible familial configurations that might be reflected in the novel, see Hawkes's introduction to Cao Xueqin and Gao E, *Story of the Stone*, 1:33–38.

59. Cao Xueqin and Gao E, *Story of the Stone*, trans. by David Hawkes, 33.150–151.

60. Hsiung, *Tender Voyage*, p. 145.

61. Compare Slote, "Oedipal Ties," pp. 443–444, and Wolf, *Women and the Family*, pp. 161–162.

62. Wolf, *Women and the Family*, p. 162.

63. See Hsiung, *Tender Voyage*, pp. 128–155; Wu Pei-Yi similarly notes the absence of the father from the autobiographical writings of the elite; see his "Childhood Remembered," pp. 131–133.

64. Hsiung, *Tender Voyage*, p. 154.

65. Slote, "Oedipal Ties," pp. 442–443.

66. See Wolf, *Women and the Family*, pp. 160–163; Cohen, *House United, House Divided*, pp. 198–199, and Hsiung, *Tender Voyage*, pp. 128–155.

67. Sangren, *Chinese Sociologies*, p. 199.

68. Malinowski has argued that the oedipal drive is missing from the matrilineal society of the Trobriand Archipelago (in New Guinea), where the animosity of the boy is directed toward his maternal uncle and his sexual attachment is to his sister. Melford Spiro (*Oedipus in the Trobriands*), however, has contended that the Freudian cluster is evident in the Trobriand Archipelago; compare Malinowski, *Sex and Repression in Savage Society*, with Spiro, *Oedipus in the Trobriands.*

69. Boretz, *Gods, Ghosts, and Gangsters*, p. 16.

70. Ibid., p. 206.

71. Tseng and Hsu ("Chinese Attitude," p. 34) argue that in China "the issue of triangular conflict within the family is less prominent than in the West because of the acceptance of uninterrupted closeness between mother and son under the concept of filial piety."

4 Teenage Delinquent or Revolutionary Martyr

1. Cao Xueqin and Gao E, *Honglou meng,* 19.184 and 7.75 respectively. The play is titled "Jiang Taigong Beheads the Generals and Canonizes the Gods" ("Jiang Taigong zhan jiang feng shen"); compare Hawkes's translation, *Story of the Stone,* 1:376 and 1:177.

2. On the Nezha figure in the theater, see Huang Jingqin, "Nezha xiju xingxiang tansuo," and Xu Xinyi, "Lun Suo mo Jing yu Nezha san bian zaju." On his role in Peking Opera martial plays, see Ying Yukang, "Lun Jingxi wuda ju zhong de Nezha." On his image in Taiwanese drama (including puppet, and shadow puppet, theater) see Shi Guangsheng, "Taiwan xiqu zhong de Nezha xingxiang kehua."

3. On the diversity of "performance-related" versus "literary" drum ballads and lute ballads, see Wan, *Green Peony,* pp. 23, 136–140.

4. Two manuscript copies of the same *Fengshen bang* drum ballad have been preserved at the Chewangfu collection. One (which I examined) is currently stored at the Beijing University Library (it is titled *Fengshen yanyi*); the other is preserved at the Zhongshan University Library. The manuscripts' orthographic errors have been corrected in the 1992 reprint edition to which reference is given here: *Chewangfu quben Fengshen bang.* Internal evidence indicates that the manuscripts originated in Tongzhi-period (1862–1874) Beijing; see the editors' preface to *Chewangfu quben Fengshen bang,* p. 2.

5. The Taiwanese *gezai* ballad survives in three related printed editions, dating from 1929, 1931, and 1957. The third bears the different title of *Li Nezha chou long jin ge* (Li Nezha pulling out the dragon's tendons). Copies of all three are preserved at the Academia Sinica, Institute of History and Philology Library (Taibei). References are given below to the reprint of the first and third editions in Chen Zhaonan's careful textual study: "Taiwan Shuochang de Nezha chuanshuo."

6. Titled *Nezha nao hai* (Nezha wreaks havoc in the ocean), the Fuzhou *pinghua* narrative was issued in a lithographic edition (printed in Shanghai) by the Fuzhou publisher Yixin shuju. A copy is available in the folk literature (*su wenxue*) collection of the Academia Sinica, Institute of History and Philology (Taibei), number Pe22-207; a photographic reprint is available in *Su wenxue congkan,* vol. 367, pp. 1–22.

7. Compare *FSYY,* 12.107 and Chen Zhaonan, "Taiwan Shuochang de Nezha chuanshuo," p. 515, lines 63–64, p. 522, lines 63–64.

8. Chen Zhaonan, "Taiwan Shuochang de Nezha chuanshuo," p. 518, lines 134–139, p. 524, lines 129–133.

9. Chen Zhaonan, "Taiwan Shuochang de Nezha chuanshuo," p. 518, lines 134–135.

10. *Nezha nao hai* (Fuzhou *pingshu* ballad), p. 5b.

11. *Nezha nao hai* (Fuzhou *pingshu* ballad), p. 7a.

12. *Nezha nao hai* (Fuzhou *pingshu* ballad), p. 7a.

13. Freud, *Totem and Taboo,* p. 141.

14. Compare *FSYY,* 12.101–14.128 with *Chewangfu quben Fengshen bang,* 85.701–101.835.

15. *Chewangfu quben Fengshen bang,* 98.806.

16. Chinese cosmology considers the flesh a manifestation of the female *yin* principle, regarding bones as a reflection of the male *yang* force. Hence Nezha returns his flesh to his

mother and his bones to his father; see Watson, "Of Flesh and Bones." See also the discussion in chapter 7 below.

17. *Chewangfu quben Fengshen bang,* 96.796.

18. Ibid., 97.797.

19. Ibid., 98.808.

20. Ibid., 97.798–799.

21. Ibid., 96.795; the crow had been used as a filial exemplar as early as the first centuries CE; see Knapp, *Selfless Offspring,* pp. 129–130.

22. *Chewangfu quben Fengshen bang,* 97. 797.

23. Ibid., 97.798.

24. This is the case with the late-Qing novel *Storyteller's Jigong* (*Pingyan Jigong zhuan*), which derives from mid-nineteenth-century Beijing *guci;* see Shahar, *Crazy Ji,* pp. 151–157.

25. One Peking Opera version of *The Canonization of the Gods* omits the oedipal tale altogether, even though it does feature Nezha as a warrior in the righteous Zhou camp; see *Fengshen tianbang* (The heavenly roster of the gods). Palace manuscript edition. Photographic reprint in *Guben xiqu congkan di jiuji* (Beijing: Zhonghua shuju, 1964).

26. *Chentang guan,* in *Su wenxue congkan,* 58:85.

27. Compare the two *Chentang guan* fragments reproduced in *Su wenxue congkan,* vol. 58, pp. 83–84 and 117 respectively.

28. Booth, *Rhetoric of Fiction,* pp. 245–249.

29. *Nezha chuanqi* is the title of the broadcast animation as well as of the ten-volume printed cartoon that has been based upon it; see the latter, vol. 10, p. 82. Detailed plot summaries, and links to all the episodes, are available online under the entry "Nezha chuanqi" in *Baidu baike.* On the evolution of the Lady Rock cycle, see also chapter 5 below.

30. The *Fengshen yanyi* (Japanese: *Hōshin engi*) is available in at least two Japanese translations: by Kijima Seidō (published in 1977) and by Anō Tsutomu (1988). Fujisaki's animation draws upon the latter.

31. Fujisaki Ryū, *Houshin engi,* episode 12, p. 10.

32. See, among others, Cui Yunlan, "Chuantong yishu de jinghua."

33. Cui Yunlan, "Chuantong yishu de jinghua," p. 24.

34 See Sangren, *Chinese Sociologies,* pp. 205, 210–211; Sangren (p. 186) aptly quotes Claude Lévi-Strauss (*The Elementary Structures of Kinship*): "To this very day, mankind has always dreamed of seizing and fixing that floating moment when it was permissible to believe that the law of exchange could be evaded, that one could gain without losing, enjoy without sharing . . . a world in which one might keep to oneself."

35. Luo Tongbing, "Tichu Edipusi."

36. The *Nezha chuanqi* script is included in volume 2, pp. 839–850 of *Gezaixi juben zhengli jihua baogao shu.* On the play, see Shi Guangsheng, "Taiwan xiqu zhong de Nezha xingxiang kehua," pp. 173–176; and Ding Zhaoqin, "Cong sange xiandai wenben kan Nezha de xingxiang," pp. 312–316. Both authors have failed to notice the play's indebtedness to the mainland cartoon. On the Xinhexing company and its director Jiang Qingliu, see the respective entries in the online *Encyclopedia of Taiwan* (*Taiwan dabaike quanshu*).

37. Compare *Nezha chuanqi* in *Gezaixi juben zhengli jihua baogao shu,* p. 850, with the oral ballad (discussed above) *Nezha nao donghai ge,* in Chen Zhaonan, "Taiwan Shuochang de Nezha chuanshuo," p. 515, lines 63–64; p. 522, lines 63–64.

38. Shi Guangsheng, "Taiwan xiqu zhong de Nezha xingxiang kehua," p. 176.

39. Xi Song, *Fengshen bang li de Nezha,* p. 4. On this story, see Ding Zhaoqin, "Cong sange xiandai wenben kan Nezha de xingxiang," pp. 316–323.

40. Xi Song, *Fengshen bang li de Nezha,* pp. 30–31.

41. Ibid., p. 23.

42. See Yoshimura, *Tianren dansheng tu,* pp. 22–63.

43. Xi Song, *Fengshen bang li de Nezha,* p. 33.

44. See the movie's screenplay: *Qing Shaonian Nezha* (Taibei: Yuanliu, 1992); see also Ding Zhaoqin, "Cong sange xiandai wenben kan Nezha de xingxiang," pp. 323–327.

45. *Qing Shaonian Nezha,* scene 31.

46. For some reason, the inscription he writes is missing from the movie's printed screenplay; *Qing Shaonian Nezha,* scene 69.

5 Divine Warrior

1. *FSYY,* 33.277–278.

2. *FSYY,* 34.287–291.

3. *FSYY,* 34.288

4. See respectively, *FSYY,* 34.289, 34.291, 36.308.

5. *FSYY,* 60.533, compare 34.289.

6. Ying Yukang, "Lun Jingxi wuda ju zhong de Nezha," p. 595.

7. The compendium survives in a Ming edition titled *Sanjiao yuanliu shengdi fozu sou shen daquan,* and in a Qing edition titled *Huitu sanjiao yuanliu soushen daquan.*

8. See, respectively, Dudbridge, *Legend of Miaoshan,* pp. 67–72, and Li Xianzhang, "Yi *sanjiao soushen daquan.*"

9. *Xinbian lianxiang soushen guangji.*

10. On this question see Dudbridge, *Legend of Miaoshan,* pp. 67–69.

11. See the Ming edition, *Sanjiao yuanliu shengdi fozu sou shen daquan,* pp. 326–327, and the Qing edition *Huitu sanjiao yuanliu soushen daquan,* pp. 330–331. The text transcribes Tārā as Duoli, rather than the more common Duoluo.

12. See Peri, "Hārītī: La Mère-de-Démons"; on the Mother-of-Demons in Chinese visual art, see Murray, "Representations of Hārītī"; see also Strickmann, *Chinese Magical Medicine,* pp. 67, 136.

13. See *Erlang shen zui she suomo jing;* the play is the subject of a study by Xu Xinyi, "Lun *Suomo Jing* yu *Nezha san bian* zaju."

14. I amend this monster's name following the *Menglie Nazha san bianhua.*

15. The Marshal of Heavenly Reeds (Tianpeng dajiang) originated in early Daoist literature. By the sixteenth century, he found his way into *The Journey to the West* in the form of Zhu Bajie (Pigsy); see Anthony Yu's translation, 8.192.

16. *Erlang shen zui she suomo jing,* 1b.

17. *Menglie Nazha san bianhua.* The play's Ming-period date is ascertained by the invocation of the dynasty's prosperity in its concluding lines (p. 10a); see also Xu Xinyi, "Lun *Suomo Jing* yu *Nezha san bian* zaju," p. 378, note 19.

18. *Menglie Nazha san bianhua,* p. 3a.

19. Ibid., p. 8b; see also Xu Xinyi, "Lun *Suomo Jing* yu *Nezha san bian* zaju," pp. 389–392.

20. Ibid., p. 5b.

21. See, for examples, Conze, *Large Sutra of Perfect Wisdom,* pp. 38–39. A digital search of the Chinese canon yields hundreds of references to the Buddha emitting rays of golden light (*fang da guangming*).

22. *Can Tang Wudai shi yanyi*, 5.13 and 38.157 respectively. Another late Ming novel that features Nezha (written Nacha) is the *Journey to the South*, in which he battles the god Huaguang; see *Quanxiang Huaguang Tianwang Nanyou zhizhuan*, 3.19b–20b.

23. *Wenshu pusa xiang shizi*; see also Idema, *Dramatic Oeuvre of Chu Yu-Tun*, pp. 46, 52–54.

24. Nezha (written as Nachi) battles Sun Wukong in a twenty-four-act dramatic version of *The Journey to the West*, which, albeit attributed to a Yuan author, likely dates from the Ming period; see scene 9 of the *Yang Donglai xiansheng piping Xiyou ji*, 3.38–3.42; on the play's dating see Dudbridge, *Hsi-yu chi*, pp. 76–80. The battle figures prominently in the 1592 prose masterpiece, attributed to Wu Cheng'en, *Xiyou ji*, 4.43–45, and Anthony Yu's translation, *The Journey to the West*, 1:127–130.

25. Anthony Yu's translation, *The Journey to the West*, 1:128–129; the original is Wu Cheng'en, *Xiyou ji*, 4.43.

26. Anthony Yu's translation, *The Journey to the West*, 1:128–129; the original is Wu Cheng'en, *Xiyou ji*, 4.44.

27. Anthony Yu's translation, *The Journey to the West*, 1:172; the original is Wu Cheng'en, *Xiyou ji*, 7.73.

28. Sangren, *Chinese Sociologies*, p. 211; compare Sangren, *Myth, Gender, and Subjectivity*, pp. 79–81.

29. *FSYY*, 13.112–117.

30. *FSYY*, 13.114.

31. See the Ming edition, *Sanjiao yuanliu shengdi fozu sou shen daquan*, p. 326, and the Qing edition, *Huitu sanjiao yuanliu soushen daquan*, p. 330.

32. See Ecke and Demiéville, *Twin Pagodas of Zayton*, p. 35 and plate 26; and Dudbridge, *The Hsi-yu chi*, pp. 47–49 and plate 5.

33. The Quanzhou scholar Wu Youxiong has suggested to me that Nezha figures on its renowned pagodas (which are discussed in more detail below). In their *Twin Pagodas of Zayton* (p. 68 and plate 45), G. Ecke and P. Demiéville cite a local tradition to identify the three-headed and six-armed guardian as an *asura* demon, and its opposite image as the dragon king Sāraga. But they account neither for the two figures' association nor for the latter's belt and bow.

34. Compare *Menglie Nazha san bianhua*, p. 8a, and *FSYY*, 13.117.

35. Hong Mai, *Yijian zhi*, pp. 1429–1430.

36. At least five manuscript versions of the Kunqu play *Qianyuan shan* survive; four are preserved at the Academia Sinica, Institute of History and Philology (Taibei). Numbered K-838, K21-221-4, K60-631, and Pi96-1092, they are reprinted in vol. 58, pp. 1–69 of the *Su wenxue congkan*. Another manuscript version is reproduced (photographically as well as on microfilm) in case 57, volume 1, of *Qing Meng'gu Che wang fu cang qu ben*.

37. On the "Qianyuan shan" in Peking Opera, see Ying Yukang, "Lun Jingxi wuda ju zhong de Nezha" (the reference to skating is on p. 602).

38. *Nezha chuanqi* is the title of the broadcast animation as well as of the ten-volume printed cartoon that has been based upon it. Detailed plot summaries, and links to all the episodes, are available online under the entry "Nezha chuanqi" in *Baidu baike*.

39. Citing Sun Wukong and Nezha as examples, Avron Boretz ("Martial Gods and Magic Swords," p. 96) has noted that "representations of efficacy and prowess manifest their power through the use of some tool, weapon, or esoterically transmitted skill."

40. See *FSYY*, 12.102, 14.122.

41. This is Edward Davis's translation, *Society and the Supernatural*, pp. 47–48 (slightly

altered); the original is Hong Mai, *Yijian zhi,* pp. 1429–1430. Davis identifies Master Cheng as a village ritual master, as distinguished from Daoist priests. Li Fengmao ("Wuying xinyang," pp. 573–574), however, highlights the orthodox Daoist elements in his ritual performance.

42. Compare the Ming and Qing editions of *The Grand Compendium: Sanjiao yuanliu shengdi fozu sou shen daquan,* p. 326, and *Huitu sanjiao yuanliu soushen daquan,* p. 330; see also *Wenshu pusa xiang shizi,* 2a–b, 3b; and Wu Cheng'en, *Xiyou ji,* 4.44, translated by Anthony Yu, *The Journey to the West,* 1:129.

43. This is Anthony Yu's translation, *The Journey to the West,* 1:129; the original is Wu Cheng'en, *Xiyou ji,* 4.44; compare the Ming and Qing editions of the *Grand Compendium: Sanjiao yuanliu shengdi fozu sou shen daquan,* p. 326, and *Huitu sanjiao yuanliu soushen daquan,* p. 330; and *Wenshu pusa xiang shizi,* 2a–b, 3b.

44. See *Daofa huiyuan, DZ* 1220, 240.11a, 138.13a; and *Fahai yizhu, DZ* 1166, 15.17a; see also chapter 5 of Meulenbeld, *Demonic Warfare.*

45. *Daofa huiyuan, DZ* 1220, 138.13a.

6 The Child-God

1. See, respectively, Zeng Guodong, "Xinying Taizi Gong"; Xu Bingkun, "Taiwan minjian Nezha Taizi xinyang"; Xu Xianping, "Tainan xian Taizi ye miao"; and Yang Tianhou and Lin Likuan, "Jinmen Taizi ye xinyang."

2. See Christina Cheng's essay "In Search of Folk Humor," which was followed by her book of the same title; and Chen Xuelin, "Ao'men Nezha miao."

3. Elliott, *Chinese Spirit-Medium Cults,* pp. 76–77; and Cheu, *Nine Emperor Gods,* pp. 30, 36–37, 39, 93–95.

4. Jordan, *Gods, Ghosts and Ancestors,* pp. 71–73; Stafford, *Roads of Chinese Childhood,* pp. 130–139; Hong Shuling, "Nezha xinyang yu nüxing shenmei"; Hu Taili, "Shen gui yu dutu," pp. 413–415; Boretz, *Gods, Ghosts, and Gangsters,* pp. 14–15, 103–104.

5. See, for example, Willem Grootaers, Li Shiyu, and Wang Fushi, "Rural Temples around Hsüan-Hua (South Chahar)." Nezha temples do not figure in recent monographs on northern Chinese religion, such as Overmyer, *Local Religion;* Johnson, *Spectacle and Sacrifice;* and Chau, *Miraculous Response.*

6. See Chen Xuelin, "Beijing waicheng Nezha miao tansu." Chen's study is partially based upon the field notes of the Japanese historian Niida Noboru, who in 1944 transcribed the (now extinct) temple's inscriptions; see also Li Qiao, *Zhongguo hangye shen,* pp. 199–200.

7. On the geographic distribution of Sun Wukong and Zhu Bajie temples in the poorer subregions of the Putian plains, see Kenneth Dean and Zheng Zhenman, *Ritual Alliances,* 1:205; on Jigong see Shahar, *Crazy Ji.*

8. *Xixia xianzhi,* p. 576.

9. See *Nezha guli,* pp. 65–67.

10. *Nezha guli,* p. 45.

11. Ibid., pp. 24–26, 41–42.

12. Adjacent to the 2001–2002 sumptuous temple is a modest red brick shrine dating from 1994. Both have been constructed with financial support from Taiwanese Zhanghua County parishioners. Steles dating from 1997, 2001, and 2003 record the patrons' names and their donations; see also *Nezha guli,* pp. 50–56.

13. See Christina Cheng's essay "In Search of Folk Humor," followed by her monograph *In Search of Folk Humor,* pp. 195–216; see also Chen Xuelin, "Ao'men Nezha miao."

14. See Cheng, *In Search of Folk Humor,* p. 199, and Chen Xuelin, "Ao'men Nezha miao."

15. Cheng, *In Search of Folk Humor,* p. 213.

16. Ibid., p. 214.

17. Legge, trans., *Sacred Books of China, Texts of Confucianism, Part 1: The Hsiao King,* 1.466.

18. Stafford, *Roads of Chinese Childhood,* pp. 142–143.

19. Greenlees, "Americans in the Action."

20. The originals read "*yi qiu ji zhong*" and "*you wo sheng cai*" respectively; see Cheng, *In Search of Folk Humor,* p. 215; on his involvement in gambling, see also Li Nezha at godchecker.com.

21. See Hu Taili, "Shen gui yu dutu," pp. 414–415; and Shahar, *Crazy Ji,* pp. 180–184.

22. Boretz, *Gods, Ghosts, and Gangsters,* pp. 104 and 33 respectively.

23. Cheng, "In Search of Folk Humor," p. 93; see also her *In Search of Folk Humor,* pp. 209–201; Cheng sees in the miniscule Nezha shrine a challenge to foreign dominance no less than to the hegemony of the large and established Chinese temples such as Mazu's.

24. Cheng, *In Search of Folk Humor,* p. 215.

25. Interview at the Taizi miao (also known as the Taizi gong), Danshui, June 24, 2012.

26. Steven Sangren, oral communication, June 2012.

27. Cheng, *In Search of Folk Humor,* pp. 212–214; see also Saso, "The Nezha Daoist shrine of Macao protects an ancient Catholic cathedral," on his webpage www.micahelsaso.org, accessed on May 7, 2010.

28. Wang Ch'iu-Kuei provided me with a Jinmen County official survey listing the addresses and telephone numbers of 178 registered shrines ("Jinmen xian simiao yilanbiao"). Based on their fieldwork, Yang Tianhou and Lin Likuan ("Jinmen Taizi ye xinyang," p. 466) arrive at the much larger number of 263 temples and shrines.

29. See the list in Yang Tianhou and Lin Likuan, "Jinmen Taizi ye xinyang," pp. 470–473.

30. Yang Tianhou and Lin Likuan ("Jinmen Taizi ye xinyang," pp. 466–470) list five Jinmen shrines dedicated to Nezha as the principal deity. In October 2011, I visited another, the Qixin Tang, at the village of Xiyuan. It dates from 2003.

31. Yang Tianhou and Lin Likuan, "Jinmen Taizi ye xinyang," pp. 467–468, 475–477.

32. Ibid., pp. 467–468; at the Dongshawei shrine Nezha is hosted by Chi Wangye and Zhu Wangye.

33. Yang Tianhou and Lin Likuan, "Jinmen Taizi ye xinyang," p. 476.

34. Cai Rongying is writing her MA thesis at Jinmen University on the Five-Villages Prince. I am most grateful to her, as well as to Zhuang Zhengong and Chen Tianqi, for their generous help during my visit to the island.

35. See Zeng Qinliang, *Taiwan minjian xinyang,* pp. 152–157, and the color photos of Nezha painted beams on pp. 14–15.

36. Chen Yiyuan, "Jiayi xian simiao."

37. On Bo Yikao in Taiwanese murals, see Zeng Qinliang, *Taiwan minjian xinyang,* p. 154.

38. Chen Yiyuan, "Jiayi xian simiao," p. 297.

39. *Taipei Times,* October 3, 2011, p. 1.

40. On Nezha as the protector of wheeled vehicles, see *Nei zhengbu shenzhi jieshao ziliao shuoming,* p. 16; see also Brian Kennedy and Elizabeth Guo, "Taiwanese Martial Motifs." James Robson has told me that his Taiwanese friends have nicknamed his bike "Nezha."

41. Xu Xianping, "Tainan xian Taizi ye miao," p. 611.

42. Ibid., pp. 611–614.

43. Qiu Dezai, *Taiwan miao shen zhuan,* pp. 361–370; and Qu Haiyuan, *Chongxiu Taiwan sheng tongzhi,* quoted in Zeng Guodong, "Xinying Taizi Gong," p. 135 (dating from 1992, the *Chongxiu Taiwan sheng tongzhi* draws upon 1981 figures).

44. *Zhonghua daojiao zhongtan yuanshuai hongdao xiehui tuanti huiyuan mingce.*

45. Liu Zhiwan, "Taiwan de minjian Xinyang," p. 91; compare also Yang Tianhou and Lin Likuan, "Jinmen Taizi ye xinyang," pp. 453–455.

46. Zeng Guodong, "Xinying Taizi Gong," pp. 120–121, 126–127.

47. Zeng Guodong, "Xinying Taizi Gong," p. 128; the proverb is "*jian xin miao, zhong rong shu.*"

48. Zeng Guodong, "Xinying Taizi Gong," pp. 129–130.

49. Informants at the Xinying Taizi Gong have told me that as many as one million pilgrims attended the god's 2008 birthday celebrations. I suspect that the number is exaggerated. The temple records list some nine thousand different shrines that, between 1993 and 2002, came there on pilgrimage. These must have included temples that feature Nezha as an ancillary (rather than principal) deity; see Xu Xianping, "Tainan xian Taizi ye miao," p. 608.

50. Interview conducted on October 10, 2008; on the Nezha toy offerings, see also Hong Shuling, "Nezha xinyang yu nüxing shenmei," p. 231, and photo on p. 239.

51. July 20, 2010, visit to the Taizi Ling Gong, in the village of Houlucun, on Mount Damao, some twenty miles north of Xiamen City, Fujian.

52. "Qiu zi wang huanyuan."

53. October 7, 2011 visit; see also below.

54. I was given at the Xinying Taizi Gong a VCD recording of the Min'nan-language speech that Chen Shuibian gave on the occasion of his visit. On the construction of the community center and library, see Zeng Guodong, "Xinying Taizi Gong," p. 126.

55. See *Jidian suiyue.*

56. Chen Yichuan, *Shenqi huoxian,* pp. 16–19; on oracle divination sticks, see Strickmann, *Chinese Poetry and Prophecy.*

57. Zeng Guodong, "Xinying Taizi Gong."

58. According to another version, the mysterious infant appeared day after day and played with the local kids. One day he bid them adieu and disappeared on his wind-and-fire wheels; see Cheng, *In Search of Folk Humor,* p. 198; and Chen Xuelin, "Ao'men Nezha miao."

59. See Xu Bingkun, "Taiwan minjian Nezha Taizi xinyang," pp. 244–246, and photo on p. 264.

60. Xu Bingkun, "Taiwan minjian Nezha Taizi Xinyang," pp. 255–256.

61. Lagerwey, *Taoist Ritual,* p. 34. (I have substituted "armies" for Lagerwey's "camps.")

62. Xu Yucheng, *Taiwan minjian xinyang zhong de wuying,* pp. 2–3.

63. Ibid., pp. 235–237.

64. Schipper, "Vernacular and Classical Ritual," p. 28.

65. Schipper, "Vernacular and Classical Ritual."

66. Xu Yucheng, *Taiwan minjian xinyang zhong de wuying,* p. 233; see Sangren, *Chinese Sociologies,* p. 211.

67. Graff, "Meritorious Cannibal," p. 8. Graff suggests that the general was cited for heroism because his cannibalism had sent the right message, namely, that loyalty to the state preceded the welfare of one's family members, who might well have been eaten for its sake.

68. Kenneth Dean describes a similar ritual across the Taiwan Straits in Tongan County, Fujian Province; see his *Taoist Ritual,* pp. 65–66.

69. Dean, *Taoist Ritual,* p. 181.

70. Li Fengmao, "Wuying xinyang," pp. 554–561; see also Meulenbeld, *Demonic Warfare,* ch. 2.

71. Li Fengmao, "Wuying xinyang," pp. 578–586; see also Xu Yucheng, *Taiwan minjian xinyang zhong de wuying,* p. 238.

72. Li Fengmao, "Wuying xinyang," pp. 572–577, 586–594.

73. *Haiqiong Bai zhenren yulu, DZ* 1307, 1.11a–b; see Davis, *Society and the Supernatural,* pp. 128–133; 283–290.

74. See *Daofa huiyuan, DZ* 1220, 224.4b; 229.27b–28a; 230.1a; 231.8b; 232.3a; 233.5b; see also Davis, *Society and the Supernatural,* p. 288; on the *Daofa huiyuan* and Bai Yuchan's Shenxiao lineage, see Davis, *Society and the Supernatural,* p. 29; and Kristofer Schipper and Yuan Bingling, "Daofa huiyuan," in Schipper and Verellen, *Taoist Canon,* pp. 1107, 1110–1111; Nezha battles Zhao Gongming in *FSYY,* 47.407–408.

75. Hong Mai, *Yijian zhi,* pp. 1429–1430. Edward Davis (*Society and the Supernatural,* pp. 47–48) identifies Master Cheng as a village ritual master, as distinguished from a Daoist priest. In contrast, Li Fengmao ("Wuying xinyang," pp. 573–4) highlights the orthodox Daoist elements in his ritual performance.

76. Fava, "Rapport de mission dans la province du Hunan."

77. Han Xin was executed on Empress Lü's orders; see Sima Qian, *Shiji,* ch. 92 (biography of the Marquis of Huaiyin).

78. On Han Xin in Hunan ritual drama, see Fava, *Aux ports du ciel,* pp. 100–113.

79. See *Daofa huiyuan, DZ* 1220, 138.13a; 240.11a; compare *Fahai yizhu, DZ* 1166, 15.17a; see also above, chapter 5.

80. Alan Elliott (*Chinese Spirit-Medium Cults,* p. 46) notes, for example, that in Singapore youths under the age of twenty are the most suitable candidates for possession.

81. See Stafford, *Roads of Chinese Childhood,* pp. 135–136, 142–143.

82. Stafford, *Roads of Chinese Childhood,* pp. 133–134; compare Jordan, *Gods, Ghosts, and Ancestors,* p. 71; Shahar, *Crazy Ji,* pp. 177–178.

83. Some scholars have suggested that the character *tong* in *jitong* is used for its phonetic (rather than semantic) value to transcribe a loan word of Vietnamese origin; see Lin Fushi, *Guhun yu guixiong,* pp. 163–164. I succumb, however, to the more common view that highlights its semantic significance of a "child" or a "youth"; see the opinions of Li Yiyuan, Song Longfei, and Liu Zhiwan, as quoted in Lin Fushi, *Guhun yu guixiong,* pp. 160–161; compare Jordan, *Gods, Ghosts, and Ancestors,* p. 71.

84. Schipper, *Le Corps Taoïste,* p. 68.

85. See Elliott, *Chinese Spirit-Medium Cults,* pp. 76–77; Cheu, *Nine Emperor Gods,* pp. 30, 36–37, 39, 93–95; Jordan, *Gods, Ghosts, and Ancestors,* pp. 71–73; Stafford, *Roads of Chinese Childhood,* pp. 130–139; Hong Shuling, "Nezha xinyang yu nüxing shenmei"; Hu Taili, "Shen gui yu dutu," pp. 413–415; Boretz, *Gods, Ghosts, and Gangsters,* pp. 14–15; 103–104.

86. See Stafford, *Roads of Chinese Childhood,* p. 131.

87. The *wangzi xian* are flat plastic figurines. The players take turns tossing them against each other. Hitting his adversary's figurine, the player gains it.

88. Hong Shuling, "Nezha xinyang yu nüxing shenmei," p. 231.

89. Interview conducted in October 2011.

90. Stafford, *Roads of Chinese Childhood,* p. 132.

91. Cheu, *Nine Emperor Gods,* p. 95.

92. Schipper, *Le Corps Taoïste,* pp. 69–70.

93. The Tantric possession techniques (called *āveśa*) are discussed in Strickmann, *Chinese Magical Medicine,* pp. 194–227; see also his *Mantras et Mandarins,* 213–241; Edward Davis discusses the Song-period Daoist and Buddhist techniques for the enchantment of a child by a priest in his *Society and the Supernatural,* pp. 87–114 and 115–152.

94. Lin Fushi has pointed out to me Daoist techniques similar to the Tantric (Buddhist) ones in the writings of the Daoist physician Sun Simiao (?–682). In Sun's *Book of Spell-binding* (*Jin jing*) (included in chapter 30 of his *Qianjin yifang*) inflicting demons are transferred into the body of a possessed child to be identified and expelled.

95. This is the case at the renowned Quanzhou Tianhou Gong, in which the Nezha altar is situated to the left of Mazu's, that is, on her right. (At the Lianchi Gong it is situated on her left.) I do not know when the Nezha altar was established at the Quanzhou temple (which dates back to the Southern-Song period).

96. *Jinmen Shamei Wan'an tang suici jichou caiji jishi wenji lu,* pp. 119–124.

97. *Jinmen shamei Wan'an tang ge zun wangye jishi wenji lu,* p. 9.

98. On the incorporation of Tantric divinities into Song-period Daoism, see Davis, *Society and the Supernatural,* pp. 128–136, 283–290. On Tantric divinities in contemporary Taiwanese rituals, see Xu Yucheng, *Taiwan minjian xinyang zhong de wuying,* pp. 278–289. On Vajrapāṇi's connection to the Chinese martial arts, see Shahar, "Diamond Body" and his *Shaolin Monastery,* pp. 36–42.

99. Legge, trans., *Sacred Books of China, Texts of Confucianism, Part 1: The Hsiao King,* 1.466.

100. Stafford, *Roads of Chinese Childhood,* p. 138.

101. Ibid., pp. 142–143.

102. Boretz, *Gods, Ghosts, and Gangsters,* pp. 14–15, compare also p. 104.

103. On possession and the expression of emotion in China, see Shapiro, "Operatic Escapes: Performing Madness in Neuropsychiatric Beijing."

7 Biological and Spiritual Fathers

1. Kunio, "Filial Piety and 'Authentic Parents,'" p. 114.

2. Wu Cheng'en, *Xiyou ji,* 83.948.

3. See Ch'en, *Chinese Transformation of Buddhism,* pp. 14–60.

4. This is Leon Hurvitz's translation of the Sanskrit original, which is appended to his translation of the Chinese text; see his *Scripture of the Lotus Blossom,* p. 378 note 4.

5. This is Luis Gómez's translation in his *Land of Bliss,* p. 187; the original is *Wuliang shou jing, T.* no. 360, 12:272b.

6. Ning, *Art, Religion, and Politics,* pp. 39–40; the original text is *Guan Wuliangshou jing* (Amitāyus Visualization Sutra), *T.* no. 365, 12:344c–346a. On the pictorial rendition of the sutra at the Central Asian Toyok Caves, see Yamabe, "Examination of the Mural Paintings," pp. 40–41.

7. Yoshimura, *Tianren dansheng tu,* pp. 22–63.

8. The flower of the Uḍumbara (*Ficus racemosa*) is hard to spot because—as in all fig trees—it is hidden within the fruit. Hence, it serves as a metaphor for an occurrence of rare good fortune, such as meeting with a buddha; see, for example, *Miaofa lianhua jing, T.* no. 262, 9:60a; and Hurvitz's translation, *Scripture of the Lotus Blossom,* p. 327.

9. Su Zhe, "Nazha," in his *Luancheng ji, sanji,* 1.12b.

10. Feng Menglong, *Jingshi tongyan,* 28.464.

11. The earliest record is the story "Bai Niangzi yong zhen Leifeng ta," in Feng Menglong, *Jingshi tongyan* (story number 28). It has been dated by Patrick Hanan to the fourteenth, or early fifteenth, century; see his *Chinese Short Story,* pp. 140, 156, 241.

12. *Jingde chuandeng lu, T.* no. 2076, 51:319c.

13. *Jingde chuandeng lu, T.* no. 2076, 51:408a; compare also Mu An's early twelfth-century Chan lexicon *Zuting shiyuan,* 6.399c.

14. See *The Journey to the West* version discussed in this chapter, and *The Roster of the Gods* version in chapter 4.

15. See Watson, "Of Flesh and Bones."

16. See Dudbridge, *Legend of Miaoshan,* pp. 21–35; on the legend's dating, see pp. 5–20.

17. This is Wilt Idema's translation in his *Personal Salvation and Filial Piety,* pp. 110–111; see also his discussion on pp. 20–21. The original is the short version of *The Precious Scroll of Incense Mountain* (*Xiangshan baojuan*). Albeit dating from the nineteenth century, the *baojuan* is related to a much earlier one that likely circulated as early as the first half of the sixteenth century (and might have contained still earlier materials).

18. See the early eighth-century *Lengjia shi zi ji,* compiled by Jingjue, *T.* no. 2837, 85:1284c; compare *Jingde chuandeng lu, T.* no. 2076, 51:217a.

19. Wu Cheng'en, *Xiyou ji,* 15.171; and Anthony Yu's translation, *The Journey to the West,* 1:322.

20. See the version included in the *Xianyu jing* (The Sutra of the wise and the foolish), *T.* no. 202, 4:352c.

21. Dudbridge, *Legend of Miaoshan,* pp. 95–98.

22. Pelliot manuscript, 3564; the translated passage is transcribed in Guo Junye, "Tuo ta Tianwang yu Nezha," p. 36. The manuscript was authored by a monk named Yuanqing, whose father has been responsible for the cave's restoration. The father, an official named Liang Xingde, is mentioned in a Dunhuang manuscript dated 907 and is the subject of a eulogy dated 935. Hence the manuscript likely dates from the first decades of the tenth century; see *Catalogue des manuscrits chinois de Touen-Houang,* vol. 4, p. 57.

23. Guo Junye, "Tuo ta Tianwang yu Nezha," p. 36.

24. Quoted in Guo Junye, "Tuo ta Tianwang yu Nezha," p. 36.

8 Esoteric Buddhism

1. On the contested terminology of esoteric Buddhism (and the question of whether or not the term should be capitalized), see the introduction by Charles Orzech, Richard Payne, and Henrik Sørensen to *Esoteric Buddhism and the Tantras.* On Chinese esoteric Buddhism, see, among others, Chou Yi-liang, "Tantrism in China"; Osabe Kazuo, *Tō Sō Mikkyōshi ronkō;* Strickmann, *Mantras et Mandarins;* Strickmann, *Chinese Magical Medicine;* Orzech, *Politics and Transcendent Wisdom;* Lü Jianfu, *Zhongguo mijiao shi;* and Yan Yaozhong, *Han chuan mijiao.* Archeological discoveries (of *dhāraṇī* pillars for instance) are shedding new light on the school's prevalence in medieval China; see Liu Shufen, *Miezui yu duwang.* On the significance of esoteric Buddhism to the evolution of the Nezha cult, see Li Xiaorong, *Dunhuang mijiao,* pp. 343–352.

2. On Kubera/Vaiśravaṇa's Indian origins, see Coomaraswamy, *Yakṣas,* pp. 35–44; Hopkins, *Epic Mythology,* pp. 142–147; Sutherland, *Disguises of the Demon,* pp. 61–68; and Iyanaga, *Daikokuten Hensō,* pp. 443–502.

3. See Shahar, *Shaolin Monastery,* p. 59. In late imperial Chinese fiction the *yakṣas* are usually described as minions in the underwater administration of the dragon kings. In *The Canonization of the Gods,* Nezha, whose own *yakṣa* origins have been forgotten,

kills such a creature; see *Fengshen yanyi,* 12.104; see also Wu Cheng'en, *Xiyou ji,* 10.104; and Pu Songling's (1640–1715) story "Yakṣa Kingdom" (Yecha Guo) in his *Liaozhai zhiyi,* 3.348–354.

4. On Vaiśravaṇa's East Asian cult, see, among others, "Bishamon," in *Hōbōgirin,* 1:79–83; Granoff, "Tobatsu Bishamon"; Hansen, "Gods on Walls," pp. 80–88; Zheng Acai, "Lun Dunhuang xieben 'Longxing si Pishamen Tianwang lingyan ji'"; and Iyanaga, *Daikokuten Hensō,* pp. 391–442. On the northern connection of the Daoist god Zhenwu, see Xiao Haiming, *Zhenwu tuxiang yanjiu,* p. 20.

5. *Jin'guang ming jing* (*Suvarṇaprabhāsottama-sūtra*), translated by Dharmakṣema between 414 and 421 CE, *T.* no. 663, 16:340c–344c.

6. Strickmann, *Mantras et Mandarins,* p. 41.

7. *Beifang Pishamen Tianwang suijun hufa zhenyan, T.* no. 1248, 21:227a.

8. Hansen, "Gods on Walls," pp. 80–88.

9. Granoff, "Tobatsu Bishamon," p. 146; and Iyanaga, *Daikokuten Hensō,* p. 360.

10. Duan Chengshi, *Youyang zazu,* 8.2a and 8.2b–3a; see also Zheng Acai, "Lun Dunhuang xieben 'Longxing si Pishamen Tianwang lingyan ji,'" p. 432.

11. The purse made of the mongoose's (Sanskrit: *nakula*) fur was named *nakulaka* after it; see A. Foucher, "Sur un attribut de Kuvera." On the gem-spitting mongoose in Vaiśravaṇa's Tibetan iconography, see De Nebesky-Wojkowitz, *Oracles and Demons of Tibet,* pp. 19, 68–69.

12. Iyanaga, *Daikokuten Hensō,* pp. 339–343, 370–373.

13. On Vaiśravaṇa's Dunhuang iconography, see Dang Yan'ni, "Pishamen Tianwang xinyang," pp. 99–104; on his iconography see also Stein, *Serinida,* 2:870–876; Getty, *Gods of Northern Buddhism,* pp. 156–160, 164–168; and Frédéric, *Dieux du bouddhisme,* pp. 242–246.

14. The dating of the process requires further investigation. In the Ming compendium *Sanjiao yuanliu shengdi fozu sou shen daquan,* p. 326, Nezha's father is already identified as the Heavenly King Li Jing (as noted above the compendium likely derives from a Yuan source). Liu Cunren (Liu Ts'un-Yan) suggests that storytellers were ignorant of Pishamen being the transcription of Sanskrit Vaiśravaṇa. Therefore they mistook Pisha to be the name of a gate (*men*) where Li Jing was supposed to have kept guard; see his "Pishamen tianwang fuzi," 2:1048, 2:1092 note 2, and Liu Ts'un-Yan, *Buddhist and Taoist Influences,* p. 219; see also Li Xiaorong, *Dunhuang mijiao,* pp. 345–346.

15. Sen, *Buddhism, Diplomacy, and Trade,* pp. 55–102, where the author discusses Empress Wu Zetian's identification with the Buddha Maitreya.

16. This is Xuanzang's (602?–664) account in his *Da Tang xiyu ji, T.* no. 2087, 51:943b; Xuanzang, *Great Tang Dynasty Record of the Western Regions,* trans. Li Rongxi, p. 377.

17. The legend is preserved in the medieval Tibetan "Prophecy of the Li Country"; see Emmerick, *Tibetan Texts Concerning Khotan,* pp. 15–16; see also Stein, *Ancient Khotan,* pp. 156–166, where he compares the Chinese and Tibetan versions.

18. See Walshe's translation, *Long Discourses of the Buddha,* 32:476. Esoteric Buddhist scriptures often attribute to Vaiśravaṇa five sons only; see, for example, *Mohe Feishiluomonaye tipohe luoshe tuoluoni yigui, T.* no. 1246, 21:219b–c; and *Asaba shō,* compiled by Shōchō (1205–1281), *T. Zuzō,* 9:419b.

19. The complete title is "Da weide Pishamen Tianwang congming taizi zhenyan" ("The Spell of the great and awesome Vaiśravaṇa clever heir-apparent"). Pelliot Chinese manuscript number 2322.

20. Hong Mai, "*Yongshi nü,*" in his *Yijian zhi* (*Yijian zhi bu*), p. 1691.

21. See Shahar, "Legacy of the Tantric Angels."

22. *Pishamen Tianwang jing, T.* no. 1244, 21:215b.

23. See his *Hongjiatuoye yigui, T.* no. 1251, 21:239b–c.

24. See his *Yiqie jing yinyi* (Dictionary of the Buddhist canon), *T.* no. 2128, 54:501b, in which Huilin identifies She'ni'suo / Chan'ni'shi as Vaiśravaṇa's second son.

25. See the *Dīrgha Āgama*'s Chinese translation *Chang'a'han jing,* in which Janeśa is transliterated as She'ni'sha (*T.* no. 1, 1:34c–36b). The scripture was translated into Chinese by Buddhayaśas (Fotuoyeshe) and Zhu fonian in 412–413; compare the parallel Pāli *Dīgha Nikāya,* sutta 18, in which Janeśa (Janavasabha) is identified as a member of Vaiśravaṇa's (Vessavaṇa's) entourage, rather than explicitly as his son; see Walshe's translation, *Long Discourses of the Buddha,* 18.293–294. The suggestion that Amoghavajra's She'ni'suo and Vajrabodhi's Chan'ni'shi are the same as the *Dīrgha Āgama*'s (*Chang'a'han jing*'s) She'ni'sha, all three being transliterations of the Sanskrit Janeśa (Pāli: Janavasabha) was made by the Shingon monk Gōhō (1306–1362) in his *Dainichi kyōsho enō shō* (Explicating the mysteries of [Yixing's] Commentary on the Mahāvairocanasaṃbodhi sutra), *T.* no. 2216, 59:170b–c; see also "She'ni'sha" in *Foguang da cidian,* 7:6529.

26. *Asaba shō,* in *T. Zuzō,* 9:421b.

27. My interpretation of the Pelliot 4514 print (copies of which are preserved at the Bibliothèque Nationale de France and the British Museum alike) follows Li Ling, "Pishamen tuxiang."

28. See Peri, "Hāritī"; on the Buddhist conversion of Indian demons, see Strickmann, *Chinese Magical Medicine,* p. 67.

29. See Li Ling, "Pishamen tuxiang."

30. Hsing I-Tien, "Heracles in the East." Hsing does not recognize the youth in question as a Vaiśravaṇa offspring. Following the British Museum cataloguing, he identifies him as a Gandharva, see Whitfield, *Art of Central Asia,* 2:111. I concur with Li Ling ("Pishamen tuxiang) that the youth in question is Vaiśravaṇa's son.

31. See Henrik Sørensen's photo of the ninth-century Dazu Vaiśravaṇa in *Esoteric Buddhism and the Tantras in East Asia,* p. 117. The original *Scroll of Buddhist Images* was painted between 1173 and 1176 by Zhang Shengwen. Vaiśravaṇa and kin appear in section 63; see Li Lincan, *Nanzhao Dali guo xin ziliao,* plate XX. On the Scroll of Buddhist Images, see also Chapin, *Long Roll of Buddhist Images.*

32. See Nakano Gensou, *Kurama dera,* pp. 16–18. Statues of Vaiśravaṇa, his consort, and child-messenger are also extant at the Hagaji Temple (Fukui prefecture); at the Seiunji Temple (Fukui prefecture); at the Hakusan Shinto shrine (Kamakura); at the Sekkeiji Temple (Kōchi prefecture); and at the Chogosonshi ji on Mount Shigi (Nara prefecture).

33. *Pishamen yigui, T.* no. 1249, 21:228b–c.

34. As Lü Jianfu has suggested to me, it is possible that Dujian is the shortened form of Mo*du*-sai*jian*tuo, who is mentioned as a Vaiśravaṇa offspring in some Chinese scriptures. The relevant information is collated in Hongzan's (1611–1685) *Sifen lü mingyi biaoshi,* pp. 652c–653a, where it appears under the heading of the Rājagṛha City gate of which Modu-saijiantuo served as a guardian. The likely Sanskrit reconstruction of the name would be Madhu-Skandha. It has been variously translated into Chinese as Mifu and Miqi.

35. Demiéville, "Le Bouddhisme et la guerre," pp. 375–376.

36. *Beifang Pishamen tianwang suijun hufa zhenyan, T.* no. 1248, 21:227a–b.

37. The Buddhist historian Zan'ning (919–1001) attributed the practice of placing Vaiśravaṇa images on city walls to Dujian's victory over the barbarians; see his *Song*

gaoseng zhuan, T. no. 2061, 50:714a, trans. Chou Yi-liang, "Tantrism in China," pp. 305–306. The Japanese monk Gōhō (1306–1362) cited Zan'ning in his account of the Vaiśravaṇa image that protected Kyoto's main gate; see Granoff, "Tobatsu Bishamon," pp. 150–151; see also Zhipan (ca. 1200), *Fozu tongji, T.* no. 2035, 49:295.

38. See Matsumoto Bunzaburō, "Tōbatsu Bishamon kō," pp. 285–290; and Chou Yi-liang, "Tantrism in China," p. 305 note 103.

39. See Beal's translation, *Buddhist Records of the Western World,* 12:315–316. The original is Xuanzang, *Da Tang xiyu ji,* chapter 12, *T.* no. 2087, 51:944a–b. The relation between the two mice legends has been pointed out by Matsumoto Bunzaburō, "Tōbatsu Bishamon kō," p. 290.

40. The story is pictorially narrated in the scroll's second section. The scroll contains illustrations only, the written portion having been lost. However the text might be reconstructed from the parallel accounts in the *Ujishūi Monogatari* (Tales from Uji) and the Umezawa version of the *Kohon Setsuwashū* (Collection of Ancient Legends); see Shibusawa Keizo, *Multilingual Version of "Pictopedia of Everyday Life,"* pp. 82–83.

41. See his translation of the *Mahāmāyūrī vidyārājñī* (Great Peacock-Queen Spell), *Fomu da kongque mingwang jing, T.* no. 982, 19:425b; compare the Sanskrit original in Takubo Shūyo, *Ārya-Mahā-Māyūrī Vidyā-rājñī,* p. 23, and Lévi, "Catalogue géographique des yakṣa," p. 55. Saṃghavara (460–ca. 524) transcribed Nalakūbara as Naluojiupoluo, whereas Yijing (635–713) chose Naluojubaluo; see respectively *Kongque wang zhou jing, T.* no. 984, 19:451b, and *Foshuo da kongque zhou wang jing, T.* no. 985, 19:466b; see also Mochizuki, *Bukkyō daijiten,* 4:3994–3995; on the *Mahāmāyūrī vidyārājñī,* see Sørensen, "Spell of the Great, Golden Peacock Queen."

42. *Beifang Pishamen Tianwang sui jun hufa yigui, T.* no. 1247, 21:224c–225c.

43. Diverse *Mahāmāyūrī* manuscripts have Nalakūvara, Nalakūvala, and Narakuvera; see respectively Lévi, "Catalogue géographique des yakṣa," p. 55; the *Taishō* editors' gloss in *T.* no. 982, 19:425b; and Takubo Shūyo, *Ārya-Mahā-Māyūrī Vidyā-rājñī,* p. 23. The *Buddhacarita* manuscripts consulted by Cowell have Nalakūvara; see Asvaghosha, *Buddha-Karita,* English 1.16, Sanskrit, p. 1.11. The Pali Kākāti-Jātaka has Naṭakuvera; see Cowell, ed., *Jātaka,* vol. 3, trans. H. T. Francis and R. A. Neil, pp. 60–62.

44. *Gnod sbyin gar mkhan mchog gi rgyud, Tôh.* no. 767; and *Mahā yakṣa senāpati nartakapara kalpa,* (*Gnod sbyin gyi sde dpon chen po gar mkhan mchog gi brtag pa*) *Tôh.* no. 766. The Qing-Dynasty patronage of Tibetan Buddhism led to the introduction of Nalakūbara's Tibetan name, Gar-mkhan-mchog ("Best of Dancers"), to China. Produced at the imperial palace in Beijing, the *Zhu Fo Pusa sheng xiang zan* (p. 326) renders his name Miaowu (Wonderful Dancer).

45. Zheng Qing, *Kai Tian chuanxin ji,* 13a–b; compare Zan'ning (919–1001), *Song gaoseng zhuan, T.* no. 2061, 50:791a.

46. Reischauer, *Ennin's Diary,* p. 303; see also Xiao Dengfu, "Nezha suyuan," pp. 20–23.

47. Strong and Strong, "Tooth Relic."

48. *Pishamen yigui, T.* no. 1249, 21:228c.

49. Ibid.

50. Nezha's Tang-period iconography was far from settled. In some of his writings Amoghavajra's instructions for the drawing of the third prince do not allude to the pagoda; see *Beifang Pishamen tianwang suijun hufa yigui, T.* no. 1247, 21:224c–225a, and Hok-Lam Chan's translation in his *Legends of the Building of Old Peking,* p. 70.

51. *Beifang Pishamen tianwang suijun hufa yigui, T.* no. 1247, 21:224c–225a. This is Hok-Lam Chan's translation in his *Legends of the Building of Old Peking,* p. 69 (slightly revised).

On Nezha's military functions see also Chen Xiaoyi, "Nezha renwu ji gushi zhi yanjiu," pp. 19–23.

52. "Wenchuan xian Tang weirongjun zhizao Tianwangdian ji" (Record of the Heavenly-King hall established by the Tang Weirong Garrison in Wenchuan County), in *Quan Tang wen,* 620.2774–2775. Nothing is known of the inscription's author Yuan Youliang except that he was a nephew of the official Yuan Jie (ca. 723–772), by whom his approximate eighth-century dates might be inferred.

53. *Nazha Taizi qiu chengjiu tuoluoni jing,* and *Nazhajuboluo qiu chengjiu jing;* see *Yiqie jing yinyi, T.* no. 2128, 54:549c.

54. *Byakuhō kushō,* by Ryōson, recording the sayings of his teacher Ryōzen (1258–1341). *T. Zuzō,* 3119, 7: 136c, 137a; on Nalakūbara the *yakṣa* general, see also Chen Xiaoyi, "Nezha renwu ji gushi zhi yanjiu," pp. 19–23.

55. *Gnod sbyin gar mkhan mchog gi rgyud, Tôh.* no. 767, and *Mahā yakṣa senāpati nartakapara kalpa* (*Gnod sbyin gyi sde dpon chen po gar mkhan mchog gi brtag pa*), *Tôh.* no. 766.

56. The title of "great *yakṣa* general" (Sanskrit: *mahā-yakṣa-senāpati*; Chinese: *da yaocha jiang*) had been bestowed upon Nalakūbara in earlier Tantric scriptures such as the *Great Peacock-Queen Spell;* see the Sanskrit text edited by Takubo Shūyo, *Ārya-Mahā-Māyūrī Vidyā-rājñī,* p. 24, and Amoghavajra's translation *Fomu da kongque mingwang jing, T.* no. 982, 19:426a.

57. *Maṇibhadra-nāma-dhāraṇī* (*'Phags pa nor bu bzang po'i gzungs*), *Tôh.* no. 764, and *Maṇibhadra yakṣa sena kalpa* (*Gnod sbyin nor bu bzang po'i rtog pa*), *Tôh.* no. 765.

58. Even though at that early stage their names differed; see Coomaraswamy, *Yakṣas,* p. 35.

59. On the Sanskrit fragments of the Maṇibhadra *dhāraṇīs* see Hoernle, "Three Further Collections," pp. 242–243; Hoernle, "Weber Manuscripts," pp. 1–40; and Hoernle, "Note on the British Collection," pp. 151–185. The Chinese Maṇibhadra sutra is *Foshuo Baoxian tuoluoni jing,* translated by Devaśantika (Tianxizai) (?–1000), *T.* no. 1285, 21: 353c–354b. Independently of his father (and brother), Maṇibhadra (Maṇibhadda) figures, for example, in the Pali *Samyutta-Nikāya;* see Davids, *Book of the Kindred Sayings,* 1:266.

60. De Nebesky-Wojkowitz, *Oracles and Demons of Tibet,* pp. 76–77.

61. *Fenyang Wude Chanshi yulu, T.* no. 1992, 47:598a.

62. *Biyan lu, T.* no. 2003, 48:212a.

63. *Shuihu quanzhuan,* 29.448.

64. *San Sui pingyao zhuan,* p. 90. Vincent Durand-Dastès has argued convincingly that the story mirrors the Tantric iconography that characterized the renowned Xiang'guo Temple; see his "Rencontres hérétiques," pp. 39–47.

65. Chan, *Legends of the Building of Old Peking,* pp. 63–85. Dating likely from the eighteenth century, another tradition identified the layout of the Chinese capital with the Tantric deity Yamāntaka ("He who has put an end to death"). The latter likely reflected the impact of Tibetan Buddhism on Qing-period Beijing; see Lessing, "Topographical Identification."

66. Chan, *Legends of the Building of Old Peking,* pp. 79–85.

9 Nezha, Nalakūbara, and Kṛṣṇa

1. See the collected essays in Hiltebeitel, *Criminal Gods.*

2. *Rāmāyaṇa, Uttarakāṇḍa,* chapter 26.

3. Cowell, ed., *Jātaka,* vol. 3, trans. H. T. Francis and R. A. Neil, p. 61.

4. See Tagare's translation, *Bhāgavata-Purāṇa,* x.10 (pp. 1308–1315). As an example of the story's visual representations, see the eighteenth-century plate no. 5, in Archer, *Loves of Krishna.*

5. See, respectively, Piṅgaḷi, *Sound of the Kiss;* and Shulman, "Concave and Full," p. 40, and plate 6.

6. See, among others, Hardy, *Viraha-Bhakti;* Hawley, *At Play with Krishna;* Hawley, *Krishna, The Butter Thief;* Archer, *Loves of Krishna;* Bryant, *Krishna: A Sourcebook.* On Kṛṣṇa and Viṣṇu, see also Gonda, *Aspects of Early Viṣṇuism,* pp. 154–163. On the role of pilgrimage in the Kṛṣṇa cult, see Haberman, *Journey through the Twelve Forests.*

7. This is the *Bhāgavata Purāṇa* episode as translated by O'Flaherty, *Hindu Myths,* p. 220.

8. Goldman, "Fathers, Sons and Gurus," pp. 350, 364; see also Masson, "Childhood of Kṛṣṇa"; on the Indian oedipal pattern, see also Ramanujan, "The Indian 'Oedipus'"; and Silk, *Riven by Lust,* pp. 164–170.

9. On Kṛṣṇa and Kāliya, see Hawley, "Krishna's Cosmic Victories"; and Matchett, "Taming of Kāliya."

10. Compare *Harivaṃśa* 52.1 and *Viṣṇu Purāṇa,* V.6.35 (quoted in Matchett, "Taming of Kāliya," p. 116), with *Fengshen yanyi,* 12.103; admittedly Nezha is merely five *days* old when he performs the same feat in the Ming compendium *Sanjiao yuanliu shengdi fozu sou shen daquan,* p. 326.

11. Compare *Bhāgavata-Purāṇa,* x.16.6; and *Fengshen yanyi,* 12.103–105.

12. This is Tagare's translation, *The Bhāgavata-Purāṇa,* x.16.9 (p. 1360).

13. O'Flaherty, *Hindu Myths,* p. 221; on Viṣṇu's dragon, see also Sharma, "Significance of Viṣṇu Reclining on the Serpent."

14. See the *Harivaṃśa,* 71.37–54, trans. Dutt, *Prose English Translation of the Harivamsha,* pp. 350–351; and *Bhāgavata Purāṇa* 10, 42.15–21, trans. Tagare, vol. 4, pp. 1511–1512.

15. See Goldman's translation, *Rāmāyaṇa of Vālmīki,* 1: 248–252 (*Bālakāṇḍa,* 65–66).

16. See *Fo benxing ji jing* (*Abhiniṣkramaṇa-sūtra*), trans. Jñānagupta (523–600), *T.* no. 190, 3:710c–711a; and Liu Ts'un-Yan's translation, *Buddhist and Taoist Influences,* p. 231.

17. Iyanaga Nobumi, *Daikokuten Hensō: Bukkyō Shinwagaku I,* pp. 45–56; see also Brian Rupert's illuminating review of Iyanaga's work, p. 180.

18. See Yang Qinzhang, "Quanzhou yindujiao diaoke yuanyuan kao"; Guy, "Lost Temples of Nagapattinam and Quanzhou"; Guy, "Tamil Merchant Guilds and the Quanzhou Trade"; and Sen, *Buddhism, Diplomacy, and Trade,* pp. 227–231.

19. See Wu Wenliang, *Quanzhou zongjiao shike,* pp. 453–460; and Yang Qinzhang, "Quanzhou yindujiao pishinu shen xingxiang shike."

20. The Kṛṣṇa legend is pictorially rendered on fifth- or sixth-century woolen carpets from Khotan (in today's Xinjiang Province); see Zhang He, "Figurative and Inscribed Carpets from Shanpula, Khotan."

21. On Devaśāntika, see Sen, *Buddhism, Diplomacy, and Trade,* pp. 120–132; and Lü Jianfu (*Zhong'guo mijiao shi,* pp. 551–555), who demonstrates that he should probably be identified with Faxian; on Devaśāntika's translations of the *Rituals of the God Vināyaka* (T. 1272) and *Rituals of the Bodhisattva Mañjuśrī* (T. 1191), see, respectively, Strickmann, *Mantras et Mandarins,* 261–266, and Osabe, *Tō Sō Mikkyōshi ronkō,* pp. 298–326; on Song-period Tantric Buddhism, see also Yan Yaozhong, *Han chuan mijiao,* pp. 37–51, and Willemen, *Chinese Hevajratantra.*

22. The character *na* usually transcribes the Sanskrit retroflex *ṇa,* or less commonly

ḍa. Kṛṣṇa is commonly transcribed Qilisena, sometimes with the phonetic instruction to combine the consonants (*erhe*).

23. *Luoye* was the Chinese name for the garment that Indian men tied under the armpit, leaving their right shoulder bare; see Xuanzang, *Da Tang Xiyu ji*, *T.* 2087, 51: 876b, and Li Rongxi's translation, *Great Tang Dynasty Record*, p. 53; compare also Beal, *Si-yu-ki*, p. 75.

24. Nanda, Upananda, and Takṣaka appear in various Buddhist lists of the eight dragon kings; see *Foguang da cidian*, pp. 6378, 6405.

25. The *rākṣasas* and the *piśācas* are two types of Hindu ogres, whom Buddhist demonology incorporated. Both types feed on human flesh; see respectively *Foguang da cidian*, pp. 6673–6674 and 3851; Monier-Williams, *A Sanskrit-English Dictionary*, pp. 871 and 628; see also Strickmann's survey of Buddhist demonology in his *Chinese Magical Medicine*, pp. 62–68.

26. The term *geboluo* (Sanskrit: *kapāla*) figures prominently in the contemporaneous Chinese translation of the *Hevajra Tantra* (Foshuo dabeikong zhi jin'guang dajiaowang yigui jing), *T.* no. 892, vol. 18: 587–601; see also Willemen, *Chinese Hevajratantra*, p. 172.

27. *Zuishang mimi Nana tian jing*, *T.* no. 1288, 21:358b–c.

28. Mochizuki Shinkô (*Bukkyō daijiten*, 4:3994–3995) was the first to associate the *Zuishang mimi Nana tian jing* with Nezha. Xiao Dengfu ("Nezha suyuan," p. 19 note 10) has disputed the connection because of Naṇa's elevated position; see also Chan, *Legends of the Building of Old Peking*, pp. 72–73.

29. On the identification of the originally distinct god Nārāyaṇa with Viṣṇu, see Matchett, *Kṛṣṇa: Lord or Avatāra*, pp. 4–8; Admittedly, the epithet Naluoyan (Nārāyaṇa) is applied in some Chinese texts to another powerful divinity, Vajrapāṇi. See Shahar, *Shaolin Monastery*, p. 40; see also "Naluoyantian," in *Foguang da cidian*, pp. 3029–3030.

30. See, for example, *Bhāgavata-Purāṇa*, x.63.23, Tagare's translation, p. 1659; compare Bryant's translation, *Krishna: The Beautiful Legend of God*, p. 273.

Epilogue

1. See chapter 6; Xu Yucheng discusses the Tantric pedigree of the commanders of the five spirit armies in his *Taiwan minjian xinyang*, pp. 278–289.

2. On the Horse-Headed Avalokiteśvara, see van Gulik, *Hayagrīva;* on his relation to Indian and Chinese lore, see Iyanaga, *Kannon henyōtan*, pp. 497–550; on his relation to the Chinese Horse King, see Grootaers et al., "Rural Temples around Hsüan-Hua," pp. 54–57.

3. See Meulenbeld, "Civilized Demons," pp. 78–90; and Hsia, *C. T. Hsia on Chinese Literature*, pp. 149, 154, and 488 note 30.

4. See Dudbridge, *Hsi-yu chi*, pp. 18–21; and Strickmann, *Chinese Magical Medicine*, pp. 312–313 note 47.

5. See Shahar, "Diamond Body"; Paul Katz (*Demon Hordes*, pp. 79–80) has suggested that the Tantric demon turned demon queller Āṭavaka contributed to the emergence of the Chinese plague god Marshal Wen; the Tantric aspect of the *Fengshen yanyi* is discussed by Liu Ts'un-yan, *Buddhist and Taoist Influences*, pp. 181–186.

6. On Śiva in Tantric Buddhism, see Iyanaga Nobumi, *Daikokuten Hensō*, and his "Récits de la soumission de Maheśvara."

7. Asvaghosha, *Buddha-Karita*, trans. Edward Cowell, English text, 1.16; Sanskrit, 1.11, and Dharmakṣema's (385–433) Chinese translation *Fo suo xing zan jing*, *T.* no. 192, 4:3c.

8. Following Ōmura Seigai's *Mikkyō hattatsu shi* (1918) and Chou Yi-Liangs's "Tantrism in China" (1945), the field of Chinese Tantric studies remained largely dormant all

through the 1990s. Among important recent contributions, see *Esoteric Buddhism and the Tantras*, ed. Orzech et al.; Orzech, *Politics and Transcendent Wisdom;* Osabe Kazuo, *Tō Sō Mikkyōshi ronkō;* Lü Jianfu, *Zhongguo mijiao shi;* and Sharf, "On Esoteric Buddhism in China." Another promising line of investigation—going beyond this study's scope—examines the late imperial patronage of Tibetan esoteric Buddhism; among numerous recent publications, see Shen Weirong, "Tibetan Buddhism in Mongol-Yuan China"; *Zhu Fo Pusa sheng xiang zan,* ed. Luo Wenhua; and the essays collected in Kapstein, *Buddhism between Tibet and China.*

9. See Strickmann, *Mantras et Mandarins* and his *Chinese Magical Medicine;* Yan Yaozhong's *Han chuan mijiao* similarly examines the Chinese Tantric movement as reflected in other Buddhist schools and in the popular religion.

10. It would be impossible to cite here the vast scholarship on Buddhism and the Indian-Chinese encounter; among the many notable contributions, see Zürcher, *Buddhist Conquest of China;* Ch'en, *Chinese Transformation of Buddhism;* Mair, *Painting and Performance;* Mair, "Narrative Revolution in Chinese Literature"; Kieschnick, *Impact of Buddhism on Chinese Material Culture;* Sen, *Buddhism, Diplomacy, and Trade;* see also the essays collected in Kieschnick and Shahar, *India in the Chinese Imagination.*

Glossary

Ao Bing 敖丙
Ao Guang 敖光
Bai Niangzi yong zhen Leifeng ta 白娘子永鎮雷峰塔
baixing xiao weixian 百行孝為先
Bai Yuchan 白玉蟾
bao 報
Beidi 北帝
benlai shen 本來身
bian 鞭
Bo Yikao 伯邑考
bugang 步罡
Bukong jingang 不空金剛
Bu xiao you san, wu hou wei da 不孝有三, 無后為大
buxiban 補習班
Cai Mingliang 蔡明亮
Cai Rongying 蔡容英
Cao E 曹娥
chang 嘗
Chang'geng 長庚
Chan'ni'shi 禪膩師 (Japanese: Zennishi)
chengjiu 成就
Chenlun 沉淪
Chentang guan 陳塘關
Chen Tianqi 陳天啓
chicu 吃醋
Chi Wangye 池王爺
Chogosonshi ji 朝護孫子寺 (Japanese)
Chongsheng 崇聖
Chuanqi hui kao 傳奇彙考
cong er bu jian fei xiao ye; jian er bu cong yi fei xiao ye 從而不諫非孝也, 諫而不從亦非孝也
Daji 妲己
Dajiale 大家樂
daochang 道場
daoshi 道師
Daoxuan 道宣
Da Sanba Nezha Miao 大三巴哪吒廟
Datong 大同
da yaocha jiang 大藥叉將
Dechajia 得(德)叉迦
Deshao 德韶
Dianyin taizi 電音太子
Dongyao Taizi Gong 東窯太子宮
Dujian 獨健
Duoli 多利 (Tārā)
Duoluo 多羅 (Tārā)
Duowen Tian 多聞天
du yu ai 篤於愛
du zicheng 獨自成
Edipusi qingjie 俄狄浦斯情結
erhe 二合
Etipu zarou 額提普雜糅
e you e bao 惡有惡報
Fahai 法海 (Temple)
falü 法律

falun 法輪
Fangbing keyi 放兵科儀
fang da guangming 放大光明
fashi 法師
Faxian 法賢
Fenghuo lun 風火輪
Fengshen bang 封神榜
Fenhe wan 汾河灣
fennu 忿怒
fushen xianling 附身顯靈
Gai Jiaotian 蓋叫天
Gan ji gou 趕雞溝
geboluo 葛波羅
gegu 割股
gezai 歌仔
gezaixi 歌仔戲
gong'an 公案
guai'dan bujing 怪誕不經
guai li luan shen 怪力亂神
Guangong 關公
guci 鼓詞
Guizi mu 鬼子母 (Hārītī)
Guo Ju 郭巨
Guo Jujing 郭居敬
Haga ji 羽賀寺 (Japanese)
hai 醢
Hakusan 白山 (Japanese)
Han Xin 韓信
Han Yu 韓愈
haohan 好漢
Heilong tan 黑龍潭
Helidi 訶利底
He Mengchun 何夢春
Hetian 和田
Hua fan xiang juan 畫梵像卷
Huaguang 華光
Huang Feihu 黃飛虎
Huntian ling 混天綾
Huojian qiang 火尖鎗
huolun 火輪
Huoya 火鴉
ī 伊 (Hokkien)
jianghu 江湖
Jiang Qingliu 江清柳
jian xin miao, zhong rong shu 建新廟, 種榕樹
jiao 醮 (Daoist ritual)
jiao 筊 (divination blocks)
Ji Gong 濟公
jiji rulü ling, xiafan jiuhu 急急如律令, 下凡救护
Jincun 金村
Jin'gang lishi 金剛力士
jin'gang shen 金剛身
Jin'gangzhi 金剛智
Jingshen fenxi 精神分析
Jin jing 禁經
jinlun 金輪
Jin ping mei 金瓶梅
Jinsha zhen 金沙鎮
jinxiang 進香
Jinzha 金吒
Jinzhuan 金磚
jitong 乩童
Jixiang tiannü 吉祥天女
Ken no gohō 劍の護法 (Japanese)
Kuiwen 奎文
Kurama-dera 鞍馬寺 (Japanese)
Leigong 雷公
Lei Haiqing 雷海青
Leizhen 雷震
Lianchi Gong 蓮池宮
liandu 鍊度
lianmu qingjie 戀母情結
Li Jing 李靖
Li Kui 李逵
Li Lanting 李蘭亭
Li Nezha chou long jin ge 李哪吒抽龍筋歌
lingchi 凌遲
ling'guai xiaoshuo 靈怪小說

Ling Zhuzi 靈珠子
Li Tieniu 李鐵牛
long 龍
long zhu 龍柱
Luhun fan 戮魂幡
luocha 羅刹
luoye 絡腋
Lüshan 閭山
Lu Xixing 陸西性
Lu Zhishen 魯智深
mabian 馬鞭
Mawang 馬王
Mazu 媽祖
Mei Bo 梅伯
Miaoshan 妙善
Miaowu 妙舞
Mifu 蜜膊
Mingwang 明王
Miqi 蜜器
Modu-saijiantuo 末度塞建陀
Mo-nü 魔女 (Māra's daughters)
mowang 魔王
Mulian 目連
Muzha 木吒
na 拏 (transliterating the Sanskrit *ṇa*)
Nacha 那叉
Nachi 那叱
Naluojiupoluo 那羅鳩婆羅
Naluojubaluo 捺羅俱跋羅
Naluoyan 那羅延 (Sanskrit: Nārāyaṇa)
Naṇa 那拏
Nantuo 難陀
Nazha 那吒
Nazha Cheng 那吒城
Nazhajuboluo qiu chengjiu jing 那吒俱鉢囉求成就經
Nazhajuwaluo 那吒矩韈囉
Nazha Taizi qiu chengjiu tuoluoni jing 那吒太子求成就陀羅尼經
Nezha 哪吒
Nezha Gu Miao 哪吒古廟
Nezha huoqiu zhou 哪吒火球咒
Nezha nao donghai ge 哪吒鬧東海歌
ni 逆
niancong 念叢
nichen 逆臣
Ninna 仁和 (Japanese)
nitu 逆徒
nizi 逆子
nuo 儺
Ouzi zhong 嘔子塚
Pili shizhe 霹靂使者
pinghua 評話 (also written 平話)
Pingyan Jigong zhuan 評演濟公傳
Pishamen 毗沙門
pishezuo 毘舍左
Pu'an 普安
qian 籤
Qiankun gong 乾坤弓
Qiankun quan 乾坤圈
Qianyuan shan 乾元山
Qilisena 訖哩瑟拏 (Kṛṣṇa)
qingjie 情結
"Qiuran ke" 虯髯客
Qixin Tang 齊心唐
Randeng 燃燈
Randengfo 燃燈佛
San'nai 三奶
Sanshisan Tian Duyuanshuai 三十三天都元帥
San Taizi 三太子
Seiun ji 清雲寺 (Japanese)
Sekkei ji 雪蹊寺 (Japanese)
Sham Shui Po 深水埔
Shangdi 上帝
Shansheng tongzi 善勝童子
shenbing huoji ru lü ling 神兵火急如律令
She'ni'sha 闍尼沙
She'ni'suo 赦儞娑
shenren 神人
Shensha shen 深沙神
Shenxiao 神霄

shi 弑
shi'e 十惡
shifu 弑父
Shigisan engi 信貴山縁起 (Japanese)
Shigong 師公 (Village)
shigong 師公 ([ritual] master)
shiji 石磯 (stone cliff)
shiji 石雞 (stone chicken)
Shi Jiantang 史建瑭
shijing 石精
Shiji Niangniang 石磯娘娘
shijun 弑君
Shun zi bian 舜子變
Song Qi 宋祁
Suiyang Zhujie 睢陽著節
Sun Tuxing 孫土行
Sun Wukong 孫悟空
Suomo jing 鎖魔鏡
Taiyi 太乙
taizi 太子
Taizi Gong 太子宮
Taizi Ling Gong 太子靈宮
tanci 彈詞
Taodai hang 絛帶行
thàn-tsia̍h-tsa-bóo 趁食查某 (Hokkien)
Tiangong Yuanshuai 田公元帥
Tianhou Gong 天后宮
Tian'nü 天女
Tianpeng dajiang 天蓬大將
tianyan 天眼
tongji 童乩
tongnan tongnü 童男童女
tongxin 童心
tongzi 童子
Tsai (Cai) Mingliang 蔡明亮
tu 兔 (rabbit)
tu 吐 (vomit)
tubao shu 吐寶鼠
Tu'er Zhong 吐兒塚
Wan'an Tang 萬安堂
Wang Ch'iu-Kuei 王秋桂
Wang Hua 汪華
wangliang 罔兩
Wang Shuchen 王樹忱
wangzi xian 尪仔仙
wanshi 頑石
weibi ren zhisi 威逼人致死
wei chang bu shi xin 未嘗不食新
weinu 威怒
wen 文 (literary)
Wen 文 (King)
Wenchuan xian Tang weirongjun zhizao Tianwang dian ji 汶川縣唐威戎軍制造天王殿記
wu 武 (military)
Wu 武 (King)
wuda ju 武打劇
Wuponantuo 烏波難陀
wusheng 武生
Wuxiang Taizi 五鄉太子
Wuying 五營
Wuying tou 五營頭
Wu Youxiong 吳幼雄
Xiangshan baojuan 香山寶卷
Xiangu 仙姑
Xiangyao Dayuanshuai 降妖大元帥
xiao 孝
Xiaokang 小康
Xin ganjue 新感覺
Xinhexing 新和興
Xinli fenxi 心理分析
xiuqiu 綉毬
Xuanmu 玄母
Xue pen jing 血盆經
Xue Rengui 薛仁貴
yaocha 藥叉
yecha 夜叉
Ye Derong 葉德榮 (A'de 阿德)
Yedibusi cuozong 耶的卜司错综
Yibin 宜賓
yin 陰
Yinbing 陰兵

yi qiu ji zhong 一求即中
Yixing 一行
Yongxing Gong 永興宮
Youli 羑里
you wo sheng cai 祐我生財
Yuanfu 元父
Yuan Jie 元結
Yuan Youliang 元友諒
Yuefu kao lüe 樂府考略
Yue Yang 樂羊
Yujia 瑜伽
Yu-lan-pen 盂蘭盆
yu qu ta xin gan chong jiu 欲取他心肝沖酒
yu xiao 愚孝
Zennishi Dōji 禪膩師童子 (also written 善膩師童子) (Japanese)
Zhang Ding 張仃
Zhang Shengwen 張勝溫
Zhang Xun 張巡
Zhang Yunxi 張雲溪
Zhao Gongming 趙公明
zheng 正
zhen ling 真靈
Zhenwu 真武
zhicheng 至誠
zhiqing 至情
zhong 忠
Zhong Kui 鍾馗
Zhongtan Yuanshuai 中壇元帥
zhong xiao jieyi 忠孝節義
Zhou 紂 (king)
Zhou 周 (dynasty)
Zhuang Zhengong 莊鎮忠
Zhu Bajie 豬八戒
zhufu 竹符
Zhu Wangye 朱王爺
Zhu Wen 朱溫
zi 子
zuo 胙

Works Cited

Alighieri, Dante. "The Divine Comedy." Translated by Laurence Binyon. In *The Portable Dante,* edited by Paolo Milano, pp. 1–544. New York: Viking, 1947.

Archer, W. G. *The Loves of Krishna in Indian Painting and Poetry.* London: George Allen & Unwin, 1957.

Arlington, L. C., and Harold Acton, trans. *Famous Chinese Plays.* 1937. Reprint. New York: Russell and Russell, 1963.

Asaba shō 阿娑縛抄 (Anthology of A, Sa, and Va). Compiled by Shōchō 承澄 (1205–1281). In volumes 8–9 of *T. Zuzō.*

Asvaghosha. *The Buddha-Karita or Life of the Buddha.* Edited and translated by Edward B. Cowell. 1894. Reprint. New Delhi: Cosmo Publications, 1977.

Bakhtin, Mikhail. *Rabelais and His World.* Translated by Hélèn Iswolsky. Bloomington: Indiana University Press, 1984.

Bakshi, Dwijendra Nath. *Hindu Divinities in Japanese Buddhist Pantheon.* Calcutta: Benten, 1979.

Bassett, Samuel Eliot. "The Exposure of Oedipus." *The Classical Review* 26, no. 7 (1912): p. 217.

Beal, Samuel. *Si-yu-ki: Buddhist Records of the Western World.* 1884. Reprint. Delhi: Motilal Banarsidass, 2004.

Beifang Pishamen Tianwang sui jun hufa yigui 北方毗沙門天王隨軍護法儀軌 (The Tantric rituals of the Northern Heavenly-King Vaiśravaṇa, who follows the army, protecting the Dharma). Translated by Amoghavajra 不空 (705–774). *T.* no. 1247.

Beifang Pishamen Tianwang sui jun hufa zhenyan 北方毗沙門天王隨軍護法真言 (The mantra of the Northern Heavenly-King Vaiśravaṇa, who follows the army, protecting the Dharma). Translated by Amoghavajra 不空 (705–774). *T.* no. 1248.

Birch, Cyril, trans. "The Curly-Bearded Hero." In *Classical Chinese Literature: An Anthology of Translations,* edited by John Minford and Joseph S. M. Lau, vol. 1, pp. 1057–1064. New York: Columbia University Press, 2000.

Birrell, Anne, trans. "A Peacock Southward Flew." In *The Columbia Anthology of Traditional Chinese Literature,* edited by Victor Mair, pp. 462–472. New York: Columbia University Press, 1994.

Biyan lu 碧巖錄 (Blue-cliff records). By Xuetou Chongxian 雪竇重顯 (980–1052) and Yuanwu Keqin 圜悟克勤 (1063–1135). *T.* no. 2003.

Blowers, Geoffrey. "Bingham Dai, Adolf Storfer, and the Tentative Beginnings of Psychoanalytic Culture in China: 1935–1941." *Psychoanalysis and History* 6 (2004): pp. 93–105.

Booth, Wayne C. *The Rhetoric of Fiction.* Harmondsworth: Penguin Books, 1987.

Boretz, Avron. *Gods, Ghosts, and Gangsters: Ritual Violence, Martial Arts, and Masculinity on the Margins of Chinese Society.* Honolulu: University of Hawai'i Press, 2011.

———. "Martial Gods and Magic Swords: Identity, Myth, and Violence in Chinese Popular Religion." *Journal of Popular Culture* 29 (1995): pp. 93–109.

Bo wu zhi 博物志 (Record of extensive things). Compiled by Zhang Hua 張華 (third century). *SKQS* edition.

Brook, Timothy, Jérôme Bourgon, and Gregory Blue. *Death by a Thousand Cuts.* Cambridge, Mass.: Harvard University Press, 2008.

Brown, R. Grant. "The Dragon of Tagaung." In Lowell Edmunds and Alan Dundes, *Oedipus: A Folklore Casebook,* pp. 47–55. Wisconsin: University of Wisconsin Press, 1983.

Brown, Shelby. *Late Carthaginian Child Sacrifice, and Sacrificial Monuments in their Mediterranean Context.* Sheffield: Sheffield Academic Press, 1991.

Bryant, Edwin F., trans. *Krishna: The Beautiful Legend of God (Śrīmad Bhāgavata Purāṇa, Book x).* London: Penguin Books, 2003.

Bryant, Edwin F., ed. *Krishna: A Sourcebook.* Oxford: Oxford University Press, 2007.

Bukong juansuo shenbian zhenyan jing 不空羂索神變真言經 (The mantra-sutra of the Amoghapāśa Guanyin divine transformations). Translated by Bodhiruci (?–727). *T.* no. 1092.

Byakuhō kushō 白寶口抄 (Selections from the Oral Transmission of White Treasures). By Ryōson 亮尊. Recording the sayings of his teacher Ryōzen 亮禪 (1258–1341). In vols. 6–7 of *T. Zuzō.*

Can Tang Wudai shi yanyi 殘唐五代史演義 (Historical romance of the declining Tang and the Five Dynasties period). Beijing: Baowen tang, 1983.

Cao Xueqin 曹雪芹 and Gao E 高鶚. *Honglou meng* 紅樓夢 (Dream of the red chamber). 3 vols. Beijing: Zuojia, 1957.

———. *The Story of the Stone.* Translated by David Hawkes and John Minford. 5 vols. Harmondsworth: Penguin Books, 1973–1986.

Catalogue des manuscrits chinois de Touen-Houang, Fonds Pelliot de la Bibliothèque nationale, volumes 4–5. Edited by Michel Soymié. Paris: École française d'Extrême-Orient, 1991–1995.

Chan, Hok-Lam [Chen Xuelin]. *Legends of the Building of Old Peking.* Hong Kong: Chinese University Press, 2008.

Chang'a'han jing 長阿含經 (*Dīrgha Āgama*). Translated by Buddhayaśas (Fotuoyeshe 佛陀耶舍) and Zhu fonian 竺佛念. *T.* no. 1.

Chapin, Helen B. *A Long Roll of Buddhist Images.* Revised by Alexander C. Soper. Ascona: Artibus Asiae, 1972.

Chau, Adam Yuet. *Miraculous Response: Doing Popular Religion in Contemporary China.* Stanford, Calif.: Stanford University Press, 2006.

Ch'en, Kenneth K. S. *The Chinese Transformation of Buddhism.* Princeton, N.J.: Princeton University Press, 1973.

Chen Xiaoyi 陳曉怡. "Nezha renwu ji gushi zhi yanjiu" 哪吒人物及故事之研究 (The figure and legend of Nezha). PhD dissertation, Fengjia University, 1994.

Chen Xuelin 陳學霖 [Hok-Lam Chan]. "Ao'men Nezha miao de lishi yuanyuan yu shehui wenhua yiyi" 澳門哪吒廟的歷史淵源與社會文化意義 (The historical origins and the social and cultural significance of the Macau Nezha temples). In *Aomen xue yinlun: Shoujie Ao'men xue guoji xueshu yantaohui lunwenji* 澳門學引論:首屆澳門學國際學術

研討會論文集, edited by Hao Yufan 郝雨凡, et al., vol. 2, pp. 417–452. Beijing: Shehui kexue wenxian, 2012.

———. "Beijing waicheng Nezha miao tansu" 北京外城哪吒廟探溯 (Tracing the origins of the Beijing outer-city Nezha temple). *Zhongguo wenhua yanjiusuo xuebao* 中國文化研究所學報 41 (2001): pp. 151–169.

———. *Liu Bowen Nezha cheng: Beijing jiancheng de chuanshou* 劉伯溫哪吒城—北京建城的傳說 (Liu Bowen and Nezha City: Legends of the building of Beijing). Taibei: Sanmin, 1996.

Chen Yichuan 陳易傳. *Shenqi huoxian: Nezha taizi liushisi shou qian gushi jijin* 神氣活現: 哪吒太子六十四首籤故事集錦 (Divine revelations: Sixty-four captivating Prince Nezha divinatory stories). Xinying: Xinyingshi Taizi shequ fazhan xiehui, 2005.

Chen Yiyuan 陳益源. "Jiayi xian simiao caihui zhong de Nezha gushi ji qi shenying" 嘉義縣寺廟中的哪吒故事及其身影 (The story and figure of Nezha in Jiayi county temple murals). In *Diyijie Nezha xueshu yantaohui lunwenji* 第一屆哪吒學術研討會論文 (Proceedings of the first academic conference on Nezha), edited by Guoli Zhongshan daxue qingdai xueshu yanjiu zhongxin 國立中山大學清代學術研究中心, pp. 291–304. Gaoxiong: Zhongshan daxue, 2003.

Chen Zhaonan 陳兆南, "Taiwan Shuochang de Nezha chuanshuo" 臺灣說唱的哪吒傳說 (The Nezha legend in Taiwanese oral literature). In *Diyijie Nezha xueshu yantaohui lunwenji* 第一屆哪吒學術研討會論文 (Proceedings of the first academic conference on Nezha), edited by Guoli Zhongshan daxue qingdai xueshu yanjiu zhongxin 國立中山大學清代學術研究中心, pp. 489–525. Gaoxiong: Zhongshan daxue, 2003.

Cheng, Christina Miu Bing. *In Search of Folk Humor: The Rebellious Cult of Nezha*. Singapore: Asiapac, 2009.

———. "In Search of Folk Humor: The Rebellious Cult of Nezha in Macau." *Review of Culture* (Macau) 22 (2007): pp. 77–93.

Cheng Guangxian 程光憲. "Wang'gong de jibai and yiwen" 汪公的祭拜與逸聞 (Lord Wang's cult and lore). *Jixi hui xue tongxun* 績溪徽學通訊 85, no. 2 (April 27, 2006).

Chentang guan 陳塘關 (Chentang Pass). Four manuscript fragments of a Kunqu play in the Academia Sinica's Folk Literature Collection, numbered: Sup 368–364, Sup 336, Sup 367, and K. 49–541. Photographic reprint in *Su wenxue congkan, xiju lei, shuochang lei* 俗文學叢刊, 戲劇類, 說唱類 (Folk literature: Materials in the collection of the Institute of History and Philology), edited by Huang Kuanzhong 黃寬重, 500 vols., vol. 58, pp. 70–118. Taibei: Xinwenfeng, 2001–.

Cheu, Hock Tong. *The Nine Emperor Gods: A Study of Chinese Spirit-Medium Cults*. Kuala Lumpur: Times Book International, 1988.

Chewangfu quben Fengshen bang 車王府曲本封神榜 (The Prince-Che mansion's ballad-manuscript roster of the gods). Edited by Su Huanzhong 蘇寰中, Guo Jingrui 郭精銳, and Chen Weiwu 陳偉武. 3 vols. Beijing: Renmin wenxue, 1992.

Cho, Haejoang. "Male Dominance and Mother Power: The Two Sides of Confucian Patriarchy in Korea." In *The Psycho-Cultural Dynamics of the Confucian Family: Past and Present,* edited by Walter H. Slote, pp. 277–296. Seoul: International Cultural Society of Korea, 1986.

Chong, Key Ray. *Cannibalism in China*. Wakefield: Longwood Academic, 1990.

Chou Yi-liang. "Tantrism in China." *Harvard Journal of Asiatic Studies* 8, no. 3/4 (1945): pp. 241–332.

Chunqiu lieguo zhizhuan 春秋列國志傳 (Romance of the spring and autumn feudal states). 1615 edition. Twelve chapters. Revision attributed to Chen Jiru 陳繼儒. Photographic reprint. In *Guben xiaoshuo jicheng.* 3 vols. Shanghai: Shanghai guji, 1994.

Chunqiu wuba qixiong lieguo zhizhuan 春秋五霸七雄列國志傳 (Romance of the spring and autumn five lords and seven heroes' feudal states). By Yu Shaoyu 余卲魚. Revised by Yu Xiangdou 余象斗. Santai guan 三台館. 1606 edition. Eight chapters. Photographic reprint. In *Guben xiaoshuo jicheng.* 2 vols. Shanghai: Shanghai guji, 1994.

Cohen, Myron L. *House United, House Divided: The Chinese Family in Taiwan.* New York: Columbia University Press, 1976.

Cole, Alan. *Mothers and Sons in Chinese Buddhism.* Stanford, Calif.: Stanford University Press, 1998.

Complete Catalogue of the Tibetan Buddhist Canons (Bkaḥ-ḥgyur and Bstan-ḥgyur), A. Edited by Hakuju Ui et al. Sendai: Tōhoku Imperial University, 1934.

Conze, Edward. *The Large Sutra on Perfect Wisdom, with the Divisions of the Abhisamayālaṅkāra.* Berkeley: University of California Press, 1975.

Coomaraswamy, Ananda K. *Yakṣas: Essays in the Water Cosmology.* Edited by Paul Schroeder. Delhi: Indira Gandhi National Center for the Arts & Oxford University Press, 1993.

Courtright, Paul B. *Gaṇeśa: Lord of Obstacles. Lord of Beginnings.* New York: Oxford University Press, 1985.

Couture, André. *L'enfance de Krishna: Traduction des chapitres 30 à 78.* Quebec: Les Presses de l'Université Laval, 1991.

Cowell, Edward B., ed. *The Jātaka or Stories of the Buddha's Former Births.* 1895. Reprint. 6 vols. New Delhi: Munshiram Manoharlal, 1990.

Coyajee, J. C. *Cults and Legends of Ancient Iran & China.* Bombay: Jehangir B. Karani's Sons, 1936.

Cui Yunlan 崔雲嵐. "Chuantong yishu de jinghua: dui donghua dianying Nezha naohai de fenxi" 傳統藝術的精華: 對動畫電影哪吒鬧海的分析 (The Best of Traditional Art: Analysis of the Cartoon Movie *Nezha Wreaks Havoc in the Ocean*). *Jilin yishu xueyuan xuebao* 吉林艺术学院学报 (2001, no. 4): pp. 23–26.

Da Dai li ji hui jiao jijie 大戴禮記匯校集解 (The Elder Dai Book of Rites with collated commentaries). Edited by Fang Xiangdong 方向東. 2 vols. Beijing: Zhonghua, 2008.

Damuqianlian mingjian jiumu bianwen bingtu 大目乾連冥間救母變文幷圖 (The illustrated transformation text of Mahā Maudgalyāyana rescuing his mother from hell). In Xiang Chu 項楚, *Dunhuang bianwen xuanzhu* 敦煌變文選注 (Selected and annotated Dunhuang transformation texts). Revised edition. 2 vols. Beijing: Zhonghua, 2006.

Dang Yan'ni 黨燕妮. "Pishamen Tianwang xinyang zai Dunhuang de liuchuan" 毗沙門天王信仰在敦煌的流傳 (The scope of the Heavenly King Pishamen's cult at Dunhuang). *Dunhuang yanjiu* 敦煌研究 (2005, no. 3): 99–104.

Daofa huiyuan 道法會元 (Daoist methods, united in principle). Early fifteenth century. *DZ* 1220.

Daoyuan 道原. *Jingde chuandeng lu* 景德傳燈錄 (Jingde-period record of the transmission of the lamp). *T.* no. 2076.

Davids, Caroline A. F. Rhys, trans. *The Book of the Kindred Sayings (Samyuta-Nikāya).* 1917. Reprint. 5 vols. Oxford: Pali Text Society, 1993.

Davis, Edward L. *Society and the Supernatural in Song China.* Honolulu: University of Hawai'i Press, 2001.

"Da weide Pishamen Tianwang congming taizi zhenyan" 大威德毗沙門天王聰明太子真言 (The spell of the great and awesome Vaiśravaṇa clever heir-apparent). Pelliot Chinese manuscript number 2322. Bibliothèque nationale, Paris.

Day, John. *Molech: A God of Human Sacrifice in the Old Testament.* Cambridge: Cambridge University Press, 1989.
Dean, Kenneth. *Taoist Ritual and Popular Cults of Southeast Asia.* Princeton, N.J.: Princeton University Press, 1993.
Dean, Kenneth, and Zheng Zhenman. *Ritual Alliances of the Putian Plain.* 2 vols. Leiden: Brill, 2010.
Demiéville, Paul. "Le Bouddhisme et la guerre: post-scriptum à l'"historie des moines guerriers du Japon" de G. Renondeau." In *Choix d'études Bouddhiques,* edited by Paul Demiéville, pp. 347–385. Leiden: Brill, 1973.
De Nebesky-Wojkowitz, Réne. *Oracles and Demons of Tibet: The Cult and Iconography of the Tibetan Protective Deities.* 1956. Reprint. Katmandu: Tiwari's Pilgrims Book House, 1993.
Des Rotours, Robert. "Encore quelques notes sur l'anthropophagie en Chine." *T'oung Pao* 54, no. 1–3 (1968): pp. 1–49.
———. "Quelques notes sur l'anthropophagie en Chine." *T'oung Pao* 50, no. 4–5 (1963): pp. 386–427.
Ding Zhaoqin 丁肇琴. "Cong sange xiandai wenben kan Nezha de xingxiang" 從三個現代文本看哪吒的形象 (Examining Nezha's image in three contemporary literary texts). In *Diyijie Nezha xueshu yantaohui lunwenji* 第一屆哪吒學術研討會論文 (Proceedings of the first academic conference on Nezha), edited by Guoli Zhongshan daxue qingdai xueshu yanjiu zhongxin 國立中山大學清代學術研究中心, pp. 305–330. Gaoxiong: Zhongshan daxue, 2003.
Diyijie Nezha xueshu yantaohui lunwenji 第一屆哪吒學術研討會論文 (Proceedings of the first academic conference on Nezha). Edited by Guoli Zhongshan daxue qingdai xueshu yanjiu zhongxin 國立中山大學清代學術研究中心. Gaoxiong: Zhongshan daxue, 2003.
Doolittle, Justus. *Social Life of the Chinese: With Some Account of their Religious, Governmental, Educational, and Business Customs and Opinions.* London: Sampson Low, 1866.
Duan Chengshi 段成式 (ca. 803–863). *Youyang zazu* 酉陽雜俎 (Miscellany of Youyang Mountains). *SKQS* edition.
Dudbridge, Glen. *The Hsi-yu chi: A Study of Antecedents to the Sixteenth-Century Chinese Novel.* Cambridge: Cambridge University Press, 1970.
———. *The Legend of Miaoshan.* Revised edition. Oxford Oriental Monographs. Oxford: Oxford University Press, 2004.
Durand-Dastès, Vincent. *La conversion de l'orient: une pérégrination didactique de Bodhidharma dans un roman chinois du XVIIe siècle.* Bruxelles: Institut belge des hautes études chinoises, 2008.
———. "Rencontres hérétiques dans les monastères de Kaifeng: le bouddhisme tantrique vu par le roman en langue vulgaire des Ming et des Qing." In *Empreintes du tantrisme en Chine et en Asie orientale: Imaginaires, rituels, influences,* edited by Vincent Durand-Dastès, pp. 27–62. Mélanges chinois et bouddhiques xxxii. Leuven: Peeters, 2015.
Dutt, Manmatha Nath. *A Prose English Translation of the Harivamsha.* Calcutta: H. C. Dass, 1897.
Ecke, G., and P. Demiéville. *The Twin Pagodas of Zayton: A Study of Later Buddhist Sculpture in China.* Harvard-Yenching Monograph Series, no. 2. Cambridge, Mass.: Harvard University Press, 1935.
Edmunds, Lowell. "Oedipus in Burma." *The Classical World* 90, no. 1 (1996): pp. 15–22.

Edmunds, Lowell, and Alan Dundes. *Oedipus: A Folklore Casebook.* Madison: University of Wisconsin Press, 1983.

Elliott, Alan J. A. *Chinese Spirit-Medium Cults in Singapore.* 1955. Reprint. London: Athlone, 1990.

Emmerick, R. E. *Tibetan Texts Concerning Khotan.* London Oriental Series, no. 19. London: Oxford University Press, 1967.

Erlang shen zui she suomo jing 二郎神醉射鎖魔鏡 (The God Erlang drunkenly shoots an arrow at the demon-locking mirror). (Complete title: *San Taizi da nao heifeng shan* 三太子大鬧黑風山; *erlanshenzui she suomo jing* (The third prince wreaks havoc on black-wind mountain; the god Erlang drunkenly shoots an arrow at the demon-locking mirror)). Yuan-period play. In *Guben Yuan Ming zaju* 孤本元明雜劇. 1939. Reprint. Beijing: Zhongguo xiju, 1957. Also available in vol. 2 of *Yuan qu xuan wai bian* 元曲選外編 (Beijing: Zhonghua, 1959).

Esoteric Buddhism and the Tantras in East Asia. Edited by Charles D. Orzech, Henrik H. Sørensen, and Richard D. Payne. Handbook of Oriental Studies 24. Leiden: Brill, 2011.

Fahai yizhu 法海遺珠 (Pearls retrieved from the sea of rites). Early Ming (fourteenth century). *DZ* 1166.

Fan Sheng 樊聖. "Yidipasi yu Nezha" 伊底帕斯與哪吒 (Oedipus and Nezha). *Taiwan Yijie* 臺灣醫界 39, no. 12 (1996): pp. 57–61.

Fang, Sheng 方胜. "Zailun *Fengshen yanyi* yinxi *Xiyou ji:* yu Xu Shuofang tongzhi shangque" 再論封神演義 因襲西遊記: 與徐朔方同志商榷 (Re-examining the *Fengshen yanyi*'s borrowings from the *Xiyou ji:* Discussion with Comrade Xu Shuofang). *Xuzhou Shifan daxue xuebao, zhexue shehui kexue ban* 徐州師範大學學報, 哲學社會科學版 (1988, no. 4): pp. 55–59.

Fava, Patrice. *Aux ports du ciel: La statuaire taoïste du Hunan.* Paris: Ecole Française d'Extrême-Orient, 2013.

———. "Rapport de mission dans la province du Hunan, 21 septembre—10 octobre 2003, dans le cadre du projet de recherche 'Taoïsme et société locale, les structures liturgiques du centre du Hunan.'" Unpublished report.

Feng Menglong 馮夢龍. *Jingshi tongyan* 警世通言 (Stories to caution the world). Edited by Yan Dunyi 嚴敦易. 2 vols. Beijing: Renmin, 1991.

Fengshen tianbang 封神天榜 (The heavenly roster of the gods). Qing-period palace manuscript edition. Photographic reprint in *Guben xiqu congkan di jiuji* 古本戲曲叢刊第九集. Beijing: Zhonghua shuju, 1964.

Fengshen yanyi 封神演義 (Canonization of the gods). Late Ming edition by the Suzhou Shu 舒 Family publishing house. Complete Title: *Xinke Zhong Bojing xiansheng piping Fengshen yanyi* 新刻鍾伯敬先生批評封神演義 (The newly printed, Zhong-Bojing annotated, Canonization of the gods). Preface by Li Yunxiang 李雲翔. Copy at the Naikaku bunko Library. Photographic Reprint. In *Guben xiaoshuo jicheng.* 5 vols. Shanghai: Shanghai guji, 1994.

Fengshen yanyi 封神演義 (Canonization of the gods). 1695 Sixuecao Tang 四雪草堂 edition. Preface by Chu Renhuo 褚人獲. Copies at the Beijing National Library and the Beijing University Library.

Fengshen yanyi 封神演義 (Canonization of the gods). Author given as Xu Zhonglin 許仲琳. Edited by Li Guoqing 李國慶. 2 vols. Beijing: Beijing tushuguan, 2001.

Fengshen yanyi: Xin zhengli ben 封神演義: 新整理本 (Canonization of the gods: Newly established text). Authors given as Xu Zhonglin 許仲琳, Li Yunxiang 李雲翔, and Zhong Bojing 鍾伯敬. Foreword by Zhang Peiheng 章培恆. Nanjing: Jiangsu guji, 1991.

"Fenhe wan" 汾河灣 (At the bend of the Fen river). In *Jingju congkan* 京劇叢刊, vol. 39, pp. 45–67. Beijing: Zhongguo xiju, 1959.

Fenyang Wude Chanshi yulu 汾陽無德禪師語錄 (The recorded sayings of the Chan Master Fenyang Wude [Shanzhao]). Recording the sayings of Shanzhao 善昭 (947–1024). *T.* no. 1992.

Ferdowsi. *The Epic of Kings.* Translated by Reuben Levy. London: Routledge, 1967.

Ferdowsi [Firdawsī]. *The Tragedy of Sohrab and Rostam.* Translated by Jerome W. Clinton. Seattle: University of Washington Press, 1987.

Fo benxing ji jing 佛本行集經 (*Abhiniṣkramaṇa-sūtra*). Translated by Jñānagupta (Shenajueduo 闍那崛多) (523–600). *T.* no. 190.

Foguang da cidian 佛光大辭典 (The big dictionary of the Buddha-Light). Edited by Ci Yi 慈怡. 8 volumes. Gaoxiong: Foguang, 1988.

Fomu da kongque mingwang jing 佛母大孔雀明王經 (*Mahāmāyūrī vidyārājñī*) (The great peacock-queen spell). Translated by Amoghavajra (Bukong 不空) (705–774). *T.* no. 982.

Foshuo Baoxian tuoluoni jing 佛說寶賢陀羅尼 (The Maṇibhadra dhāraṇī sutra). Translated by Tianxizai 天息災 (Devaśantika?) (?–1000). *T.* no. 1285.

Foshuo dabeikong zhi jin'guang dajiaowang yigui jing 佛說大悲空智金剛大教王儀軌經 (*Hevajra-ḍākinī-jāla-saṃbara-tantra*) *T.* no. 892.

Foshuo da kongque zhou wang jing 佛說大孔雀呪王經 (*Mahāmāyūrī vidyārājñī*) (The great peacock-queen spell). Translated by Yijing 義淨 (635–713). *T.* no. 985.

Fo suo xing zan jing 佛所行讚經 (The acts of the Buddha). Dharmakṣema's (385–433) translation of Aśvaghoṣa's (first century) *Buddhacarita. T.* no. 192.

Foucher, A. "Sur un attribut de Kuvera." *Bulletin de l'Ecole Francaise d'Extrême Orient* 3 (1903): pp. 655–657.

Franke, Herbert, ed. *Sung Biographies.* 2 vols. Wiesbaden: Franz Steiner, 1976.

Frédéric, Louis. *Les Dieux du bouddhisme.* Paris: Flammarion, 2006.

Freud, Sigmund. *The Complete Letters of Sigmund Freud to Wilhelm Fliess, 1887–1904.* Translated and edited by Jeffery Moussaieff Masson. Cambridge, Mass.: Harvard University Press, 1985.

———. "Dostoevsky and Parricide." *SE,* 21:177–196.

———. *The Interpretation of Dreams. SE,* vol. 4–5.

———. *The Standard Edition of the Complete Psychological Works of Sigmund Freud.* Translated and edited by James Strachey et al. London: Hogarth Press, 1953–1974.

———. *Totem and Taboo. SE,* 13:1–161.

Fujisaki Ryū 藤崎竜. *Houshin engi* 封神演義 (Canonization of the gods). Cartoon edition. Available online with English translation at manga.animea.net.

Gabbiani, Luca. "Insanity and Parricide in Late Imperial China (Eighteenth through Twentieth Centuries)." *International Journal of Asiatic Studies* 10, no. 2 (2013): pp. 115–141.

Gao Juefu 高觉敷, trans. *Jingshen fenxi yinlun* 精神分析引論 (Introductory lectures on psychoanalysis). By Sigmund Freud [Fuluoyide 弗洛伊德]. 1930. Revised edition. Beijing: Shangwu, 1984.

———. *Jingshen fenxi yinlun xinbian* 精神分析引論新編 (New introductory lectures on psychoanalysis). By Sigmund Freud [Fuluoyide 弗洛伊德]. Shanghai: Shangwu, 1936. Revised edition. Beijing: Shangwu, 1987.

Gay, Peter. *Freud: A Life for Our Time.* New York: Norton, 1988.

———. *Freud for Historians.* New York: Oxford University Press, 1985.

Getty, Alice. *The Gods of Northern Buddhism: Their History, Iconography and Progressive*

Evolution through the Northern Buddhist Countries. 1928. Reprint. New Delhi: Munshiram Manoharlal, 1978.
Gnod sbyin gar mkhan mchog gi rgyud (The Yakṣa Nartakavara tantra). *Tôh*. no. 767, *Dergé Kanjur*, vol. WA, folios 81v.7–88v.7. Translated by Dānagupta and Rab zhi Lo tsā ba.
Gōhō 杲寶 (1306–1362). *Dainichi kyōsho enō shō* 大日經疏演奧鈔 (Explicating the mysteries of [Yixing's] commentary on the Mahāvairocanasaṃbodhi sutra), *T*. no. 2216.
Goldman, Robert P. "Fathers, Sons and Gurus: Oedipal Conflict in the Sanskrit Epics." *Journal of Indian Philosophy* 6, no. 3 (November 1978): 349–392.
———, trans. *The Rāmāyaṇa of Vālmīki: An Epic of Ancient India*. Vol. 1: *Bālakāṇḍa*. Princeton, N.J.: Princeton University Press, 1984.
Gómez, Luis O. *Land of Bliss: The Paradise of the Buddha of Measureless Light*. Honolulu: University of Hawai'i Press, 1996.
Gonda, J. *Aspects of Early Viṣṇuism*. 1954. Reprint. Delhi: Motilal Banarsidass, 1969.
Graff, David A. "'Meritorious Cannibal:' Chang Hsün's Defense of Sui-yang and the Exaltation of Loyalty in an Age of Rebellion." *Asia Major* (third series) 8, no. 1 (1995): pp. 1–16.
Granoff, Phyllis. "Tobatsu Bishamon: Three Japanese Statues in the United States and an Outline of the Rise of this Cult in East Asia." *East and West* (new series) 20, no. 1–2 (1970): pp. 144–168.
Graves, Robert. *The Greek Myths*. 2 vols. New York: Penguin Books, 1960.
Green, André. *The Tragic Effect: The Oedipus Complex in Tragedy*. Translated by Alan Sheridan. Cambridge: Cambridge University Press, 1979.
Greenlees, Donald. "Americans in the Action as Macao Casinos Soar." *International Herald Tribune*, January 18, 2008.
Grootaers, Willem L., Li Shiyu 李世瑜, and Wang Fushi 王輔世. "Rural Temples around Hsüan-Hua (South Chahar), Their Iconography and Their History." *Folklore Studies* 10, no. 1 (1951): pp. 1–116.
Grube, Wilhelm, trans. *Die Metamorphosen der Goetter: Historisch-mythologischer Roman aus dem Chinesischen Übersetzung der Kapitel 1 bis 46*. 2 vols. Leiden: Brill, 1912.
Gu Ming-Dong. "The Chinese Filial Piety Complex: Variations on the Oedipus Theme in Chinese Literature and Culture." *Psychoanalytic Quarterly* 75 (2006): pp. 163–195.
———. "A Chinese Oedipus in Exile." *Literature and Psychology* 39, no. 1–2 (1993): pp. 1–25.
Gu Zhizong, trans. *Creation of the Gods*. 2 vols. Beijing: New World Press, 1992.
Guan Wuliangshou jing 觀無量壽經 (Amitāyus Visualization Sutra). *T*. no. 365.
Gu jin ershisi xiao 古今二十四孝 (The ancient and modern twenty-four filial exemplars). Compiled by Tan Jie 譚杰. Beijing: Zhong'guo shehui, 2008.
Guo Junye 郭俊葉. "Tuo ta Tianwang yu Nezha: Jiantan Dunhuang Pishamen Tianwang fu Nezha hui" 托塔天王與哪吒: 兼談敦煌毗沙門天王赴哪吒會圖 (The pagoda-bearer Heavenly King and Nezha: The Dunhuang paintings of the Heavenly King attending the Nezha assembly). *Dunhuang yanjiu* 敦煌研究 109 (2008.3): pp. 32–40.
Guy, John. "The Lost Temples of Nagapattinam and Quanzhou: A Study in Sino-Indian Relations." *Silk Road Art and Archeology* 3 (1993–1994): pp. 292–310.
———. "Tamil Merchant Guilds and the Quanzhou Trade." In *The Emporium of the World: Maritime Quanzhou, 1000–1400*, edited by Angela Schottenhammer, pp. 283–308. Brill: Leiden, 2001.
Haberman, David L. *Journey through the Twelve Forests: An Encounter with Krishna*. New York: Oxford University Press, 1994.

Haiqiong Bai zhenren yulu 海瓊白真人語錄 (The recorded sayings of Bai Yuchan (*hao:* Haiqiong)). *DZ* 1307.

Hanan, Patrick. *The Chinese Short Story: Studies in Dating, Authorship, and Composition.* Harvard-Yenching Institute Monograph Series 21. Cambridge, Mass.: Harvard University Press, 1973.

———. *The Chinese Vernacular Story.* Cambridge, Mass.: Harvard University Press, 1981.

Handelman, Don, and David Shulman. *God Inside Out: Śiva's Game of Dice.* New York: Oxford University Press, 1997.

Han Feizi 韓非子. *Han Feizi jijie* 韩非子集解 (Han Feizi with commentaries). Compiled by Wang Xianshen 王先慎. Beijing: Zhonghua, 1998.

Hansen, Valerie. "Gods on Walls: A Case of Indian Influence on Chinese Lay Religion?" In *Religion and Society in T'ang and Sung China,* edited by Patricia Buckley Ebrey and Peter N. Gregory, pp. 75–113. Honolulu: University of Hawai'i Press, 1993.

Hardy, Friedhelm. *Viraha-Bhakti: The Early History of Kṛṣṇa Devotion in South India.* Delhi: Oxford University Press, 1983.

Harivamśa: Being the Khila of Supplement to the Mahābhārata. Edited by Parashuram Lakshman Vaidya. 2 vols. Poona: Bhandarkar Oriental Research Institute, 1969–1971.

Hawkes, David, trans. *The Songs of the South.* Middlesex: Penguin Books, 1985.

Hawley, John Stratton. *At Play with Krishna: Pilgrimage Dramas from Brindavan.* Delhi: Motilal Banarsidass, 1981.

———. *Krishna, the Butter Thief.* Princeton, N.J.: Princeton University Press, 1983.

———. "Krishna's Cosmic Victories." *Journal of the American Academy of Religion* 47, no. 2 (June 1979): pp. 201–221.

Herodotus. *Persian Wars.* Translated by George Rawlinson. In *The Greek Historians,* edited by Francis R. B. Godolphin, vol. 1, pp. 1–563. New York: Random House, 1942.

Hiltebeitel, Alf, ed. *Criminal Gods and Demon Devotees: Essays on the Guardians of Popular Hinduism.* Albany: State University of New York Press, 1989.

Ho Kin-chung. "Nezha: Figure de l'enfant rebelle." *Études Chinoises* 7, no. 2 (Autumn, 1988): pp. 7–26.

Hōbōgirin: Dictionnaire encyclopédique du Bouddhisme d'après les sources Chinoises et Japonaises. Edited by Sylvain Lévi, J. Takakusu, and Paul Demiéville. Vol. 1. Tokyo: Maison Franco-Japonaise, 1929–1930.

Hoernle, A. F. Rudolf. "A Note on the British Collection of Central Asian Antiquities." In *Actes du XIIme Congrès international des orientalists,* vol. 1, pp. 151–185. Rome, 1899.

———. "Three Further Collections of Ancient Manuscripts from Central Asia." *Journal of the Asiatic Society of Bengal* 66 (1897): pp. 213–260.

———. "The Weber Manuscripts." *Journal of the Asiatic Society of Bengal* 62 (1893): pp. 1–40.

Holzman, Donald. "The Place of Filial Piety in Ancient China." *Journal of the American Oriental Society* 118, no. 2 (1998): pp. 185–199.

Hong Mai 洪邁 (1123–1202). *Yijian zhi* 夷堅志 (Record of hearsay). Collated by He Zhuo 何卓. 4 vols. Beijing: Zhonghua, 1981.

Hong Shuling 洪淑苓. "Nezha xinyang yu nüxing shenmei yanjiu" 哪吒信仰與女性神媒研究 (Research into the Nezha cult and female spirit mediums). In *Diyijie Nezha xueshu yantaohui lunwenji* 第一屆哪吒學術研討會論文 (Proceedings of the first academic conference on Nezha), edited by Guoli Zhongshan daxue qingdai xueshu yanjiu zhongxin 國立中山大學清代學術研究中心, pp. 215–240. Gaoxiong: Zhongshan daxue, 2003.

Hongjiatuoye yigui 吽迦陀野儀軌 (The rituals of the [Vaiśravaṇa mantra] Hong-jia-tuo-ye). By Vajrabodhi 金剛智 *T.* 1251.

Hongzan 弘贊 (1611–1685). *Sifen lü mingyi biaoshi* 四分律名義標釋 (Explanation of the names and titles in the Dharmaguptaka vinaya). *X.* no. 744.

Hopkins, E. Washburn. *Epic Mythology.* Strassburg: Trübner, 1915.

Hōshin engi 封神演義 (Canonization of the gods). Translated into Japanese by Anō Tsutomu 安能務. 3 vols. Tokyo: Kōdansha, 1988–1989.

Hōshin engi 封神演義 (Canonization of the gods). Translated into Japanese by Kijima Seidō 木嶋清道. Tokyo: Kenkōsha, 1977.

Hsia, C. T. *C. T. Hsia on Chinese Literature.* New York: Columbia University Press, 2004.

Hsieh, Andrew C. K., and Jonathan D. Spence. "Suicide and the Family in Pre-Modern Chinese Society." In *Normal and Abnormal Behavior in Chinese Culture,* edited by Arthur Kleinman and Tsung-Yi Lin, pp. 29–47. Dordrecht: D. Reidel, 1981.

Hsieh Yu-Wei. "Filial Piety and Chinese Society." In *The Chinese Mind: Essentials of Chinese Philosophy and Culture,* edited by Charles A. Moore, pp. 167–187. Honolulu: University of Hawai'i Press, 1967.

Hsing I-Tien. "Heracles in the East: The Diffusion and Transformation of his Image in the Arts of Central Asia, India, and Medieval China." Translated by William G. Crowell. *Asia Major* (third series) 18, no. 2 (2005): pp. 103–154.

Hsiung Ping-Chen. *A Tender Voyage: Children and Childhood in Late Imperial China.* Stanford, Calif.: Stanford University Press, 2005.

Hu Taili 胡台麗. "Shen gui yu dutu: Dajiale duxi fanying zhi minsu xinyang 神鬼與賭徒: 大家樂賭戲反應之民俗信仰 (Gods, ghosts, and gamblers: Popular religion in Everybody's Happy gambling). In *Zhongyang yanjiuyuan di'erjie hanxue huiyi lunweji* 中央研究院第二屆國際漢學會議論文集, section on "Minsu yu wenhua," pp. 401–424. Taibei: Zhongyang yanjiuyuan, 1989.

Huang Jingqin 黄敬欽. "Nezha xiju xingxiang tansuo" 哪吒戲劇形象探索 (An exploration of the Nezha theatrical image). In *Diyijie Nezha xueshu yantaohui lunwenji* 第一屆哪吒學術研討會論文 (Proceedings of the first academic conference on Nezha), edited by Guoli Zhongshan daxue qingdai xueshu yanjiu zhongxin 國立中山大學清代學術研究中心, pp. 331–361. Gaoxiong: Zhongshan daxue, 2003.

Huangfu Mi 皇甫謐 (215–282). *Di wang shi ji* 帝王世紀 (Chronologies of emperors and kings). Congshu jicheng edition. Shanghai: Shangwu, 1936.

Huitu sanjiao yuanliu soushen daquan 繪圖三教源流搜神大全 (Illustrated grand compendium of the three religions' original deities). Published by Ye Dehui 葉德輝 in 1909. Reprint. Edited by Wang Qiugui 王秋桂. Taipei: Lianjing, 1970.

Hurvitz, Leon. *Scripture of the Lotus Blossom of the Fine Dharma.* New York: Columbia University Press, 1976.

Idema, Wilt L. *The Dramatic Oeuvre of Chu Yu-Tun (1379–1439).* Leiden: Brill, 1985.

———. *Personal Salvation and Filial Piety: Two Precious Scroll Narratives of Guanyin and Her Acolytes.* Kuroda Institute Classics in East Asian Buddhism. Honolulu: University of Hawai'i Press, 2008.

Ikels, Charlotte. *Filial Piety: Practice and Discourse in Contemporary East Asia.* Stanford, Calif.: Stanford University Press, 2004.

Iyanaga Nobumi 彌永信美. *Daikokuten Hensō: Bukkyō Shinwagaku I* 大黑天変相—仏教神话学 (The Transformations of Mahākāla: Studies in Buddhist mythology, volume 1). Kyoto: Hōzōkan, 2002.

———. *Kannon henyōtan: Bukkyō Shinwagaku* II 观音变容譚 (Avalokiteśvara's metamorphosis: Studies in Buddhist mythology, volume 2). Kyoto: Hōzōkan, 2002.

———. "Récits de la soumission de Maheśvara par Trailokyavijaya—d'après les sources chinoises et japonaises." In *Tantric and Taoist Studies in Honor of R. A. Stein,* edited by Michel Strickmann, pp. 633–745. Mélanges chinois et bouddhiques, no. 22. Bruxelles: Institut Belge des Hautes Études Chinoises, 1985.

Jiang Liangfu 姜亮夫. *Qu Yuan fu jin yi* 屈原賦今譯 (A contemporary translation of the Qu Yuan rhapsodies). Kunming: Yun'nan Renmin, 1999.

Jiang Tao, and Philip J. Ivanhoe, eds. *The Reception and Rendition of Freud in China: China's Freudian Slip.* New York: Routledge, 2013.

Jidian suiyue: Jiaxu ke qian huguo qizhao yuan jiao yingxiang zhuanji 祭典歲月甲戌科祈安護國七朝圓醮影像專輯 (Times of offering: Commemorative album of the 1994 seven day *yuan-jiao* ritual for blessings and state protection). Xinying: Xinying Taizigong, 1995.

Jin'gang sa'duo shuo pin'na'ye'jia tian chengjiu yigui 金剛薩埵說頻那夜迦天成就儀軌經 (The rituals of the god Vināyaka explicated by Vajrasattva). Translated by Tianxizai 天息災 (Devaśāntika?) (?–1000). *T.* no. 1272.

Jin'guang ming jing 金光明經 (*Suvarṇaprabhāsottama-sūtra*) (The Golden-Light Sūtra). Translated by Dharmakṣema (Tan Wuchen 曇無讖) (385–433) *T.* no. 663.

Jinmen shamei Wan'an tang ge zun wangye jishi wenji lu 金門沙美萬安堂各尊王爺乩示文輯錄 (Record of the Quemoy Shamei Wan'an Temple various gods' spirit writings). Edited by Zhang Yunsheng 張雲盛 et al. Taibei: Da shouyin wenhua, 2008.

Jinmen Shamei Wan'an tang suici jichou caiji jishi wenji lu 金門沙美萬安堂歲次己丑彩乩乩示文輯錄 (Record of the prized oracles' spirit writings produced at the Quemoy Shamei Wan'an Temple in the year 2009). Edited by Zhang Yunsheng 張雲盛 et al. Taibei: Da shouyin wenhua, 2009.

"Jinmen xian simiao yilanbiao" 金門縣寺廟一覽表 (Table of [registered] Jinmen temples). Jinmen County government. Unpublished document, ca. 2010.

Jiu Tang shu 舊唐書 (Old history of the Tang Dynasty). Edited by Liu Xu 劉昫 (887–946) et al. Beijing: Zhonghua shuju, 1974.

Johnson, Allan W., and Douglas Price-Williams. *Oedipus Ubiquitous: The Family Complex in World Folk Literature.* Stanford, Calif.: Stanford University Press, 1996.

Johnson, David, ed. *Ritual Opera, Operatic Ritual: "Mu-lien Rescues his Mother" in Chinese Popular Culture.* Berkeley: University of California, Institute for East Asian Studies, 1989.

Johnson, David, trans. "Selections from the Twenty-Four Exemplars of Filial Piety." In *Sources of Chinese Tradition,* edited by W. Theodore de Bary and Richard Lufrano, vol. 2, pp. 138–141. New York: Columbia University Press, 2000.

Johnson, David. *Spectacle and Sacrifice: The Ritual Foundations of Village Life in North China.* Cambridge, Mass.: Harvard University Asia Center, 2009.

Jones, Ernest. *Hamlet and Oedipus.* New York: Doubleday, 1949.

———. *The Life and Work of Sigmund Freud.* 3 vols. New York: Basic Books, 1953.

Jordan, David K. "Folk Filial Piety in Taiwan: The Twenty-Four Filial Exemplars." In *The Psycho-Cultural Dynamics of the Confucian Family: Past and Present,* edited by Walter H. Slote, pp. 47–113. Seoul: International Cultural Society of Korea, 1986.

———. *Gods, Ghosts, and Ancestors: The Folk Religion of a Taiwanese Village.* Berkeley: University of California Press, 1972.

Kapstein, Matthew T., ed. *Buddhism between Tibet and China.* Studies in Indian and Tibetan Buddhism. Boston: Wisdom Publications, 2009.

Katz, Paul R. "Banner Worship and Human Sacrifice in Chinese Military History." In *The Scholar's Mind: Essays in Honor of F. W. Mote,* edited by Perry Link, pp. 207–227. Hong Kong: Chinese University Press, 2009.

———. *Demon Hordes and Burning Boats: The Cult of Marshal Wen in Late Imperial Chekiang.* SUNY Series in Chinese Local Studies. Albany: State University of New York Press, 1995.

Kennedy, Brian L., and Elizabeth Nai-Jia Guo. "Taiwanese Martial Motifs." *Journal of Chinese Martial Arts* 2 (2010): 72–81.

Kieschnick, John. *The Impact of Buddhism on Chinese Material Culture.* Princeton, N.J.: Princeton University Press, 2003.

———, and Meir Shahar, eds. *India in the Chinese Imagination: Myth, Religion, and Thought.* Encounters with Asia. Philadelphia: University of Pennsylvania Press, 2013.

Kirsner, Douglas, and Elise Snyder. "Psychoanalysis in China." In *Freud and the Far East: Psychoanalytic Perspectives on the People and Culture of China, Japan, and Korea,* edited by Salman Akhtar, pp. 43–58. Plymouth: Jason Aronson, 2009.

Kleeman, Terry F. *A God's Own Tale: The Book of Transformations of Wenchang, the Divine Lord of Zitong.* SUNY Series in Chinese Philosophy and Culture. Albany: State University of New York, 1994.

Knapp, Keith N. "The *Ru* Reinterpretaion of Xiao." *Early China* 20 (1995): pp. 195–222.

———. *Selfless Offspring: Filial Children and Social Order in Medieval China.* Honolulu: University of Hawai'i Press, 2005.

Komatsu, Shigemi, ed. 小松, 茂美. *Shigisanengi emaki* (Legends of the Mount Shigi [Monastery]). Volume 4 of *Nihon no emaki* (Japanese painted scrolls). Tokyo: Chūō kōronsha, 1987.

Kongque wang zhou jing 孔雀王呪經 (*Mahāmāyūrī vidyārājñī*) (The great peacock queen spell). Translated in 516 by Sengjiapoluo 僧伽婆羅 (Saṃghavara or Saṃghavarman). *T.* no. 984.

Koss, Nicholas. "The Relationship of the *Hsi-yu chi* and *Feng-shenyan-yi.*" *T'oung pao* 65, no. 4–5 (1979): pp. 143–165.

Kunio, Mugitani. "Filial Piety and 'Authentic Parents' in religious Daoism." In *Filial Piety in Chinese Thought and History,* edited by Alan K. L. Chan and Sor-Hoon Tan, pp. 110–121. London: Routledge, 2004.

Lagerwey, John. *Taoist Ritual in Chinese Society and History.* New York: Macmillan, 1987.

———. "Village Religion in Huizhou: A Preliminary Assessment." *Minsu quyi* 民俗曲藝 174 (2011.12): pp. 305–357.

Lai, Whalen. "Unmasking the Filial Sage-King Shun: Oedipus at Anyang." *History of Religions* 35, no. 2 (Nov. 1995): pp. 163–184.

Larson, Wendy. *From Ah Q to Lei Feng: Freud and Revolutionary Spirit in 20th Century China.* Stanford, Calif.: Stanford University Press, 2009.

Lau, D. C., trans. *Confucius: The Analects.* London: Penguin Books, 1979.

Lee, Cheuk-Yin. "The Dichotomy of Loyalty and Filial Piety in Confucianism: Historical Development and Modern Significance." In *Confucianism and the Modernization of China,* edited by Silke Krieger and Rolf Trauzettel, pp. 96–115. Mainz: Hase & Koehler, 1991.

Legge, James, trans. *The Works of Mencius.* 1895. Reprint. New York: Dover, 1970.

———. *The Sacred Books of China. The Texts of Confucianism. Part 1: The Hsiao King.* 1879. Reprint. Delhi: Motilal Banarsidass, 1988.

Lengjia shi zi ji 楞伽師資記 (Chronicle of the *Laṅkāvatāra* masters). Compiled by Jingjue 淨覺 (683–ca. 750). *T.* no. 2837.

Lessing, F. D. "The Topographical Identification of Peking with Yamāntaka." *Central Asiatic Journal* 2 (1956): 140–141.

Levenson, Jon Douglas. *The Death and Resurrection of the Beloved Son: The Transformation of Child Sacrifice in Judaism and Christianity.* New Haven, Conn.: Yale University Press, 1993.

Lévi, M. Sylvain. "Catalogue géographique des yakṣa dans la Mahāmāyūrī." *Journal Asiatique* 5 (1915): pp. 19–138.

Lévi-Strauss, Claude. *Tristes Tropiques: An Anthropological Study of Primitive Societies in Brazil.* Translated by John Russell. New York: Atheneum, 1972.

Lewis, Mark Edward. *Sanctioned Violence in Early China.* SUNY Series in Chinese Philosophy and Culture. Albany: State University of New York Press, 1990.

Li Fengmao 李豐楙. "Wuying xinyang yu Zhongtan yuanshuai: qi yuanshi ji yanbian" 五營信仰與中壇元帥: 其原始及衍變 (The Five-Armies Belief and the General of the Middle Altar: Origins and evolution). In *Diyijie Nezha xueshu yantaohui lunwenji* 第一屆哪吒學術研討會論文 (Proceedings of the first academic conference on Nezha), edited by Guoli Zhongshan daxue qingdai xueshu yanjiu zhongxin 國立中山大學清代學術研究中心, pp. 549–594. Gaoxiong: Zhongshan daxue, 2003.

Li Lincan 李霖燦. *Nanzhao Dali guo xin ziliao de zonghe yanjiu* 南詔大理国新資料的綜合研究 (Integrated research of newly discovered materials from the Nanzhao Dali Kingdom). Nangang: Zhongyang yanjiuyuan, 1967.

Li Ling 李翎. "Pishamen tuxiang bianshi: Yi Yulin 25 ku qian shi Pishamen Tian zuhe tuxiang de renshi wei zongxin" 毗沙门图像辨识: 以榆林25窟前室毗沙门组合图像的认识为中心 (Identifying the figures in Vaiśravaṇa and retinue images: Focusing on the example of the group fresco in the front chamber of Yulin cave no. 25). *Gugong Xuekan* 故宫学刊 7 (2011): pp. 180–190.

Li Qiao 李喬. *Zhongguo hangye shen chongbai* 中國行業神崇拜 (The cult of Chinese vocational gods). Beijing: Zhongguo Huaqiao, 1990.

Li Xianzhang 李獻章. "Yi *sanjiao soushen daquan* yu *Tianfei niangma zhuan* wei zhongxin lai kaocha Mazu chuanshuo" 以三教搜神大全與天妃娘媽傳為中心來考察媽祖傳説 (Employing *The Grand compendium of the three religions' deities* and *The biography of the Heavenly Consort Mazu* as principal sources for the study of the Mazu legend). In *Huitu sanjiao yuanliu soushen daquan* 繪圖三教源流搜神大全 (Illustrated grand compendium of the three religions' original deities). Published by Ye Dehui 葉德輝 in 1909. Reprint, pp. 3–33. Edited by Wang Qiugui 王秋桂. Taipei: Lianjing, 1970.

Li Xiaorong 李小榮. *Dunhuang mijiao wenxian lungao* 敦煌密教文献论稿 (Draft essays on Dunhuang Tantric literature). Beijing: Renmin wenxue, 2003.

Li Yu. *Silent Operas.* Edited by Patrick Hanan. Hong Kong: Chinese University of Hong Kong, 1990.

Li ji jijie 禮記集解 (The book of rites with commentaries). Edited by Sun Xidan 孫希旦. 3 vols. Beijing: Zhonghua, 1989.

Lin Fushi 林富士. *Guhun yu guixiong de shijie: bei Taiwan de ligui xinyang* 孤魂與鬼雄的世界: 北臺灣的厲鬼信仰 (Orphaned souls and ghostly heroes: The northern Taiwan belief in pernicious ghosts). Banqiao: Taibei xian li wenhua, 1995.

Lin, Yüan-huei. "The Weight of Mt. T'ai: Patterns of Suicide in Traditional Chinese History and Culture." PhD dissertation, University of Wisconsin-Madison, 1990.

Liu Cunren 柳存仁 [Liu Ts'un-Yan]. "Pishamen tianwang fuzi yu Zhongguo xiaoshuo zhi guanxi" 毗沙門天王父子與中國小說之關係 (The Heavenly King Pishamen and son, and their relation to Chinese fiction). In his *Hefengtang wenji* 和風堂文集 (Collected writings from Hefeng Hall), vol. 2, pp. 1045–1094. Shanghai: Shanghai guji, 1991.

Liu Shufen 劉淑芬. *Miezui yu duwang: Foding zunsheng tuoluoni jingchuang zhi yanjiu* 滅罪與度亡: 佛頂尊勝陀羅尼經幢之研究 (Atonement and salvation: Research into the *Uṣṇīṣa vijaya dhāraṇī* sutra-pillars). Shanghai: Shanghai guji, 2008.

Liu Ts'un-Yan [Liu Cunren]. *Buddhist and Taoist Influences on Chinese Novels, Volume 1: The Authorship of the Feng Shen Yen I.* Wiesbaden: Kommissionsverlag, 1962.

Liu Xiongping 劉雄平. "Edipusi qingjie yu xiandai wenxue zuopin zhong de poxi Maodun" 俄狄浦斯情結與現代文學作品中的婆媳矛盾 (The Oedipus complex and mother-in-law daughter-in-law conflicts in modern Chinese literature). Zhanjiang shifan xueyuan xuebao 湛江师范学院学报26, no. 1 (Feb. 2005): pp. 46–50.

Liu Zehua 劉澤華, ed. *Zhong'guo zhengzhi sixiang shi: Qin, Han, Wei, Jin Nanbei chao juan* 中國政治思想史: 秦漢魏晉南北朝卷 (A history of Chinese political thought: The Qin, Han, Wei, Jin, Northern and Southern dynasties). Hangzhou: Zhejiang Renmin, 1996.

Liu Zhiwan 劉枝萬. "Taiwan de minjian xinyang" 臺灣的民間信仰 (Taiwanese popular religion). Translated into Chinese by Yu Wanju 余萬居. *Taiwan fengwu* 臺灣風物 39, no. 1 (1989): pp. 79–107.

Lu Hsun. *Dawn Blossoms Plucked at Dusk.* Translated by Gladys and Hsien-Yi Yang. Beijing: Foreign Language Press, 1976.

———. *Selected Works of Lu Hsun.* Translated by Yang Xianyi and Gladys Yang. 4 vols. Beijing: Foreign Language Press, 1956.

Lü Jianfu 吕建福. *Zhongguo mijiao shi* 中国密教史 (History of Chinese esoteric Buddhism). Revised edition. Beijing: Zhongguo shehui kexue, 2011.

Lu Shihua 盧世華. *Yuan dai pinghua yanjiu: Yuanshengtai de tonsu xiaoshuo* 元代平話研究: 原生態的通俗小說 (Research into the Yuan period *pinghua:* The prototype of popular fiction). Beijing: Zhonghua, 2009.

Lu, Tina. *Accidental Incest, Filial Cannibalism, and Other Peculiar Encounters in Late-Imperial Chinese Literature.* Harvard East Asian Monographs, 304. Cambridge, Mass.: Harvard University Asia Center, 2008.

Luo, Guanzhong. *Three Kingdoms: A Historical Novel.* Translated by Moss Roberts. Berkeley: University of California Press, 1991.

Luo Tongbing 罗同兵. "Tichu Edipusi: Donghua dianying 'Nezha naohai' bianju jiexi 剔除俄狄浦斯:動畫電影哪吒鬧海編劇解析 (Rejecting Oedipus: Analyzing the screenplay of the animated 'Nezha wreaks havoc in the ocean'). *Dianying pingjia* 電影評價 23 (2006): pp. 10–11.

Mahā yakṣa senāpati nartakapara kalpa (*Gnod sbyin gyi sde dpon chen po gar mkhan mchog gi brtag pa*) (The text of the great *yakṣa* general Narta-kavara) *Tôh.* no. 766, *Dergé Kanjur,* vol. WA, folios 69r.7–81v.7. Translated by Dānagupta and Rab zhi Lo tsā ba.

Mair, Victor H. "A Medieval, Central Asian Buddhist Theme in a Late Ming Taoist Tale by Feng Meng-lung." *Sino-Platonic Papers* 95 (May 1999): pp. 1–27.

———. "The Narrative Revolution in Chinese Literature: Ontological Presuppositions." *Chinese Literature: Essays, Articles, Reviews* 5, no. 1 (July 1983): pp. 1–27.

———. *Painting and Performance: Chinese Picture Recitation and Its Indian Genesis.* Honolulu: University of Hawai'i Press, 1988.

———. *Tun-Huang Popular Narratives.* Cambridge Studies in Chinese History, Literature, and Institutions. Cambridge: Cambridge University Press, 1983.

Malinowski, Bronislaw. *Sex and Repression in Savage Society.* 1927. Reprint. Chicago: University of Chicago Press, 1985.

Maṇibhadra-nāma-dhāraṇī (*'Phags pa nor bu bzang po'i gzungs*) (The Maṇibhadra dhāraṇī). *Tôh.* no. 764. *Dergé Kanjur,* vol. WA, folios 56r.1–56v.2. Translated by Vidyākarasiṃha and Klu'i dbang po.

Maṇibhadra yakṣa sena kalpa (*Gnod sbyin nor bu bzang po'i rtog pa*) (The Text of the *yakṣa* general Maṇibhadra). *Tôh.* no. 765, *Dergé Kanjur,* vol. WA, folios 56v.2–69r.6. Translated by Mañjuśrī and Ba ri.

Marco Polo: The Description of the World. Translated and edited by A. C. Moule and Paul Pelliot. 2 vols. London: Routledge, 1938.

Masson, J. L. "The Childhood of Kṛṣṇa: Some Psychoanalytic Observations." *Journal of the American Oriental Society* 49, no. 4 (October–December 1974): pp. 454–459.

Matchett, Freda. *Kṛṣṇa: Lord or Avatāra? The Relationship between Kṛṣṇa and Viṣṇu.* Richmond: Curzon, 2001.

———. "The Taming of Kāliya: A Comparison of the Harivaṃśa, Viṣṇu-Purāṇa and Bhāgavata-Purāṇa Versions." *Religion* 16 (1986): pp. 115–133.

Matsumoto Bunzaburō 宋本文三郎. "Tōbatsu Bishamon kō" 兜跋毗沙門考 (Research into Tōbatsu Bishamon). 1939. Reprint in his *Bukkyō-shi zakkō* 佛教史雜考 (Miscellaneous essays on Buddhist history), pp. 273–313. Osaka: Sōbunsha, 1944.

Matsumura Takeo 宋村武雄. *Wenyi yu xing'yu* 文艺与性欲 (Literature and sexual desire). Tranlsated from the Japanese by Xie Liuyi 谢六逸. Shanghai: Kaiming, 1927.

Menglie Nazha san bianhua 猛烈那吒三變化 (The fierce Nazha's three transformations). (Complete title: *Cibei shefu wu guimo* 慈悲攝伏五鬼魔; *Menglie Nazha san bianhua* (The merciful conversion of the three demons; the fierce Nazha's three transformations)). Early Ming-period play. In *Guben Yuan Ming zaju* 孤本元明雜劇. 1939. Reprint. Beijing: Zhongguo xiju, 1957.

Meulenbeld, Mark R. E. "Civilized Demons: Ming Thunder Gods from Ritual to Literature." PhD dissertation. Princeton University, 2007.

———. *Demonic Warfare, Daoism, Territorial Networks, and the History of a Ming Novel.* Honolulu: University of Hawai'i Press, 2015.

Miaofa lianhua jing 妙法蓮華經 (Sutra of the lotus blossom of the fine Dharma). Translated by Kumārajīva. *T.* no. 262.

Ming shi lu 明實錄 (Ming veritable records). Manuscript edition. Photographic reprint. 133 vols. Taibei: Zhongyang yanjiuyuan, 1961–1966.

Mochizuki Shinkô 望月信享, ed. *Bukkyô daijiten* 佛教大辭典 (The big dictionary of Buddhism). 3rd ed., 10 vols. Kyoto: Sekai seiten kankô kyôkai, 1954–1971.

Mohe Feishiluomonaye tipohe luoshe tuoluoni yigui 摩訶吠室囉末那野提婆喝囉闍陀羅尼儀軌 (The Tantric rituals of the *dhāraṇī* of the great heavenly king Vaiśravaṇa). Translated by Banruokanjieluo 般若斫羯囉 (Prajñācakra). *T.* no. 1246.

Monier-Williams, Monier. *A Sanskrit-English Dictionary, Etymologically and Philologically Arranged With Special Reference to Cognate Indo-European Languages.* 1899. Reprint. Oxford: Clarendon Press, 1979.

Mozi 墨子. *Mozi jiaozhu* 墨子校注 (Mozi with collected annotations). Compiled by Wu Yujiang 吳毓江. 2 vols. Beijing: Zhonghua, 2006.

Mu An 睦庵 [Shan Qing 善卿]. *Zuting shiyuan* 祖庭事苑 (Literary selections from the patriarch's hall). *X.* no. 1261.

Murray, Julia K. "Representations of Hāritī, the Mother of Demons, and the Theme of 'Raising the alms-Bowl' in Chinese Painting." *Artibus Asiae* 43, no. 4 (1981–1982): pp. 253–284.

Nakamura Hajime 中村元. *Bukkyōgo daijiten* 佛教語大辭典 (The big dictionary of Buddhist terminology). Tokyo: Tōkyō shoseki, 1981.

Nakano Gensou 中野, 玄三. *Kurama dera* (The Kurama-Dera Temple). Tokyo: Chuuoukouron bijutsushuppan, 1972.

Naxin 納新 (fl. 1345). *Heshuo fang'gu ji* 河朔訪古記 (Antiquities north of the [Yellow] River). Congshu jicheng chubian edition. Beijing: Zhonghua, 1991.

Nei zhengbu shenzhi jieshao ziliao shuoming 內政部神祇介紹資料說明 (Government internal introductory materials on the Taiwanese gods). Unpublished document. Taiwan: 2000.

Nezha chuanqi 哪吒傳奇 (Nezha story). Gezaixi play performed by the Xinhexing 新和興 Company. Script included in *Gezaixi juben zhengli jihua baogao shu* 歌仔戲劇本整理計劃報告書, vol. 2, pp. 839–850. Taibei: Zhonghua minsu yishu jijinhui, 1995.

Nezha chuanqi 哪吒傳奇 (Nezha story). Cartoon edition based upon the Zhongyang dianshi tai television serial of the same title. 10 vols. Beijing: Renmin Youdian, 2004.

Nezha guli 哪吒故里 (Nezha's native place). Edited by Pang Dashan 龐大繕, et al. Xixia: Zhengxie Xixia xian weiyuanhui, 2004.

Nezha nao hai 哪吒鬧海 (Nezha wreaks havoc in the ocean). Fuzhou *pinghua* 評話 ballad. Lithographic edition printed in Shanghai by the Fuzhou publisher Yixin shuju 益新書局. Copy numbered Pe22–207 in the folk literature (*su wenxue*) collection of the Academia Sinica, Institute of History and Philology (Taibei). Photographic reprint in *Su wenxue congkan, xiju lei, shuochang lei* 俗文學叢刊, 戲劇類, 說唱類 (Folk literature: Materials in the collection of the Institute of History and Philology). Edited by Huang Kuanzhong 黃寬重. Vol. 367, pp. 1–22. Taibei: Xinwenfeng, 2001.

Nezha nao hai 哪吒鬧海 (Nezha wreaks havoc in the ocean). Animation Movie. Directed by Wang Shuchen 王樹忱. Figure design by Zhang Ding 張仃. Shanghai: Shanghai meishu dianying zhipian guang, 1979.

Nikaido Yoshihirō 二階堂善弘. "Nata taishi kō" 那吒太子考 (Research on Nezha, the third prince). In *Dōkyō no rekishi to bunka* 道教の歴史と文化, edited by Yamada Toshiaki 山田利明 and Tanaka Fumio 田中文雄, pp. 176–196. Tokyo: Yūzankaku, 1998.

Ning, Qiang. *Art, Religion, and Politics in Medieval China: The Dunhuang Cave of the Zhai Family.* Honolulu: University of Hawai'i Press, 2004.

O'Flaherty, Wendy Doniger. *Hindu Myths: A Sourcebook Translated from the Sanskrit.* Middlesex: Penguin Books, 1976.

———. *Śiva: The Erotic Ascetic.* Oxford: Oxford University Press, 1981.

Ōmura Seigai 大村西崖 (1868–1927). *Mikkyō hattatsu shi* 密教發達志 (The evolution of Tantric Buddhism). 1918. Reprint. Taibei: Wuling, 1993.

Orzech, Charles D. *Politics and Transcendent Wisdom: The Scripture for Humane Kings in Creation of Chinese Buddhism.* University Park: Pennsylvania State University Press, 1998.

Osabe Kazuo 長部和雄. *Tō Sō Mikkyōshi ronkō* 唐宋密教史論考 (Essays on the history of Tang and Song esoteric Buddhism). Kyoto, 1982.

Ōtsuka Hidetaka 大塚秀高. *Zōho Chūgoku tsūzoku shōsetsu shomoku* 增補中國通俗小說書目 (Supplement to the catalogue of Chinese popular fiction). Tokyo: Kifuku shoin, 1987.

Overmyer, Daniel L. *Local Religion in North China in the Twentieth Century: The Structure and Organization of Community Rituals and Beliefs.* Leiden: Brill, 2009.

Owen, Stephen. *An Anthology of Chinese Literature: Beginnings to 1911.* New York: W. W. Norton, 1996.
Peri, Noel. "Hārītī: La Mère-de-Démons," *Bulletin de l'École Française d'Extrême-Orient* 17, no. 3 (1917): pp. 1–102.
Phillips, Michael R., Huaqing Liu, and Yanping Zhang. "Suicide and Social Change in China." *Culture, Medicine, and Psychiatry* 23 (1999): pp. 25–50.
Pines, Yuri. "Beasts or Humans: Pre-Imperial Origins of the Sino-Barbarian Dichotomy." In *Mongols, Turks and Others,* edited by Reuven Amitai and Michal Biran, pp. 59–102. Leiden: Brill, 2004.
———. *Everlasting Empire: The Political Culture of Ancient China and Its Imperial Legacy.* Princeton, N.J.: Princeton University Press, 2012.
Piṅgaḷi, Sūranna. *The Sound of the Kiss, or the Story That Must Never Be Told.* Translated by Velcheru Narayana Rao and David Shulman. New York: Columbia University Press, 2002.
Pishamen Tianwang jing 毗沙門天王經 (Sutra of the Heavenly King Vaiśravaṇa). By Amoghavajra 不空 (705–774). *T.* no. 1244.
Pishamen yigui 毘沙門儀軌 (The Tantric rituals of Vaiśravaṇa). Attributed to Amoghavajra 不空 (705–774). *T.* no. 1249.
Plaks, Andrew. "The Problem of Incest in *Jin Ping Mei* and *Honglou meng.*" In *Paradoxes of Traditional Chinese Literature,* edited by Eva Hung and Robert E. Hegel, pp. 123–145. Hong Kong: Chinese University Press, 1994.
Pu Songling 蒲松齡. *Liaozhai zhiyi huijiao huizhu huiping ben* 聊齋志異會校會注會評本 (The complete collated and annotated Liaozhai's records of the strange). Edited by Zhang Youhe 張友鶴. 4 vols. Shanghai: Shanghai guji, 1978.
Qianyuan shan 乾元山 (Primordial Mountain). Four manuscript versions of a Kunqu-style play preserved at the Academia Sinica (Taibei) and numbered K-838, K21-221-4, K60-631, and Pi96-1092. Photographic reprint in *Su wenxue congkan, xiju lei, shuochang lei* 俗文學叢刊, 戲劇類, 説唱類 (Folk literature: Materials in the collection of the Institute of History and Philology). Edited by Huang Kuanzhong 黃寬重. Vol. 58, pp. 70–118. Taibei: Xinwenfeng, 2001.
Qing caihui quanben Xiyou ji 清彩繪全本西遊記 (Qing-period color-illustrated complete edition of the journey to the west). Edited by Meng Qingjiang 孟慶江. Beijing: Zhong'guo shudian, 2008.
Qing Meng'gu Che wang fu cang qu ben 清蒙古車王府藏曲本 (Performance literature preserved at the Mongolian Prince Che residence). Edited by the Shoudu (Capital) Library. Beijing: Beijing guji, 1991. 1661 volumes. Available also in a microfilm edition.
Qing Shaonian Nezha 青少年哪吒 (Teenage Nezha). (Additional English title: *Rebels of the Neon God*). Written and directed by Tsai (Cai) Mingliang 蔡明亮. Released in Taiwan in 1993 by the Zhongyang dianying shiye 中央電影事業 (Central motion pictures corporation).
Qing Shaonian Nezha 青少年哪吒 (Teenage Nezha). Screenplay of Tsai (Cai) Mingliang's 蔡明亮 movie. Edited by Zhang Jingheng 張靚菡. Taibei: Yuanliu, 1992.
Qiu Dezai 仇德哉. *Taiwan miao shen zhuan* 台灣廟神傳 (Taiwanese temple deities). 1979. Reprint. Douliu: Xintong, 1985.
Qiu Xigui 裘錫圭. "Sha shouzi jie" 殺首子解 (Interpreting the killing of the first-born). *Zhong'guo wenhua* 中國文化 (1994.1): 47–51.
Qiu Zhonglin 邱仲麟 [Ch'iu Chung-lin]. "Bu xiao zhi xiao: Tang yilai gegu liaoqin xianxiang shehui shi chutan" 不孝之孝: 唐以來割股療親現象的社會史初探 (A socio-

historical study of the phenomenon of 'cutting flesh to heal parents' from the Tang Dynasty to Modern China). *Xin shi xue* 新史學 6, no. 1 (1995): pp. 49–94.

———. "Renyao yu Xueqi: 'Gegu' liaoqin xianxiang zhong de yiliao guan'nian" 人藥與血氣: '割股' 療親現象中的醫療觀念 (The human flesh as medicine and the idea of "vitalism": The medical underpinnings of "cutting the flesh" to heal one's parents). *Xin shi xue* 新史學 10, no. 4 (1999): pp. 67–116.

"Qiu zi wang huanyuan; San Taizi tuo meng yao naizui" 求子忘還願三太子託夢要奶嘴 (Forgetting her vow if blessed with a child, the Third Prince demanding a pacifier in her dream). *Dongsen xinwen* 東森新聞 news agency, October 4, 2011.

Quan Tang wen 全唐文 (The complete prose of the Tang). 1814 edition. Photographic reprint. 5 vols. Shanghai: Shanghai guji, 1990.

Quanxiang Huaguang Tianwang Nanyou zhizhuan 全像華光天王南遊志傳 (The fully illustrated record of the Heavenly King Splendid Radiance's journey to the south). Compiled by Yu Xiangdou 余象斗. Late Ming edition.

Ramanujan, A. K. "The Indian 'Oedipus.'" In *Indian Literature: Proceedings of a Seminar*, edited by Arabinda Poddar, pp. 127–137. Simla: Indian Institute of Advanced Study, 1972.

Reischauer, Edwin O. *Ennin's Diary: The Record of a Pilgrimage to China in Search of the Law*. New York: Ronald Press, 1955.

Renwang huguo banruoboluomiduo jing tuoluoni niansong yigui 仁王護國般若波羅密多經陀羅尼念誦儀軌 (The Tantric rituals of the recitation of the *dhāraṇī* of the Benevolent-King Buddha protecting the state supreme wisdom sutra). Translated by Amoghavajra 不空 (705–774). *T.* no. 994.

Ropp, Paul S, Paola Zamperini, and Harriet T. Zurndorfer, eds. *Passionate Women: Female Suicide in Late Imperial China*. Special issue of *Nan Nü* 3, no. 1 (2001).

Rudnytsky, Peter L. *Freud and Oedipus*. New York: Columbia University Press, 1987.

Rundin, John. "Pozo Moro, Child Sacrifice, and the Greek Legendary Tradition." *Journal of Biblical Literature* 123, no. 3 (Autumn 2004): pp. 425–447.

Rupert, Brian. "Review of Iyanaga Nobumi's *Daikokuten Hensō: Bukkyō Shinwagaku I*, and Iyanaga Nobumi's *Kannon henyōtan: Bukkyō Shinwagaku II*." *Japanese Journal of Religious Studies* 30, nos. 1–2 (2003): pp. 177–186.

Sangren, P. Steven. *Chinese Sociologies: An Anthropological Account of the Role of Alienation in Social Reproduction*. London School of Economics Monographs on Social Anthropology, no. 72. London: Athlone Press, 2000.

———. "Female Gender in Chinese Religious Symbols: Kuan Yin, Ma Tsu, and the 'Eternal Mother.'" *Signs* 9 (1983): 4–25.

———. *Myth, Gender, and Subjectivity*. Hsin-chu: Program for Research of Intellectual-Cultural History, Tsing-Hua University, 1997.

———. "Myths, Gods, and Family Relations." In *Unruly Gods: Divinity and Society in China*, edited by Meir Shahar and Robert Weller, pp. 150–183. Honolulu: University of Hawai'i Press, 1996.

Sanjiao yuanliu shengdi fozu sou shen daquan 三教源流聖帝佛祖搜神大全 (The grand compendium of the three religions' original sages, Buddhas, and deities). Ming edition. Photographic reprint in vol. 3 of Wang Qiugui and Li Fengmao, eds., *Zhongguo Minjian xinyang ziliao huibian* 中國民間信仰資料彙編 (Collected materials on Chinese popular religion). Series no. 1, 31 vols. Taibei: Xuesheng shuju, 1988.

San Sui pingyao zhuan 三遂平妖傳 (The three Sui quell the demons' revolt). Author given as Luo Guanzhong 羅貫中. Edited by Zhang Rongqi 張榮起. Beijing: Beijing daxue, 1983.

Saso, Michael. "The Nezha Daoist shrine of Macao protects an ancient Catholic cathedral." May 7, 2010. www.michaelsaso.org.

Schipper, Kristofer. *Le Corpse Taoïste.* L'espace intérieur, 25. Paris: Fayard, 1982.

———. "Vernacular and Classical Ritual in Taoism." *Journal of Asian Studies* 45, no. 1 (November 1985): pp. 21–51.

Schipper, Kristofer, and Franciscus Verellen, eds. *The Taoist Canon: A Historical Companion to the Daozang.* 3 vols. Chicago: University of Chicago Press, 2004.

Seaman, Gary. *The Journey to the North: An Ethno-historical Analysis and Annotated Translation of the Chinese Folk Novel "Pei-yu-chi."* Berkeley: University of California Press, 1987.

———. "The Sexual Politics of Karmic Retribution." In *The Anthropology of Taiwanese Society,* edited by Emily Martin Ahern and Hill Gates, pp. 381–396. Stanford, Calif.: Stanford University Press, 1981.

Seaman, Gary, and Victor H. Mair, trans. "Romance of the Investiture of the Gods." Attributed to Lu Xixing. In *Hawai'i Reader in Traditional Chinese Culture,* edited by Victor H. Mair et al., pp. 467–489. Honolulu: University of Hawai'i Press, 2005.

Sen, Tansen. *Buddhism, Diplomacy, and Trade: The Realignment of Sino-Indian Relations 600–1400.* Asian Interactions and Comparisons. Honolulu: Association for Asian Studies and University of Hawai'i Press, 2003.

Shahar, Meir. *Crazy Ji: Chinese Religion and Popular Literature.* Harvard-Yenching Institute Monograph Series, 48. Cambridge, Mass.: Harvard University Asia Center, 1998.

———. "Diamond Body: The Origins of Invulnerability in the Chinese Martial Arts." In *Perfect Bodies: Sports, Medicine, and Immortality,* edited by Vivienne Lo, pp. 119–128. The British Museum Research Publications 188. London: British Museum, 2012.

———. "The Legacy of the Tantric Angels." In *Xinyang, Shijian yu wenhua tiaoshi: di sijie guoji hanxue huiyi lunwenji* 信仰實踐與文化調適: 第四屆國際漢學會議論文集 (Belief, practice, and cultural adaptation: Papers from the religion section of the fourth international conference on sinology), edited by Kang Bao 康豹 (Paul R. Katz) and Liu Shu-fen 劉淑芬, pp. 31–69. Taibei: Zhongyang yanjiuyuan, 2013.

———. *The Shaolin Monastery: History, Religion, and the Chinese Martial Arts.* Honolulu: University of Hawai'i Press, 2008.

Shahar, Shulamith. *Childhood in the Middle Ages.* London: Routledge, 1990.

Shapiro, Hugh. "Operatic Escapes: Performing Madness in Neuropsychiatric Beijing." In *Science and Technology in Modern China, 1880s–1940s,* edited by Jing Tsu and Benjamin Elman, pp. 297–326. Leiden: Brill, 2014.

Shapiro, Sidney, trans. *Outlaws of the Marsh.* Authors given as Shi Nai'an and Luo Guanzhong. 4 vols. Beijing: Foreign Languages Press, 1988.

Sharf, Robert. "On Esoteric Buddhism in China." In his *Coming to Terms with Chinese Buddhism: A Reading of the Treasure Store Treatise,* pp. 263–278. Honolulu: University of Hawai'i Press, 2002.

Sharma, Arvind. "The Significance of Viṣṇu Reclining on the Serpent." *Religion* 16 (1986): 101–114.

Shen Weirong. "Tibetan Buddhism in Mongol-Yuan China." In *Esoteric Buddhism and the Tantras in East Asia,* edited by Charles D. Orzech, Henrik H. Sørensen, and Richard D. Payne. Handbook of Oriental Studies 24, pp. 539–549. Leiden: Brill, 2011.

Shi Guangsheng 石光生. "Taiwan xiqu zhong de Nezha xingxiang kehua" 臺灣戲曲中的哪吒形象刻畫 (The portrayal of the Nezha figure in Taiwanese drama). In *Diyijie Nezha xueshu yantaohui lunwenji* 第一屆哪吒學術研討會論文 (Proceedings of the first academic conference on Nezha), edited by Guoli Zhongshan daxue qingdai xueshu yanjiu zhongxin 國立中山大學清代學術研究中心, pp. 171–196. Gaoxiong: Zhongshan daxue, 2003.

Shibusawa Keizō. *Multilingual Version of "Pictopedia of Everyday Life in Medieval Japan."* Yokohama: Kanagawa University 21st Century COE Program, 2008.

Shuihu quanzhuan 水滸全傳 (Water margin). 3 vols. Beijing: Renmin wenxue, 1954. Reprint. 2 vols. Taibei: Wannianqing shudian, 1979.

Shulman, David. "Concave and Full: Masking the Mirrored Deity at Lepākṣī." In *In the Company of the Gods: Essays in Memory of Günther-Dietz Sontheimer,* edited by Aditya Malik, Ann Feldhaus, and Heidrun Brückner, pp. 31–52. New Delhi: Indira Gandhi National Center for the Arts, 2005.

Shuo Tang hou zhuan 說唐後傳 (Sequel to the romance of the Tang Dynasty). Author given as Yuanhu yu sou 鴛湖魚叟. 1783 edition. Photographic reprint in the series Guben xiaoshuo jicheng. 2 vols. Shanghai: Shanghai guji, 1992.

Silk, Jonathan A. *Riven by Lust: Incest and Schism in Indian Buddhist Legend and Historiography.* Honolulu: University of Hawai'i Press, 2009.

Sima Qian 司馬遷. *Shiji* 史記. Annotated by Zhang Shoujie 張守節, Sima Zhen 司馬貞, and Pei Yinji 裴駰集. Beijing: Zhonghua shuju, 1992.

Sivaramamurti, Calambur. *The Art of India.* New York: Harry N. Abrams, 1977.

Slote, Walter H. "Oedipal Ties and the Issue of Separation-Individuation in Confucian Societies." *Journal of the American Academy of Psychoanalysis* 20 (1992): 435–453.

Song Maocheng 宋懋澄. *Jiu yue ji* 九籥集 (Nine bamboo writing slips). Edited by Wang Liqi 王利器. Beijing: Zhongguo shehui kexue, 1984.

Sophocles. *Oedipus Rex.* Translated by David Mulroy. Madison: University of Wisconsin Press, 2011.

Sørensen, Henrik H. "The Spell of the Great, Golden Peacock Queen: The Origin, Practices, and Lore of an Early Esoteric Buddhist Tradition in China." *Pacific World,* third series, 8 (Fall 2006): pp. 89–123.

Spiro, Melford E. "The Oedipus Complex in Burma." In Lowell Edmunds and Alan Dundes, *Oedipus: A Folklore Casebook,* pp. 203–214. Wisconsin: University of Wisconsin Press, 1983.

———. *Oedipus in the Trobriands.* Chicago: University of Chicago Press, 1982.

Stafford, Charles. *The Roads of Chinese Childhood: Learning and Identification in Angang.* Cambridge Studies in Social and Cultural Anthropology, no. 97. Cambridge: Cambridge University Press, 1995.

Stein, M. Aurel. *Ancient Khotan: Detailed Report of Archeological Explorations in Chinese Turkestan.* 2 vols. Oxford: Clarendon Press, 1907.

———. *Serinida: Detailed Report of Explorations in Central Asia and Westernmost China.* 5 vols. Oxford: Oxford University Press, 1921.

Stephens, William N. *The Oedipus Complex: Cross Cultural Evidence.* New York: Free Press of Glencoe, 1962.

Strickmann, Michel. *Chinese Magical Medicine.* Edited by Bernard Faure. Asian Religions and Cultures. Stanford, Calif.: Stanford University Press, 2002.

———. *Chinese Poetry and Prophecy: The Written Oracle in East Asia.* Edited by Bernard Faure. Asian Religions and Cultures. Stanford, Calif.: Stanford University Press, 2005.

———. *Mantras et Mandarins: Le Bouddhisme Tantrique en Chine.* Paris: Gallimard, 1996.

Strong, John S., and Sarah M. Strong. "A Tooth Relic of the Buddha in Japan: An Essay on

the Sennyū-Ji Tradition and a Translation of Zeami's Nō Play *Shari*." *Japanese Religions* 20, no. 1 (January 1995): pp. 1–33.
Su Zhe 蘇轍. *Luancheng ji* 欒城集 (Su Zhe's collected writings). Ming edition. Photographic reprint. Sibu congkan. Taibei: Shangwu, 1967.
Sun Simiao 孫思邈. *Qianjin yifang* 千金翼方 (Supplement to the prescriptions worth a thousand gold pieces). Yuan Dade period (1297–1307) Meixi shuyuan edition.
Sutherland, Gail Hinich. *The Disguises of the Demon: The Development of the Yaksa in Hinduism and Buddhism*. SUNY Series in Hindu Studies. Albany: State University of New York Press, 1991.
Sutton, Donald. "Consuming Counterrevolutionaries: The Ritual and Culture of Cannibalism in Wuxuan, Guangxi, China, May to July 1968." *Comparative Studies in Society and History* 37, no. 1 (Jan. 1995): pp. 136–172.
Su wenxue congkan, xiju lei, shuochang lei 俗文學叢刊, 戲劇類, 說唱類 (Folk literature: Materials in the collection of the Institute of History and Philology). Edited by Huang Kuanzhong 黃寬重. 500 vols. Taibei: Xinwenfeng, 2001–.
Tagare, Ganesh Vasudeo, trans. *The Bhāgavata-Purāṇa*. Ancient Indian Tradition and Mythology Series. 5 vols. Delhi: Motilal Banarsidass, 1976–1978.
Taiping yulan 太平御覽 (Imperially reviewed encyclopedia of the Taiping era). Compiled by Li Fang 李昉 (925–996). *SKQS* edition.
Taishō shinshū daizōkyō 大正新脩大藏經 (The great Buddhist canon compiled during the Taishō period). 100 vols. Tokyo: Taishō issaikyō kankōkai, 1924–1932.
Taishō shinshū daizōkyō zuzōbu 大正新脩大藏經圖像部 (The iconographic supplement of the great Buddhist canon compiled during the Taishō period). 12 vols. Tokyo: Taishō issaikyō kankōkai, 1932.
Taiwan Dabaike quanshu 臺灣大百科全書 (Encyclopedia of Taiwan). Online encyclopedia produced by the Republic of China, Ministry of Culture. http://taiwanpedia.culture.tw/.
Takubo Shūyo 田久保周譽, ed. *Ārya-Mahā-Māyūrī Vidyā-rājñī* (The venerable great peacock queen spell). Tokyo: Sankibo, 1972.
Tang, Nadine M., and Bruce L. Smith. "The Eternal Triangle Across Cultures: Oedipus, Hsueh, and Ganesa." *The Psychoanalytic Study of the Child* 51 (1996): pp. 562–579.
Tangyin xianzhi 湯陰縣志 (Gazetteer of Tangyin county). Compiled by Yang Shida 楊世達. 1738 edition.
Todorov, Tzvetan. *The Fantastic: A Structural Approach to a Literary Genre*. Translated by Richard Howard. Ithaca, N.Y.: Cornell University Press, 1975.
Tseng Wen-Shing and Jing Hsu. "The Chinese Attitude toward Paternal Authority as Expressed in Chinese Children's Stories." *Archives of General Psychiatry* 26 (1972): 28–34.
van Gulik, Robert Hans. *Hayagrīva: The Mantrayānic Aspect of the Horse-Cult in China and Japan*. Leiden: Brill, 1935.
Walshe, Maurice, trans. *The Long Discourses of the Buddha: A Translation of the Dīgha Nikāya*. Boston: Wisdom Publications, 1987.
Wan, Margaret B. *Green Peony and the Rise of the Chinese Martial Arts Novel*. Albany: State University of New York Press, 2009.
Wan, Pin Pin. "Investiture of the Gods ('Fengshen yanyi'): Sources, Narrative Structure, and Mythical Significance." PhD dissertation, University of Washington, 1987.
Wan, William. "The Fundamentals of Freud Come into Fashion in China." *Washington Post*, October 10, 2010.
Wang, Ning. "The Reception of Freudianism in Modern Chinese Literature: Part I." *China Information* 5 (1991): pp. 58–71; "Part II." *China Information* 6 (1991): pp. 46–54.

Wang Ningsheng 汪寧生. *Gu su xin yan* 古俗新研 (New research on old customs). Lanzhou: Dunhuang wenyi, 2001.

Wang Qiugui 王秋桂 and Li Fengmao 李豐楙, eds. *Zhongguo minjian xinyang ziliao huibian* 中國民間信仰資料彙編 (Collected materials on Chinese popular religion). Series no. 1, 31 vols. Taibei: Xuesheng shuju, 1988.

Wang Shufang 王淑芳. *Fahai si bihua* 法海寺壁畫 (The Fahai Temple's murals). Zhong'guo siguan bihua jingdian congshu. Shijiazhuang: Hebei meishu, 2007.

Wan xu zang jing 卍續藏經 (The continuation of the Buddhist canon). 88 volumes. Taipei: Xinwenfeng, 1975.

Watson, James L. "Of Flesh and Bones: The Management of Death Pollution in Cantonese Society." In *Death and the Regeneration of Life*, edited by Maurice Bloch and Jonathan Perry, pp. 155–186. Cambridge: Cambridge University Press, 1982.

Weller, Robert P. *Resistance, Chaos and Control in China: Taiping Rebels, Taiwanese Ghosts, and Tiananmen*. London: Macmillan, 1994.

Wen Yiduo 聞一多. *Tianwen shu zheng* 天問疏證 (Cursory comments on the heavenly questions). Beijing: Sanlian, 1980.

Wenshu pusa xiang shizi 文殊菩薩降獅子 (The Bodhisattva Mañjuśri subjugates the lion). By Zhu Youdun 朱有燉. In *Quan Ming zaju* 全明雜劇, edited by Chen Wan'nai 陳萬鼐 and Yang Jialuo 楊家駱, vol. 4, pp. 2139–2161. Taibei: Dingwen shuju, 1979.

Wenyuange Siku quanshu 文淵閣四庫全書 (All the books from the four treasuries stored at the Wenyuan hall). 1782. Photographic reprint. 1500 vols. Taiwan: Shangwu, 1983–1986.

Whitfield, Roderick. *The Art of Central Asia: The Stein Collection in the British Museum*. 2 vols. Tokyo: Kodansha, 1982.

Willemen, Charles. *The Chinese Hevajratantra: The Scriptural Text of the Ritual of the Great King of the Teaching The Adamantine One with Great Compassion and Knowledge of the Void*. Orientalia Gandensia, no. 8. Leuven: Peeters, 1983.

Wolf, Margery. *Women and the Family in Rural Taiwan*. Stanford, Calif.: Stanford University Press, 1972.

———. "Women and Suicide in China." In *Women in Chinese Society*, edited by Margery Wolf and Roxane Witke, pp. 111–141. Stanford, Calif.: Stanford University Press, 1975.

Wu Cheng'en 吳承恩. *Xiyou ji* 西遊記 (Journey to the west). 2 vols. Beijing: Zuojia chubanshe, 1954.

Wu Pei-Yi. "Childhood Remembered: Parents and Children in China, 800 to 1700." In *Chinese Views of Childhood*, edited by Anne Behnke Kinney, pp. 129–156. Honolulu: University of Hawai'i Press, 1995.

Wu Wenliang 吳文良. *Quanzhou zongjiao shike* 泉州宗教石刻 (Religious stone carvings from Quanzhou). Revised and enlarged by Wu Youxiong 吳幼雄. Beijing: Kexue, 2005.

Wu Zhangyu 吳彰裕. "Taiwan minjian xinyang zhong de Li Nezha" 臺灣民間信仰中的李哪吒 (Li Nezha in Taiwanese popular religion). In *Diyijie Nezha xueshu yantaohui lunwenji* 第一屆哪吒學術研討會論文 (Proceedings of the first academic conference on Nezha), edited by Guoli Zhongshan daxue qingdai xueshu yanjiu zhongxin 國立中山大學清代學術研究中心, pp. 401–422. Gaoxiong: Zhongshan daxue, 2003.

Wuliang shou jing 無量壽經 (The larger sutra of the Buddha of Immeasurable Life (Amitāyus)). Translation attributed to Saṃghavarman (Kang Sengkai 康僧鎧). *T.* no. 360.

Wu wang fa Zhou pinghua 武王伐紂平話 (The popular tale of King Wu punishing King Zhou). Shanghai: Zhongguo gudian wenxue, 1957.

Xi Song 奚淞. *Fengshen bang li de Nezha* 封神榜裏的哪吒 (The roster of the gods' Nezha). Taibei: Dongrun, 1991.

Xiang Chu 項楚. *Dunhuang bianwen xuanzhu* 敦煌變文選注 (Selected and annotated Dunhuang transformation texts). Revised edition. 2 vols. Beijing: Zhonghua, 2006.

Xianyu jing 賢愚經 (The sutra of the wise and the foolish). Translated by Huijue 慧覺 et al. *T.* 202.

Xiao Dengfu 蕭登福. "Nezha suyuan" 哪吒溯源 (Tracing Nezha's origins). In *Diyijie Nezha xueshu yantaohui lunwenji* 第一屆哪吒學術研討會論文 (Proceedings of the first academic conference on Nezha), edited by Guoli Zhongshan daxue qingdai xueshu yanjiu zhongxin 國立中山大學清代學術研究中心, pp. 1–66. Gaoxiong: Zhongshan daxue, 2003.

Xiao Haiming 肖海明. *Zhenwu tuxiang yanjiu* 真武圖像研究 (Research into Zhenwu's iconography). Quanzhen Daojiao yanjiu zhongxin, no. 2. Beijing: Wenwu, 2007.

Xiao jing, ershisi xiao zhuyi 孝經二十四孝注譯 (The annotated and translated *Classic of filial piety,* and *Twenty-four filial exemplars*). Annotated by Tang Songbo 唐松波. Beijing: Jindun, 2008.

Xinbian lianxiang soushen guangji 新編連像搜神廣記 (Newly edited and illustrated extensive record of the gods). Yuan-period edition. Copy at Beijing Library.

Xixia xianzhi 西峽縣志 (Xixia County gazetteer). Compiled by Xixia xianzhi bianji weiyuanhui. Zhengzhou: Henan renmin, 1990.

Xu Bingkun 許炳坤. "Taiwan minjian Nezha Taizi xinyang tantao: Yi Xinzhushi Dongyao Taizi gong wei li" 台灣民間哪吒太子信仰探討: 以新竹市東窯太子宮為例 (Exploration of Taiwanese Prince Nezha popular beliefs: Using the Xinzhu Eastern-Kiln Prince Palace as an example). In *Diyijie Nezha xueshu yantaohui lunwenji* 第一屆哪吒學術研討會論文 (Proceedings of the first academic conference on Nezha), edited by Guoli Zhongshan daxue qingdai xueshu yanjiu zhongxin 國立中山大學清代學術研究中心, pp. 241–263. Gaoxiong: Zhongshan daxue, 2003.

Xu Xianping 許獻平. "Tainan xian Taizi ye miao de fenbu yu xitong" 台南縣太子爺廟的分佈與系統 (The distribution and organization of the Lord Prince's temples in Tainan county). In *Diyijie Nezha xueshu yantaohui lunwenji* 第一屆哪吒學術研討會論文 (Proceedings of the first academic conference on Nezha), edited by Guoli Zhongshan daxue qingdai xueshu yanjiu zhongxin 國立中山大學清代學術研究中心, pp. 607–643. Gaoxiong: Zhongshan daxue, 2003.

Xu Xinyi 徐信義. "Lun *Suomo Jing* yu *Nezha san bian* zaju" 論鎖魔鏡與哪吒三變雜劇 (On the *Demon-locking mirror* and *Nezha's three transformations* zaju plays). In *Diyijie Nezha xueshu yantaohui lunwenji* 第一屆哪吒學術研討會論文 (Proceedings of the first academic conference on Nezha), edited by Guoli Zhongshan daxue qingdai xueshu yanjiu zhongxin 國立中山大學清代學術研究中心, pp. 373–400. Gaoxiong: Zhongshan daxue, 2003.

Xu Yucheng 許宇承. *Taiwan minjian xinyang zhong de wuying bingjiang* 臺灣民間信仰中的五營兵將 (The Five Armies' soldiers and generals in Taiwanese popular religion). Taibei: Lantai, 2009.

Xuanzang 玄奘. *Da Tang xiyu ji* 大唐西域記 (The great Tang Dynasty record of the western regions), *T.* 2087.

———. *The Great Tang Dynasty Record of the Western Regions.* Translated by Li Rongxi. BDK English Tripiṭaka, no. 79. Berkeley: Numata Center, 1996.

Yamabe, Nobuyoshi. "An Examination of the Mural Paintings of Toyok Cave 20 in Conjunction with the Origin of the *Amitayus Visualization Sutra,*" *Orientations* 30, no. 4 (April 1999): pp. 38–44.

Yan Yaozhong 嚴耀中. *Han chuan mijiao* 漢傳密教 (Chinese Tantric Buddhism). Shanghai: Xuelin, 1999.

Yang Donglai xiansheng piping Xiyou ji 楊東來先生批評西遊記 (*The Journey to the West* with commentary by Mr. Yang Donglai). Twenty-four act *zaju* play. Author given as Wu Changling 吴昌齡. Reprinted in *Shibun* 斯文 9, no. 1–10, no. 3 (1927–1928).

Yang Erzeng. *The Story of Han Xiangzi: The Alchemical Adventures of a Daoist Immortal.* Translated and introduced by Philip Clart. Seattle: University of Washington Press, 2007.

Yang Qinzhang 楊欽章. "Quanzhou yindujiao diaoke yuanyuan kao" 泉州印度教雕刻淵源考 (Research into the origins of the Quanzhou Hindu stone carvings). *Shijie zongjiao yanjiu* 世界宗教研究 (1982.2): pp. 87–94.

———. "Quanzhou yindujiao pishinu shen xingxiang shike" 泉州印度教毗濕奴神形象石刻 (The Quanzhou stone images of the Hindu god Viṣṇu). *Shijie zongjiao yanjiu* 世界宗教研究 (1988.1): pp. 96–105.

Yang Tianhou 楊天厚 and Lin Likuan 林麗寬. "Jinmen Taizi ye xinyang" 金門太子爺信仰 (The Lord Prince's cult on Jinmen Island). In *Diyijie Nezha xueshu yantaohui lunwenji* 第一屆哪吒學術研討會論文 (Proceedings of the first academic conference on Nezha), edited by Guoli Zhongshan daxue qingdai xueshu yanjiu zhongxin 國立中山大學清代學術研究中心, pp. 451–487. Gaoxiong: Zhongshan daxue, 2003.

Yang Xianyi and Gladys Yang, trans. *The Courtesan's Jewel Box: Chinese Stories of the Xth-XVIIth Centuries.* Beijing: Foreign Language Press, 1957.

Ying Yukang 應裕康. "Lun Jingxi wuda ju zhong de Nezha" 論京戲武打劇中的哪吒 (Nezha in the martial plays of the Peking Opera). In *Diyijie Nezha xueshu yantaohui lunwenji* 第一屆哪吒學術研討會論文 (Proceedings of the first academic conference on Nezha), edited by Guoli Zhongshan daxue qingdai xueshu yanjiu zhongxin 國立中山大學清代學術研究中心, pp. 595–605. Gaoxiong: Zhongshan daxue, 2003.

Yiqie jing yinyi 一切經音義 (Dictionary of the Buddhist canon). By Huilin 慧琳 (737–820). *T.* 2128.

Yiwen leiju 藝文類聚 (Collection of classified literature). Compiled by Ouyang Xun 歐陽詢 (557–641). *SKQS* edition.

Yoshimura, Rei 吉村怜. *Tianren dansheng tu yanjiu* 天人诞生图研究 (Research into the illustrations of heavenly beings' birth). Translated into Chinese by Bian Liqiang 卞立强. Shanghai: Shanghai guji, 2009.

Youli cheng zhi 羑里城志 (Gazetteer of Youli fort). Compiled by Yin Shixue 殷時學 and Tao Tao 陶濤. Zhengzhou: Henan renmin, 2007.

Yu, Anthony, trans. *The Journey to the West.* 4 vols. Chicago: University of Chicago Press, 1977–1983.

Yu, Jimmy. *Sanctity and Self-Inflicted Violence in Chinese Religions, 1500–1700.* Oxford: Oxford University Press, 2012.

Yuan Changying 袁昌英. *Kongque dongnan fei ji qita dumuju* 孔雀東南飛及其他獨幕劇 (The peacock flies southeast and other, one-act, plays). Changsha?: Shangwu, ca. 1930.

Yuanwu Foguo Chanshi yulu 圓悟佛果禪師語錄 (The recorded sayings of Yuanwu [Keqin] (1063–1135)). (Completed in 1133). *T.* no. 1997.

Zamperini, Paola. "Untamed Hearts: Eros and Suicide in Late Imperial Chinese Fiction." In Ropp et al., eds., *Passionate Women.* Special issue of *Nan Nü* 3, no. 1 (2001): pp. 77–104.

Zan'ning 贊寧 (919–1001). *Song gaoseng zhuan* 宋高僧傳 (Biographies of eminent monks compiled during the Song period) (988). *T.* no. 2061.

Zeng Guodong 曾國棟. "Xinying Taizi Gong de lishi yanjiu" 新營太子宮的歷史研究 (Research into the history of the Xinying Taizi Gong). In *Diyijie Nezha xueshu yantaohui lunwenji* 第一屆哪吒學術研討會論文 (Proceedings of the first academic conference on Nezha), edited by Guoli Zhongshan daxue qingdai xueshu yanjiu zhongxin 國立中山大學清代學術研究中心, pp. 117–145. Gaoxiong: Zhongshan daxue, 2003.

Zeng Qinliang 曾勤良. *Taiwan minjian xinyang yu "fengshen yanyi" zhi bijiao yanjiu* 台灣民間信仰與封神演義之比較研究 (A comparative study of Taiwanese popular beliefs and "the canonization of the gods"). Taibei: Huazheng, 1985.

Zhang He. "Figurative and Inscribed Carpets from Shanpula, Khotan: Unexpected Representations of the Hindu God Krishna. A Preliminary Study." *Journal of Inner Asian Art and Archeology* 5 (2012): 59–94.

Zhang Jingyuan. *Psychoanalysis in China: Literary Transformations 1919–1949*. Cornell East Asia Series. Ithaca, N.Y.: Cornell University Press, 1992.

Zhang Peiheng 章培恆. "*Fengshen yanyi* zuozhe bukao" 封神演義作者补考 (Supplementary research on the authorship of "the canonization of the gods"). *Fudan xuebao, shehui kexue bao* 复旦學報, 社會科學報 (1992.4): 90–98.

Zhang Shizhao 張士釗, trans. *Fuluoyide xuzhuan* 弗罗乙德叙傳 (Selbstdarstellung). By Sigmund Freud. Shanghai: Shangwu: 1930.

Zhao Jingshen 趙景深. "Zhongguo xin wenyi yu biantai xingyu" 中國新文藝與變態性欲 (New Chinese literature and deviant sexual desires). *Yiban* 一般 4, no. 1 (1928): pp. 204–208.

Zheng Acai 鄭阿財. "Lun Dunhuang xieben 'Longxing si Pishamen Tianwang lingyan ji' yu Tang Wudai de Pishamen xinyang" 論敦煌寫本"龍興寺毗沙門天王靈驗記"與唐五代的毗沙門信仰 (On the Dunhuang manuscript "The divine efficacy of the Longxing Temple's Heavenly King Vaiśravaṇa" and the Vaiśravaṇa cult of the Tang and Five Dynasties period). In *Zhong'guo Tang dai wenhua xueshu yantaohui lunwen ji, di san jie* 中國唐代文化學術研討會論文集, 第三屆, pp. 427–442. Taibei: Zhong'guo Tang dai xuehui, 1997.

Zheng Qing (?–899) 鄭綮. *Kai Tian chuanxin ji* 開天傳信記 (Truthful anecdotes from the Kaiyuan and Tianbao reigns). *SKQS* edition.

Zheng Yi. *Scarlet Memorial: Tales of Cannibalism in Modern China*. Translated and edited by T. P. Sym. Boulder, Colo.: Westview Press, 1996.

Zhengtong daozang 正統道藏 (The Daoist canon published during the Zhengtong reign 1438–1449). Photographic reprint. 60 vols. Taibei: Xin Wenfeng, 1990.

Zhipan 志磐 (ca. 1200). *Fozu tongji* 佛祖統紀 (Record of the lineages of buddhas and patriarchs). *T.* no. 2035.

Zhongguo tongsu xiaoshuo zongmu tiyao 中國通俗小說總目提要 (Comprehensive catalogue and synopses of Chinese popular fiction). Edited by Jiangsu sheng shehui kexue yuan, Ming Qing xiaoshuo yanjiu zhongxin 江蘇省社會科學院,明清小說研究中. Beijing: Zhongguo wenlian, 1990.

Zhonghua daojiao zhongtan yuanshuai hongdao xiehui tuanti huiyuan mingce 中華道教中壇元帥弘道協會團體會員名冊 (List of members of the temples of the Chinese Daoist General of the Middle Altar association for the promotion of the way). Taiwan, 2008.

Zhou Yibai 周貽白. "*Wu wang fa zhou pinghua de lishi genju*" 武王伐紂平話的歷史根據 (The historical sources of the popular tale of King Wu punishing King Zhou). In his *Zhou Yibai xiaoshuo xiqu lunji* 周貽白小說戲曲論集. Edited by Shen Xieyuan 沈燮元. Jinan: Qilu, 1986.

Zhou Zuoren 周作人. *Ziji de yuandi; yutian de shu* 自己的園地; 雨天的書 (My own garden; a book from a rainy day). Beijing: Renmin wenxue, 1988.

Zhu Fo Pusa sheng xiang zan 諸佛菩薩聖像贊 (Hymns to the sacred images of the buddhas and bodhisattvas). Edited and prefaced by Luo Wenhua 羅文華. Beijing: Zhongguo zangxue 2008.
Zizhi tongjian 資治通鑒 (Comprehensive mirror for the aid of government). By Sima Guang 司馬光. 20 vols. Beijing: Zhonghua: 1995.
Zuishang mimi Nana tian jing 最上祕密那拏天經 (Scripture of the Supreme Secrets of Naṇa Deva). Translated by Tianxizai天息災 (Devaśāntika?) (?–1000). *T.* no. 1288.
Zürcher, E. *The Buddhist Conquest of China: The Spread and Adaptation of Buddhism in Early Medieval China.* Leiden: Brill, 1959.

Index

Page numbers in **bold** refer to illustrations.